Cambridge Studies in Oral and Literate Culture 15

TO SPEAK IN PAIRS

Cambridge Studies in Oral and Literate Culture

Edited by PETER BURKE and RUTH FINNEGAN

This series is designed to address the question of the significance of literacy in human societies: it will assess its importance for political, economic, social and cultural development, and examine how what we take to be the common functions of writing are carried out in oral cultures.

This series is interdisciplinary, but with particular emphasis on social anthropology and social history, and encourages cross-fertilisation between these disciplines; it also is of interest to readers in allied fields, such as sociology, folklore and literature. Although it will include some monographs, the focus of the series will be on theoretical and comparative aspects rather than detailed description, and the books will be presented in a form accessible to non-specialist readers interested in the general subject of literacy and orality.

Books in the series

1 NIGEL PHILIPPS: *'Sijobang': sung narrative poetry of west Sumatra*
2 R. W. SCRIBNER: *For the sake of simple folk: popular propaganda for the German Reformation*
3 HARVEY J. GRAFF: *Literacy and social development in the West: a reader*
4 DONALD J. COSENTINO: *Defiant maids and stubborn farmers: tradition and invention in Mende story performance*
5 FRANÇOIS FURET and JACQUES OZOUF: *Reading and writing: literacy in France from Calvin to Jules Ferry*
6 JEAN-CLAUDE SCHMITT: *The Holy Greyhound: Guinefort, healer of children since the thirteenth century*
7 JEFF OPLAND: *Xhosa oral poetry: aspects of a Black South African tradition*
8 RICHARD BAUMAN: *Let your words be few: symbolism of speaking and silence among seventeenth-century Quakers*
9 BRIAN V. STREET: *Literacy in theory and practice*
10 RICHARD BAUMAN: *Story, performance, and event: contextual studies of oral narrative*
11 AMY SHUMAN: *Storytelling rights: the uses of oral and written texts by urban adolescents*
12 PETER BURKE and ROY PORTER (Eds): *The social history of language*
13 JOEL SHERZER and ANTHONY C. WOODBURY (Eds): *Native American discourse: poetics and rhetoric*
14 ARON IAKOVLEVICH GUREVICH: *Medieval popular culture: problems of belief and perception*
15 JAMES J. FOX (Ed.): *To speak in pairs: essays on the ritual languages of eastern Indonesia*

TO SPEAK IN PAIRS

Essays on the ritual languages
of eastern Indonesia

Edited by
JAMES J. FOX

Department of Anthropology
The Research School of Pacific Studies
The Australian National University

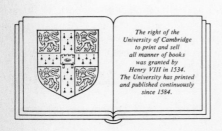

The right of the
University of Cambridge
to print and sell
all manner of books
was granted by
Henry VIII in 1534.
The University has printed
and published continuously
since 1584.

CAMBRIDGE UNIVERSITY PRESS

CAMBRIDGE

NEW YORK   NEW ROCHELLE   MELBOURNE   SYDNEY

Published by the Press Syndicate of the University of Cambridge
The Pitt Building, Trumpington Street, Cambridge CB2 1RP
32 East 57th Street, New York, NY 10022, USA
10 Stamford Road, Oakleigh, Melbourne 3166, Australia

First Published 1988

Printed in Great Britain by Woolnough Bookbinding, Irthlingbrough

British Library cataloguing in publication data

To speak in pairs: essays on the ritual languages
of Eastern Indonesia –
(Cambridge studies in oral and literate culture; 15).
1. Indonesian language
I. Fox, James J.
499′.22   PL5071

Library of Congress cataloguing in publication data

To speak in pairs.
(Cambridge studies in oral and literate culture; 15)
Bibliography. p.
Includes index.
1. Languages – Religious aspects.   2. Ritual.
3. Indonesia – Languages – Religious aspects.
I. Fox, James J., 1940–   II. Series.
BL65.L2T6 1987   401′.9   87-6563

ISBN 0 521 34332 1

CS

To the memory of Roman Jakobson

CONTENTS

		page
Illustrations		viii
The contributors		ix
Acknowledgements		xi
Introduction JAMES J. FOX		1

1 *Etiquette in Kodi spirit communication: the lips told to pronounce, the mouths told to speak*   29
JANET ALISON HOSKINS

2 *Method in the metaphor: the ritual language of Wanukaka*   64
DAVID MITCHELL

3 *Li'i marapu: speech and ritual among the Wewewa of west Sumba*   87
BRIGITTE RENARD-CLAMAGIRAND

4 *The Pattern of Prayer in Weyéwa*   104
JOEL C. KUIPERS

5 *Fashioned speech, full communication: aspects of eastern Sumbanese ritual language*   129
GREGORY FORTH

6 *Manu Kama's road, Tepa Nilu's path: theme, narrative, and formula in Rotinese ritual language*   161
JAMES J. FOX

7 *The case of the purloined statues: the power of words among the Lionese*   202
ERIKO AOKI

8 *The journey of the bridegroom: idioms of marriage among the Endenese*   228
SATOSHI NAKAGAWA

9 *A quest for the source: the ontogenesis of a creation myth of the Ata Tana Ai*   246
E. D. LEWIS

10 *The Tree of Desire: A Toraja ritual poem*   282
CHARLES ZERNER and TOBY ALICE VOLKMAN

Notes	306
References	325
Index	334

ILLUSTRATIONS

Photographs

A singer (*tou yaigho*) beating the drum as he sings an invocation to its spirit   46

A Rindi priest performing an invocation at the river's edge (*hamayangu la ngamba luku//hingi wai*) on the occasion of a mother's first bath after childbirth.   137

Rotinese chanters doing *bapa* – chanting to the beat of the drum – at a mortuary ceremony in honour of the deceased Head of the Earth from Termanu, S. Adulanu   163

The *tana puan* of Tana Wai Brama 'chisels' a classificatory sister's son as part of the 'cooling' of his new house (1978)   251

Men gather around the base of the *bate*, firmly planting it in the ground   283

Figures

4.1. Expelling the guilt from the village   106
5.1. Disposition of speakers in oratorical performances   140
7.1. Lionese views of their society   222
8.1. The village structure (*nua*)   237
8.2. The house structure (*sa'o*)   237
8.3. Outline representation of the bridegroom's journey   240

THE CONTRIBUTORS

ERIKO AOKI
Department of Cultural Anthropology, Division of Sociology, Graduate School, The University of Tokyo.
Fieldwork: Lio, central Flores.

GREGORY FORTH
Assistant Professor, Department of Anthropology, University of Alberta, Edmonton.
Fieldwork: Rindi, eastern Sumba; Nage-Keo region, central Flores.

JAMES J. FOX
Professorial Fellow, Department of Anthropology, Research School of Pacific Studies, The Australian National University, Canberra.
Fieldwork: Roti, west Timor.

JANET ALISON HOSKINS
Assistant Professor, Department of Anthropology, University of Southern California, Los Angeles.
Fieldwork: Kodi, west Sumba.

JOEL C. KUIPERS
Assistant Professor, Seton Hall University, South Orange, New Jersey.
Fieldwork: Weyéwa, west Sumba.

E. D. LEWIS
Lecturer in Anthropology, Department of Sociology, La Trobe University, Melbourne.
Fieldwork: Tana Ai, Sikka, Flores.

DAVID MITCHELL
Willsmere Hospital, Melbourne.
Fieldwork: Wanukaka, west Sumba.

SATOSHI NAKAGAWA
Research Fellow, Center for Southeast Asian Studies, Kyoto University.
Fieldwork: Ende, central Flores.

BRIGITTE RENARD-CLAMAGIRAND
Chargée de Recherche au Centre National de la Recherche Scientifique, Paris.
Fieldwork: Wewewa, west Sumba.

TOBY ALICE VOLKMAN
> Staff Associate, Social Science Research Council, New York.
> Fieldwork: Tana Toraja, Sulawesi.

CHARLES ZERNER
> Senior Lecturer, Department of Design, Massachusetts College
> of Art, Boston.
> Fieldwork: Tana Toraja, Sulawesi.

ACKNOWLEDGEMENTS

This volume is not based on a conference. It consists of papers that were solicited from researchers who have done fieldwork in eastern Indonesia. Putting this volume together has taken longer than any one of us initially expected. As a result, contributors who were among the first to produce their papers have had the longest wait. As editor, I would like to thank these contributors, in particular, for their patience.

Support and assistance in preparing this volume has come from the Research School of Pacific Studies of The Australian National University. The careful typing of the various drafts of the volume was done by Ita M. Pead and Ria van de Zandt. Paula Harris assisted with the bibliography and helped with work on the final draft. However, the major work of copy-editing, co-ordinating papers, and corresponding with contributors was done by Judith A. Wilson. Her assistance has enormously enhanced this volume as a cumulative endeavour. On behalf of the contributors, I would like to thank her and the other members of the Department of Anthropology for their assistance.

INTRODUCTION

JAMES J. FOX

The ten essays that compose this volume are directed to a examination of an ethnographic phenomenon of singular importance: the prevalent use of strict forms of parallelism in traditional oral communication. In communication of this kind, parallelism is promoted to the status of canon, and paired correspondences, at the semantic and syntactic levels, result in what is essentially a dyadic language – the phenomenon of 'speaking in pairs'.

Since such forms of parallelism are widely attested in the oral poetry and elevated speech of a variety of peoples of the world, comprehension of this linguistic phenomenon is crucial to an understanding of oral literature. Moreover, since patterns of dyadic composition are implicated in diverse forms of communication, consideration of this phenomenon is equally important to an understanding of the ethnography of rhetoric and ritual.

The essays in this volume all deal with forms of dyadic language that occur within a single broadly defined ethnographic area, namely the islands of eastern Indonesia. Each essay is concerned with the particularities of dyadic composition in a separate cultural setting. This is in itself strategically important since it allows the possibility of co-ordinated comparison among related languages and cultures. As a whole, therefore, the volume represents a concerted attempt to focus examination on dyadic language as a special linguistic phenomenon in a comparative ethnographic context.

Eastern Indonesia, the context for this comparison, is an area of considerable linguistic diversity – a common feature of many of the areas of the world where complex forms of parallelism are particularly prominent. Eastern Indonesia's linguistic diversity is due to both geographical and historical factors. A mix of large and small islands, a mountainous hinterland on several of the larger islands, ample possibilities for migration, the lack of political hegemony by any one linguistic group, an historical division among colonial powers – Dutch and Portuguese – and colonial policies ranging from self-rule accorded numerous petty rulers to near indifference or outright neglect, combined with internal pressures within many small polities to enhance differences to distinguish themselves from neighbouring groups; and all these factors have contributed to creating a culturally diverse region.

Current evidence points to the islands of eastern Indonesia as a region into which distinct subgroups of Austronesian-speaking peoples migrated in the distant past. Thus the overwhelming majority of the languages of the area are Austronesian, but these languages show considerable divergence. The islands of the Sumba–Flores–Timor area, on which most of this volume is concentrated, have by conservative estimate at least twenty-one distinct Austronesian languages. And as one expands the boundaries of eastern Indonesia to include the Moluccas and Sulawesi, the number of Austronesian languages more than doubles. In terms of dialects, the region becomes even more complex. In addition, a number of non-Austronesian languages are to be found on Alor, Pantar, Timor, and Halmahera, adding further diversity to the region.

Within the region literacy has until recently been limited to certain elites. As a result, the cultures of the area are noted for their lively and diverse oral traditions; but they are equally, and perhaps even more importantly, noted for the cultural importance attached to dyadic speech. Oral composition in a binary mode is an essential means of social as well as ritual communication. Dyadic language is, however, more than a means of special communication; it has become, for many of the societies of the region, the primary vehicle for the preservation and transmission of cultural knowledge. Thus, in eastern Indonesia, fundamental metaphoric structures of culture are embedded in forms of dyadic language.

The contributors to this volume have all done extensive fieldwork among the peoples whose dyadic language they describe and, as a result, have come to recognise the critical importance of an understanding of dyadic language to an understanding of the culture that they had committed themselves to comprehend. Hence a major impetus for the study of dyadic language can be seen to derive from the cultural centrality of the phenomenon itself. One of the chief purposes of this collection of essays is to establish this point by portraying a variety of cultural analyses that take the linguistic phenomenon of dyadic composition as fundamental to an ethnographic understanding of the region.

Parallelism as a linguistic phenomenon

Since 1753, when Robert Lowth first noted and defined the use of parallelism in relation to Hebrew verse, the concept of parallelism has come to mean many things. In some contexts parallelism is used to refer to nothing more than a limited rhetorical device; in other contexts, as in the case of this volume, parallelism refers to the distinctive, indeed defining, feature of specific forms of oral communication. Both of these definitions of parallelism, however, merely represent aspects of a wider understanding.

Early in his career, in an essay in 1919 on the new Russian poetry, Roman Jakobson enunciated a sweeping definition of parallelism (Jakobson 1973). In almost aphoristic form, he asserted that 'poetic language consists of an elementary operation: the bringing together of two elements ...'. This 'bringing together of two elements' he defined as parallelism. And with this definition he went on to argue that comparison, metamorphosis, and metaphor were all 'semantic variants' of the operation of parallelism. Comparison was 'a particular instance of parallelism'; metamorphosis was 'parallelism projected in time'; and metaphor, 'parallelism reduced to a point'. 'Euphonic variants' of this same process of juxtaposition were rhyme, assonance, and alliteration (Jakobson 1973:21).

Almost fifty years later Jakobson returned to his earlier insights having discovered that the poet G.M. Hopkins had preceded him in advancing a similar argument about parallelism. In a major article, 'Grammatical parallelism and its Russian facet', Jakobson observed:

> one is irresistibly compelled to quote again and again the path-breaking study written exactly one hundred years ago by the juvenile Gerard Manley Hopkins: 'The artificial part of poetry, perhaps we shall be right to say all artifice, reduces itself to the principle of parallelism, ranging from the technical so-called parallelisms of Hebrew poetry and the antiphons of Church music to the intricacy of Greek or Italian or English verse'. (1966:399)

Thus, following Hopkins, Jakobson reasserted his own earlier argument that 'on every level of language the essence of poetic artifice consists of recurrent returns' (1966:399). By this definition, parallelism is an extension of the binary principle of opposition to the phonetic, syntactic, and semantic levels of expression. Poetic language is the most elaborate and complex expression of this phenomenon.

Useful as this definition may be at a general level, it does not satisfactorily distinguish the specific forms of parallelism that Lowth originally defined. As numerous scholars have observed, in many cultures of the world tradition demands that certain compositions be given dual expression. Words, phrases, and lines must be paired for a composition to be defined as poetry, ritual language, or elevated speech. Moreover, many of these traditions also prescribe, always with varying degrees of freedom, what words, phrases, or other elements of language are to be paired in composition. Jakobson has described this form of parallelism 'where certain similarities between successive verbal sequences are compulsory or enjoy high preference' as 'compulsory' or 'canonical' parallelism – what

Hopkins referred to as 'the technical so-called parallelisms of Hebrew poetry' (see Fox 1977:59–60).

Although widespread, canonical parallelism as a strict, consistent, and pervasive means of communication is limited to specific cultures. Its importance, however, is not restricted by this occurrence. The theoretical significance of canonical parallelism lies in the glimpses it provides of fundamental aspects of linguistic composition.

In the concluding section of *Fundamentals of language* (1956:58ff.), Jakobson defined, by a series of parallelisms of his own making, two poles or axes of language: a paradigmatic axis based on selection and a syntagmatic axis based on combination. The first of these axes defines the creation of metaphor by means of similarity; the second the creation of metonymy by means of contiguity. Despite Jakobson's lucid presentation, the significance of these distinctions cannot be fully appreciated without an understanding of his notion of parallelism and particularly the phenomenon of canonical parallelism which he alludes to in his discussion. The same is true of Jakobson's often-quoted statement that 'the poetic function projects the principle of equivalence from the axis of selection into the axis of combination' (1960:358). Whereas in other forms of poetry the 'poetic function' is subtly concealed or implicit, only in canonical parallelism is this function given direct and explicit expression. Culturally defined linguistic equivalences, both semantic and syntactic, must be fully expressed. Hence if poetic language is the most complex expression of the application of the principle of binary opposition, canonical parallelism has to be regarded as its most manifest aspect. As such, it offers an elementary starting point for study of all forms of poetic language.

Initial observations on parallelism

Parallelism as a phenomenon was first formally noted and defined in the middle of the eighteenth century by the Professor of Hebrew Poetry at Oxford, the Reverend Robert Lowth. In his nineteenth lecture on the 'Sacred poetry of the Hebrews', delivered in Latin at Oxford in 1753, Lowth observed that the poetry of the Old Testament consisted of 'versicles or parallelisms corresponding to each other', and he defined this parallelism as follows:

> The poetic conformation of the sentences, which has been so often alluded to as characteristic of Hebrew poetry, consists chiefly in a certain equality, resemblance, or parallelism between members of each period; so that in two lines (or members of the same period) things for the most part shall answer to things, and words to words, as if fitted to each other by a kind of rule or

measure. This parallelism has much variety and many gradations; it is sometimes more accurate and manifest, sometimes more vague and obscure. (Lowth 1971:II,32–34)

Later, in his 'Preliminary dissertation' on a new translation of Isaiah, published in 1778, Lowth set forth, in a more explicit fashion, a terminology for what he identified as *parallelismus membrorum*:

> The correspondence of one verse or line with another, I call parallelism. When a proposition is delivered, and a second is subjoined to it, or drawn under it, equivalent, or contrasted with it in sense, or similar to it in the form of grammatical construction, these I call parallel lines; and the words or phrases, answering one to another in corresponding lines, parallel terms. (Lowth 1834:ix)

With this by no means simple definition of a complex phenomenon, Lowth, in effect, established the study of parallelism and, in the process, an entire tradition of scholarship. Interestingly, in concluding his earlier historical lecture on Hebrew poetry Lowth offered the simple but prescient remark:

> I scarcely know any subject which promises more copiously to reward the labour of such as are studious of sacred criticism, than this one in particular. (Lowth 1971:II,57)

The impact of Lowth's research was immediate and pronounced. It inspired the writing of English poetry in a Hebrew vein and influenced J.G. Herder, who popularised Lowth's notion of parallelism in his *Vom Geist der ebraischen Poesie* (1782). Lowth's writings were translated and appeared in numerous editions. Lowth himself was made Lord Bishop of London in 1777 and was later, in 1783, offered the position of Archbishop of Canterbury, an honour which he declined.

More importantly, as Lowth himself predicted, his research gave rise to voluminous scholarship. Following Lowth's early observations, scholars have continued to study the parallelism of Hebrew poetry. G.B. Gray's *The forms of Hebrew poetry* (1915), devoted in large part to a 'restatement' of Lowth's work, carried this research into the twentieth century; L.I. Newman and W. Popper's *Studies in biblical parallelism* (1918–23) marked a further advance; and Newman's introduction to his study, 'Parallelism in Amos' (1918), surveyed a wide range of Near Eastern traditions of parallelism – ancient Egyptian, Sumerian, Babylonian, Assyrian, and Arabic – and examined as well the diminished reliance on parallelism in the New Testament, and in rabbinical, medieval, and modern Hebrew literature.

In 1928 the remarkable discovery, at Ras Shamra, of Canaanite or Ugaritic texts opened a new area of study. The existence of these critical texts led a host of scholars to examine, in meticulous detail, the extent to which Lowth's 'parallel terms' constitute, in the ancient oral traditions of Syria and Palestine, a standardised body of fixed word-pairs by means of which verse forms were composed. A particularly useful study in this regard was S. Gevirtz' s *Patterns in the early poetry of Israel* (1963). More recently, D.N. Freedman in his 'Prolegomenon' to the reprinted edition of Gray (1972) has compiled an annotated bibliography on the developments in this specialised textual research, including references to the work of such scholars as Albright, Cross, Dahood, Driver, Ginsburg, Gordon, and Rin. In this field of textual scholarship, Dahood's extensive reconstruction of 'pairs of parallel words' common to both Hebrew and Ugaritic marks a critically important development in the study of parallelism (see, for example, Dahood and Penar 1970:445–446).[1]

The occurrence of canonical parallelism

With a few exceptions, however, the tradition of biblical scholarship has confined its attention principally to the consideration of parallelism within Semitic languages. It has not taken cognisance of the existence of parallelism in other major languages, although it was Lowth's recognition of Hebrew parallelism that initially gave rise to the comparative study of parallelism. Already in the nineteenth century, linguists, literary scholars and, not infrequently, Bible translators encountered traditions of parallel composition in widely scattered areas of the world. The enormous accumulation of these studies has created a rich comparative literature.

The Ural–Altaic region is one area remarkable for its use of parallelism. Roman Jakobson, in particular, has pointed to the importance of parallelism in an admirable survey of the principal literature on this linguistic phenomenon in the region (1966:403–405). Studies of Finnish oral poetry offer a classic case. The *Kalevala*, for example, is probably the most frequently cited example of parallel poetry after that of the Old Testament. Prior to Lowth, Cajanus (1697), Juslenius (1728), and Porthan (1766–68) all noted the similarities between Finnish and biblical poetry, though Marmier (1842) appears to have been the first Finnish scholar to adopt Lowth's terminology to characterise these verse forms.

W. Steinitz' s major monograph, *Der Parallelismus in der finisch–karelischen Volksdichtung* (1934), traces the development of these studies. Ahlqvist's dissertation (1863), Steinitz's pioneering study and his further work on Ostyak (1939–41), followed by Austerlitz's monograph on Ostyak and Vogul folk poetry (1958), the continuing work of Hungarian scholars such as Zsirai (1951) and Fokos (1963), and recent research by Schulze

(1982) and Lang (forthcoming) have all advanced this study of parallelism.

In the epic poetry of the Mongolians, parallelism was first remarked on by H.C. von der Gabelentz in 1837. This research on Mongolian has been carried forward particularly by N. Poppe (1958). Similar valuable research has also been done on parallelism in Turkic poetry by Kowalski (1921) and Schirmunski (1965). As Lotz has argued, 'parallelism is a common phenomenon in Ural and Altaic folkpoetry' (1954:374). In fact, the Ural–Altaic region in its complexity of oral traditions is one of the major areas of the world for the study of parallelism.

Another major area for the study of parallelism is Middle America, some of whose complex oral traditions can be traced to an earlier pre-Columbian period. Garibay, in his monumental history of Nahuatl literature (1953), lists parallelism as the first principle of Maya poetry, a point that J.E.S. Thompson had already remarked on in his introduction to Maya hieroglyphic writing (1950:61–63). Recognition of this principle has led to the retranslation of old texts. Edmonson, for example, has retranslated the *Popol vuh*, demonstrating that this long poem is based on a formal canon of traditional lexical pairs (1970, 1971), and R. de Ridder (1979) has extended this study of canonical parallelism in the *Popol vuh* to a general examination of Quiche Maya traditions.

A considerable amount of research has also been devoted to the study of parallelism in the oral traditions of the region. Bricker has written on the 'couplet poetry' of the Zinacantecos of Chiapas (1974); Gossen on the use of 'metaphoric couplets' in Tzotzil speech genre (1974a, 1974b); Siskel on the couplets used in Tzotzil curing (1974) and Field on similar couplets in Tzotzil prayers (1975); Boster on prayer couplets among the K'ekchi' Maya of British Honduras (1973). Kramer (1970) and D. and J. Sherzer (1972, 1974) have investigated parallelism in Cuna oral literature.

One of the earliest observations of another important tradition of parallelism was made in a long essay by J.F. Davis, 'On the poetry of the Chinese' (1830), published in the *Transactions of the Royal Asiatic Society*. In his essay Davis noted 'a striking coincidence' between the construction of Chinese and Hebrew verse. He contended that a 'synthetic' or 'constructive' parallelism, which he defined, following Lowth, as 'a marked correspondence and equality in construction of the lines – "such as noun answering to noun, verb to verb, member to member, negative to negative, interrogative to interrogative" ... was by far the most common species of parallelism with the Chinese' (1830:414). This parallelism, he maintained, was 'much more exact' in Chinese than in Hebrew, owing to the structure of the language and the writing system of the Chinese. Davis contended that parallelism 'pervades their poetry universally, forms its chief characteristic feature, and is the source of a great deal of its artificial beauty' (1830:415), but he also noted that parallelism was not strictly confined to verse:

> The constructional parallelism of sentences extends to prose composition, and is very frequent in what is called *wun-chang*, or fine-writing, which is measured prose, though written line by line, like poetry. (1830:416)

Davis's observations initiated a substantial tradition of sinological studies of parallelism. The use of parallelism in Chinese has been noted in a variety of linguistic forms: in the earliest of written documents (Granet 1919), in the *fu* or 'rhyme-prose' of the Han period (Watson 1971), in the later literary style, *p'ien-wen*, known as 'parallel prose' (Hightower 1966), in love songs (Clementi 1904), in proverbs (Scarborough 1875; Smith 1902), and in popular poetry (Jablonski 1935).[2] Similar usages also occur throughout Tibetan literature (Stein 1972:252ff.).

For mainland southeast Asia, the missionary linguist O. Hanson was among the first to recognise the importance of parallelism. In his dictionary of Katchin, Hanson noted that the 'most marked characteristic' of Katchin religious language was *'parallelismus membrorum*, or the attempt to unfold the same thought in two parallel members of the same verse or stanza' (1906: 33). Since Hanson, various anthropologists have pointed to the existence of similar forms of parallelism among the Garo, Shan, Burmese, Mon, Karen, and Thai peoples. It is Vietnamese, however, of all the languages of mainland southeast Asia, whose tradition of parallelism has been best studied. Nguyen Dinh Hoà, who has written papers on parallelism, has observed:

> A characteristic feature of Vietnamese literary utterances is parallelism, which is found not only in verse but also in prose. This parallel structure requires the use of two phrases, or 'two sentences, that go together like two horses in front of a cart'. The nature of the parallelism may reside in the content and/or the form. Parallelism of form or structure is minimum, however. (1955:237)

Although Chinese influence on Vietnamese parallel poetry is undeniable, this tradition of parallelism appears to be indigenous and goes well beyond what is found among the Chinese. Nguyen notes the occurrence of parallelism as a 'prominent feature' not only in folk literature but in all literary forms: in poetry, in funeral orations, and in the formal language of inscriptions. Vietnam's great literary classic, *Tryuen Thuy Kieu*, belongs in this tradition. Quoting Vietnamese sources, Nguyen asserts: '"two successive sentences become poetry as soon as they are parallel"' (1965:133).

For Austronesian languages, the evidence of parallelism is enormous.

In the nineteenth century the missionary linguist, A. Hardeland, in his *Versuch einer Grammatik der Dajackschen Sprache* (1858), was the first to point to the parallelism in Dayak 'spirit language' (*basa Sangiang*); another nineteenth-century missionary linguist, J. Sibree, made a similar observation about Malagasy: 'in the more formal Malagasy speeches the parts of every sentence are regularly balanced in construction, forming a kind of rhythm very closely resembling the parallelism of Hebrew poetry' (1880:148).

Parallelism is so prominent a feature of Austronesian languages that a proper survey of all of the evidence would be a major undertaking. (For a brief survey, see Fox 1971:217–19.) Parallelism is strikingly evident in extensive collections of texts gathered from among the Merina of Madagascar, from the Rhade of central Vietnam, from the peoples of Nias, from a variety of Dayak groups throughout Kalimantan, from among Toraja groups in central Sulawesi, and from Bolaang Mongondow of northern Sulawesi, as well as from many of the populations of eastern Indonesia.

A listing of texts, however, hardly begins to cover the evidence of parallelism throughout Indonesia, the Philippines, and the Pacific.[3] Van der Tuuk for the Batak, Matthes for the Bugis, Adriani for the Bare'e Toraja, and Onvlee for the Sumbanese, all indicated the importance of parallelism in the languages they studied, but none of these linguists ever published extensive texts (Fox 1971:218). Parallelism in the work of Dutch Bible translators was, for example, a subject of discussion in missionary journals because of its singular importance in the oral traditions of the Indonesian peoples (see van der Veen 1952; Onvlee 1953). Kern pointed out the importance of parallelism in the Malay dialect of Kutai, suggesting that such parallelism was also a prominent but often overlooked feature of other Malay dialects (1956:17–18).

Parallelism is also evident in Philippine oral literature. As Wrigglesworth notes, 'even the most unskilled Manobo, in singing or in story-telling, will repeat for days an attractive couplet of parallelism which he has just heard expressed in a tale, while savouring its every word' (1980:50). There is also good evidence of parallelism among Oceanic language speakers of the Pacific. The *Kumulipo*, the long Hawaiian creation chant, translated by Beckwith (1951), provides an excellent example of the extended use of parallelism. Yet for the Philippines and areas of the Pacific, as indeed for parts of western Indonesia, parallelism is not as prominent or as rigorously maintained as in parts of Borneo, Sulawesi, and eastern Indonesia. This is itself a fact that requires explanation.

The large collection of texts, mainly in parallel verse, that were gathered by Berthe (1972) from among the Bunaq, a non-Austronesian population in the mountains of central Timor whose linguistic links are to Irian Jaya, are of considerable comparative importance and extend the occurrence of parallelism to yet another large language family. Of similar importance is the study by Sankoff (1977) of parallelism in the poetry of the Buang of Papua New Guinea. Within the general region, however, the single most important contribution to the study of parallelism is T.G.H. Strehlow's masterly examination of Aranda songs, *Songs of Central Australia* (1971). The son of a missionary, Strehlow was raised among the Aranda and had a native speaker's knowledge of the language. The depth of his knowledge of Aranda and the clarity of his insights lend particular weight to his analysis, which clearly establishes parallelism as fundamental to Aboriginal oral composition. Strehlow describes the structure of this form of composition as follows:

> in a native song words and word-weaving receive as much attention as the rhythms and tonal patterns which accompany them ... the Aranda couplets (or quatrains) tend to consist of two individual lines which, musically and rhythmically, stand in a complementary relation to each other: the second line of a couplet is either identical in rhythm and construction with the first line, or it balances the first line antithetically and rounds off the couplet by a contrasting rhythm of its own. This relation of parallelism and antithesis also characterizes the language of songs. As a general rule each couplet, like a Hebrew psalm verse, falls into two halves: the second half either reiterates or restates, in slightly different words, a subject already expressed by the first half, or it introduces a new thought or statement, thereby advancing or completing the subject that has been expressed in the first half ... The structure of these couplets is of the utmost simplicity; and yet it is most effective. (1971:109–110)

From India the evidence of parallelism is mixed. Allen (1978), for example, has pointed to the binary structure of the ritual language of the Thulung Rai of East Nepal. Parallelism is also indicated in the ritual texts of the Sadars of Jashpur published by Rosner (1961) and suggested by other sources. But it is only in Emeneau's studies of the 'formulaically fixed pairs' of song units among the Todas of south India that parallelism has been specially noted. According to Emeneau, 'If we combine the Hebrew parallelism and the use of stereotyped phraseology of the epics or the Vedas, and push the combination to its farthest point, we have Toda poetry' (1937:560).

Parallelism in Indo-European languages also presents a less determinate case. Both Bloomfield in *Rig-Veda repetitions* (1916) and Gonda in *Stylistic repetition in the Veda* (1959) have compared Vedic verse structures with the parallelism in Hebrew poetry, but the 'catenary structures' or 'carmen style' they adduce in evidence include so many instances of simple repetition, anaphoric phrasing, and the recurrence of set formulae that it is difficult to accept their contention without altering the general understanding of the concept of parallelism. By the same token, the frequent occurrence of 'twin formulae' or 'Zwillingsformeln', 'polar expressions', or, in more recent parlance, '(irreversible) binomials', common in Indo-European languages, does not constitute, by itself, evidence of a tradition of pervasive canonical parallelism.[4] According to Jakobson, 'the only living oral tradition in the Indo-European world which uses grammatical parallelism as its basic mode of concatenating successive verses is the Russian folk poetry, both songs and recitatives' (1966:405). In other Slavic languages, parallelism possesses varying degrees of importance, but among none of these is parallelism as consistent a principle of composition as in the Russian case. Undoubtedly parallelism of various sorts is a significant feature of other Indo-European poetic traditions as well, but often its occurrence is optional, sporadic, or at times subordinate to the requirement of rhyme, alliteration, assonance, and a variety of complex metrical rules.

Consideration of the prominence of canonical parallelism in oral traditions as varied as those of the ancient Near East, of the Ural–Altaic region, of the Maya, of the Chinese, and of the Aranda of central Australia point to a linguistic phenomenon which Jakobson referred to as a 'near universal' – a general phenomenon that is all the more interesting because of the fact that its variable occurrence also requires explanation. Steps in the direction of an understanding of this phenomenon must be based on initial comparative investigations of regional traditions of canonical parallelism and it is to this task that the essays in this volume are directed.

Formal features of ritual languages in eastern Indonesia

Although the essays in this volume address important issues in the study of canonical parallelism, each individual essay is primarily concerned to examine the specific characteristics of parallel poetry as a living tradition of oral composition in a particular cultural setting. The cumulative effect of these essays is to delineate the significance of canonical parallelism in eastern Indonesia and to indicate its comparative relevance.

That the formal structures of the ritual languages of eastern Indonesia bear comparison with similar forms of parallelism in other areas of the world is the initial point of departure for all of the essays. Writing of Kodi in west Sumba, Hoskins describes an 'etiquette of spirit communication' that has as its first characteristic 'the exclusive use of paired couplets' which the people of Kodi regard as the 'words of the ancestors': 'the language that is passed down through the generations//the words that are sewn up into couplets'. In a similar vein, Mitchell describes four features of ritual language in Wanukaka: special vocabulary, distinctive rhythm, the use of metaphor, and a word-for-word parallelism. As in Kodi, ritual language is the appropriate mode of expression on occasions where spirits are regarded as participants in ritual communication. Similarly, Kuipers notes that the 'Weyéwa themselves consider couplets (*ngobba*) to be the outstanding and distinctive feature of ritual speech'. Writing about the speech community in west Sumba, Renard-Clamagirand defines the *li'i marapu*, the ritual speech of the Wewewa,[5] as 'the words that relate the living to the dead, to their ancestors, and to all the forces of the invisible world which are referred to as *marapu* ... These words are expressed in a ceremonial language, *tenda*, which is composed of formulae using images and metaphors ... These formulae form pairs using synonymous or related words and expressions which are not always found in everyday life.'

The characterisation of the ritual languages of the peoples of Flores and of the Toraja of Sulawesi is similar to the descriptions of the ritual languages of Sumba. Writing of the Ata Tana Ai of Flores, Lewis defines the *bleka hura* as '"patterned speech", where the pattern is in the parallelism of words, phrases, and lines that comprise a couplet of ritual language ... The phrase *bleka hura*, itself exhibiting the semantic pairing of ritual language, is used synonymously with *latu lawan "to* speak boldly" ... *Latu lawan* is bold, because addressing the ancestors and the deity is a dangerous business with the potential for inauspicious consequences.' Forth translates the east Sumbanese paired term for their ritual language as 'fashioned speech, full communication'; an equivalent translation of the Tana Ai phrase would be 'patterned speech, bold utterance'. According to Zerner and Volkman, the 'high speech' of the Toraja is associated with the ritual priest, *tominaa*, who has mastered the language by learning '"ancestral words" that enter as "breath" or "spirit" (*penaa*) and are stored in his "stomach" ... It is the *tominaa* who calls in high speech to the spirits to bless the house or rice fields, and it is he who knows the special language to chase away plagues or cure the sick.' In the high speech of the *tominaa*, 'phrases are typically repeated, with parallel meanings or closely related variations ... the speech of the *tominaa* must be full, made powerful through the repetition of words and images'.

Thus, despite widely differing cultural contexts, the ritual languages of eastern Indonesia share common characteristics. They are all 'formal, formulaic, and parallelistic' (see Fox 1971:215). Elevated and highly metaphoric in nature, these languages are culturally regarded as consisting of 'ancestral words' whose power must be boldly mastered to achieve full communication.

Ritual language as the 'words of the ancestors'

This widespread conception of ritual language as the 'words of the ancestors' implies a conception of ritual language as the pre-eminent vehicle of social discourse. Ritual language is seen to stand above, and often in contrast to, ordinary individual speech. In describing the etiquette of spirit communication among the people of Kodi, Hoskins stresses the 'merging of individual responsibility with the destiny of the group'. Phrased in a different way, this could characterise ritual language use throughout the region.

Recourse to ritual language allows performers to impersonalise and externalise precisely what is most extraordinarily personal. On the one hand, ritual language may be used to convey critical assertions of advice, instruction, or reprimand from the ancestors or spirits; on the other hand, it may be used to express the prayers, hopes, fears, rivalries, anxieties, or grievances of particular individuals that might otherwise not be openly divulged. Thus ritual language constitutes an elevated.mode of discourse that is able to give public voice to what might otherwise be unspeakable. As a consequence, poetic compositions in ritual language are concerned with revelation and disclosure.

This view of ritual language affects the cultural view of the poet, performer, or ritual specialist. Without in any way discounting the role of learning, most of the peoples of eastern Indonesia consider mastery of ritual language as a special endowment either given by a spirit, bequeathed from an ancestor, or transmitted along specific genealogical lines. According to Renard-Clamagirand, for example, in Wewewa, 'during the performance of its rituals, every house asks that a man "skilled in speaking" should be born in their midst'. Simple skill in speaking is not, however, sufficient to establish a ritual language specialist.

What is required is linguistic ability wedded to a special knowledge. As the Wewewa insist, 'movements of the lips must accord with thoughts that come from the liver'. Lewis describes this culturally conceived process of selective endowment among the Tana Ai as follows:

> Young chanters acquire their knowledge of ritual language not by study or by memorising chants but by receiving their knowledge of the language of the histories and the histories themselves in a single flash of insight and understanding when, it is said, they *himo wa dea li'ar*, 'receive the tongue and take the voice' of their ancestors' knowledge. Thereafter, having received knowledge of the language of ritual, they can add to that knowledge the skills of performance that come from practice and from hearing the performances of other experienced chanters. Only a few men

are chosen and there is no predicting who, among the living members of the community, the ancestors will choose to receive the voice.

Acquiring the impersonal 'voice' of the ancestors, however, does not of itself confer high status. In the rivalrous societies of west Sumba, mastery of ritual language confers considerable social prestige, but such competence must be combined with the appropriate performance of ritual feasts to effect any elevation of status. Among the people of Lio on Flores, the status of ritual speakers is mediated by a priesthood based on clan affiliation. Similarly the social standing of ritual specialists in Tana Ai is bound up with clan affiliation. According to Zerner and Volkman, the *tominaa*, or ritual priest of the Toraja, need not be 'a man of great ancestry or riches', and often this priest holds his respected position in relation to a village head or *ambe' tondok*, whose position requires both wealth and a noble lineage. In the rigidly stratified societies of east Sumba, priests and ritual orators are distinguishable, though one and the same man may perform both functions. In the domain of Rindi, as Forth notes, 'there are a number of priests who never perform orations'. Although expertise in ritual language can confer respect and prestige, it offers no possibility of advance in social position. The same is true among the Rotinese: ritual language ability does not alter one's social standing. Many of the finest chanters are poor men of commoner descent. Yet high rank, important office, great wealth, and ritual language expertise represent pinnacles of the human condition. The rare coincidence of these attributes in a single individual assumes mythic significance.

Poetic voice and individual performance

Whatever social valuation is given to ritual speakers in the different societies of the region, an individual's performance as a poet is seen not so much as a personally creative act but as an inner receptivity to inspiration. This 'taking of the voice' allows the poet a social versatility that transcends any particular social position.

In focusing either on a particular performance (or related series of performances) or on the ritual composition of a single individual, various essays in this volume illustrate this 'taking of the voice' and the potential of its expression. In her paper on Wewewa, Renard-Clamagirand describes the offerings to the *marapu* spirits by the officiants who are to perform a *zaizu* ceremony. Among these offerings, a chicken is dedicated to the *marapu* of the chanter and this spirit is addressed as his partner in oratory:

I pull out the thorn from my own foot,
I remove the blade of grass from my own eye,
...
My words may be like clear water,
My utterances may be like life-giving water.
You confront my speech,
You are partner to my discourse.

Kuipers illustrates a further aspect of this 'poetic partnership' or impersonation of spirit in his examination of a Weyéwa expiation ritual. As the ritual proceeds, the voice that speaks in the first person is not the poet but a messenger spirit:

So that I
    walk the trail,
So that I
    follow the spoors;
...
The Spiritual Messenger
The Ghostly Envoy;
...

In the Kodi divination ceremony described by Hoskins, the diviner-poet assumes the voice of a hamlet deity whose physical representation – a tree trunk set in the stone altar of the village – has withered and died. Speaking as the deity, the poet can express his grievance, reprimand the community, and demand appropriate retribution:

How can I be the trunk that you lean back upon?
How can I provide the leaves that offer you shade?
Says the Lord of the Land.
And yet now you let me be attacked by these pains in the head,
And yet now you let me suffer the fevers in the body.
Holding a chicken augury for me,
When the death force came into me
There was no one to hold a chicken augury for me.
Blowing on the divination ropes,
When I felt my life energies disappearing
There was no one to blow on the divination ropes for me.
So that now – you should make up for this by making
A shrimp to replace me on the mat,
A pikefish to stay in my place.
You should build for me
A spot for my name to stand,
A replacement for my namesake.

In the first part of the creation myth of the Ata Tana Ai, as told by the *tana puan* of clan Ipir, there is no identification of voice by personal pronoun. But even without such markers, identification is clearly with the 'earth diver' at the time of creation:

> Dive, dive below,
> Below, go downward and carry the lumps,
> Swim, swim below,
> Beneath, go downward and collect the piles.

Suddenly, however, in the concluding lines of the poet's composition, a first-person pronoun dramatically announces an identification of voice with the clan of Ipir and the entire domain of Wai Brama:

> I am clan Ipir, the great ebony tree,
> I am exalted like the large birds of the mountains,
> The domain of Wai Brama and Wolobola,
> Raja as far as Balgnatar,
> Speaking to the sky and earth,
> Addressing the sun and moon,

The Rotinese provide another example of the variety of the 'taking of voice' in the ritual languages of eastern Indonesia. In the death chants of the Rotinese, the deceased is always identified with a chant character drawn from a large repertoire of possible characters. In this way, through the medium of the poet, on the night preceding the burial the deceased may return momentarily to address the living:

> For I am the man Ndi Lonama
> And I am the boy Laki Elokama.
> My boat is about to lift
> And my perahu is about to rise,
> For I am going to search for my mother
> And I am going to seek my aunt
> In the receding west,
> And at the tail's edge
> ...
> My boat will not turn back
> And my perahu will not return.
> The earth demands a spouse
> And the rocks require a mate.
> Those who die, this includes everyone,
> Those who perish, this includes all men.[6]

This multiplicity of voices that the poet is able to assume provides a unique means of public intervention in all manner of personal or social crises.

Performative aspects of ritual language

In so far as ritual language is conceived of as a capacity granted to particular individuals to give public voice to specific cultural utterances, the activity of composition itself becomes more than an individual act. It becomes a collective enterprise. In addition to the spirits who are regarded as participants in ritual situations, a lead performer is almost always assisted in the 'taking of voice'. Understanding composition requires an understanding of how such collective performances are put together.

Several papers in this volume examine the process of performance in some detail. In Sumba, for example, there is considerable emphasis on a public speech etiquette that requires what Hoskins refers to as 'mediated communication'. Forth, in his paper, describes and diagrams the formal communication procedures of the nobles of Rindi that involve a balanced complement of speakers and deputies: major and minor orators, those who are stationary and those who are mobile.

The Sumbanese of Rindi liken this complex passing of speech to a kind of 'weaving' of words, thus invoking a common Austronesian cultural contrast between two distinct communicative systems: a visual system represented by textiles (and often, as well, by colourful food offerings) produced by women for public display on ceremonial occasions, and an oral system represented by a verbal virtuosity that is dominated by men (see Forth 1981:19–20; Fox 1983a).

Renard-Clamagirand gives an account of a specific Wewewa ritual that illustrates how collective performances are put together. In the *zaizo* ceremony which she describes, the lead chanter, who is referred to as 'the base of the tree//the source of the water', is assisted by a number of different speakers, including accomplished orators, as well as young men ('water buffalo with tender necks//horses with fragile backs'), who are given an opportunity to develop their speaking skills in a ritual prologue that cannot jeopardise the proper performance of the main ceremony. All of these men speak on behalf of a ceremonial sponsor, 'the master of the horse//the owner of the boat', who remains silent. Chanting is accompanied by drum and gong, instruments that are regarded as yet another 'voice', and punctuated by the modulated cries of women who attended the feast. The joining of all these voices is described, in a botanic metaphor, as so many 'luxurious leaves//abundant fruit'.

In Wewewa, the rules of performance require that everyone speak twice during the prologue to the ceremony. Gradually, the ritual moves to its main phase, which is denoted by a distribution of betel to the chief participants to mark 'the boundary of speaking'. While other orators lend support, this main phase becomes a 'mediated dialogue' between a chanter who is in communication with the *marapu* spirits and an orator who is in communication with the chanter. To describe this complex performance, the Wewewa use three appropriate concepts: that of 'pair' or 'opponent' to describe the reciprocity of balanced speaking, that of 'bridge' to describe the processes of 'mediated dialogue', and that of 'ladder' to describe the hierarchical progression in speaking.

Sumba appears remarkable for the degree and complexity of verbal mediation required in particular performances. Elsewhere in eastern Indonesia there is no lack of group involvement in performance, but this often takes the form of collective support by a group of speakers who focus their assistance successively on a progression of lead speakers, each of whom contributes to the 'construction' of a total performance. Performances of this kind may continue for some days. The underlying idea is that such performances are the collective expression of all the various parts of a single body of sacred knowledge differentially held by constituent groups of the community. Any individual's performance is part of a succession of related performances.

Zerner and Volkman provide an excellent example of this type of performance, although they examine only one segment of a week-long *maro* recitation of a major periodic Toraja ritual. In this segment a young priest leads a chant, supported by other older priests who follow his cues. His role is to annunciate the wishes of the family group. As the ritual progresses, anyone can shout suggestions of what they want from the spirits and, accompanied by the steady beating of a drum, the task of the lead priest is to orchestrate these suggestions and sort his way through 'the diverse desires and conflicting claims within the group'. As in the case of the Wewewa, botanic metaphors – 'those of one thousand slender bamboo trees' or 'the whole cluster of coconuts' – are called upon to describe the collectivity of separate individuals.

Aoki's paper on the Lio of Flores examines another kind of performance: the sequence of rituals enacted by a confraternity of priests in the attempt to regain two stolen sacred statues. The main ritual she describes is a traditional ordeal held to determine the truth of conflicting statements. For this ritual, one old priest was designated to 'voice' a long malediction after consuming the spleen of a sacrificial dog and administering to both accused and accuser a specially prepared drink of palm wine mixed with earth, rusty shavings from a ritual knife, and a fine powder from the village altar stones. In concluding the chant, the priest dramatically adopted the first person to identify the 'voice' he had taken:

> I, who am doing *bhéa*,
> Am a brother-in-law of the thunder and the lightning,
> Am allied to the rain and the wind,
> Succeeded to the authority,

Inherited the prestige:
Wolo and Mité.

As Aoki points out, when the ordeal proved inconclusive commentators on the performance argued that it was the priest's incorrect invocation of the ancestral voice that deflected the power of the words and rendered the whole of the ritual ineffective.

Lewis's paper on ritual language in Tana Ai is of singular interest because it considers the structure of an 'unvoiced' text and the response to it by ritual specialists in their performance of a major ceremony. The text in question was specifically written (or, more precisely, dictated) by the *tana puan* or ritual leader of Wai Brama. Shortly thereafter, having 'spoken the words' to initiate preparations for the performance of the most important of Tana Ai ceremonies, the *gren mahé*, the *tana puan* died. His dictated text for the ceremony, produced under special circumstances in response to the requests of the anthropologist, became the first written record of its kind and provided other ritual specialists with a 'libretto' for the future *gren mahé*. It is this libretto, with various insertions and emendations added by other chanters, that eventually formed the basis for the full set of ceremonial performances which Lewis was able to record.

In a similar vein, the paper on Rotinese ritual language deals with local responses to the anthropologist's recitation and revival of a text recorded for a Dutch linguist at the beginning of the century. The formal nature of ritual language and the cultural understanding of performance are such that what may appear, from an outside perspective, to be innovation is interpreted merely as a 'return of voice'.

Perhaps among the peoples of eastern Indonesia it is the Rotinese understanding of ritual language that has become the most individualised. As the old Protestants of the area, whose conversion began at the beginning of the seventeenth century, the Rotinese do not use ritual language to communicate with the spirits. Yet sermons, songs, and prayers in Christian church services may all be spoken in ritual language form (see Fox 1982). No clan histories are told in ritual language, but the myths of the origin of important cultural objects, such as fire, tools, rice and millet, the water buffalo, the house, dye-stuffs, and the loom, can still only be told in ritual language. Into this traditional canon some poets have begun to assimilate elements of Christian origin, such as the story of Adam and Eve (see Fox 1983b). More significantly, however, Rotinese have begun to dislodge individual recitation from collective performance. Earlier compromises that allowed traditional performances to be combined with Christian services are now increasingly suspect. As the notions of traditional performance change, the role of poet-performer who would appear at ceremonies anywhere in his dialect area – or his neighbouring dialect area – has begun to alter. It is possible now to call on a poet to hear his recitation of a specific canon without the full paraphernalia of performance. As they learn to bifurcate their world view, the Rotinese describe this change as a shift of ritual language from the realm of religion (*agama*) to the realm of culture (*kebudayaan*). Preserved as 'culture', the vestiges of the power of former ritual performances are allowed to continue.

Structural contrasts: ritual 'dialogues' and 'recitations'

Lewis, in his paper, draws a distinction between two categories of chant in Tana Ai: (1) 'invocations' that are addressed to the spirits, and (2) 'histories and genealogies' that recount origins. As a starting point for comparison, this distinction is useful. The invocations of the Tana Ai, which Lewis notes are the most frequently performed chants, resemble the interrogations, prayers, and entreaties to the spirits described by Hoskins, Renard-Clamagirand, Kuipers for west Sumba, and Aoki for central Flores.

All of these uses of ritual language involve or presume a form of dialogue. Kuipers, for example, notes the 'high percentage of quotative utterances; such as "I say", "you say"' which punctuate Weyéwa prayers. This use of ritual language is also similar to the protocols of ritual language in the formal negotiations described by Forth for east Sumba.[7] 'Ritual dialogue' would seem an appropriate descriptive label for these various forms of speaking: individual utterances are relatively short; they presume a response; and, they are open to a variety of possible developments. Adopting Kuipers's words, they constitute 'a turn at talk, a sequence of conversation'.

By contrast, there are the chants that recount clan histories and myths of origin. These are what the Tana Ai refer to generically as *sejara* and what Mitchell describes for Wanukaka as the *kanuga*. They are like the origin myths of the Rotinese, the stylised accounts of the wanderings of the clans of the Timorese, or the monumental ritual recitations of the Toraja. They are structured on the basis of extended narrative; they are performed infrequently at an annual or periodic ceremony; and they cohere as a recognised sequence and must be told from beginning to end in the proper order. Mitchell provides a good description of what such performances involve:.

> The performance of a clan history is a considerable feat, since it continues without a break from about two hours after sunset until sunrise the next day. It consists of 900 to 1600 couplets, in what is supposed to be a fixed sequence. Each passage is first chanted by one performer, unaccompanied, and then, while the

chanter regains his breath, a second performer sings the passage to the accompaniment of gongs and dancing. The sung version is intended for the attending spirits, but the unaccompanied chanted version is usually more intelligible to the human audience.

In contrast to 'ritual dialogues', such 'ritual recitations' neither tolerate interruption nor permit response. Although embellishment – or what Mitchell calls 'padding' – is commonly relied on to enhance a performance, the intended purpose of the recitation is to complete a generally agreed upon sequence.

Whereas in ritual dialogues a mistake in wording is believed to have a deleterious effect on performers, in ritual recitations any deviation from the proper sequence, as well as any mistake in wording, is considered a serious and dangerous fault in performance.

This contrast between ritual dialogues and ritual recitations highlights significant differences in ritual speaking. It conforms well with native distinctions in some eastern Indonesian societies but it does not cover the variety of ritual speaking in others.[8] Many major ritual performances that are conducted over several days require both dialogue and recitation. Moreover, both forms share certain common structural features.

Metaphors of sequence and narrative

In eastern Indonesia a common organising metaphor for any elaborate sequence is that of the 'journey' – an interposed movement through time or space. This general metaphor is supported by numerous more specific metaphors: walking, climbing, soaring, diving, mounting ladders, following paths, riding horses, or setting sail. Such metaphors are particularly apparent in the narrative structure of ritual recitations. In this volume, for example, the metaphor of the 'journey' forms the basis both of the creation myth of Tana Ai cited in Lewis's paper and of the Rotinese funeral chant in the paper by Fox. The action in these two ritual recitations is represented as a continuing 'search'. For the Ata Tana Ai, this constitutes the process of creation; for the Rotinese, it is an image of the course of human life.

The metaphor of the journey is also common in ritual dialogues, although it is generally one among several organising structures. As Hoskins points out, for the people of Kodi the drum is regarded as the vehicle that carries a singer's voice to the spirits of the upper world, and the elaborate journey of the drum's beat through the 'six levels of the earth//the seven levels of the sky' is magnificently recounted in ritual language. Renard-Clamagirand, in her paper on Wewewa, describes the progression in ritual discourse as a 'ladder' of words spoken to the *marapu*. Kuipers, in his analysis of a particular prayer sequence in a Weyéwa expiation ceremony, argues cogently that the structure of its constituent 'scenes' resembles the 'pattern of organisation of a social visit'. Although visiting itself implies a journey, what is especially interesting is Kuipers's examination of the various subsidiary journeying metaphors involved in the expiation prayer. Thus, for example, the final segment of the prayer introduces the metaphor of 'hunting'. This becomes a pursuit of transgression and the ritual speaker adopts the first-person pronoun, 'assuming the role of the Messenger Spirit who "walks the trail//follows the spoor"'. Kuipers makes clear the density of meanings implied in this journey.

> The altars at which offerings are placed in the course of this journey are represented as 'footprints' or 'tracks'. While these holy sites act as landmarks along the stages of the Messenger's journey, they also stand for many other things as well. They stand for the specific sins which caused the misfortunes; they stand for the misfortunes themselves...; and they are also the altars at which various verbally-offered oblations are provided in retribution. Thus the 'trail' refers not only to the series of steps taken to right the wrongs, but to the sequence of misdeeds and transgressions which originally resulted in the tragedy. This hunting expedition is represented as a kind of journey of moral purification.

Aoki's paper examines an equally dense use of journey metaphors in the priestly invocations spoken in the course of a Lionese ordeal ceremony. In the maledictions of the priests, the major threat to the thief who stole the sacred statues is that the spirits may make him lose his way and that, once having lost his way, the spirits will destroy him.

> May *nitu*-spirits make you lose your way,
> May *pa'i*-spirits bend your way,
> *Pa'i*-spirits who walk along the rivers,
> *Juu*-spirits who walk along the mountains,
> ...
> We order you,
> We command you,
> *Pa'i*-spirits who go along the rivers
> ...
> Gather at the altar stones,
> Assemble the members,
> And he who stole,
> Who is a little child,

Who has quick hands,
...
If he goes on a road,
Kiku-snakes will bite him,
Rocks will press him.
If he stole *'iné naju 'amé naka* with quick hands,
May his boat capsize,
May his ship sink,
...

In this regard the paper by Nakagawa on the *mbuku* or 'jointed' narratives of the Endenese of central Flores takes on special significance. As a form of ritual speaking, *mbuku* are not easily classified. They are sets of couplets used during the course of bridewealth negotiations. The utterance of each set is followed by a demand from the woman's side for a particular payment. Only when this payment has been satisfactorily negotiated can the next set of couplets be spoken. Although these *mbuku* are each relatively short and require a form of response, they clearly do not belong to the category of ritual dialogue. As Nakagawa argues, they are a form of narrative and belong to the category of ritual recitation. *Mbuku* form a fixed sequence, organised by the metaphor of a journey, that must be followed through from beginning to end in order to conclude a proper bridewealth negotiation. Each set of couplets is thus a succinctly phrased signpost in a long implied narrative.

The canonical structure of ritual language compositions

Ultimately it is the nature of composition and the obligatory parallel structure of the ritual languages of eastern Indonesia that are of particular theoretical interest. Many of the essays in this volume provide the beginnings of an analysis of composition, and thereby set the stage for the detailed comparative analysis of composition within particular speech communities and between different speech communities.

One of the questions raised by these essays concerns the degree to which there is a canonical, or in some sense 'obligatory', pairing of words in ritual compositions. Understanding the 'pairing requirements' of particular compositions is essential to understanding the nature of composition itself.

To begin, it is essential to note that in no ritual language of eastern Indonesia is there anything that approaches a strict one-to-one correspondence of all words of the lexicon. In Rotinese, for example, a substantial number of words pair with only one other word. For this portion of the lexicon, pairing requirements do produce a one-to-one correspondence of terms. But a larger number of words pair with more than one other word, producing a range of possibilities. There is, however, a recognised limit to the range of words with which any word may pair. The use of a word that does not belong to that range will prompt knowledgeable Rotinese to click their teeth and even stop a recitation. Thus there are culturally recognised arrangements of pairs, and in a series of papers (Fox 1971, 1974, 1975) an analytical apparatus has been devised to begin to describe these arrangements. To apply this apparatus requires the systematic study of a large corpus of compositions and the construction of an appropriate lexicon of ritual language.

Rotinese usage may not be the most appropriate standard of comparison for other ritual languages in eastern Indonesia. Several authors allude to this in their papers. Zerner and Volkman state, in a note, that Toraja parallelism is 'not nearly so thorough or precise as in Rotinese speech'. Similarly Forth argues, in a note, that 'a greater variety of types of elements form dyadic sets in Rotinese, and that eastern Sumbanese, accordingly, appears to make greater use of repetition in paired lines'. These observations are of critical importance because they point to differences that may relate to the organisation of composition.

The overwhelming bulk of Rotinese compositions belong to the general category of 'ritual recitation'. The Rotinese, perhaps through their long encounter with Christianity, may have lost the spirit 'dialogues' described for other peoples of the area. Even those negotiations which informants insist were conducted exclusively in ritual language only a generation ago, are now at best merely punctuated with quotations from long canonical poems. Nor do the Rotinese possess the variety of ritual language use that some of the other peoples of the area possess. What they do preserve, however, pertains to a strict and formal body of cultural knowledge.

Here Weyéwa presents an excellent case for comparison. Kuipers, in his dissertation, *Weyéwa ritual speech* (1982:89ff.), distinguishes eleven named 'genres' or 'events' requiring ritual speech. As Kuipers notes, Weyéwa ritual speech is not equally 'formal' across these different genres, which cover topics and occasions that extend from the light-hearted to the serious and include spontaneous as well as 'relatively fixed' compositions. The question this raises for future research is whether it is possible to detect a greater degree of 'tightening' in formal pairing requirements over different genres in different speech communities. In the Jakobson model discussed earlier in this introduction, this would require a finer analytic precision in our understanding of semantic relations of a paradigmatic or metaphoric nature.

In studying semantic relations among languages of eastern Indonesia, it may be possible to emulate some of the comparative work on parallelism that has been carried forward by biblical scholars on Semitic languages.

Dahood and Penar's 'The grammar of the psalter' contains a 'list of some one hundred and fifty seven pairs of parallel words ... collocations, and juxtapositions' in Hebrew and Canaanite that are intended to indicate the extent to which 'the psalmists and Canaanite poets drew from a common literary fund' (1970:445ff.). Similar lists could now be compiled for many languages in eastern Indonesia, though these lists would illuminate not so much a common literary tradition as a common metaphoric inheritance.

A simple illustration of this common metaphoric inheritance is the pairing of 'banana'//'sugar cane', which occurs in many ritual languages of eastern Indonesia. Unlike more general pairs, this highly specific linking of two particular plants often has special ritual significance. A comparative lexicon of similar specific pairings for birds, fish, plants, and a variety of cultural objects might begin to illuminate the common structuring of ritual conceptions in eastern Indonesia.

Other more detailed comparisons might also be attempted. Forth, who in his paper devotes careful attention to the structure of pairing, lists the various words that pair with the term *tana*, 'earth, land, soil, country, ground'. The Rotinese equivalent of this term, *dae* ('earth, land, below'), is a core term that has an extensive range of terms with which it forms pairs in ritual language (see Fox 1975:111ff.). A comparison of these terms in east Sumbanese and Rotinese may serve to illustrate the similarities and differences in their mutual 'embeddedness' in semantic networks.

Rindi	*Gloss*	*Roti*	*Gloss*
tana//ai	tree, wood	*dae//ai*	tree, wood
wai	water	*oe*	water
watu	stone	*batu*	stone
awangu	sky	*lai (n)*	sky, above
rumba	grass	*tua*	lontar palm
luku	river	*dale*	inside
pindu	gate	*de'a*	outside
paraingu	domain	*dulu*	east

From this simple example it becomes clear that both Rindi and Roti share a common set of ritual associations that link earth, water, stone, and tree. For both terms there exists the contrastive association between earth and sky – what is below and what is above. For the east Sumbanese, other associations of earth or land are with grass and rivers; whereas among the Rotinese there is an association of earth with the lontar palm. In Rotinese the term *dae* can function as a directional indicator meaning 'below', and through this sense it links to other directional terms such as inside, outside, and east. By contrast, in Rindi the association of *tana* focuses on the domain and the gate as a defining feature. Formal comparisons of this sort open new understandings and permit more rigorous analyses of different but related systems.

The capacity exists to chart formal relationships – the 'embeddedness' of terms – in complex semantic networks across the entire lexicon of a ritual language. This complex 'embeddedness' – itself the product of canonical pairing requirements – renders the 'taking of voice' in ritual language significantly different from speaking in ordinary language. The dyadic features of ritual language, manifest as a 'speaking in pairs', provide the basis for a more complex underlying structure.

Dyadic languages and systems of dual classification

Many of the cultures of eastern Indonesia are noted for their thoroughgoing systems of complementary dual classification. The pervasive parallelism that characterises the majority of the languages of the area undoubtedly contributes to a dualistic perception of the world. The canonical structure of particular pairs also provides and preserves a rich resource of dual categories. Yet, despite what may seem to be obvious connections, the relationship between the dyadic structures of ritual language and the structures of dualism still remains to be carefully investigated.

The systems of social and cosmological dualism described for eastern Indonesia do not consist of a simple pairing of elements but rather of an analogical concordance of elements within pairs according to some criterion that establishes an asymmetry between them. In other words, one term of a pair has to be 'marked' or designated as somehow different from the other. To create even the simplest of dualistic systems, a consistent relationship is required among sets of dual categories. 'Right', for example, might be distinguished as superior to 'left'; 'wife-giver' as superior to 'wife-taker'; 'elder' as superior to 'younger', and so on. In short, dual systems must consist of ordered pairs.

By contrast, the pairing of terms in ritual languages is unordered. Although individual poets may develop their own habits of expression, it generally makes little or no difference which term of a canonical pair is expressed first. Cultures may well adopt a dualistic attitude to their ritual speech and express the view that all words that form pairs ought to be distinguished according to some criterion, such as 'male' and 'female'. Forth reports that the people of Rindi take this view of their ritual language, even though such a view is impossible to sustain except selectively. Not only is it difficult to apply a single criterion to all pairs in the lexicon, it also generates internal contradictions in cases where words form a variety of pairs.

The pairings of ritual languages include not just nouns, but also verbs, adverbs, and adjectives. Thus, for example, Rotinese ritual language pairs verbs, such as *pe'u//sungu*, 'to lie still'//'to sleep', or adverbials, such as *kuku//tidi*, 'rippling'//'splashing', which it would be difficult to order according to a consistent dual principle. But even pairs such as 'right'//'left' or 'east'//'west', which are important culturally ordered dual categories among the Rotinese, remain neutral in ritual language. No marking is accorded to either term of such pairs. (In this volume, double oblique lines, //, are used to distinguish the terms of a canonical pair. This follows a convention established in Biblical exegesis; see G. Gevirtz 1963. By contrast, a single oblique line, /, is used to distinguish elements of an analytic opposition.)

At this level, investigation depends, not on linguistic analysis, but rather on cultural analysis. The question is how the unordered pairs in ritual language become ordered pairs in particular systems of dual classification. The cultural criteria used to order a system of dual classification are rarely explicitly given. It is notable, however, that, compared with the total lexicon of a ritual language, only a relatively limited set of pairs is utilised in systems of dual classification. For eastern Indonesia, it is also worth noting that this select set of pairs is basically much the same throughout the region, a feature that reflects both a common cultural inheritance and a communication of shared ideas. It is these shared cultural conceptions that also figure prominently not just in the ordering of linguistic categories but in the basic organisation of ritual itself.

Metaphors of 'heat' and the 'power' of performance

A ritual in eastern Indonesia is intended to generate 'heat'. As Zerner and Volkman describe the Toraja view of ritual, 'a ritual must be *marua*': crowded, noisy, alive with a bustling multitude of people. In a similar way, the speech of *tominaa* must be full, made powerful through the repetition of words and images.' As they argue, to use repetition and to invoke multiples is a way of generating 'power'.

To the resonant expression of these multiple words is added the rhythmic beating of drum and gong. All of the major ritual performances described in the papers of this volume feature either the drum or gong or a combination of these two instruments. This is often combined with the shouts and cries of bystanders, particularly women, and with dancing, even by leading orators who wish to emphasise their involvement. The Rotinese describe this concatenation of sound and commotion with the verbal pair *doto//se*, which connotes the image of a hot, bubbling cauldron.

The pattern of such celebrations calls for a gradual build-up of ritual 'heat' which must then be cautiously dispelled by ritual 'cooling'. In ceremonies involving oration, speaking follows a similar pattern, rising to a crescendo and then subsiding. Important utterances, given 'heat' by the ritual, mark the pinnacle of a ceremony and lend weight to the general view that the 'taking of voice' is a powerful and dangerous undertaking.

Other uses of ritual language are far simpler. These may be no more than slow incantation of couplets accompanied by the steady beating of a single drum. The people of Kodi, for example, regard the drum as an essential vehicle for carrying the voice of a singer to the heavens. For the Rotinese, songs in ritual language can be sung to the music of the *sesandu*, a stringed instrument set within a bucket-shaped lontar leaf. While the *sesandu*-player manipulates the strings, a second player will use the *sesandu* leaf structure to beat out a rhythm for the singing of the ritual couplets. Although there are no strict metrical rules to ritual language recitations, the rhythm of a ritual language performance is one of its most essential and compelling features.

Recognising the complexity both of the steady stream of superimposed, highly metaphoric parallel imagery and of the variety of verbal, instrumental, and phatic means of marking rhythms and counter-rhythms in spoken performances, it is reasonable to conclude on a speculative note. In a brief paper, 'Syntactical metaplasia in stereoscopic parallelism', Peter Boodberg remarked that 'parallelism is not merely a stylistic device of formularistic syntactical duplication; it is intended to achieve a result reminiscent of binocular vision, the superimposition of two syntactical images in order to endow them with solidity and depth, the repetition of the pattern having the effect of binding together syntagms that appear at first rather loosely aligned' (1954–55). If, as has been suggested by some researchers, the brain's processing of verbal information is of the same order as its processing of visual information, then there may well be a neurophysiological underpinning for the almost hypnotic appeal of ritual language performances. To the study of the cultural production of parallel imagery we would have to add the study of the parallel processing of this imagery.

1

ETIQUETTE IN KODI SPIRIT COMMUNICATION: THE LIPS TOLD TO PRONOUNCE, THE MOUTHS TOLD TO SPEAK

JANET ALISON HOSKINS

Introduction

This paper explores the etiquette used for communicating with the spirits among the Kodi people of west Sumba. It examines speech rules and forms of address in order to discern an underlying division within Kodi cosmology and the hierarchical structure to which it is related. The focus is on the Kodi articulation of the universe as made up of both natural and supernatural interlocutors who must be approached in a specific manner, and whose relations to each other are structured and expressed in language. These relations may variously be cast in the metaphors of parent to child, host to guest, speaker to messenger, companion to companion, and intermediate authority to supreme power. In each of the various contexts of ritual interactions certain kinds of relationship are stressed, and there is a discernible pattern which distinguishes the types of spiritual being addressed and the style of interaction appropriate for each. I shall argue that this pattern is worked out in relation to the cultural boundary between the forces of the 'inside' and 'outside', and I shall then present the style of ritual etiquette which is appropriate for each. In a final sense, this paper is an effort to arrive at more general ideas of social and cosmic order through an examination of the use of ritual language and its constitutive principles. Although the use of formal language is not strictly confined to communications with the spirit world, this paper will treat it primarily within that context, as this is where its traditional patterns remain most salient in the still largely unconverted communities of west Sumba.

The people of Kodi

The people of the Kodi district number about 45,000 traditional swidden cultivators living in the lowland coastal region at the western tip of Sumba. Roughly 80 per cent of the population identify themselves as followers of the religious ways of their ancestors, usually identified on

29

government census cards as *agama marapu. Marapu* is a Sumbanese term used to refer to the community of the dead ancestors, who continue to show an interest in the welfare and conduct of their living descendants and enforce the code of traditional law established when the villages were first founded. In Kodi, the term is also applied to the local spirits who inhabit the forest and fields, the seashore and the coral reefs, as well as to various altars and sacred objects. The whole system of worship of these local spirits and deified ancestors involves a complex of prayers, invocations, ritual offerings and ceremonies which are now opposed to the more recently arrived creeds of the Protestant and Catholic churches. *Marapu* beliefs, although obviously concerned with mediating the relationship between men and the divinity, encompass much more than the domain traditionally assigned to religion, containing within them the germ of the political division of power, the legal system, and the essentials of kinship organisation.

One particularly striking aspect of Kodi belief is the fact that the elaborate series of levels of spirits worshipped are most clearly articulated in speech rules.[1] *Marapu* worship is based on a chain of communication in which messages sent between men and deities are mediated through a network of intermediate spirits. The ultimate audience for all these complex verbal performances is the Creator, maker and sustainer of human life, whose power is seen to overshadow that of the *marapu*. He, however, can never be addressed directly. In ritual contexts, he is referred to as 'the one whose namesake cannot be mentioned//whose name cannot be pronounced' (*nja pa taki camo//nja pa numa ngara*). Although his omniscient presence can be discussed and honoured, it can never be directly invoked.[2] Instead, the living are forced to seek the help of the local spirits of the house and clan, their spirit deputies, and the dead ancestors, to serve as messengers to the upper world. They become the spokesmen of their human patrons, 'the lips told to pronounce//the mouths told to speak' (*wiwi canggu tene//ghoba tanggu naggulo*) who carry these entreaties phrased in humble language up to the higher levels. From the top downwards, the various spirits are arranged in an order where their power and authority is inversely correlated with their accessibility and the directness with which they can be addressed. Smooth relations in the spirit bureaucracy can only be established by placating the lower-level messenger spirits who then carry the words up to the loftier echelons of power.

The number of intermediaries is expanded at the human end of the chain because ritual communications with the spirit world must always be phrased in the traditional couplets of *panggecango* or Kodi ritual language. The term comes from an abbreviated version of the words *paneghe pa panggapango*, language which is arranged into pairs, since this is the prescribed verse form of all prayers and invocations addressed to *marapu* in the house and village. The couplets are seen as the 'words of the ancestors', and are accorded unusual status and authority through their use in the formal expression of traditional values, precedent and custom law. The Kodinese speak of the *paneghe pa helu//patera pa katu*, 'the language that is passed down [through the generations]//the words that are sewn up [into couplets]' as if this formalised speech offered an unchanging mandate from the time that the Kodi villages were first founded.

Even today, disputes over land rights or ritual prerogatives may be settled by determining the proper ceremonial name for a given area or office, and the authority implied by ritual naming carries over into other transactions. Whenever an official declaration is made which requires the attendance of the *marapu* as invisible listeners, the formality of standardised couplets and a structured ritual interaction is obligatory. For those who have not achieved fluency in this intricate style, it is necessary to seek the services of priests and ritual orators, who act as spokesmen and messengers, carrying the words of their patrons up to the divinity. The structure of Kodi spirit worship emerges as a chain of many intermediaries, both human and spiritual, who relay the messages to the higher powers.

Knowledge of these poetic conventions is highly esteemed and valued, and although the words themselves are not kept secret, their interpretation is seen as a delicate and esoteric art. When asked to translate these couplets into Indonesian, the Kodinese will often explain that this is not really possible, since they are phrased in *bahasa dalam*, a language whose real meanings are hidden deep inside.

The 'inside' character of Kodi ritual language does not remove it from the public domain to the property of a clandestine mystery cult, but it does situate it with reference to the wider Sumbanese notions of inside and outside, and the geographical relations of centre to periphery. The power of the 'inside', for the Kodinese, is located in the lineage centres of ancestral authority, while that of the 'outside' is identified with the wild spirits who roam the forests and fields. This distinction is given a mythological justification in Kodi oral tradition. According to local accounts, the cultural order was brought to Sumba in the form of rock and tree altars belonging to each of the founding clans who travelled to the island from overseas. Once these altars were planted and ritually consecrated, they made the land surrounding them 'cool' and farmable, removing it from the original owners and bringing it inside the circle of ancestral protection. From these first centres of human communities and worship, later outposts were established at smaller garden altars in the scattered inland hamlets, thus further extending the boundary of cultivated land. Up to the present, the frequent shifts in residence necessitated by shifting cultivation have made the redefinition of the boundaries between inside and outside a continuing theme of ritual activity.

Instead of directly labelling their spirits with terms for 'inside' and 'outside' (*dalo* and *loho*), as is the case, for example, in the classification of the Rotinese spirit world (Fox 1973:346), the people of Kodi speak of a gradual series of enclosures. Moving from the most 'inside' spirits in the enclosed lofts of the high-peaked cult houses (*marapu la uma dalo*), to the spirits which inhabit the house in general (*marapu la uma*), they gradually shift to include all the spirits inside the walls of the ancestral villages (*marapu la parona dalo*), then those within the consecrated garden settlements (*marapu la kalimbyatu dalo*), and finally the spirits dwelling in cultivated land (*marapu la mango dalo*). Within each enclosure we also find an internal ranking built up around a stationary deity resident in the rock and tree altar (or sacred house pillar) and a number of intermediate spirits arranged around the periphery. Those spirits which lie outside all these cultural boundaries are the wild spirits of the forests and fields, of the seashore and the ocean (*marapu la kandaghu la marada, la kahudo la wei myahi*). They are seen as the autochthonous inhabitants of the region, original owners of the land, rivers and caves. Their power is often associated with witchcraft, fertility and the dispersed matriclans – in contrast to the localised patrilineages, whose clan altars represent hierarchical relations and ancestral authority.[3]

The argument of this paper is that the specific rules for naming and addressing the spirits provide the most salient means of distinguishing between those spirits associated with the 'inside' world of ancestor worship and custom law, and the others whose allegiance belongs to the 'outside' forces of nature. Kodinese informants themselves express the principles of order governing their cosmology in the terms of a communication system. For them, it is the structuring of the word which has the final authority.

The contrast in spirit etiquettes revealed in religious practice is a more reliable guide than any mapping of geographical relations, although the two kinds of spirits are also separated spatially. In the strictest sense, it is only the deities of the clan village and their spirit deputies who can be classified as *marapu pa bara* – the powers which are officially worshipped. Official worship is understood as involving the scattering of rice and the pronouncing of prayers designed to promote the health and well-being of the whole group. These deities are the guardians of the lineage houses, the consecrated garden settlements, and the ceremonial system based on large-scale prestige feasts. Their relations with the human community are vertical, hierarchical and collective. This is marked in communicative terms because individuals can communicate with the higher inside deities only through their spirit deputies: a host of intermediate spirits who skirt the margins and boundaries of the human settlements, functioning as sentries and go-betweens carrying out orders issued from the centre. Moreover, it is not even possible for most people to address these intermediate spirits directly. They must instead defer to religious specialists who, for reasons of age or fluency in ritual speech, are better qualified to speak on their behalf: traditional elders, priests, diviners, or representatives of a specific descent line.

Outside the boundaries of cultivated land live the *marapu pa kahele* – troublesome spirits of the wild, teasers and tempters who establish relations with men, and are much more individualistic and capricious. Any person may go off into the forests to pray or sacrifice to them secretly, braving the dangers involved in the hopes of acquiring later wealth or prominence. The spirits of the outside offer, therefore, an alternative to the hierarchical structure of official ancestor worship, and provide an avenue for achievement in a more direct and worldly sense. In their wider symbolic function, the diffuse, uncontrolled vitality of the wild spirits expresses the autonomy and spontaneity that threaten to dissolve the social order, so they are opposed by the priests of the lineage centres. The traditional couplets of Kodi ritual language condemn praying to the outside spirits in these words:

Ambu bara marapu la kapumbu	Do not worship the spirits in the long grass,
Ambu wiha marapu la marada	Do not scatter rice [in invocations to] the spirits in the fields,
Ambu wabingoka na Manola danga bara a patera	Do not worship falsely with your words like the people of Manola,
Ambu wabingoka na kahale teba kadu a paneghe	Do not trim the horns [of sacrificial buffalo] wrongly with your speech.

Contact with the wild spirits offers, in essence, an illicit arena for personal advancement, which complements the collective rituals of the ancestral centres by providing a riskier, but perhaps more rewarding, pathway to riches and renown.

The etiquette of the inside

We shall begin our examination of Kodi ritual etiquette with the official 'etiquette of the inside': the series of rules which governs appropriate interactions with the ranking deities of the ancestral villages and ritual centres, and the format of the ceremonies through which they can be approached. We shall survey three specific ritual contexts in which men communicate with the spirit world of the inside: a divination, an all-night singing ceremony (*yaigho*), and a full-scale buffalo feast (*woleko*). Although the terms of address used and the rules for speaking remain basically the same in each case, there are marked differences in the levels of elaboration of other forms of symbolic statement: the use of music, dance, visual displays and food distributions. The different messages carried by verbal and visual channels provide an interesting angle on the problem of the 'inside' orientation of formal language, as opposed to the 'outside' incorporation of less discursive forms of symbolic statement.

Divination

A divination is primarily a litany of spirit names, recited in a fixed order, with questions interspersed, in the hope of eventually discovering which of the many spirits assembled was the angry one responsible for this human misfortune. In Kodi, the name of the spirit is itself seen as an invocation, and the longer ceremonial names, in particular, cannot be bandied about carelessly in inappropriate contexts. Ritual names are generally praise names, which serve didactically to remind the listener of the general functions of each spirit concerned, as well as foreshadowing requests to come, by attributing qualities of kindness and generosity to him. For this reason, honorific titles and flattering references are particularly frequent in the longer versions of the spirit names. Later on in the rite, the same spirit may be pictured far more simply, as a messenger or errand boy who carries out a specific task which overshadows his own importance.

Each divination begins with an invitation extended to the spirit world to attend first as guests, as honoured persons offered 'water to drink and rice to eat' (*wei pa inu//ngagha ha muyo*) along with their human counterparts. A diviner is called in from another hamlet or even from another clan to serve as the mediator between the house owner and the spirits. He seats himself beside the head pillar in the right front corner of the house, a spot known as the *mata marapu* or source of spiritual power. Holding a spear outstretched in both arms, with the right thumb extended, he asks questions of the pillar, then lunges towards it. If the thumb touches the pillar directly, the spirits have given a positive answer. If it does not reach all the way, the answer is negative.

Significantly, for the Kodinese this interaction is seen as involving three separate intermediaries, all of whom must be paid with betel-nut offerings: the diviner, spokesman of the human community; the spirit of the spear, who serves to ask the questions; and the house deity resident in the front pillar, who relays that message up to the higher powers. The purpose of the divination must be stated at the beginning, and various ritual injunctions pronounced to exhort the spirits to reply willingly to the questions asked of them.

I quote below some selections from a divination held in the garden hamlet of Kalembu Kaha in March 1980, after the sudden death, from high fevers, of a young girl. For the Kodinese, every death must have its cause in some spirit's displeasure, but this unexpected and rapid loss was especially alarming. The entry of death into the house is always a disturbing intrusion. Even when older people die quietly, their passing is said to tear holes in the very walls and floorboards of the home, creating a dangerous opening in the boundary of ancestral protection. The divination is held for two purposes: to determine, through interrogation, which of the spirits was upset, and to find the appropriate ritual means to appease him and restore the sanctity of the house as a cult centre. The Kodi name for it is the rite to 'mend the tears in the walls and close the gap in the floorboards' where the dead soul slipped out.

The diviner begins by scattering rice and calling out to the spirit community in general:

Deke baka wiha rongo baka liyo!	Take this rice and hear our voices!
Todi byoki kiyaka mono wolo handa kiyaka henene	Let us close the gap in the floorboards and mend the tears in the walls,
Tanaka ha ngge kalunikya	So that wherever he [the angry spirit] is,
Na wolo huda koko	Who tightened his throat in anger,
Na rawi raka ate	Who embittered his liver with rage,
Na boghe halili ana wawi	So that he let the piglet fall from his armpit,
Na weiha kapa ana manu	So that he let the chick slip from his wing,
Ba duki waingo a mate	Until death was able to come in,
Ba toma waingo a mbunge	Until disappearance arrived,
Ba duki Pyoke la kadoki	Until Pyoka came to the banyan tree,
Ba duki Mbyora la maliti	Until Mbyora came to the *waringin* tree.[4]
Tana hena – la wiha pa pandalarongo	So that now – at this rice which is scattered,
La kapuda pa rappa	At the spear held in outstretched arms,
Tana ambu tonda bali kyoro	So do not hide yourselves behind the room,
Ambu tanongo taki mu	Do not bury your message from us,
Ambu mbuningo paneghe mu!	Do not hide your speech from us!

The diviner then addresses the spirit of the spear directly, before he begins to go down the roll call of the other spirits invited.

Deke baka wiha – yo mone haghu	Take this rice – you, the Savunese man,[5]
Rongo baka liyo – yo mone urato	Hear our voices – you, the divination man,
Tana kole pa luna rara	So that we will get [an answer] on the pathway of the headrest,
Tana hena bongoka ela nopo pa kaghakaro	So that we will find it [the reason] on the mat that is opened up.
Yo dikya na pa dukingo liyo	You are the one to carry our voices
Tana hena bongoka ela wiha pa pandalarongo	So that we will find it [the cause] in the rice that is scattered.
Yo dikya na pa tomango taki	You are the one to bring in our message
Tana ambu kako tana dana	So they won't just wander off to other lands,
Tana ambu kumbuni wulu mata	So that they won't hide coyly behind their eyelashes.
Ya dikya ha mbani engenghu wenggu ba wena	I am the one who was angry with you, you should tell them to say,
Ta dikya ba hari dengenghu wenggu ba wena	I am the one who was upset at you, you should tell them to say,
Tana ghoba we kingo a kambuna	So that we can stroke their stomachs,
Tana ami we kingo a atena	So that we can caress their livers.

After explicitly enlisting the help of the spear as an intermediary, the diviner calls on the house deity, guardian of the fertility of the crops and of the descendants of that lineage. This double-gendered deity is said to live in the sacred divination pillar where the ceremony is being conducted.

Mala hena we yo – Inya Bokolo, Bapa Bokolo	So that you now – Great Mother, Great Father,
Na tundu kabihu bihya	Who travels down the sacred corner,
Na tane karangga hari	Who braces her/himself on the holy beam,
Na wongo ana minye, ana mone	Who gives girl children and boy children,

Na wongo manengge wuli, mandapo polano	Who gives thick rice sheaves and heavy ears of corn,
Na wongo labiri myanu, labongga wawi	Who gives us plentiful chickens and abundant pigs,
Na ponggango ela awango	Whose pillar reaches to the heavens
Na ndukango ela tana	And stretches down to the earth –
Nengyo ha mbani ha ri mu?	Is there anything that you are angry or upset about?

This deity, like all of the higher-ranking spirit powers, is addressed with a double name that reflects a relationship of parental nurturance and guardianship towards his or her human charges. While the lower-level intermediaries may be classed as male (such as the spear) or female (such as the drum), the higher deities encompass both male and female attributes in a metaphor of regenerative union. When pleading with this deity for blessings of children and better crops, human spokesmen expand upon this image of an indulgent parent: 'Stretch out your breasts full of cucumber milk, Great Mother[6]//Open up your lap of wide thighs, Great Father' (*Pa malembe a huhu wei karere, Inya Bokolo//Pa ndilyakoni a baba kalu kenga, Bapa Bokolo*), they will say. When illness and misfortune indicate a measure of spiritual disfavour, they are implored 'not to twist away the breast//not to turn aside the lap' (*ambu pa kalengga a huhuna// ambu pa kahoni a babana*).

But while the *Marapu Bokolo* or Great Spirit is praised and venerated as the guardian of human welfare, that spirit's residence in the main house pillar is still presented as only a ladder to the upper world, the ultimate source of wealth and good fortune. Blessings from the *Marapu Bokolo* are referred to as cooling waters (*wei myaringi//wei myalala*, 'cool water// fresh water') which nourish the human community, but originate in the upper world, the rain kingdom of the Creator. In receiving messages from the living addressed to the main house pillar, the *Marapu Bokolo* is also a middleman who transfers these blessings to them as if they were wood or water.

Dikya na hoke weiyo pa himbiango	He/she is the one who fetches water so that we may receive it,
Dikya na pata ghaiyo pa nokotongo	He/she is the one who chops firewood so that we may hold it,
Dikya na ndende la paraduana	He/she is the one who stands in the middle,
Dikya na londo la amba letena	He/she is the one who sits between the mountains.

This shifting of roles from the admired protector to the simple messenger is a repeated occurrence in Kodi prayers addressed to the higher deities, as each one is seen as both the divine parent who oversees his or her children, and the servant of a higher and more distant power. The same ambiguity is observable when the diviner addresses the second major deity found in the ancestral centres, the *Marapu Matuyo* (Elder Spirit), resident in the rock and tree altar at the centre of the ancestral villages.

Dikya ba hene yoyo – Inya Matuyo, Bapa Maheha	So that now, you – the Elder Mother, Ancient Father,
Na pa lohongo ba lodo	Who leads us out in the daytime,
Na pa tamango be hudo	Who brings us in the night-time,
Katu pa kalele	In the sewn-up circle of rocks,
Watu pa kalibye	Among the heaped stone foundations,
A kalanda panda hari	The sacred mat of pandanus leaves,
A kalele mboro bihya	The holy ring of *mboro* leaves,
Na totoko pa ngado	Who oversees us from afar,
Na nggelako pa eli	Who watches over us from above.

Here, the Elder Spirit is portrayed as the guardian of his or her human charges, much as the shepherd tends his flock, walking them to the pastures during the day and bringing them back at dusk. The altar of the Elder Spirit encircles and encompasses the ceremonial centre, setting the stage for the prestige feasts and protecting the heirloom objects stored in the attics of the lineage houses. Since the rock and tree altar which is this spirit's home is said to have been brought from overseas by the founding ancestors, it continues to represent and enforce their authority.

The diviner proceeds to ask the Elder Spirit if he has been offended by any inappropriate behaviour among his charges, who are again compared to domesticated animals.

Uru ya awaka na hawundo wura kari	Perhaps there was a reason to swell the buffalo's lungs,
Uru ya awaka na ha reke ate dalo	Perhaps there was a cause to sour the inside of the liver,
Uru ya awaka na mbani na ha riyo	Perhaps there was something to make you angry or upset with us,
Uru nei awango pa lada hawuku	Perhaps someone went one node too far
Ha manungo manu	Among those you keep as chickens,

Uru nei awango pa dowada ha ndallu	Perhaps someone overstepped a bamboo joint
Ha wawingo wawi	Among those you keep as pigs,
Tana ambu tanongo takimu	So do not bury your message from us,
Tana ambu mbuningo liyomu	So do not conceal your voice from us.

Since there has not yet been a positive response, the interrogation goes on to address the souls of the dead founders of the clan village, who are also included as parental guardians of the living.

Ndewa ambu ndewa nuhi	Souls of grandparents, souls of forebears,
Ndewa inya ndewa bapa	Souls of mothers, souls of fathers,
Na kawungo toghi ali	Who first dug the house foundation pillars,
Na kede rawingo kambattu linjako	Who formed the first even surface of stones,
Ngara na duki la hondi wu panduku	All those who came to the tombstones in a line,
Ngara na toma la rate wu palolo	All those who entered the large graves in a row,
Na layo ela nduha ngali mbyoghi	Who remain inside the turned earth and rot,
Na layo ela rehi cana ndamu	Who remain under the heaped land and decay,
Ambu mate nuhi mate	Dead grandparents, dead forebears,
Inya mate bapa mate	Dead mothers, dead fathers.

The souls of the dead are most likely to cause trouble among their living descendants if they remain committed to performing a ceremony or erecting a large tomb, and if that obligation has not yet been carried out by their children. Promises are thus passed down through the generations, and the weight of ancestral disapproval increases with each year that they are not fulfilled. Responsibilities to carry out the proper prestige feasts are borne by the collectivity, not just the individual most directly concerned. Thus, the death of the young girl that this divination was intended to investigate was not caused by any wrongdoing on her part, but rather by a collective guilt incurred through ignoring the ceremonial obligations of the group.

The real cause of death was revealed when the next major deity was questioned: the hamlet deity, *Mori Cana*, guardian and 'local landlord' of the small settlements near the gardens, where people live for most of the year. The spear finally struck the pillar at the extended thumb when that name was called. In the following passage, the questioning has shifted to concern the causes for his anger. Although the diviner continues to speak in a normal tone of voice and does not go into trance, his task as an intermediary demands that he move from speaking for the human community to serving as the mouthpiece of the deity concerned. As a result, half-way through this section he begins to express the displeasure of the hamlet deity in the first person.

Maka yo dana – wudi pa hamulla watu pa pandende
So you there – the planted *wudi* tree, the stone standing upright,

Inya mangu tana, Bapa mangu loko
Mother of the Land, Father of the Rivers,

Madangga rongo rara
The mighty yellow kapok tree,

Madeta rehi wyatu
The even taller stone

Pa hangoghingo buku
Where the snails come to gather together,

Pa kanihyongo nggengge
Where the spiders crawl to assemble,

Pandou daringo tana, katungo karewe
The place where we dig the land and mend our old rags,

Pandou batungo rumba, tatungo kambala
The place where we weed the grass and beat the bark cloth,

Kalimbyatu wataro
The stone enclosure for holding corn,

Bondo lihu pare
The large granary for storing rice,

Ngge nikya oa hambani ha rimu?
What is the reason for your anger and rage?

Ngge nikya pa koko nja hambeimu?
What is it that your throat cannot swallow?

Ngge nikya pa ate nja mbuhamu?
What is it that your liver cannot accept?

Nengyo ha waingo lodo ndanga na waingo hudo ndoku?
Were there those who used the height of the day or the middle of the night?[7]

Nja do wena, njaing kedu
No, he says, it was not stealing.

Nengyo kaka nggiro nggoro mono wondo ngihu ndoku?
Were there cockatoos shaking their ankle bells or *gosong* birds beating their chests?[8]

Nengyo kura tadungo teiyo mono kawico olengo hamenga?
Were there shrimps with excrement in their heads and octopuses with filth in their bellies?[9]

Njado – nja ghenaka	No, it still doesn't strike.
Ba na otu la gharuni wyatu	When they went off to drag the gravestone
Ela tana nale, tana padu	In the land of sea worms and prohibitions,
Ba na otu la tingu tugha	When they went off to pull in the vines
Ela katu kalele, watu kalibye	At the sewn-up rock circle and heaped stones,
Inde kede nja pa ghondo?	Did they get up without eating beforehand?
Inde halako nja pa na?	Did they walk off without taking their leave?[10]
Nja do wadi	Not that either.
Inde londo mondongo ela handa?	Are you not sitting soundly beside the wall?
Inde ndende ndicako ela koro?	Are you not standing firmly in the room?
Ghenaka!	It struck!
Di douka pa ha mbani mu wemu?	You say that is what you are angry about?
Ghena wadi!	It struck again![11]
Pena ba ya doyo ha hendengo polana?	How can I be the trunk that you lean back upon?
Pena ba ya doyo pa ngindingo rouna?	How can I provide the leaves that offer you shade?
Wena a Mori Cana	Says the Lord of the Land [the hamlet deity].
Mono dikya henene duki nggu a hadu kataku	And yet now you let me be attacked by these pains in the head,
Mono dikya henene toma nggu a kalawaro ihi	And yet now you let me suffer the fevers in the body.
Pende nggu manu	Holding a chicken augury for me,
Ba duki nggu la mate myota	When the death force came into me
Nja ha pende nggu manu	There was no one to hold a chicken augury for me.
Parupu nggu kaloro	Blowing on the divination ropes,
Ba toma nggu mbunga hotu	When I felt my life energies disappearing
Nja pa parupu nggu kaloro	There was no one to blow on the divination ropes for me.

Dikya ba henene – tana rawi do kingguka	So that now – you should make up for this by making
Kura helu teppe	A shrimp to replace me on the mat,
Kamboko helu pinya	A pikefish to stay in my place.
Tana wolo do kingguka	You should build for me
A ndende ngara nggu	A spot for my name to stand,
A hada tamo nggu	A replacement for my namesake.

In this last interchange the hamlet deity spoke through the diviner to compare the gradual rotting of his altar tree to the human experience of illness and malarial fevers. Although there is no immediately evident change in the diviner's speaking style or tone of voice, he shifts to expressing directly the deity's distress that, ever since the decay started, no ritual attention was paid to the fact. No auguries were held, and there was no divination to determine the cause. Thus, finally, when the trunk itself was dead, it took along a human victim to announce its anger. Now the hamlet deity or *Mori Cana* uses the conventional phrases of ritual language to ask for a formal burial of his arboreal carcass (including the funeral sacrifice of a young calf) and demands that a replacement tree be erected in its place. The full consecration of the new spirit landlord will require an elaborate ceremony to reinstate the tree and ensure that it will offer its protective shade to the inhabitants.

The human side of the dialogue resumes with offers, again phrased in ritual language, of a pig and goat to bind them to the promised ceremony. Two chickens must also be killed to verify the results of the divination through an examination of their entrails. As always, the community of the living pleads poverty and hardship, stressing that they cannot afford to hold such a ceremony unless next year's harvest is good. The goat is offered to placate the angry spirit for the time being, so that the spirit will 'lean back and rest//pillow the head for a while', awaiting the preparations to be made for the feast to come.

Deke baka wiha, rongo baka liyo	Take this rice, hear our voices,
Inya mangu tana, Bapa mangu loko	Mother of the Land, Father of the Rivers.
Pandou daringo tana, pandou batungo rumba	The place we dig the land, the place we weed the grass.
Tana hena waingo kawimbi	So please receive this goat here
Tana na hende horo we jomoka	To lean your head back to rest and wait
A hada tamo mu	For the replacement of your namesake,

Njana mbara mbica witti pyango	Since all the crossed feet are not present,
Tana na luna deta we jomoka	To pillow your head for a while,
A ndende ngara mu	For the spot where your name shall stand,
Njana hangga mbera limya pango	Since all the folded arms are not here yet.
Dikya ba kalokongo a rumba rara	Thus, when the yellow grass grows scarce,
Labiri myanu we donghu	We ask you to give us abundant chickens
Mono labongga wawi we donghu	And we ask you to give us plentiful pigs.
Dikya ba na kambukongo a mara tana	Thus, when the dust of the dry season starts to blow about,
Mangengge wuli we do kingo	We ask humbly for thick paddy sheaves,
Mono mandapo pola we do kingo	And we ask modestly for thick corn ears.
Mono ba njana ghemelo do kiyo a weiyo pa hoke la pandalu	And if the water that we fetch from the urn has not dried up,
Ba na njana ndudu do kiyo a ghai ha pata la kambu luna	If the firewood that we chop under the floorboards is not lacking,
Apa diyo ba ky ndende ghu ndikacko ela koro	Only then can we stand you firmly in the room
Dikya hanjoka wu kawallu	With a calf of candlenut-length horns,
Apa diyo ba ku londo ghu mondongo ela handa	Only then can we sit you soundly by the wall
Dikya hinjalu mete mata!	With a yearling with jet-black eyes!

These sorts of promises and commitments bind all living communities in a never-ending chain of obligations to their dead ancestors and spirit protectors. Since many of the promised feasts are never carried out, such failures can also be used as an explanation for the sudden death or illness of another person in the village, and the chain itself is extended into another generation.

Each major stage of Kodi ceremonies – the divination, the all-night singing ceremony and the several-day buffalo feast – requires an increase in the number of offerings, an increase in the number of religious specialists present as human intermediaries, and an increase in the number of spirits invited and made to serve as message bearers to the higher powers. In the *yaigho* or singing ceremony the main 'bearer of the voice' is the drum – but it must 'receive the words' in a dialogue format between a ritual orator (*tou ta liyo*) who traces the history of the problem in ritual couplets, and a singer who sets these phrases to the rhythm of the drums and gongs. For the *woleko* or large-scale feast, a full set of six gongs is hung on a rack in the village square and used to complement the drum. The cast of ritual officiants is much larger and more complex. One is charged with scattering rice at offerings (*tou wiha*), one with circling the sacrificial animals (*tou kanikingo*), one with pronouncing the spoken invocations (*tou ka'okongo*), several with contributing to the oratorical commentary on the causes of the event (*tou ta liyo*), and one with singing while people dance in the ceremonial field (*tou lodo*).

These increases in scale and complexity still repeat the same patterns of pleading, deference and indirect address that we observed in the more simple divination. The role-shifting, where a deity such as the hamlet deity is presented as the 'lord of the land' within his own domain but as only a mere servant in relation to the higher powers, is also found in striking form in the invocations made to the spirit of the drum. We shall focus on its role as an intermediary in man–spirit relations in our description of the singing ceremony or *yaigho*.

The yaigho: singing to the drum

The drum, like the divination spear and the gongs, is one of the Kodi ritual objects dignified with a ceremonial name and various anthropomorphic characteristics. It is charged with the important mission of carrying the 'words' of its human masters up to the divinity. Carved in a shapely *S* form, the drum is presented as symbolically female and forms the counterpart or travelling companion to the voice of the male *yaigho* singer. Both of them are said to travel off together on a night-long journey to the upper world, guided by the double-gendered hamlet deity (*Mori Cana*) who will show them the way to the ancestral village.

Often the ceremony itself starts with a long invocation to the drum, in which the full story of its origins is recounted: how it was found as a piece of driftwood floating off the sacred tip of the western half of the island, then carved into its present form by two now deified ancestors. Once this 'genealogy', if we could call it that, is recited, the singer says: 'Now we can call upon you with names of fishes//now we can summon you with names of pigs.' Now it is proper to address the drum with its full ceremonial name and allow it to begin its shamanistic journey.

Yoyo na tamboro kuru	You with the full chest,
Yoyo na taranda kenda	You with the slender waist,
Pa hono mone Ngawi	Carved out by old man Ngawi,
Pa hono pa kalekongo limya	Carved until his hand was twisted,

La pipi watu kaka	Beside the incline of white stones,
Pa tapi mone Nende	Sculpted by old man Nende,
Pico pa kambidingo mata	Sculpted until his eyes began to squint
La ngendo ngamba ndende	By the upright slope of the cliff,
Pa toghi kyaka marou ngandu	Pierced by the cockatoo with long teeth,
Ha bola a pero manumba ghoba	Bored by the parrot with the large beak.
Yo dikya a kahilye pa ha puningo	You are the bird that we set singing,
Yo dikya a kapudu pa palerango	You are the butterfly that we set flying,
Tanaka ta halako mbola lara kiyo	So let us walk down the same path together,
Tanaka ta kalete dunggu ndara kiyo	So let us ride astride the same horse together.

The singer's final words ask the drum to carry his own voice up into the highest reaches of the upper world, where these words, set to the rhythm of the drums and gongs, will be heard by the ancestral deities. As the final offerings are made to the drum (usually in the form of betel-nut and the sacrifice of a single chicken), its task is made more explicit.

Yo dikya pa tanggu ndoru mbaha ngoya	You are the one who is charged with bringing our words across the waters,
Yo dikya pa hambewa do menanga ngoya	You are the one who is sent to carry our message over the bay,
Yo na pa tomango taki ela Inya Wolo Hungga	You are the one who will bring this speech to the Mother Binder of the Forelock,
Yo na pa dukingo liyo ela Bapa Rawi Lindu	You are the one who will carry these voices to the Father Creator of the Crown.

The drum is said to arrive at the upper kingdom by the time that the morning star makes its first appearance, in the first hours of dawn (around 5 a.m.). At this time there may also be signs that the souls of dead men, rice or houses, which had perished in some misfortune, have descended from the heavens: traces of footprints in the ashes scattered at the base of a bamboo 'spirit ladder' erected in front of the house, loud crashing sounds, a rustling in the thatch rooftops, or the sighting of a falling star. This is taken as proof that the deities have been appeased and have

A singer (*tou yaigho*) beating the drum as he sings an invocation to its spirit

agreed to release the lost souls. Then the drum can begin its return journey, accompanied by the harvest deity, bringing a packload of blessings for future prosperity.

Dikya pa woti mundi ngandi njara inya	This is what Mother carries in on her horse,
Pa taiyo ela kemba waru ndara	Loading it at the back of the horse's withers,
Dikya pa ngahu bokona baba bapa	This is what Father holds in the rice bag on his lap,
Pa la taiyo ela kaluka limya tonda	Grasping it in his hand like a shield,

Manengge wuli, mandapo polana	Thick paddy sheaves, heavy corn ears,
Labiri myanu, labongga wawi	Plentiful chickens, abundant pigs.

The promise of increased fertility comes from the source of rainfall, the lush kingdom of the upper deities (*marapu deta*). It is described as a green, fertile field of wet rice and overflowing streams, where the crops are always bountiful and the people feast regularly on large amounts of meat. The hamlet deity and the drum travel there together through the seven layers of the Kodi cosmos in order to seek a direct answer to their pleas. Since Kodi is in fact a region prone to famine and drought, this description of their journey presents an image of heavenly splendour and opulence.

Wali ome la nomo ndani cana	From the six levels of the earth,
Minye pa tongorongo tana	Woman who plunges through the earth,
Wali ome la pitu ndani awango	From the seven levels of the sky,
Mone na kombokongo awango	Man who pierces through the sky,
Ola pandouna wolo inya	To the home of the Mother Binder,
Ola Byokokoro kori lyoko	To Byokokoro by the river's dam,
Ola pandouna dari byapa	To the home of the Father Creator,
Ola Manjalur nduka ndende	To Manjalur who only stands guard,[12]
Na kawendengo wulu manu	With a roof thatched with chicken feathers,
Na kandilengo ule wawi	With a rack hung with pigs' tusks,
Ola ngawuho kawendo	In the cooking smoke that swirls thickly
Ola nggiringo katonga	On the veranda darkened by fumes,
Ola rende wei kapihyako	In the swamps of wet rice fields
Pandou manombona kamale rende rara	Where the yellow drakes frolic,
Ola homba wei lyambora	In the waters of the lake at Lambora
Pandou manggole katura kuka kaka	Where the white water birds roll,
Na kahupungo lala wawi	Whose firelogs are made with pigs' fat,
Na talurongo kataku toyo	Whose hearthstones are made of human skulls.[13]

According to Kodi mythology, the first ancestors of the various clans travelled to this upper world to seek wives, and came back bringing with them the sacred objects used to pray for rainfall and fertility: heirloom water urns, plates to catch the raindrops, and unusual weapons. These objects were distributed among the members of various descent lines, and have remained important in the local cult of each lineage house. At certain critical junctures, when the well-being of all is endangered, they can also be drafted to serve as intermediaries and messengers, sent back up to their homeland with pleas and entreaties. The drum itself was originally a gift from this upper world, and there are still several villages in Kodi where a sacred drum, supposedly once covered with human skin, is kept among the heirloom objects in the attic. Legends claim that the drum was given along with a bride and her personal slave, who was later sacrificed to replace the drum's skin covering. According to Kodi traditions, the hollow inside of the drum is still inhabited by the soul of the slave woman who died. But in more recent years, the hide of a young buffalo calf has been used, since human skin did not prove durable enough for a feast which continued over several nights. It is the human soul inside which qualifies the drum to serve as ritual intermediary in communicating with the higher powers.

Woleko feasting

In moving from the *yaigho* or singing ceremony to the large-scale buffalo feasts or *woleko*, the crucial role of the drum is supplanted by a new elaboration of visual and dramatic modes of presentation. Instead of the small group gathered around the singer and ritual orator near the garden altar, we now find a full cast of ritual specialists performing in the central ceremonial field of the ancestral villages. The host and sponsor of the feast must also join in the performance, usually with a vigorous display of his own forcefulness, generosity and power. Before the buffalo are brought out into the slaughter field, the hosts of the feast dance in front of their guests dressed in elaborate headcloths of red and orange, bedecked with gold pendants (*mamoli*) and neckpieces (*marangga*) which have been hidden in the attic for years. Wealth is paraded before the spectators in the form of livestock, cloth, plates and dishes, and unusual weapons: imported sabres topped with black plumes, and spears and machetes with ivory handles.

While the women's dancing is composed of a series of graceful, undulating hand movements and fluttering feet, the men's dances consist mainly of strutting about with a fierce war-like expression and brandishing a weapon. A mock battle is occasionally staged when a large party arrives from another village bringing contributions to the sacrifice. The host must first challenge them and determine that their share of the livestock contributed to the feast will be no greater than his own. The greetings and replies are phrased in the formal oratorical style traditionally used to enemy intruders or when returning from headhunting raids.

In a quite blatant sense, therefore, the scale and visual displays of the *woleko* feasts are designed to celebrate the riches and renown of the feast-giver. They also form a stage on a ladder of ceremonial obligations leading to the traditional title of *rato* or 'great man', 'ritual lord'. The full series required by the ancestors includes the rites of pulling a huge stone to build a megalithic grave, of constructing a lineage house in the traditional village, of holding harvest feasts in both the village and the garden hamlet, and of consecrating the house and gravestone with full-scale buffalo feasts in the ancestral centre. Although the number of men who manage to complete all of these ceremonial stages is quite small (perhaps only four or five were living at the time of my fieldwork), the title *rato* assures them of a position within the roster of prominent ancestors called on by name at specific ritual events. The permanent attachment of this honorific title to their personal names provides formal social legitimation of their power and prestige, and allows their 'names to live on' (*pa mopiro a ngarana*) in oral tradition.

But while the human spectators are the audience to a display of their host's wealth and generosity, quite a different message is conveyed in the verbal section of the ritual. There is a contradiction between the message of the long orations addressed to the *marapu* and the flashy exuberance of the dancing and feasting the next day. The sacred words spoken to the ancestors and local deities present them with a description of hardship, poverty and suffering, designed to 'soften their hearts and cool down their livers' so that the harvest will continue to be bountiful. However opulent the feast at which they are pronounced, the rhetoric of *woleko* orators must be laced with denials of riches and abundance. Instead of celebrating their accomplishments, the speakers must plead that the human community has been forced into holding the rite by illness and misfortune.

The following passage provides an illustration of a feast where protestations of poverty and hardship are coupled with extravagant visual displays of wealth. The rite was held to repair damage caused at an earlier feast which had dissolved into a jealous fight between two brothers.[14] Although some of the animals brought for the sacrifice were slaughtered, they did not receive the formal invocations necessary to help their souls arrive at their final destination in the upper world. In all the confusion surrounding the event, their souls were lost, wandering off to haunt the village as they waited 'beside the thatch and the house drains', causing recurrent illness and fevers among the inhabitants. It was to repair this earlier error in procedure, and to show the new solidarity and unity of the kin group, that this rite was held. The confusion and bitterness which had erupted within the village some three years before was transposed onto the cosmological plane. The following passage is in the form of an imagined dialogue among the deities of the upper world, wondering what the cause of all the commotion is.

Payaka ole, no wa nyonno	What is that, friend, going on down there
Pa kawulla pa yaigho waingo?	Which causes them to sing wildly up to the moon?
Engge nanikya a kapudu la pola	Are there grasshoppers hopping merrily on the rice stalks
Ela bondo lihu pare?	In the granary to store the paddy?
Tana ambu wena a wolo inya	Do not say that to the Mother Binder.
O payaka ole, no wa nyonno	What is that, friend, going on down there
Pa mari ndere dandi waingo?	Which makes them beat the gongs and drums to dance?
Deto nanikya a panighi la rou kalogho	Are there bats balancing gaily on banana leaves,
Ela kalimbyatu wataro?	In the stone enclosure holding the corn?
Tana ambu wena a rawi bapa	Do not say that to the Father Creator.
Na walla nanikya a katinyaho la noha	Abundant blossoms in the bushes of the dense undergrowth,
A ndara nggallu nggu?	Among the horses in my corral?
Tana ambu wena	Do not say that.
Na wu nanikya a kapumbu la Malando	Copious fruits in the long grass at Malando [a seashore region],
A wawi wyanno nggu?	Among the pigs of my village?
Tana ambu wena	Do not say that.[15]
A-anikya ha tunu ha manaho	It is only because of that which was roasted and boiled,
A-anikya ha mbaku ha labba	It is only because of the tobacco and the areca nut,
Ha pondako hangango	Who wait yawning at the gateway,
Ha kalambo habba hula	Who impatiently adjust their loincloths,
A mandere la ura	Wandering through the rain,
La wangge rou kawendo	Beside the thatch edges of the roof,
A kandoko la lodo	Baking underneath the sun,

La lete pamba uma	By the steps near the side of the house.[16]
Na marara denge nikya a bahi la kahangga	This is what made the metal red-hot on the rack,
Na mangoda denge nikya a kamba la kapepe	This is what made the cloth in the basket full of holes,[17]
Pa katoghi dengeni a mundu koro	Making the room itself open to dangers,
Pa kataka dengeni a lara pongga	Wounding the carved divination pillar,
Engana marewako malanggana	Causing the constant burning of the logs on the fire,
Engana mbanaho kambipi	Causing the constant heat of the pots in the kiln.[18]
Maka yiwa yiya a kadolihya la	So this is what forced our hands to pull,
Dikya rawi kibyandikya a katuku ndende bendu	In order to pull together the post for the upright drum,
Tana ambu enga bandakya la lete pamba uma	So they would not be left there by the steps beside the house.
Mono yiwa yiya a tuduhukya la witti	So this is what pressed our feet to move
Dikya wolo kibyandikya a kandanga landa tala	In order to set up the stand where the gongs would hang,
Tana mabu enga bandakya la hangango rou kawendo	So they would not be stuck yawning beside the thatch edges of the roof.[19]
Pa hei waingo ha wei wira	This is the reason for the flowing of the mucus.
Inya mangu tana	Mother of the Earth,
Pa tane witti byuandikya	We place what we have at your feet
Tana pa inu mi weiyo	So that you can drink it as water.
Pa hei waingo ha wei myata	This is the reason for the flowing of the tears.
Bapa mangu loko	Father of the Rivers,
Pa ghughu limya bandikya	We put what we have in your hand's grasp
Tana pa ha mu mi ngagha	So that you can eat it as rice.[20]

In the final words of this passage, the hamlet deity – and, by extension, all the other spirits invited to attend – is invited to partake of the feast foods provided, and beseeched to look more mercifully upon the human

community. The account of human suffering presented is supposed to move them to restore their protection and nurturance to all of the inhabitants of the garden hamlet. The elements of flattery and even deception involved are frankly acknowledged in the instructions given to the hamlet deity and the drum, as they journey up to speak to the Creator.

Tana paneghe eghetto minya manu	So speak with words as slippery as chicken fat
Ela inya wolo hungga	To the Mother Binder of the Forelock.
Tana patera lalato wei kawallu	So speak with language as slick as candlenut oil
Ela bapa rawi lindu	To the Father Creator of the Crown.

The Kodinese themselves are conscious of the fact that each rite is in fact addressed to two audiences: a spirit audience which listens primarily to the words uttered, and a human audience which pays more attention to visual symbols (dancing, elaborate costumes, large-scale sacrifices). The words are concerned with mediating relations between men and gods, while the visual display indexes the status and generosity of the host. Christian critics of the *marapu* religion have often considered this a sign of hypocrisy or of the ignorance and stupidity of the ancestral deities. Kodinese informants, on the other hand, stress that it is a necessary consequence of the rules of deference and respect which separate the human and the spirit world. The human community should not presume to compete with the splendour of the supernatural kingdom of the upper world, so all their descriptions of sacrificial offerings and riches must be phrased in modest terms.

Since the language used in ritual is seen as the 'words of the ancestors', its form and even its content must remain relatively standardised. Each speaker moves from the names of important deities and the highly formalised invocations to the freer format of generalised entreaties and short histories, also cast into paired couplets, of recent events in the village. Although the order in which a diviner or ritual singer can call on the higher deities is rigidly determined at the start, he can then proceed to roam a bit more freely through minor deputy spirits in the house and village, the guardian spirits of the gateway and garden altar, and the local spirits of the sacred springs and groves surrounding them. At the end of his roll-call he may have named twenty or thirty specific spirits resident in named hills, rivers or outcroppings of rock, the fierce guardians of sacred forest or wells which defy violations by human intruders.

The whole direction of ritual oratory is to begin with the 'inside' deities and move outwards to the more diffuse and loosely structured realm of intermediate spirits and finally to the capricious inhabitants of wild territory. It involves a parallel movement from a fixed (or relatively fixed) verbal 'text' to a series of improvised communications, albeit still cast in the style of traditional rhetoric. The Kodinese explain this transition as a repetition of the principle that order is most important on the inside. Religious taboos and restrictions are most strictly enforced at the centre, and often neglected in the peripheral garden settlements. In the ancestral villages, for instance, it would be impossible to sample any of the new rice or corn crop until the appropriate offerings had been made. In more distant settlements minor violations of these rules often occur, and are sanctioned in *de facto* fashion as long as later offerings are brought in, with a confession and apology, to the deities concerned.

Similarly, the prayers addressed to the innermost deities of the house and village have a standardised form that is immediately recognisable (in spite of some variations in style from speaker to speaker) and must contain a number of the same phrases as earlier rites. The words used to coax intermediate spirits are somewhat less fixed, and the specific ones which a given diviner may choose to invoke for each occasion may vary widely. There is therefore a good deal more room for 'play', for strategic choices, and for stylistic self-expression for the parts of each oration which concern the middle-level spirits.

The scale and opulence with which each rite is performed provide the greatest range for variation and even for innovation. Gimmicks such as introducing new forms of dance or costume, inaugurating a new slaughter field, a multi-levelled cult house, or modern status objects such as motor cycles and tape-players, are tolerated in the relatively free-form displays of the visual parts of the rite. Even when such flashy novelties are introduced, however, the verbal content of the prayers is kept rigorously traditional.[21] The Kodinese explain that the words form the core of the rite; without them, one would only have a parading of wealth and influence, with no spiritual or religious justification. Thus each time a large ceremony is performed the participants must protest their own innocence of the implied charge of reckless consumption and ostentation. They do so in the humble words of ritual language, attempting to legitimate their own claims to higher status by bringing them inside the realm of ancestral protection and control.

We are now in a position to summarise the characteristics of the system of 'spirit etiquette' which governs interactions with the supernatural forces of the inside. Appropriate communications must always conform to these norms of style when the deities of the ancestral centres and their spirit deputies are addressed:

(1) Exclusive use of paired couplets. The formalised conventions of the 'language of the ancestors' are prescribed for all ritual interactions. When

paired speech is used in a non-ritual context (as in welcome speeches or political rhetoric), it usually brings with it the implication that the ancestral deities may be listening.

(2) Mediated communication in a public forum. No head of household may argue his own case before the ancestral deities, however skilled he may be in ritual speech. He must always call in a speaker from another hamlet or lineage house to make the offerings on his behalf, and this debt must be acknowledged with a public payment. All interactions with the spirits of the inside occur with an audience present, whether this is the small group of family members gathered around the diviner or the several thousand people invited to a feast to consecrate a new megalithic stone grave. An audience of human spectators is essential to one of the key functions of the prestige feasts, which is to parade one's wealth before others and gain ancestral recognition for one's generosity and leadership of other men.

(3) Indirectness. None of the higher deities may be named or summoned directly, and even requests to their spirit deputies must be phrased in a manner which does not make them appear too insistent. Deference and respect for the spirit world are shown through metaphorical phrases which clothe the description of previous offences in the language of humble contrition.

(4) Hierarchical stratification of both the human and spirit world. The various deities must be addressed in a strict order. The highest-ranked ones may only be approached through an intermediary, such as the divination spear or upright drum. In similar fashion, guests at prestige feasts are served according to prescribed order, which recognises their seniority, lineage rank and social position.

(5) An attitude of submission and pleading. Even the most respected ritual specialists must assume a humble, self-deprecating manner when addressing the spirits of the inside. They repeatedly apologise for their own ignorance and incompetence, even in the midst of an otherwise flamboyant display of verbal skill. This is done because, as they say, the living must always consider themselves like small children in relation to their dead ancestors. Their attitude is illustrated in this excerpt from a prayer spoken by an old and respected white-haired priest, who nevertheless protests his youth and inexperience before the deities.

Njaingo na matungo pola pare	There is no one left as mature as ripe paddy,
Njaingo na marara rou tandeiyo	There is no one left as golden as *kambili* leaves,
Ghica kanehengoka ha nggengge nja pa ate	Only we are left, [as ignorant as] spiders with no livers.[22]

Ghica kanehengoka ha buku nja pa koko	Only we are left, [as stupid as] snails with no throats.
Na kaka pango ha wungandu ma	Our teeth are still too white,
Na moro pango a longge ma	Our hair is still too blue.[23]
Njaingo na kedeko pa danga	There is no one here to tell us the many long myths,
Njaingo na nughalo pa rehi	There is no one here to teach us more of our customs.
Di kaluka yayo enga pada pokatao kalaiyo	I alone am like a child holding the net for a discus toy,
Di kaluka yayo enga pada lereho kadiyo	I alone am like a child grasping the rope on a spinning top,
Kaco pa kadughu ngguni a patera ambu	The pointing stick that we extend out from the language of our grandparents,
Kaloro pa lamenda ngguni a paneghe nuhi	The rope that we lengthen from the speech of our forebears.
Ghica pimoka wiwi canggu tene	We are only the lips told to pronounce,
Ghica pimoka ghoba tanggu naggulo	We are only the mouths told to speak.

(6) A merging of individual responsibility with the destiny of the group. In the divination concerning a death, discussed above, a single girl in the garden hamlet died suddenly because the group as a whole had neglected to keep up the tree altar near the consecrated stone. As a result, while the fault was not hers in any personal sense, her death was used as a message to the whole settlement. The anger of the spirits of the inside is often expressed by illness or misfortune which afflicts only one member of the community. That person's suffering is used as a device to communicate with them all. Minor ailments, such as an infected, sore or swollen limb, are referred to as small 'warning pinches' which alert the members of the hamlet that the deities are dissatisfied with them. They are said to 'pull downward on the nerve ends, so the spirits won't enter to catch people in their nets//cause the skin to twitch, so epidemics won't come in to destroy the pigs with illness' (*pa kawico kadoru tana amba tama a marapu mangu dala//pa tuikyo kambihya tana ambu duki a kapore wawi diri*). It is only when these warnings are not heeded that more serious illness, or even death, may come.

The etiquette of the outside

All of these conventions contrast sharply with the style of interaction considered appropriate for dealing with the spirits associated with the outside – the wild inhabitants of the forests and fields, the seashore and the ocean (*marapu la kandaghu la marada//la kahudo la wei myahi*). Encounters with wild spirits occur in contexts very different from the public ceremonial setting of most Kodi ritual, and this may help to explain why they are less strictly stratified and less strictly governed by rules of order and deference.

Speaking to wild spirits

Instead of calling on them in the elaborate ritual language of the ancestors, the person desiring a wild-spirit familiar will wander off into the usually dangerous terrain of the forest or the coral reefs along the coast. There he may be surprised by the sudden appearance of a hairy man-goat (*kawimbi mbyulu*), a swollen puff adder (*tumbango*), a witch-woman with long fingernails and a single pendulous breast (*warico ha wu huhu*), a giant crab (*kura mbiyo*), or a python, bird or crocodile, willing to form an intimate pact with a human being.

He must confront the wild spirit or *yora* directly, and never show his fear, for in such interactions boldness, cunning and ambition are his only weapons.[24] In contrast to the attitudes of submissiveness and pleading that pervade the humble prayers addressed to the ancestors, in speaking to the wild spirits individual courage and resourcefulness are prized. Most reported conversations begin in ordinary language and do not use praise names or indirect forms of address. The formal paired couplets of the 'language of the ancestors' are used only if the person wishes to ward off the wild spirits. In order to approach them and negotiate a contract of mutual benefit, claims must be made and exchanged in ordinary speech.

Usually the human interlocutor will simply try to persuade the wild spirit to leave him alone, either by offering to share his food with him or by appealing to his feelings of sympathy for a lone wanderer. The following passage from a longer epic shows the generally informal speech styles used in their interactions.

> While he was eating, a giant wild spirit came by with long sharp fingernails.
> 'Who is that there?' said the giant man.
> 'Oo, it is just me, grandfather.'
> 'What are you doing there?'
> 'Oo, I was just wandering aimlessly, because my mother and father died, grandfather.'
> 'I am a fingernail witch,' said the giant man. 'That means that if I stab you with my fingernail, you will die immediately!'
> 'Oo, please have pity on me, grandfather. My mother left me an orphan, and my father left me all alone.'

'Give me one of your tubers,' said the fingernail witch.

He handed over one of the tubers. The witch peeled it, took a bit out of the inside and set it down beside him. Then he made his voice heard in an invocation: 'Take this here and eat it, for all our anuses and penises!'

'Why do you say that, when you make invocations, grandfather?'

'Those are the spirits that I pray to', said the fingernail witch. Then, when he had finished, he disappeared.[25]

In this passage the only echoes of ritual language are in the plea of the young orphan for the sympathy and compassion of the wild spirit, whom he flatters by addressing as grandfather. The use of any sort of paired speech indicates the ancestors. Had the boy wished to work out a contract for some sort of personal goal, such as the acquisition of livestock or a particular bride in marriage, he would have continued the conversation in ordinary speech.

A different code is used for formulating requests for sacrifices and gifts, one based on persistent animal metaphors. Thus, while a human wife in official ritual language is described as 'the kernel at the heart of the house, who serves the guests//the banana at the centre of the home, who becomes one's own coconut shell' (*lendu atu umana wawa ana kula//kalogho ndomo uma na koba tanggu mete*), in the language used by and to the wild spirits she is a *bei wawi uta*, a large wild sow. An important man will be referred to as a *bei marangga*, the gold horned headdress of a warrior, a phrase which is also used as a metaphor for a wild boar. The code used for negotiations with a wild spirit is very similar to the *paneghe kalola* or 'hunting language', a series of substitute names for wild animals, foods and movements which are used by hunters to keep their plans secret from their projected victims. The assumption, of course, is that the wild creatures can understand ordinary human speech but not these special, culturally convoluted forms.

In dealing with volatile wild spirits, human beings do not have the options of deception and denial that are often used in coaxing favours out of the ancestral deities. The demands made must be immediately agreed to, and there are no procedures for delaying a promised sacrifice with tales of hardship and woe. The Kodinese say that initially the *yora* or wild-spirit familiar will ask for only an occasional pig or chicken sacrifice, and he will reciprocate with gifts of magical animals and huge increases in wealth. After several years, however, if his human partner is not as attentive as he should be, the wild spirit may come to ask for the sacrifice of a spouse, child, or close relative. Those who enter into such pacts, while known for the splendour of their houses and herds, are said not to live very long – unless they prove unusually clever.

Significantly, debts incurred to a wild-spirit familiar are personal debts, which are not passed on to succeeding generations as are the ceremonial obligations of the feasting system. Whatever commitments an individual makes to his python or bird friend are made in secret, without the presence of others or even spirit deputies summoned as invisible witnesses. Contacts with the *yora* serve to advance individual ambition rather than the collective well-being, so they are seen as fundamentally antisocial. While prominent men are known to have such 'secret friends' that they meet in secluded places, few of them will readily confess. Many fear that by revealing these illicit encounters as the source of their wealth, they may anger the wild spirit and thus cause their own downfall.

The signs that death has been caused by an angry *yora* are the same as those that suggest the human use of witchcraft or poison: unusual swelling or a particularly foul smell coming from the victim's belly, bluish eyes and fingernails, or – most clearly – a bluish ring around the navel and an opening there. These are clear marks of outside interference, but the blame in these cases must be laid on the individual concerned, since it was a personal choice to stray away from the protective circle of ancestral protection. Funeral lament songs or dirges (*hoyo*) often dwell on the dangers of the wild, reproaching the dead person for his obvious disregard of social conventions and his desertion of the leafy shade of the clan's tree altar.

Ta yo domongoka na halako inja doli	But you still wandered off without pausing,
Ela pundu wu kandaghu	Into the depths of the forest.
Ta yo domongoka na kaka inja handaka	But you still walked away with no sense of direction,
Ela marada wu marapu	Among the wild spirits in the fields.
Maka inde mate mangguna egheto kadoki	So you didn't die playing safely at the base of the smooth banyan tree,
Maka inde heda maghana lalako maliti	So you didn't pass away amusing yourself by the sleek *waringin* trunk.
Mateka la vidu poto rara	You died at the top of the yellow bamboo stalk,
Hedaka la ghoba lingo ndattu	You passed away at the mouth of a deep cave,
Na kataongong a tana mete	Laying your body on the black earth,
Na nopongo a rumba rara	Resting your head on the yellow grass.

Similar lines could be repeated concerning the death of anyone who died outside the home – by drowning, falling from a tree, being struck by lightning, attacked by enemies or wild animals – since he also fell victim to the forces of the outside.

The boundaries separating the domain of the inside ancestral spirits from the outside can be altered and extended through the agricultural rituals which accompany the system of shifting cultivation. In order to open up new lands, sacrifices must be made to the spirits of the wild so that they will release their control over the fields, making them ritually cool and 'bland' (*kaba*) enough to cultivate. Each year, before any rice or corn can be consumed inside the ceremonial centres, it must first be offered to the ancestral deities by the priests of the clan. Before these offerings have been made, the rice is still 'bitter' (*padu*), charged with the fertile energies of the original inhabitants of the land. Once it has been ritually cleaned, and a share consecrated to ceremonial use, then it becomes 'bland' and edible.

The original inhabitants of the land are directly addressed in these prayers to transfer their territory to human use, but they are called as companions and neighbours rather than with the parental metaphors usually applied to the deities of the inside. There is also no use of intermediaries or hierarchically arranged levels. The wild spirits are bribed into co-operation with the human community, but they are never incorporated into its system of social relations.

The following passage from a harvest offering shows how such charms, designed to keep the forces of the wild at a distance, are constructed.

Tanaka yo dana – a tagheghe mori lyoda
So for you, then – the forest fowl, lord of the area,

Na ole ndikya ha kaledeko marada
Whose companions are the fruit-flies in the fields,

Tanaka yo dana – a wondo mori pyada
So that for you, then – the *gosong* bird, lord of the region,

Na ole ndikya ha loloto kandaghu
Whose companions are the grasshoppers in the forests,

Yemi kolongo malagho
You, the cuckoo birds and the mice,

Ha rote kahodo
You, the rice weevils and red ants,

Ka nggengee palakico
The spiders and the scorpions,

Ha kalipye talidiko
The centipedes and the green snakes,

Nja pa didi ela nggorengo
Who did not push the bottle,

Nja pa tonda ela pengga
Who did not touch the plate,

Nja pa kikulo rou karaba rara
Who did not disturb the golden gourd leaf,

Nja pa tonda lugha kadu koba	Who did not touch the horn shell tubers,
Tana hena a ngagha, a weiyo	Please take this rice and this water
Inu baka mono mu baka!	To drink and eat [in payment]!

The only other contexts in which the spirits of the wild are directly addressed and appeased are in the charms used by travellers who must cross through dangerous forests or fields. The unwary may be attacked by wild animals on such trips, or tempted to follow the lovely forest nymphs (*lemba karingge*) who live along the river banks and are said to drive the men who pursue them crazy with lust. True to the inverted character of many of the spirits of the outside, these false spirit-women are unable to satisfy their human partners because their genitals have actually grown backwards – but the truly besotted may even be driven to engage in bestial practices. Thus, the challenge presented to the traveller is to escape such antisocial temptations and arrive safely at his destination. Usually these charms are just a few short words spoken as a bit of betel-nut is left at the base of a tree. But occasionally more elaborate examples surface, such as this text taken from a myth about a lonely orphan who wandered through the forest, pleading with the wild spirits for help and guidance.

Ba hema do kinggumi, ndilu ghu tilu	If you are out there, lend me your ears,
Yo ma kandi katuku tana	You who guard the posts in the land,
Nggengge milye ate kalu kinjaka	Be the spider with the sympathetic liver to me.
Ba hema do kinggumi, mata gha ice	If you are out there, look with your eyes,
Yo na dagha manggehilo watu	You who watch over the holes in the stones,
Rowa tabu ngahu kalu kinjaka	Be the dove who taps his chest in compassion for me.
Ambu wolo kalu kinjaka limya ha pa ngora	Do not put the hands on my snout,
Ambu rawi kalu kinjaka witti ha rembio wawa	Do not put my feet down into the net,
Ambu caka lo kiyaka	Do not send me out there
La kahoha wawi mbyani	In front of the fierce forest pigs.
Ambu caka lo kiyaka	Do not send me out there
Ngape ndara rara	Between the stampeding bay horses.
Ambu ngandigha ela loko ndunga woyo	Do not bring me to the rivers full of crocodiles,

Ambu erugha ela limbu palu kura!   Do not take me to the waterholes
                                        where the crabs may strike!

Such a direct entreaty, in the world of mythology at least, is often enough to soften the hearts of the wild spirits so that the young hero gains the assistance of a wild-spirit familiar or *yora*. Popular stories go on to describe how this wild spirit, in the form of a snake, bird or monkey, travels with the hero as his companion, helps him to marry a beautiful woman and to pay her sumptuous bride-price, and finally to found his own house and village. Cast off from his own family and descent line, the orphaned hero of these myths is forced to seek assistance from the spirits of the forests and fields. At the end of the tale, however, he returns to the graves of his parents to rebury them in the proper manner. By using his new wealth to sponsor a stone-dragging ceremony which will culminate in the consecration of a new megalithic grave, he brings his newfound riches 'inside' and legitimates his standing with the ancestral spirits.

The prestige feasts, in everyday life as well as in mythological accounts, transform individual renown achieved on the 'outside' (through feats of daring and great riches) into social position recognised on the 'inside'. In the sacrifice of livestock and the distribution of meat, the hero must again humble himself before his ancestors and ask for their blessings to continue his line. Once he has achieved the prominence he desires, he no longer needs to rely on the charismatic powers that he derived from the wild and can instead enjoy the traditional authority of the ancestor cult.

What, then, are the characteristics of the 'etiquette of the outside' which distinguish these spirits from those of the ancestral centres and lineage houses? In direct contrast to the style of interaction discussed earlier, the wild spirits are addressed according to the following conventions:

(1) Use of relatively unmarked language forms. Most communications with the wild spirits occur in ordinary speech, especially if some sort of contract is being negotiated between the person and his spirit familiar. The code used to articulate demands for sacrifices is different from the paired couplets of ritual language and expresses human relations by the metaphoric substitution of wild animals.

Formal ritual speech is only appropriate for charms designed to ward off the wild spirits and keep their disruptive powers at a distance. While reported conversations often incorporate paired couplets to keep away the spirits concerned, informants agreed that in secret conversations these were dispensed with. In this way, individuals who have no fluency in ritual speech enjoy equal access to the powers of the outside.

(2) Personal conversations held in a secluded place. In contrast to the public ceremonial of the inside, there is no audience present at the meeting between an individual and his *yora* or wild-spirit familiar. Details of such

meetings are kept secret, at least until the person concerned has achieved social prominence. Even then they are acknowledged only in intimate conversation and by small offerings made in the wild.

(3) Directness. Spirits inhabiting the forests and fields can be addressed without the elaborate deference which is paid to the ancestral deities, and when they are called upon it is as companions and helpmates rather than as parental figures.

(4) An egalitarian assumption that personal daring may pay off. The wild spirits are scornful of rank and privilege, and often seem most inclined to help those who have been cast off from formal social groups and forced to make it on their own.

(5) An attitude of boldness and assertiveness. Value is placed on individual courage and resourcefulness. Often a series of specific tests is set for the hero, and the wild spirits themselves may be outwitted by a clever person willing to take a chance. Should all other strategies fail, a skilful speaker may also appeal to their feelings of sympathy for orphans and the downtrodden.

(6) An ethic of individual responsibility. The contract entered into with a wild spirit is personally binding, but does not necessarily involve the other members of the person's household, and still less his descendants in generations to come. Obligations to perform certain sacrifices are undertaken for reasons of personal ambition, not collective duty. The charismatic powers that an individual may acquire from outside spirits include not only the ability to amass wealth and livestock, but also invulnerability in battle, skill in ritual speaking, and medicines for use in courtship and healing. These powers, however, are not inheritable by his sons, who must prove themselves worthy before they can establish their own relationships with spirit familiars.

Interactions with the Kodi spirit world are carried out according to two separate sets of rules: one attuned to the official centres of traditional law and custom, the other tied to the idiosyncratic demands of personal advancement. It is the tension between the two systems, often mutually contradictory, which pervades the ritual arena and requires the mediation of priests, diviners and elders to analyse the situation in Kodi terms and work out a solution, balancing the force of individual ambition and drive against the collective needs of the social body. In Kodi, this drama is played out on a cosmological scale, and its various aspects are incarnated in specific named deities whose powers may be appealed to through rite and ceremony.

The view presented of Kodi traditional belief as a communication system allows us to distinguish these two modes of interaction, and to isolate their characteristics through an analysis of the forms of address used to name and summon the various spirits. The overall picture of Kodi cosmology that emerges combines elements of hierarchy and structured levels with a complex series of spirit deputies who move between levels, and a contrasting network of wild spirits who move outside them – in occasionally disruptive fashion. Overall, it could be said to offer a parable on Kodi theories of the struggle between collective pressures and individual achievement. While the laws of the ancestors present a supposedly unchanging template for social life, ambitious individuals continue to use their own talents to advance their positions. The interactions between the human community and the fixed levels of the inside spirits are infused with a new dynamism and energy by the competing interactions with the wild spirits of the outside. It is this contrast in styles which provides an indigenous commentary on the changing order of the world, and an explanation for individual shifts in social rank and group.

2

METHOD IN THE METAPHOR: THE RITUAL LANGUAGE OF WANUKAKA

DAVID MITCHELL

Malapa na kabu hoba radi-mu?	What is in the bellies of the ducks on the pond?
Malapa na kaweru loku jangi-mu?	What lies behind the overhanging leaves at the riverside?

A simple scene of ducks on a pond, against a background of overhanging leaves, may at first suggest to us no more than a sense of the peace and beauty of the natural world. But there may well be cues in this peaceful scene which bring about a shift in our perspective and radically transform the significance that the scene has for us. Are the ducks taking fish of a kind that men too might harvest? Do those overhanging leaves conceal a waiting crocodile?

So, too, when a Sumbanese villager receives an unexpected visitor at his house, the initial focus of attention is on the warm greeting and the observance of the proper courtesies: the offering of a betel-chew, a woven mat to sit on in the shade of the veranda, and then a mug of freshly ground coffee. After these pleasantries comes a shift in attention to the real business of the occasion. What opportunities, and what threats, does this scene of quiet hospitality portend? Why has the visitor come? When the host asks the reason for the visit, he will in all probability shift into the poetic language which the Sumbanese use for such occasions, and put his question with the classical couplet quoted above. The ducks' bellies and the overhanging leaves are his metaphors for his own situation.

Indeed, it is likely that the whole of the serious discussion between host and visitor will be conducted in this way, as each draws on the classic metaphors to make his point, and a prolonged poetic dialogue will ensue. Whether it is a trading agreement to be entered into, a marriage to be proposed, a dispute to be settled, or any other serious dealings between the people of different villages, the Sumbanese abandon the simplicity and directness of ordinary speech and conduct their discussion in this complex and elegant manner. This form of poetic speech has come to be referred to as the 'ritual language' (Fox 1971), or *ceremonielle taal*

(Onvlee 1973) because it is prescribed for use in such formal social situations.

As well as being used in formal dealings between two human parties, the ritual language is used in communications with supernatural beings. Thus, most of the important moments in Sumbanese social life are accompanied by at least a few phrases in the ritual language. Even outside the situations where ritual language is prescribed as the normal and proper means of communication, its images and metaphors have a pervasive influence on Sumbanese thought.

Adams, for instance, has interpreted some of the designs on east Sumbanese textiles as a reference to the imagery of the ritual language (1971). The example she quotes is a schematic turtle-shell design which to a naïve observer would be no more than a decorative abstract pattern. To the east Sumbanese, however, this design invokes the traditional couplet:

Kaba kara	Golden turtle-shell,
Wuya rara	Red-toned crocodile.

The turtle is thought of as an extraordinarily fertile creature, just as the crocodile is an extraordinarily dangerous one. Metaphorically the couplet is used as a reference to the noble rulers of east Sumba, depicting the ruler as a source of comparable powers over life and death. In this way the simple visual design gives rise to a complex chain of associations, through the mediation of the ritual language couplet.

In this essay it is part of my intention to provide a general description of the ritual language of Sumba, but more specifically I am concerned to understand why this poetic form is used at all. To express a thought metaphorically is more devious and more difficult than to state it directly, and there is always the risk that the metaphor may be misunderstood. These problems are obvious. What then are the compensating advantages of the poetic form?

One might answer very simply that the poetic language is used for the sake of its beauty, and I do not doubt that there is some truth in this answer. But to leave the matter there surely would be equivalent to leaving our scene of ducks and overhanging leaves as a representation of the peace and beauty of nature. Like the Sumbanese villager, we must ask more penetrating questions. What deeper meanings lie concealed behind the elegant surface appearance of things? What other meaningful connections can be found between the structure of the ritual language and the role that it plays in Sumbanese life?

Some of the issues I wish to raise have been referred to by Onvlee in his discussion of Sumbanese language in general (1973), and by Adams in her paper on the east Sumba area (1973), so it is necessary to stress that, in spite of significant differences in dialect and custom in the different parts of Sumba, there appears to be a basic uniformity, from one end of the island to the other, both in the form of the ritual language and in its role in social life. At the same time, where matters of detail are concerned it becomes more difficult to deal with the island as a whole and a narrower focus seems more appropriate. In this essay the ritual language couplets will be quoted in the Wanukaka dialect, as spoken by the community of some 6000 persons who occupy the Wanukaka valley on the south coast of west Sumba. The pattern of use of the ritual language is as I observed it during the period from 1973 to 1975 when I was living in Wanukaka.

The social context

> ... it is a linguistic convention in eastern Indonesia that social wisdom and indeed significant knowledge of a ritual sort must be expressed in dual terms – in a binary or dyadic form. (Fox 1980a:16)

The Sumbanese ritual language is but one example of the special forms of language used in the islands of eastern Indonesia. These islands also provide many examples of dyadic forms of social organisation and dyadic systems of classificatory thought which have been the object of much attention, firstly from the Dutch structuralist school of anthropology, and subsequently in a series of more recent detailed studies (Fox 1980c).

Fox's statement points to the linking of the ritual language to certain social situations. This means that we can identify a category of social situations by the fact that ordinary language is avoided and ritual language is prescribed. It is not always clear how this category is conceived by the people themselves, but one interesting possibility is that the ritual language is used where supernatural spirits are a party to the communication. I have not heard this notion expressed by the Sumbanese, but it is true in practice that in most of the situations where ritual language is used in Wanukaka today there is communication between men and supernatural beings. Thus one must use ritual language in making offerings to ancestral spirits (*taungu marapu*), or to nature spirits (*taunga moritana*), in divination (*uratu*), in begging mercy (*kalierung*), and in the recitation of clan histories (*kanuga*). All of these performances are explicitly addressed to spirits, and the spirits concerned are mentioned by name or by other identifying characteristics, although there is usually a human audience listening in as well. We have also seen that the ritual language is used in formal negotiations between two parties (*panewe dengang*, 'talking together') but in this situation too, although each communication is addressed to the other human party, it is believed that the ancestral spirits of the two households involved (*marapu uma*) are listening to the negotiations, and indeed are interested parties in the matters being dealt with. The attendance of these spirits is marked by the placing of small offerings of betel and areca for the invisible participants to chew.

There are two further forms of public verbal performance in Wanukaka where ritual language is not used, but in neither of these is there participation by spirits. The first of these forms is the love-song. It is built around the subtle use of metaphor, but not in the parallel form which characterises the ritual language. It is composed by an individual in response to some poignant real-life incident, to be remembered and sung for a few years until the incident and the song are gradually forgotten.

The second form is a more substantial performance, the *paneka*, an extended traditional narrative about the culture heroes *Umbu Deilu* (male) and *Rambu Kahi* (female). These are romantic tales, and are sung as a night-long entertainment by a group of people who have been working together in the fields during the harvest season. The narrative passages are sung by the principal singer, separated by a chorus of workers singing the repetitive refrain.

The two most substantial performances in the ritual language are the clan histories (*kanuga*) and the negotiations (*panewe dengang*); both of these require more extensive discussion. The clan histories are sung only on a small number of occasions. In many villages they are reserved for the major annual ceremony when the whole village comes together at the end of the harvest season to make offerings to and seek the blessings of the ancestral spirits and the spirits of the land. Each clan history begins with an account of the creation of the world. It then tells how the ancestors of the clan descended from heaven to earth and travelled across the land seeking a suitable place to live, until, after various adventures, they arrived at the ideal spot: the present village site.[1] The history provides an explanation for the name and distinguishing attributes of the clan, and of the rights and duties which it has in the wider community. There is considerable rivalry between the clans of the Wanukaka valley, so each clan history devotes much attention to the claims to fame of its own ancestors, and to subtle denigration of the other clans of the valley (Mitchell 1981).

The performance of a clan history is a considerable feat, since it continues without a break from about two hours after sunset until sunrise the next day. It consists of 900 to 1600 couplets, in what is supposed to be a fixed sequence. Each passage is first chanted by one performer, unaccompanied, and then, while the chanter regains his breath, a second performer sings the passage to the accompaniment of gongs and dancing. The sung version is intended for the attending spirits, but the unaccompanied chanted version is usually more intelligible to the human audience. The format used allows the first performer, who knows the history best, to set it up, passage by passage, for the second performer, who has the better singing voice. It thus gives the listeners two chances to understand. Once the performance has ended, the interested listener will have to wait a full twelve months before he has the opportunity to hear it again, since usually it is forbidden for the key passages to be sung at all outside this single annual ceremony. There are separate forms of the history to be sung on other occasions. For the building of a new house, for instance, the history would focus on how the ancestors acquired the tools and knowledge to build houses. Fortunately there are some overlapping passages which are sung on several occasions, as well as those passages specific to the ceremony of the day. As well, there are 'padding' passages, which may be used at the discretion of the chanter and thus allow him to prolong or to shorten the total length of the performance.

In learning his art, a new chanter must memorise the whole corpus of his own clan's histories by simply listening repeatedly to the performances of his predecessor. There is no opportunity for practice, and he is specifically forbidden to pronounce the sacred couplets 'in vain', that is, outside the context of the proper public performance. The only compensation for the infrequent opportunities to hear the histories is that the learner has many years during which he can listen to performances. The process of learning probably begins in earnest in early teenage years, but it is only in his forties or fifties that he must 'shoulder the burden', as they say, of performing the sacred histories.

It says a great deal for the qualities of the ritual language that it is capable of being memorised at all under such circumstances. Each couplet must be sufficiently striking and meaningful to survive unrehearsed in the memory of the candidate chanter. And when he does come to perform, he does so under the constant threat that if he makes an error he may at once be struck down by the angered spirits. I observed one old man suddenly fall faint to the ground after making a mistake, and it was twenty minutes before he was well enough to continue. It was considered fortunate that his mistake had been a minor one and that the spirits had responded promptly to placation.

Of course, all forms of poetry have specific devices which make them more easily remembered. Sumbanese couplets make very little use of rhyme or alliteration, but they are characterised by a word-for-word parallelism of the type which Robert Lowth designated as *parallelismus membrorum* in his eighteenth-century commentaries on Hebrew poetry (see Fox 1977). It is clear that this parallelism helps to limit errors in performance, since any word substituted for the correct one would not only have to sound like the original word and preserve some meaning in the line, but should also correspond to it in the number of syllables and grammatical type, since these two features are also matched with the paired word in the other line of the couplet.

Parallelism is a concept as well established within the discipline of poetics as is dualism within the discipline of social anthropology. Fox (1977) has published a comparative paper setting the parallelism of eastern Indonesian languages within the broader context of other parallel traditions around the world. For the present we need only note that the 'memorable' quality of the parallelism in Sumba provides one link between the structure of the ritual language and its role in social life. This is only one small fragment of the total answer to our question; we must assemble some of the larger pieces.

In the other major area of use of the ritual language – the formal negotiations – the performers are not exposed to retribution from angry spirits, but their task is only a little lighter. The atmosphere during negotiations is one of high formality, and a misjudged couplet may give offence to the other party. There may then be a demand for an apology before negotiations can continue, and mere words are not enough. To have substance an apology must take the form of a substantial gift, ranging from a knife or cloth, at the lower end of the scale, to a large buffalo or pig at the other. Thus accuracy in use of the ritual language is of great importance and, just as in the sacred context, an expert practitioner is required.

The principal parties to the negotiations are represented by intermediaries, two to represent each side (see Mitchell 1981:328–66). Each pair of intermediaries consists of a 'listener', *kadehang*, and a 'speaker', *ma-pa-newi*. During consultations with their principals both the intermediaries may play an active role in helping to formulate the propositions to be put to the other side, but when they go out to meet their counterparts from the other side the 'speaker' puts the proposition and the 'listener' simply listens passively to the response, saying 'ah-ha' from time to time. It is worth noticing in passing that this formal arrangement of the *dramatis personae* into pairs with complementary functions is yet another manifestation of the dualism theme.

Even if no mistakes are made by the intermediaries, the matters under negotiation may be of considerable importance. The arrangement of marriages always requires such negotiations, and marriages must be accompanied by the exchange of goods on a large scale. The standard bride price in Wanukaka is thirty head of buffalo and horses; the bride's family responds with a counter-gift of pigs and cloths of equivalent value. The total size of the bride price and counter-gift and the composition of each instalment are subjects of intense and detailed negotiation, with not only the economic advantage of the participants but also their social prestige hanging in the balance.

Although the arrangement of marriage is the most typical subject of negotiation, and has the greatest economic and human consequences, many other matters are also handled in the same way if they involve a transaction between people of different clans. These include matters of trade and the settlement of conflict. A great deal of borrowing of pigs, buffalo and horses goes on in Wanukaka, and trade in land in the form of rice paddies and coconut groves is also common. Some, but not all, of this is negotiated in the ritual language. In trade matters there seems to be a choice between doing things in the proper grand manner and just working them out informally; so matters often will be handled face to face without the use of intermediaries, using ritual language couplets for the key points but mixed with much ordinary language commentary as well. This kind of compromise approach is quite unthinkable, however, in the case of marriage. The settling of conflict by negotiation occurs, for instance, when a member of one clan has caused harm to members of another, by theft of property, by adultery, or by being responsible for an accidental death. These situations are resolved by the payment of a fine, as agreed upon in negotiation.

Whereas in the sacred rituals the emphasis is on the faithful reproduction of the couplets prescribed for each particular occasion, in secular matters the emphasis is on the clever choice of the couplets most appropriate to the situation and to the negotiating tactics of the moment. The intermediaries are paid for their services, *hi-aa-na* ('to buy his mouth'), and the more skilled intermediaries spend a lot of their time at this task. No one in Wanukaka traditional society ever entirely gives up subsistence agriculture, but for some the income from working as an intermediary makes a very useful contribution to their livelihood.

The massing of skilled manpower in negotiations suggests how important the proper use of ritual language is, but what function can poetic metaphor have in this serious situation? We might first note that there is a set of couplets which we may not unreasonably describe as a legal terminology. Each category of transaction, each legally significant event and each status of legal significance can be designated by a specific couplet.

Wuatu regi ta kalitu ina	Place a mantle on mother's skin,
Hailang rowa ta katiku ama	Put a head-cloth on father's head.

This couplet refers to a standard symbolic gesture of submission to a person of superior rank within one's own village, expressed concretely by the presentation of a small gift. If a person claims this status he is claiming the right to take decisions on behalf of those of lower status in relation to himself. This status is expressed most generally and succinctly by the mini-couplet *ina-ama*, which literally means 'mother-father' but is best translated as 'person in authority'. This mini-couplet is often used in ordinary language discussions, as an odd dyadic element in a sentence of unpaired words, but in ritual language it usually occurs in more extended phrases, such as:

Ina papa-lohung	Mother who gives things out,
Ama papa-tamang	Father who takes things in.

This couplet refers to the right to dispose of and accept property on behalf of the group.

Within each clan there is an inherited status of highest-ranking member, and although in normal circumstances each segment of the clan has its own leader, the highest-ranking member of the clan may choose to claim the right to represent all the clan members in their dealings with outsiders. It so happens that there is no precise term in the ordinary language to designate this highest status within the clan. In ritual language, however, there is a precise term.

Na-ma pakang-waingu karabau ma-bani	He who tames the wild buffalo,
Na-ma pahudu-waingu jara ma-hawadda	He who breaks the spirited horse.

In fact, every event and every status of significance in traditional law must be designated by a specific couplet. Thus the question of consummation of a marriage is referred to by the couplet:

Katikuku 'dingu na penangu	Squeaking of the floor slats,
Karu'uku 'dingu na wei ta pajalu	Splashing of water in the water jar.

The concept of being below the age of legal responsibility, frequently advanced to excuse adolescent sexual liaisons, is covered by the couplet:

Ta'u rou kabukilu	[Eating from] plates of *kabukilu* leaf,
Kakoba tipi tana	Winnowing [grains of] earth with a *kakoba* husk.

The following set of three couplets is of key importance. It invokes the scene of all the participants in a negotiation sitting down to a meal together, as a sign that agreement has been reached.

Kottu-ya na api	Smoke is curling from the fire,
Heriku na ikit	Hawks are circling above,
Ngodu-nya mabokulu ta lenang	Old men sitting on the veranda,
Madidi-nya mangoma ta uma	Old women sitting in the house,
Angu wihi kamemi	Eating goat meat,
Angu wihi ahu	Eating dog meat.

The participation in such a meal is tantamount to entering into a binding contract, the terms of which have been spelled out in the preceding negotiations, with the four intermediaries as witnesses to the details and all those who partake in the meal as participants in the contract. Every element in the transaction between the two parties must be expressed by one or other of the couplets of the 'legal terminology', since the ritual language, as carried by the intermediaries, is the only medium of communication used in hammering out the agreement.

In negotiations the ritual language is equally the language of diplomacy. The use of two sets of intermediaries and the proper metaphoric couplets is a mechanism quite effective at modifying any unacceptable expressions of feeling. When negotiations are at a tense stage it is quite common to hear one party muttering angrily together and striking a defiant posture, but these spontaneous outbursts of feeling have time to settle before the intermediaries are given the formal response, and whatever is said has to be contained within the limits set by the available couplets. The other side may happen to overhear a few ill-judged remarks muttered in the ordinary language, and indeed it may do no harm for them to know that feeling is running high, but they should close their ears to these private, ordinary-language remarks and attend only to the public response in the ritual language.

Although it has a mellowing influence, the ritual language does not prevent strong expressions of attitude or the making of subtle points. For instance, it is possible to ask the other party to stop dissimulating and state their true intentions by means of the couplet with which I began this essay. One delicate task is to tell the other party that they are close to the bounds of proper behaviour and are risking their reputation by persisting in their attitude. This may be achieved by the following couplet:

Haniri baku wawa	Traversing a narrow ledge on a cliff face,
Leti wei ma-joruku	Stepping along the slippery edge of a waterfall.

As a legal terminology and a language of diplomacy, it is clear that the role of ritual language is absolute in Sumbanese traditional law, since no ordinary language is used in the dialogue between the contending parties. There seems to be a contrast here with the role of *umpama* aphorisms, as described in Vergouwen's account of Batak traditional law. The Batak *umpama* do take a similar form as metaphoric couplets or quatrains, and they do express the principal concepts of Batak traditional law, but it appears that they are presented and perhaps qualified by accompanying dialogue in the ordinary language (Vergouwen 1964:138–40).

As we have noted, the individual performer is supposed to reproduce each couplet exactly as he originally heard it. He is not permitted to introduce variations or 'improvements'. In this way the ritual language is supposed to have been transmitted unchanged from one generation to the next, from the time of the original ancestors of the Sumbanese people. The idea prevails in Sumba that all Sumbanese are descended from the same group of ancestors. This idea is expressed in different ways in different areas, and is always qualified in some way to accommodate social class differences and the ideal of clan exogamy, but some notion of common origin is widely held. It follows from this that the ritual language ought to be the same all over the island, and this indeed is what is claimed in Wanukaka and elsewhere. The ritual language is said to function as a kind of diplomatic lingua franca for communication between people from distant areas, and enables them to have satisfactory formal dealings with one another even in the presence of considerable difficulties in understanding when ordinary language forms are used.

This is a fairly remarkable claim since, by the criterion of mutual unintelligibility, there are four distinct languages spoken on Sumba. Eastern Sumbanese is spoken over the eastern three-quarters of the island, with the Wanukaka dialect as one of the variations occurring in the most westerly part of the east Sumba language area; while in the more densely populated western quarter of the island the Weyéwa, Lamboya and Kodi languages are found. Since these Sumbanese languages are all related to one another, it is relatively easy for speakers of one Sumbanese language to learn the others; but nevertheless, unintelligibility is such a real problem that today Sumbanese from different language areas will normally communicate with one another using the Indonesian national language. Since the ritual language in each area is basically made up of the words of the ordinary language plus a small special vocabulary of its own, it follows that many words in the ritual language will not be intelligible to people from other language areas. It seems likely that the greater intelligibility of the ritual language is due to the ability of expert speakers of the ritual language to recognise the couplet as a whole even when they do not know all of the component words. It is also true that the ritual language experts do have greater language skills than most other members of their own communities, and will have picked up some knowledge of the other languages of Sumba.

Thus the ideal of a common ritual language shared by divergent language communities is partly an illusion, but we should not dismiss it altogether. It seems reasonable to suppose that the *parallelismus membrorum* of Sumbanese ritual language has worked to provide a body of oral tradition which is relatively stable over time, in the same way as are written texts in literate societies. The belief that the ritual language is the unchanging and unchangeable words of the ancestors gives it the dignity and authority which in other cultures belong to the written word.

Form and meaning in the Sumbanese couplet

> [It] proceeds through a series of couplets using figurative images
> in pairs to convey a common meaning. (Adams 1973:271)

We can readily identify four special features of Sumbanese ritual language: its special vocabulary, distinctive rhythm, use of metaphor, and word-for-word parallelism.

Of these the special vocabulary can be most briefly dealt with. It is only a minority of the words in the ritual language which are not shared with the ordinary language, and for the most part these special words are simple synonyms of ordinary words. Nevertheless these words do contribute to the perception of the ritual language as an esoteric and ancient means of expression. Many of the special words are known to be part of the ordinary language in other parts of Sumba, so this fact contributes to the notion of the ritual language as part of the shared heritage of the whole Sumbanese people. Most listeners who are not themselves able to perform in the ritual language will have a passive understanding of most of the special words, but there are a few words that even the most expert performers do not understand.

I will return to a discussion of rhythm at the end of the essay, but there are some points to be made briefly at this point. There is no prescribed metre in ritual language, and the length of the lines varies greatly. Rhythm is still important, however, since the normal stress pattern is heightened in the chanting of ritual language and the rhythm of each line is reinforced by being repeated in the parallel line.

We have previously referred to both the parallelism and the metaphorical character of the ritual language. It would be possible to continue to deal with these two features separately: relating Sumbanese parallelism to that found in other east Indonesian languages, and relating the Sumbanese metaphorical devices to those found in the metaphorical traditions of western Indonesia, such as the Malay *pantun* and the Batak *umpama*. This could lead to some insights, but also it could be fundamentally misleading. It is my contention that Sumbanese ritual language is best interpreted in terms of a model in which both metaphor and parallelism are inextricably linked. In this model two metaphorical statements are placed in parallel so that in combination they indicate a single hidden meaning. It is as if an arrow were pointing at a target which is not directly visible, and there is also a second arrow pointing at the same target from a different direction, so that our task of locating the target is made much easier. This is an intriguing and very fertile poetic device, and it does occur in many other poetic traditions, but the Sumbanese case is remarkable for the rigid and systematic fashion in which it is applied.

The essential features of the model have been noted previously by both Onvlee (1973) and Adams (1973), but in my view it is of such central importance to the study of Sumbanese culture that it bears further detailed analysis. First of all, it is worth stating the model as precisely as possible. This might be done as follows:

(1) the ritual language is composed of a series of couplets;

(2) within each couplet each word in the first line is matched to the corresponding word in the second line by metre and grammatical type; and

(3) each line contains a concrete statement such that the two statements of the couplet metaphorically represent a single intended meaning for the couplet as a whole.

From this model follow certain implications, which ought to be made clear. First, it is the parallelism which binds the two metaphors together. A ritual language passage consists of a long string of metaphors, so the parallelism is necessary in order to indicate which metaphors belong together as a pair. Secondly, the fact that a statement occurs in parallel with another indicates that it is to be interpreted metaphorically. It would be possible, for instance, to use the phrase *heriku na ikit*, 'the hawk is circling', on its own and as a direct statement describing a bird out hunting for mice in the fields. But if this same phrase were used in parallel with another, then it would take on its standard metaphorical reference to a ritual meal. In fact, it creates confusion to use such phrases from the ritual language in ordinary speech in their non-metaphorical sense, so the Sumbanese would normally avoid doing so.

A third implication is that the meaning of the couplet is hidden. To say that the meaning is 'hidden' is in a sense redundant, since it is the nature of metaphor that the intended meaning is not explicitly expressed and the listener has to guess what the speaker intends. But this 'hidden' quality needs to be emphasised, since we must give due attention to discovering how the intended meaning can be made known. There is a clear difference here between Sumbanese metaphor and the metaphor in Malay *pantun* and Batak *umpama*. In those traditions a quatrain is characteristic, with the first two lines stating the metaphor and the final two lines revealing the intended meaning in direct language. In the Sumbanese tradition the meaning is never revealed in this way.

For the majority of the couplets the problem of knowing the intended meaning may not be immediately apparent, since the imagery of each line is clear, the intended meaning is already known beforehand, and the link between them is readily grasped. Although the performer of a ritual language passage has no way of explaining the couplets during the performance, once the performance has finished he is usually able to explain each couplet in the ordinary language. The situation is complicated in the case of the sacred passages, where fear of supernatural danger inhibits discussion; but this fear does not apply to the couplets used in the context of negotiations, and one can readily establish that there is a widely shared consensus as to the meaning of each couplet. Since the Wanukakans themselves view this meaning as being irrevocably fixed, we may speak of a conventional meaning. This conventional meaning may or may not coincide with the meaning the couplet had for previous generations or in other parts of Sumba, but it does represent the intention of present-day users within the one language community.

The relationship between the imagery of the couplet and its conventional meaning can be made clearer by a simple example.

| *Maturu-na-nya-ka na tapu* | He is lying on the mat, |
| *Kadenga-na-nya-ka na api* | He has his back to the fire. |

This couplet has the conventional meaning 'he is seriously ill', which can be stated clearly in the ordinary language as *hidu-bakul-na-nya-ka*. The two concrete statements in the couplet refer to the traditional position of a person who is seriously ill, lying by the hearth in the house. The conventional meaning is much narrower than a logical interpretation of these lines would imply. One might think that these lines could refer to a person lying down to sleep by the fire, or to a person suffering from a mild and passing illness, but this would be incorrect. By convention the couplet can only be applied to life-threatening illness. Furthermore, since the couplet means that the person is seriously ill, it does not mean that he is actually lying down on a mat with his back to the fire. Even if he were sitting up, without a mat, and facing the fire, it would still be perfectly correct to apply the couplet to him.

If the conventional meaning is narrow in some couplets, it is broad in others. *Tuwa padita//tuwa comida*, for example, must have been coined after the arrival of the Dutch colonial government in Sumba (in west Sumba this happened in 1909). This is a Wanukakan phonetic transformation of the Malay words:

| *Tuan pendeta* | Mister pastor, |
| *Tuan komandan* | Mister commandant. |

Although this looks like a list of two kinds of Dutchmen, in fact it conventionally applies to the Dutch in general, to women and children, tourists and teachers, as well as to pastors and commandants.

These two examples demonstrate the need to interpret the couplets in accordance with the model. Both couplets would be likely to be misunderstood if their metaphorical character were overlooked and they were taken as descriptive statements. I would not wish to claim that all Sumbanese couplets conform precisely to the model proposed, and indeed several of the couplets already quoted have deviated from strict parallelism, but it should be apparent from the examples how misleading a naïve interpretation of the couplets could be.

In part, these two examples have been misleading because of their prosaic imagery; most couplets are more colourful, taking full advantage of the metaphorical mode of expression. The following examples display something of the range of Sumbanese metaphor.

The images may be striking in their originality.

Korahu kataraku	The rat-tat-tat of sand,
Ladihu palibangu	The cross-legged pandanus.

Imagery: grains of sand poured onto a rigid surface, such as a banana leaf, making a characteristic sound; the pandanus palm, found along the sandy ridges of the coast, has angular protruding roots which look like bent knees.

Conventional meaning: the beach.

In other cases onomatopoeia adds to the imagery used to evoke the intended emotional state.

Gaga bohi bata	Startled as the oar snaps,
Gela tena bera	Scared as the hull cracks open.

Imagery: a boat in danger at sea, made more vivid by the abrupt sound of *bata*, 'snap', and *gaga*, 'startle', which mimics the incoherent stutter emitted by a startled person.

Conventional meaning: fear for one's life.

The ritual language also has its lighter moments, and the tone of the metaphors may be whimsical or cynical.

Jami ahu	Pat the dog,
Gowa wawi	Scratch the pig.

Conventional meaning: to persuade by flattery.

The following couplet elaborates a somewhat jaundiced view of love. It was used to refer to the case of a noble lady who was prepared to face humiliation and ruin as the price for going to live with her lower-class lover.

Agalu na wunitu mabela	A strangling fig embracing a banyan tree at Mabela,
Lapa-lodu mati-na na wunit	Until the banyan dies in its embrace,

Na wunitu Mabela.	The banyan at Mabela.
Koluru kaboku libbu ranni	A fish entangled in the roots of a mangrove clump,
Lapa-lodu wou-na na kaboku	Until the fish stinks in its entanglement,
Na kaboku libbu ranni	The fish in the mangrove clump.

Imagery: the strangling fig is a parasitic plant which does eventually strangle its host in a deadly embrace.

Conventional meaning: infatuation.

The use of a local place name here suggests that this particular couplet is a Wanukakan addition to the repertoire.

Discovering the conventional meaning

The most obvious way to discover the conventional meaning of a couplet is to ask a number of knowledgeable informants. After I had discovered that it was impossible reliably to guess the meaning, this was the procedure that I followed. No doubt Sumbanese sometimes discover the conventional meaning in this way, but it is the exception. Usually the meaning of a couplet can be readily grasped when it is heard in context, so it is not necessary to ask. There is no tradition of critical discussion of the couplets and no didactic teaching; anyone learning the ritual language must simply listen to performances and intuitively grasp what he can of the meaning. An example will clarify what is involved.

Potiru pajengang na uli tena lajang	Swing around the rudder of the long canoe,
Wigiru habaling na ngora jara rara	Pull about the nose of the red horse.

While the general intent of this pair of metaphors is obviously a reversal of direction of some kind, it is not obvious which kind. Does it refer to a vehicle turning around, an armed band retreating on the battlefield, a traveller deciding to return home, or the abandonment of a plan before even beginning to carry it out? The metaphor could equally well be aimed at any of these events, or it could cover all of them. In fact, none of these uses of the couplet is acceptable. When we hear this couplet in the context of a prayer for the recovery of a sick man it is at once apparent that it applies to the moment of crisis in his illness, the moment when progressive worsening gives way to the beginning of recovery. Usually a single hearing in context would be sufficient for a listener accustomed to the style of Sumbanese couplets to grasp its meaning, but sometimes it may take several hearings before the intention becomes clear. The previous couplet is one that I have not heard in any other context, so it appears that it has a very narrow focus of meaning.

The following couplet has a slightly broader application.

Duking keka nalu	Reach the perch of *nalu* wood,
Tumang raa ritta	Come to the feeding-trough of *ritta* wood.

This couplet evokes the image of hens coming home to roost under the eaves of the house at nightfall, and pigs returning at their feeding time. Both these domestic animals forage freely during the day and are always counted when they return in case any of them have been lost. This couplet is also used in the context of illness, and refers to the recovery from delirium to clear consciousness, since it is thought that this phenomenon is due to the person's spirit returning from its wanderings away from the body and entering its proper place once again.

In a different context this couplet refers to the eagerly awaited swarming of marine worms, an event which occurs each year at the beginning of the rainy season. The meaning of the couplet is still the same, however, since a rice crop is believed to possess a spirit which gives it life. After the rice crop has been harvested each year, the spirit wanders across the seas, returning in the form of the swarm of worms just at the time when the rains are beginning to fall and the rice is being planted. Once again it is a matter of a wandering spirit returning to its proper place, so that the normal forms of life may be resumed.

So far we have considered couplets where the meaning is relatively easy to grasp. Alas, this is not always easy. There are many couplets where the link between the images presented in the couplet and the context is quite elusive, and it is only after hearing the couplet several times that the learner reaches some sense of what is intended. The following couplet refers to death.

Tadulla dapa-hepangu	Mountain peak unmovable,
Karaja dapa-heilangu	Armband never taken off.

There is nothing obvious about the metaphor here, but it becomes a little more comprehensible in the light of Wanukakan customs. When making an irrevocable vow, of revenge for instance, Wanukakans have an armband of tough strips of vegetable fibre woven onto the arm in such a way that no loose ends are visible. The appearance thus suggests that the band cannot be taken off, and indeed it is not removed until the vow has been carried out completely.

The mountain peak is an image that my informants found hard to explain. Though a mountain may inspire our awe by its massiveness and its permanence, by its domination of the landscape, a connection with death is not immediately obvious. But in Sumbanese culture mountains also have significance as boundaries between neighbouring territories, as the point at which ancestors descend from heaven to earth, and where the spirits of the dead pass on their return to the heavens. There are thus suggestions of crossing a major boundary, or irreversible change, but it must be said that the imagery remains ambiguous and obscure.

There are other cases where the obscurity is even greater because of the use of words which are not part of the everyday language. Even a quite arbitrary or nonsensical sequence of syllables can adequately serve the purpose of signifier of a conventional meaning, and some couplets in current use are quite devoid of any metaphorical meaning to the present generation of Wanukakans.

In the case of the Batak *umpama*, Vergouwen suggested that the unknown words are nonsense words inserted to maintain the rhythmic pattern (1964:138). In Wanukaka, however, it seems likely that historically there was once a metaphorical meaning which has since become lost. More typical in Wanukaka is a case like that of the mountain peak and the armband, where there is some connection between clear images and the conventional meaning but the connection is an ambiguous one.

Such ambiguity is not, of course, something to be regretted, since it is the hallmark of the 'creative leap' which has been proposed as the source of all art, wit and creative scientific thought. The idea that creativity is essentially the paradoxical or unexpected linking of two concepts which are basically unlike one another has been formulated in different ways by many different authors (De Bono 1970; Guildford 1967; Koestler 1964; Rothenberg 1971) and has been applied in both the aesthetic and scientific domains. Any metaphorical statement is creative, since it is the nature of metaphor that two entities, alike but not identical, are compared. Some ambiguity is inherent in any metaphorical mode of expression, and it is important to note that the couplets with the clearest link between imagery and meaning are often less interesting than those with the more ambiguous imagery.

The couplet as an explanation

There remains to be considered one final aspect of the relationship between the couplets and their conventional meanings. Up to this point we have largely been treating each couplet as if it were a puzzle to be solved by discovering the abstract concept which it signifies. This is indeed the problem for the learner who wishes to understand and make use of the ritual language, but solving it is only the first step, the means of gaining access to the esoteric knowledge which the ritual language expresses.

So far, in dealing with this first step, it has been sufficient glibly to label each couplet as a means of referring to 'death' or 'serious illness', and so forth, but now we must turn our attention to each couplet as an explanation of 'death' or 'serious illness' – or whatever the subject of the couplet may be. We must appreciate that many of the couplets deal with complex areas of abstract thought. They make statements about social status, legal rights and duties, states of mind or supernatural powers. In fact, they lay out, in synoptic form, all the key features of the Sumbanese view of the world. We must therefore put aside any notion that the couplets are complicated ways of saying something simple. They are, on the contrary, a simple means of bringing clarity and order to inherently complex matters.

The poetic explanations that the couplets provide derive their power from their capacity to condense subtle abstractions into concrete examples, to remind us, by the immediacy of their images, of what is the heart of the matter. Two examples of the legal concepts already mentioned are worth recalling to illustrate the point. The notion of 'brinkmanship' in conducting social relations is clearly grasped from the couplet evoking a narrow ledge and the edge of the waterfall. The concept that children's behaviour must be considered differently from adult behaviour, and that they should not bear the same responsibility for their acts as adults do, is well captured in the couplet evoking children playing at cooking and preparing food.

It is interesting that, although the ordinary language in Sumba has no shortage of abstract nouns, the ritual language characteristically avoids them. It is constructed instead of concrete statements about the empirical world, so that the mental images evoked by the couplets are solidly rooted in perceptual experience. Vivid visual images are typical, but sometimes sounds or tactile sensations are employed, and, where there is change or process to be indicated, this is achieved by reference to physical action. Thus, although the intended conventional meaning may be abstract and difficult to comprehend, it can be approached through imagery that is clear and concrete.

Almost all of the couplets presented so far might be usefully studied in this reversed perspective, but the following example is particularly useful in bringing out these aspects of the ritual language.

Tilu kobu moru	Eggs of the green gecko,
Woya lai karara	Crocodile reddish in the current.

This couplet refers to the supernatural, and its conventional meaning may be stated in the ordinary language phrase *na ma biha*, 'that which is supernatural'.

There are some difficulties in the way of a non-Sumbanese attempting to understand how the synoptic representation works, since we are not exposed to the same experiences of daily life on which the imagery draws and we cannot hope to track precisely the train of thought that is triggered in a Sumbanese mind by the paired images of the couplet. Indeed, part of the problem is that no two Sumbanese will react to the couplet in exactly the same way. When I asked what gecko eggs had to do with supernatural forces, one informant explained that the green gecko lives in the rafters of houses but lays its eggs in little clusters close to the ground where the air is more humid. They are hidden from view, and one usually discovers them accidentally when engaged in some incidental activity such as picking up a rock to use as an anvil or recovering a disused wooden pig-trough that had been left lying undisturbed for some time. Thus, I was told, the odd little cluster of eggs is an unexpected reminder of the irrepressible processes of life going on around us all the time, but hidden from our gaze.

I knew that crocodiles had lived in the Wanukaka river in significant numbers until recent times, and were often used as a symbol of dangerous supernatural powers. I asked why the crocodile was 'reddish' rather than 'red', as it is in other couplets; and I was surprised at the sense of immediacy of experience as I was told how, standing at the edge of the flooded river, wondering whether it was safe to cross, one might notice a reddish patch in the swirling discoloured water and feel a shudder of fear, whilst not being quite sure whether it really was a crocodile or not. Once it has been unpacked in this way, the compact little couplet can be seen as quite a powerful evocation of the mysterious forces, which humankind is so prone to see, hidden just behind the exposed surfaces of the natural world.

However, the couplet is not simply to be understood in terms of vivid imagery and random associations of thought. There is some system in the packing of images in the couplet. It is the Sumbanese dialectical style to oppose an egg, giving rise to life, to a crocodile, threatening death. By opposing these images the couplet proposed life-giving and life-ending as dual aspects of the same ill-comprehended forces. Similarly, it is not an accident but the hallmark of Sumbanese design that green is opposed to red, and the gecko is opposed to the crocodile, as opposite aspects of the category 'colour' and the category 'reptile'. It would take too long a diversion to do justice to this Sumbanese notion of each whole being made up of two opposed complementary parts, but the contributions of Onvlee (1977), Adams (1973) and Needham (1980) provide us with a range of further examples and analyses.

I have chosen this particular example of a couplet dealing with the supernatural because it is one of the more eloquent examples of the art, and I have quoted the explanation given by one particular informant who was both articulate and a devoted connoisseur of the tradition of his people. Not all couplets are as eloquent, and not all Sumbanese are as interested in decoding them, but the ritual language is rich in similar constructions and this particular couplet is only remarkable as one of the more intricate examples. The following couplet is simple, widely used, and understood and appreciated by all Sumbanese.

| *Karei wei* | To ask for water, |
| *Karei ohu* | To ask for cooked rice. |

Conventional meaning: to ask for a wife.

Even in this uncomplicated pattern, containing three words only, we can see once again the opposition of two complementary elements, and we have once again a synoptic representation of a complex area of Sumbanese thought concerning marriage. To the Sumbanese this is a powerful poem about women faithfully nurturing their children and their husbands, and about the humbleness and gratitude that a family owes to that other family who may give to them the greatest possible gift (Mitchell 1981:159–85). It carries with it a similar weight of sentiment to that attached to the English language lines

> for better for worse,
> for richer for poorer,
> in sickness and in health,

and it has the same virtue of bypassing abstract thinking about marriage and establishing a concrete base in reality.

It seems, then, that in these couplets we can recognise a recurring pattern, a methodical approach to the presentation of these abstract ideas. To define this method fully would require a systematic examination of a large collection of couplets, but even on the basis of the small sample already discussed we can characterise the method as concretising, synoptic and dialectical. Although these three features are fully compatible with the basic model of conjoined parallel metaphors, and indeed seem to flow from it, it would be too artificial to identify them in all the couplets. They are probably best described as favoured principles which may be brought into play when the couplet deals with a complex or abstract subject. Even though they are not constantly applied, these three features should be recognised as constituting a systematic method for the manipulation of ideas.

A note of caution is appropriate here. Much of the time these couplets are used quite instrumentally in negotiations or public prayer, with the attention of the performer and the audience focused on the needs of the moment. Each couplet has been heard many times before and in such a setting it must function as a rather tired cliché for most of the listeners.

But for all the mindless repetition of such occasions, there are other moments when the Sumbanese pause to pay more thoughtful attention to the words of the couplet, and it is then that it stands as a means of clarifying the nature of the supernatural, the meaning of marriage, or whatever is the subject to which it refers.

Rhythm

We have now analysed enough couplets to understand a complete statement in the ritual language. The following passage was recorded in the course of a prayer addressed to the spirits of the ancestors asking that a sick man be allowed to recover from the illness they have brought upon him. In the translation of the passage only the conventional meanings are given, but all four couplets have already been literally translated and their imagery has been discussed on pages 76, 78 and 79. Stress marks indicate the rhythm.

Ya, Dummu Anu	Oh, Honoured One,
bá-na matúru-nya na tápu	
bá-na kadénga-nya ápi	as he lies seriously ill,
Ya,	Oh,
bá-na láu-ya ta tadúlla dá-pa	
hépang	
bá-na láu-ya ta karája dá-pa	as he approaches death,
héilang	
Nei nammu jaku	Then let it be
ká-na pótiru pajéngang na úli	
téna lájang	that his spirit turns back in its
ká-na wígru habáling na ngora	journey,
jára rára	
ká-na dúking kéka nálu	that it returns to its proper
ká-na tómang ráa rítta.	place.

It is important to consider such a passage as a pattern of sounds, since the ritual language is always chanted or sung with a strong emphasis on the stressed syllables. The chanting style is vigorous and its rhythm is compelling. The Sumbanese value boldness in most things, and the chanted words are intended to ring out to reach a large assembled audience of men and spirits. It is a proud public performance, and if the people in the next village can hear it as well, then so much the better. Most Sumbanese words have two syllables with a stress on the first, so that a sequence of two-syllable words produces a dense alternation of strong and weak beats. But another feature of Sumbanese speech rhythms is the use of trains of affixes and suffixes which are unstressed and thus provide a variation in rhythm by filling in the interval between the strong beats with a varying number of unstressed beats. Thus there is very great variety of rhythm from one couplet to the next, and this contrasts with the rigidity of repetition of rhythm within each couplet.

These rhythmic qualities are something for the children in the audience, and for those not interested in the verbal content. They provide an undemanding level of entertainment for anyone whose concentration is not sustained through the whole of the performance.

But there is more to rhythm than this. Many writers have noted the attention-catching or, alternatively, the hypnotic qualities of rhythmic sound, though the psychological mechanisms involved here are speculative. It seems that one of the more important answers to the question why a poetic form is used in the ritual language is simply that spoken verse is rhythmic and rhythm commands attention. If our understanding of ritual language as a vehicle for creative abstract thought is correct, then the suggestion of W. B. Yeats is especially intriguing.

> The purpose of rhythm is to prolong the moment of contemplation, the moment when we are both asleep and awake, which is the moment of creation, by hushing us with an alluring monotony, while it holds us waking by variety, to keep us in that state of perhaps real trance, in which the mind, liberated from the pressure of the will, is unfolded in symbols. (Yeats 1903:247–48)

Conclusions

As we have seen, the ritual language is used in Sumba as the medium of expression for the most abstract levels of thought: the cosmology and history, the legal and moral order. We may now assemble together such answers as we have found to our opening question: what has been gained by expressing this thought in poetic form?

At the most elementary level we have noted the role of rhythm in compelling attention and providing some simple satisfaction in its own right. At a higher level we have explored the creativity of the associations generated by the ordered interplay of image with image, and image with context. These creative associations have sometimes had a quiet humour, sometimes been striking in their originality, and usually been aesthetically satisfying. Sometimes the couplets have seemed to make quite a profound statement about life as the Sumbanese experience it, and have done so with the immediacy of art rather than the meticulous working-out of science.

In so far as the ritual language does achieve some profound statements, this does not arise through happy chance but rather from the systematic character of the Sumbanese couplet. By their metaphoric, synoptic, dialectical method of thought, the Sumbanese systematically deploy images of the concrete in order to apprehend the abstract.

We have seen how the error-resisting character of the parallel form provides these great truths of Sumbanese tradition with a source of stability across time and space. And, finally, we should not neglect the most obvious of all the properties of the ritual language, its distinctive difference from the ordinary language. The parallel form serves to mark the special status of what is being said. It gives to a statement a cast of unique authority, identifying it as part of a body of traditional wisdom passed down from ancient times, and distinguishes it from the passing and changeable thoughts of common men.

3

LI'I MARAPU: SPEECH AND RITUAL AMONG THE WEWEWA OF WEST SUMBA

BRIGITTE RENARD-CLAMAGIRAND

On my arrival in the field, in March 1979, I attended feasts that showed clearly the richness of oral expression among the Wewewa and their fondness for extended verbal performance. There was not much to be seen but there was a lot to be heard, and hours of recording were followed by the hard work of transcribing and translating. The primacy of words over gestures and the social prestige granted to those who master ritual speech make the study of ritual language a prerequisite to an understanding of Wewewa society.

Signs, speech and sacrifice

Li'i marapu refers to the words that relate the living to the dead, to their ancestors, and to all the forces of the invisible world which are referred to as *marapu*. But *li'i* also has the sense of promise: *katuku li'i*, 'to plant the word', refers to the contract established between someone who asks for an abundant crop or abundant offspring and a specific *marapu* who is promised in return the sacrifice of an animal, after a certain period of time.

These 'words' are expressed in a ceremonial language, *tenda*, which is composed of formulae using images and metaphors. Each of these formulae carries a precise meaning and can be used in different contexts. For example, the invitation to speak freely in a ritual or during discussions about the amount of bridewealth can be worded in the same terms:

Nda'iki bongga kedu ate	There is no dog with an envious liver,
Nda'iki manu buza koko[1]	There is no chicken with a tight throat.

These formulae form pairs using synonymous or related words and expressions which are not always found in everyday life. The purpose, however, of this paper is not so much to study the formal aspect of this ceremonial language as to grasp the articulation of the ritual and the different stages of the dialogue between people and the *marapu*. Perhaps the principal characteristic of this dialogue is that it is carried out like a battle in which the *marapu* 'demands' his due: that custom be followed, that a promise be fulfilled, or that reparation for a transgression be made, by men who are forced to explain and justify their acts in interpreting the signs sent by the *marapu*.

These signs (*tanda*) are a fundamental means of communication. Whether positive or negative, these signs are the word of the *marapu* in response to the words addressed to them by men. These signs both begin and end rituals, because it is often under the pressure of an ill omen (sickness, death or accident) that a ritual takes place. Signs therefore engender words from men which are accompanied by music, singing and dancing, according to the solemnity of the ritual, which always ends with the sacrifice of an animal whose entrails or liver is examined to decipher the signs sent by the *marapu*. Thus signs, words and sacrifice are deeply bound together.

A ritual activates a whole series of social ties: kinsmen and affines aid the master of the feast in collecting the animals needed for sacrifice. Moreover, it is necessary to call upon those who specialise in the spoken word: *ata urata*, *ata zaizo* and *ata woleka* – men who officiate at the three types of ceremonies that designate different degrees of ritual. These degrees are similar to the rungs of a ladder that must be climbed step by step – the 'ladder of spoken words [addressed] to the *marapu*', *nauta li'i marapu*.

Urata is the first step, and can be accompanied by a simple sacrifice of chicken without the beating of drums and gongs.

Zaizo is a more elaborate ritual celebration which is necessary, for example, to recall the 'soul' of the rice or the soul of a man which has been struck by lightning. The words addressed to the *marapu* are accompanied by a chant enhanced by the beating of drums and gongs and more important animal sacrifices.

Woleka is the final step where the living and the *marapu* are made 'serene'. This is a feast of thanksgiving and of homage to the *marapu* who have accorded their blessings so that the master of the house can 'redden the village with blood', thus demonstrating that he is a man of importance, an *ata mboto*, 'a man who carries weight'.

Linked to this hierarchy of rituals, in which the solemnity of the spoken word corresponds with the importance of the sacrifices, there is also a hierarchy of houses expressed in space, the older ones occupying the higher location. The houses of the high villages – customary villages built on hills overlooking irrigated rice fields – are the houses of the lineages who represent the elders in the genealogy of the clans. They cannot, without losing prestige, perform rituals 'at the same price' as houses that were founded later. This doubtless accounts for the vitality of the rituals that take place in those secondary houses which, in contrast to the more important ones, find in these rituals a validation of their status and an affirmation of their permanence which their 'natural' place in the genealogy does not confer on them.

It is within the framework of villages of secondary origin – 'corral villages' or 'field villages', where different clans live interspersed, contrary to what generally occurs in customary villages in which only one clan is represented – that most rituals are observed. These rituals are performed in the house and under the authority of the head of the house, supported by his kin and affines. They are, for the most part, rituals of healing and redress. Thus this study of speech will only focus on certain kinds of ritual, excluding the collective rituals, which, though still vividly remembered, are no longer performed in the spatial and ritual framework of customary villages where, generally, they used to take place.

A particular ritual may often announce a series of ritual engagements, but it can also serve different purposes (as in the case that will be discussed in this study). It is impossible, within the limited context of this paper, to follow the ritual word by word. Instead, by selecting examples, I have attempted to illustrate the role of each ritual actor and the way in which ritual speech unfolds, even though this may fail to convey the full incantatory character of the oral expression.

The way of the spoken word: the ritual of pakako zala – 'the banishment of transgression'

This particular ritual took place on 7 and 8 April 1979 in the village of Bondo Kapoda and in the house of N.K., who belongs to the Umbu Koba Wini Lere clan. After discussing matters with the head of the house, the officiator tried to find out through divination the meaning of the ill omen (in this case, the illness of a member of the house) sent by the *marapu*. Although there appeared to be several reasons for the anger of the *marapu*, an attempt was made to solve only one problem: the resolution of other conflicts was postponed by setting a date 'to speak once more to the *marapu*'. The ritual to be performed was a purification ritual, made necessary because prohibited sexual relations had taken place in the house. An *urata* should have been enough, but in this case a *zaizo* celebration was also decided upon. At dawn all 'transgressions' were to be cast out of the village and thereafter everyone was to return to the house, to 'cleanse' it by different sacrifices and then to conclude the ritual.

The evening of 7 April began with an offering of newly harvested rice and maize to the *marapu* to lift the prohibition on consuming these foods. It is possible that the coupling of these two rituals was neither accidental nor simply convenient, since the offering of newly harvested rice cannot take place in a house that is considered soiled, especially where the presence of a sick person is a visible sign of transgression. Moreover, certain collective rituals cannot take place before each house has totally fulfilled its promises of sacrifices to the *marapu*.

The way of the chicken

Before the *zaizo* ceremony began, six chickens were successively sacrificed, each for a particular purpose. The first was dedicated to the *marapu* of the man who was to act as chanter, the *zaizo* man (*ata zaizo*). The following is a summary of this dedication in which I have translated the more important and recurrent formulae:

> Eat this betel and areca nut, you who follow me, who accompany me, you who always stand beside me, you who send me to care for people, to beat the drum and to perform this feast in a house of my lineage.

Kuika tara wa'i dounggu	I pull out the thorn from my own foot,
Kukairo ruta mata wekinggu	I remove the blade of grass from my own eye.

> Do not impede me, give me liveliness and knowledge. Dapa Loka, you who have brought forth numerous offspring,

Awewarana uwana	Who have strewn fruit,
Atalarana ro'ona	Who have spread leaves.

> You are the place on which to lean, the site that protects. Tonight may my language be sharp, may my voice be clear. Come down without being impeded. Be my help and my protection so that

Panewe we'e malala	My words may be like clear water,
Kandouka we'e maringi	My utterances may be like life-giving water.
Yemi papakona panewe	You confront my speech,
Yemi nggobakona kandouka	You are partner to my discourse.

> Kindly accept this red cock, may it be agreeable to you and fragrant.

Ngungu numbu	Sharpen the spear,
Tiri ponda	Divide the pandanus,
Lalai lengi	Sprinkle the coconut oil,
Ware ndana	Grate the sandalwood.

All these requests are made so that everything goes well when reading the omens in the entrails of the chicken. The part of the entrails that is examined is called the *ai manu* and is composed of three distinct elements: the 'mouth' (*ngora*), the part which is associated with the living and, by its shape, shows what may happen in the future; the 'body' (*weki*), the part which depicts the world of the living; and the 'river' (*loko*), the line on the 'body' which marks the boundary between the living and the *marapu*. Holes, lines, red dots and fuzzy shapes are considered bad omens. Thus, the *ai manu* ought to have a 'sharp mouth' so that the lot of the living exceeds that of the *marapu*; it ought to be smooth as well (with no blemishes or unevenness); and its parts ought to be clear and well-defined, like pandanus which is smoothed and divided into fine strips before plaiting. It should also be polished in appearance as if it had been oiled and scented like sandalwood.

The second chicken was given to the *marapu* of the officiating *ata urata*, who belonged to an allied clan. The *marapu* of this *ata urata* was

Pakalete ndara ia	Asked to mount his horse,
Pakawa'a numbu nggazu	Invited to carry his sword.

Thus carrying his sword, he set off to help

Ana kambu linde	The children of the terraces,
Ana kambu atura	The children of the steps of stone,

namely, his wife-takers, who had established themselves in the land of their wife-givers.

The third chicken announced the rite of redress:

Ba na delakangge tana	At daybreak,
Ba na wanggarangge lodo	At sunrise,
We'e mangu nggengge	The water full of spiders,
Ruta mangu ndabo	The grass full of worms,
Manu tutuka tolu	The hen that pecks her own egg,
Bongga nga'a laiko	The dog that eats first [before its masters].

All these transgressions were brought down from the house and thrown out of the village.

The fourth chicken was offered to the souls of the dead who protect the house. They were asked to give their help so that

Nda'iki kadenge nduka wura	The lungs are not constricted,
Nda'iki kapoda nduka ngau	Breathing is not suffocating.

Thus the words may reach their goal and be transmitted to all the *marapu*.

The fifth chicken accompanied the rice and maize so that these offerings would be received joyfully:

Nda'iki ndiri mata	The eyes do not turn away,
Nda'iki peli po'o	The cheeks do not tighten.

The last chicken announced the *zaizo* feast that was to follow. All problems would be disentangled:

Talara kadinda mere tanabandi	Spread out like slices of cassava put out to dry in the dry season,
Wewara maroto mburu urabandi	Strewn about like mandarin leaves fallen during the rainy season.

The wish was that there should be

Nda'iki ita kere	No painful bottoms,
Nda'iki paro mata	No closed eyes,

but that everyone should follow the voice of the drums and gongs.

So ended the 'way' of the chicken. After the offering of some cooked food to the *marapu*, everyone ate.

The zaizo ceremony

It was 11.30 at night when the drums and gongs sounded to announce the beginning of the *zaizo*. The head of the house was 'the master of the horse// the owner of the boat' (*mori ndara//mangu tena*). He had arranged the drums and hung the gongs, and he had assembled his kin and affinal relatives like

Wandora wawi ta mareda	Pigs herded from the open fields,
Oruta kedu ta kalunga	Monkeys chased out from the young shoots.

It was he who was supposed to conduct the ritual, but he could delegate his role to a representative if he were not fully competent. The person who leads the ritual speech is 'the base of the tree//the source of the water' (*pu'una wazu//matana we'e*). One turns to him to request explanations or to begin a new topic. The 'man who is under the lips' (*ata kambu wiwi*) is the one who receives the words of another person either to assist him or to act as a go-between with the other officiators.

The chanter begins the ritual assisted by different speakers, 'men who speak' (*ata tau li'i*), who provide him with the substance of his chant. The chant is accompanied by the sound of drums and gongs, and also from time to time by the modulated cries (*pakalaka*) of the women who attend the feast. The chanter serves as a mediator and solemnly informs the *marapu* of the reasons and circumstances that have led to the performance of the ritual. The first speaker in the ritual shows the way. He is 'the small pigeon who leads//the little dove who precedes' (*kapopoka pairu//kadidika palaiko*). This is a reference to the pigeons and doves[2] which fly above the fields of rice and millet, thus warning the sparrows by their songs.

A kind of prologue precedes the core of the ritual, in which the particular reasons for the performance are made clear. These preliminaries act as a training ground where young men can venture to speak without fear of ruining the ceremony or of being punished for their mistakes. Everyone normally must speak twice (*panggoba*) before reaching the core of the ritual, where the emphasis is rigorously directed to proper speaking.

The speaker announced the beginning of the *zaizo* ritual:

Tapalengge kere	We move our bottoms,
Tapakede mata	We raise our faces.

And he recalled his role as mediator:

Andende pera mata	Who stands opposite [the *marapu*]
Azada kambu wo'u	Who stands under the chin [to receive their words].

He called the people to take their places:

Palimbandi kenga	Line up your thighs,
Pandukundi teke	Put your heads together.

They were to join the feast because the men of the village which is 'surrounded with a boundary of stones//encompassed by a fence of *kawango* [*Hibiscus tiliaceus*] trees' (*kilora kangali//woleta kawango*) had gathered with men from elsewhere like 'sheaves of bundled rice//streams of rejoining water' (*apabundu pare pamba//apawangu duki deta*). Everyone must speak up because 'all the lips are here//many eyes are present' (*tanga wiwi//matu mata*).

No one can be angry.

Nda'iki bongga kedu ate	There is no dog with an envious liver,
Nda'iki manu buza koko	There is no chicken with a tight throat.

Together they must follow the feast like

Apambonu tena detana	A boat filled to the gunnels,
Apabundu niri laingona	Sand packed upon the shore.

Thus all those who attend are urged to become speakers so that the chanter can accomplish his task. They must help him 'to support his bottom//to strengthen his knees' (*tema kere//ruka kundo*). However, they are not all equally skilled. Young and inexperienced men are like

Kambola tana mete	Handfuls of black topsoil,
Kapundu ro'o mapódu	Bundles of *mapodu* leaves [a medicinal plant used for newborn babies].

These men speak of their fear of speaking, for they are still like

Kuda koko kari	Water buffalo with tender necks,
Mbera lipi ndara	Horses with fragile backs.

Men who know, on the other hand, are

Ana paina	Children of an important mother,
Ana paama	Children of an important father.

They invite the young men to speak because

Nda'iki kiku la patenda	There is no tail that strikes,
Nda'iki ngora la pakati	There is no mouth that bites.

These knowledgeable men are 'the men who observe//the men who watch' (*ata pareda*//*ata paelo*) the unfolding of the feast, and they take responsibility for any mistakes that are made. They know how to straighten the course of ritual speech:

Awazi kere numbu	They restrain the base of the spear,
Andabi zazi ndara	They pull on the reins of the horse.

No one must be reluctant to speak:

Ndau remakani ndaramu	Do not wait for your horse,
Ndau manggakani bonggamu	Do not long for your dog [to begin the hunt].

The young, unskilled men should take a turn at speaking; they should not be afraid of the criticisms of those who know how to speak properly and accurately:

Aremba koba kalu	They display the beautiful coconut cups,
Ateba tabo lindaka	They align the plates.

The young should join in speaking so as not to remain out of the feast like

Kaka mbali lete	The parrot on the other side of the mountain,
Wondo mbali ala	The forest hen at the edge of the wood.

These new men, who are like 'betel that has begun to twine itself//to-
bacco that has just come forth' (*uta wudi akarangge//mbaku wudi aka-
beba*), do not wish to be accused of only waiting for their share of meat
and of pursuing goals, like

Ndara kendu wela	A horse racing to the rear,
Bongga mbeika eka	A dog sleeping outside its own place.

They have to contribute to the success of the feast, where all voices
must be like

Mbokota paro'o	Luxurious leaves,
Mbidura pauwa	Abundant fruits.

They must not remain silent like someone who is too old to move; nor
must they be like inconsiderate youths. They are therefore urged:

Ndu pata'iko bei kaweda kana lundu mate na mareda	Do not shit on the pasture so that the grass dies, as does an old buffalo,
Ndu pataliki bei kabondi kana lundu mbowona kapumbu	Do not piss on the straw until it rots, as does a young buffalo.

So that the remarks they express are not in vain, they are also urged not
to behave

Ndu pakaparoka wondo ro'o karikita	Like the forest hen that flaps its wings among the dry leaves [making a lot of fuss about nothing],
Ndu pakazewaka wawi roma dana	Like the pig that grunts in the fields [talking nonsense].

Their views are to be in accord with one another so that they all follow
the same path.

Thus, all through the prologue, emphasis was on the necessary participation of everyone and a certain liberty of speech was permitted. Allusions were made to matters extraneous to the ritual itself, such as my
presence:

> Let us not keep waiting someone who expects something, for the
> *ibu* ['mother', as they called me] who wants to learn is here and
> what we are doing is new to her. Why has she crossed the sea? Let
> us all, 'companions in misery and misfortune', give her what she
> has come to request ...

Very little was said about the reasons for the ritual itself: only that there
was a sick person and that gongs and drums were being sounded to expel

the 'transgression of the robber' (*zala kedu*), the 'transgression committed with the brother, the transgression committed with the sister'. It is only at the heart of the ritual that the reasons for the anger of the *marapu* are revealed. It is then important to make known the various transgressions that have been committed, and how they are linked to one another, by recalling what has already been discovered by the process of divination.

The transition to the second phase was marked by a distribution of areca nuts to the main actors in the ritual, the *pamama tapala panewe*, 'the betel quid as the boundary of speaking'. Those who now took part were skilled men capable of directing their speech, through an ordered succession of explanations, to a proper conclusion, thus gaining the approval of the *marapu*. After everything had been revealed, a further distribution of areca nut indicated that the ritual was heading towards its conclusion. A final discussion took place to decide on the number of animals to be sacrificed and on the share that was to go to each *marapu*. The chanter then informed the *marapu* of his share before ending the *zaizo* feast.

The actors in the ritual were now reduced in number. There was virtually a dialogue between the chanter, whose task was to communicate with the *marapu*, and the principal orator, who promised to conceal nothing:

Nda kukamborokinggu beto rara	I am not like the red ant that wraps itself in a cocoon [whose bite is cruel],
Nda kuponikinggu malawo tana	I am not like the mouse that hides underground [and provides itself with several exits].

Other orators intervened, but they did this mainly to encourage and relieve the lead orator and to express their support for and admiration of the chanter, who has 'gathered in his net//borne on his shoulders' (*pademe tete//paturu bale*) all the problems that had to be transmitted to the *marapu* and thus appeared as a powerful man:

Ana inabau alendaka ndara pakatuku	Son of a mother who unties the bridle of a horse tied to a stake [thus, by his knowledge, delivering the living from the grip of the *marapu*],
Ana amabau awopa pare ta kalenda	Son of a father who gathers rice on a large mat [thus like a strong man whose presence keeps the soul of the rice from fleeing when it is about to be stored away].

They urged the chanter to ask for clear explanations from the leader, who must 'cut [the wood] straight//pull [the liana] straight' (*ponggo luruta//rata nggonaka*) to discover who was angry:

Aparangge pu'una	Who strikes at the base,
Apobangge lawina	Who twists the tip.

The chanter also stressed the seriousness of what was being said. He called on both the other participants and his own ancestors to protect him and give him their attention because the lead orator had already given clear explanations:

Langgura pabetiba li'ina	Already the voice has fallen like the sheath surrounding a cluster of areca nuts,
Kamboka patumbaba lomana	Already the word has been thrown forth like a packet of betel [revealing the motives for the ritual].

The lead orator was asked by the chanter to be precise in his remarks:

Pende manu	Choose the chicken,
Tau kanduti	Throw the lance [at the target].

By questioning the *marapu*, the lead orator revealed the different factors that had provoked their anger. These had all been revealed in the course of the divination ritual, but the goal of the *zaizo* feast was to unfold these explanations solemnly, going back over the whole chain of causes which led to the celebration of the ritual – 'to banish the transgression' – in the hope of obtaining a cure.

The sickness was a sign of the anger of the *marapu*. This wrath was caused by the failure to keep a promise, and it had already caused a death. The promise itself had been made following the 'transgression of the robber' – 'the transgression with the brother, the transgression with the sister'.

Mandatingge ndou	The years have gone by,
Marorungge wula	The months have passed.

The unfulfilled promise had provoked the anger of the mother and the father:

Na pawolangga bongga la kalola inanggu	My mother who pursues me with a hunting dog,
Na pandutungga ndara la mareda amanggu	My father who tracks over the open fields with a horse.

That is why this day the drums and gongs have sounded. The ritual to banish the transgression is being performed.

Waingge we'e mata	With tears in the eyes,
Waingge we'e wira	With snot running from the nose.

Thus the present illness appeared as the very latest indication of an unresolved conflict with the *marapu*. To obtain release from a transgression that they themselves had not committed, the living had to perform a purification ritual that had been promised by a father and mother who were already dead. Since the living and the dead are bound together, the present generation, in order to continue to live and prosper, had to rid themselves of the 'traces' left by their predecessors.

Besides these explanations of the reasons for the ritual, the ritual language formulae show the way in which discourse proceeds. One must 'card the cotton//draw the thread' (*wunda kamba//louta lelu*) so that speech may take ordered form. This is compared to

Katondo ngi'i wino	Tying stems of areca,
Kaloko lolo uta	Winding vines of betel.

All problems were to be gathered together so that they were

Wunggu lima	Held between the hands,
Bilu bengge	Inserted in the belt.

Then they were to be given to the *marapu*:

Leiro lima	Laid in their hands,
Baba kenga	Placed in their laps.

In particular they were to be given to the recently deceased fathers and mothers who 'faced the speech//were partners in the discourse'. They were to inform all the *marapu*, those from within the house and those outside,[3] that the faults were to be brought down from the house and cast out of the village:

Patundungge loko Loura	Scattered in the river Loura,
Pazobangge wara Ngaura	Swept by the waves at Nggaura,
Na deke lawora toda ndende	Seized by the *lawora* lizard that stands upright,
Na ngale lamboku mbani mata	Taken away by the *lamboku* civet with the fearless eyes.

The *marapu* were requested not to create an obstacle to hinder the performance of the ritual:

Ila ndana palondakana kalere	No outstretched rope,
Ila ndana palakakana karinggi	No stick that impedes.

But there were still other problems, and their origin had to be revealed before a solution could be found:

Wini tando pare	The rice grain is planted in the earth [to grow forth],
Ndara ndeke lola	The horse starts at the bottom [to climb a hill].

A promise had been made to offer a sacrifice to the *koni* rice and to the *ndima* rice,

Amangolo we'ena	Whose water is so tasty,
Aminaka ina	Whose substance is so delicious.

Similarly, a promise had been made to build a tomb:

Katitini tana	To dig the earth,
Kawowani watu	To break the stone,

for the great *kaboko* snake

Akako waina ti'ana	That moves on its stomach,
Apalawe waina karana	That slithers on its chest,

because it had been found burnt. Both of these matters were put aside until later, but they were not forgotten and thus continued to be

Pakatowa todu teke	Carried on the head,
Pakaboti bale deta	Placed on the shoulders,

until what was necessary had been accomplished.

Finally, the *marapu* of the house were called upon to provide their assistance in

Padedena ndewana	Gathering the soul,
Pambalina mawona	Recovering the spirit,

of the man of the house who has fallen and whose soul has escaped. This was likened to

Zodo ana rande kere omba	Seizing the duck at the far end of the lake,
Odeta kaboko kere lango	Twisting the snake at the bottom of the cave,

so that the man would continue to live. The wish was expressed that no one would

Apote upu nggungga	Twist the hair at the top of the head,
Amando lai kadanu	Seize the string of the betel bag,

thus causing death.

In his final chant the chanter informed each *marapu* of the share he would receive and asked that no mistakes be made in the distribution, like

Manu kazala pandura	The chicken that sleeps in the wrong place,
Keila kazala kekora	The bird that goes to the wrong nest.

All were to stay near the drums, gongs and betel that was being offered:

Lindaka mandi'imi	They should sit in line [on the mat],
Luruta palomani	They should stretch out their legs,

because the speaking was about to end:

Ndende ba ndara	The horse has stopped,
Ngaru ba bongga	The dog is at rest.

All that was done was done

Uku benge modu	According to the old way,
Pata lara dinga	Following ancient custom,

so that all might be like

We'e amaringi loko	The fresh water of the river,
We'e amanggabo tana	The refreshing water of the earth.

These are the revitalizing waters provided by the performance of the ritual.

The sending away of the transgressions

At daybreak, about 6 o'clock, the ritual performers descended from the house to go and expel the transgressions from the village.

Near the entrance a small shelter had been built under which squatted the men of the house. When this shelter was set on fire they had to flee, and as they fled others tried to hit them with pieces of the *kabota* plant, a plant whose flower stinks and which causes itching if it is eaten. This plant symbolises the ill effects of the 'robber's transgression'. A goat was sacrificed in compensation for the transgression, as was a dog that was supposed to bark at it so that it would

Lera kikipa	Fly high,
Kako kindola	Go straight forward.

Once back in the house, various sacrifices were made 'to cleanse' the house. The chanter received a chicken, which he would sacrifice, once back home, to his own *marapu* to obtain their protection. An offering was also made to the drums and gongs, which were identified with buffaloes and horses, and which were requested

Kana benu doukona we'e	To drink water again by themselves,
Kana manopa doukona ruta	To graze again on the grass by themselves [in between rituals, gongs and drums have to fend for themselves, they are no longer 'fed'],

until the time of the next feast. And during the course of each sacrifice, the *marapu* were asked to signal their satisfaction when the omens were read so that everyone could leave in good spirits.

Ritual speech, knowledge, power

Either on its own or accompanied by the sound of drums and gongs, speech is at the centre of the ritual and its efficacy in obtaining the approval of the *marapu* depends, in large part, on the way in which this speaking is performed.

Three important notions seem to be embodied in ritual speech. The first is the notion of *nggoba*, 'pair, partner' (conceived also as 'opponent'). Ritual formulae form pairs in which one phrase is balanced by the other; drums and gongs are partners; the living and the *marapu* are partners in speech.

The second notion, which is linked to the first, is that of the intermediary or go-between: the officiator, the chanter, the recently dead, 'allow speech to pass' from one side to the other; they are the 'bridge' joining the two shores of discourse.

The third notion is that of *nauta*, 'ladder'. This is definitely an image of hierarchy – the hierarchy of importance attached to speech addressed to the *marapu* – but it is also the image of a step-by-step approach, of a progression in ritual discourse which, having arrived at its conclusion has achieved its goal: to cast away 'that which is hot' (*ambutu ambangata*) and synonymous with danger, and to receive 'the cool water, the fresh water' (*we'e maringi we'e manggabo*) which are symbols of health and prosperity.

The specialists who perform the ritual appear, first of all, as masters of speech, clever men with 'acute minds'. But this mastery of ritual speech involves not just a facility in the use of language but also a knowledge of custom. It is not enough to know the formulae; one must be able to use them properly to address specific situations and resolve particular problems. Many expressions describe this knowledge, which combines skill and understanding, virtuosity of the lips, and understanding of the heart:

'movements of the lips must accord with thoughts that come from the liver'. Words are dangerous. One must not speak carelessly and, even outside of a ritual context, useless words, lies and slander can be serious and have disastrous consequences. There even exists a ritual for expelling all ill-considered remarks or incorrect rumours, for example those that spread after an accident. Similarly, one must not believe everything that is said like someone 'whose ears are thin' and who accepts, without discrimination, everything he hears.

Thus, whoever knows how to conduct ritual speech enjoys great social prestige and the most renowned specialists are in great demand. Some of these specialists have this role because of the place given them by tradition within their own clan, but many have acquired their positions by demonstrating their competence. During the performance of its rituals, every house asks that a man 'skilled in speaking' should be born in their midst. Hence one may give to a new-born child the name of a relative known for his exceptional gifts, the most precious of which is that of skill in speaking. This namesake (*tamo*) will encourage the transference of these gifts to the child. Thus everyone tries to acquire this knowledge. If he cannot hope to become a *rato* (the master of a *marapu* house in a traditional village, or in a 'corral village', if the traditional village no longer exists), who is always supposed to be knowledgeable about custom and a master of speech, he can aspire 'to become a father' (*paama*) and thus an important man. Wewewa society is not rigidly stratified, especially in the framework of more recent villages where roles are less strictly defined. A younger brother can surpass his elder brother in prestige if his skill allows his house to perform rituals, such feats as elevate its status, even though the genealogical pre-eminence of the elder brother is recalled in the ritual. The house that possesses a master of speech is certain to prosper, for the benevolence of the *marapu* will endow it with children and wealth and remove all misfortune. Speech will be fully effective in its positive aspect, which tends to ensure harmonious communication among the living, and between them and the forces that rule them – the *marapu*.

But speech can also be used negatively: instead of attempting to free men from the anger of the *marapu*, it can call on the *marapu*'s sanctions in an oath or deliver men to punishment in a curse: 'May I and all my family disappear if I lie' ('may he who contradicts me perish if I am telling the truth'). The threat of such statements often calls forth a compromise solution. The person who is the object of a curse is placed in the hands of the *marapu*. The curse is a kind of negative contract that is established with the *marapu*, who will sow death and desolation instead of fertility and prosperity. To contravene such a curse, one must ritually 'tear the tongue//pull out the word' (*lizu loma//kouka li'i*) by making a sacrifice.

The mastery of speech and the knowledge attached to it bring its bearer social prestige that makes him an influential man in a society where competition appears to be an important feature, even at the highest level, where the clan hierarchy is a subject of permanent dispute.[4]

However, the mastery of speech, which distinguishes whoever possesses it, confers a power which can only be used in a concerted effort that must lead to an accord between all parties. Thus this power appears to be, above all, a cohesive force. It is based on the recognition of supremacy, but a supremacy that must always be put to the test and must always be reaffirmed.

4

THE PATTERN OF PRAYER IN WEYÉWA

JOEL C. KUIPERS

In the western highlands of Sumba, incest and adultery seriously disturb the social order, necessitating verbal and economic retribution in a ritual context. During one rainy season, a man named Mbulu Mada carried on an illicit love affair with his uncle's wife, a woman called Lyali Leba. They had not only violated a strict rule against adultery enforced among the approximately 70,000 people inhabiting the Weyéwa-speaking districts, but, since Lyali was also a distant agnate to Mbulu, they had also committed incest (*sála*). In February 1979, about ten years after the affair was terminated, a series of misfortunes struck their families. Lyali tripped and fell while fetching water and hurt her knee; her father was killed suddenly in a fire of suspicious origin; and Mbulu's son became ill with a disease which caused his arms, legs and face to swell up like balloons. A diviner was called in, their confessions elicited, a placation rite was staged, and several chickens, three pigs and a water buffalo lost their lives as sacrifices to soothe the angered spirits.

This oblation was accompanied by a 'prayer' (*bára*), delivered by a specialist spokesman, Mbulu Renda, in the richly metaphorical, parallelistic style of 'ritual speech' (*panéwe ténda*) required in all Weyéwa ceremonial occasions. His attempt to expiate verbally the guilt, on behalf of the two sinners, is recorded below and is the subject of this analysis. Typical in form and content, this prayer translates, with vivid metaphors, the sexual transgression into terms concordant with their cosmology and symbolism. However, I want to argue in this paper that the linear organisation by which these metaphorical themes unfold lends this text to interpretation not as an expository monologue guided solely by individual choices and decisions, but as part of a dialogue, a turn at talk. Although it appears as a solo performance, the prayer is a stretch of communicative activity which clearly reflects Weyéwa norms for co-ordinated communicative interaction and verbal interchange. The basis for this claim is an examination of the units and themes of the prayer which yield a clear resemblance to the everyday sociolinguistic act, 'the social visit' (*pakúlla wékkina*). It can be further demonstrated that the social visit pattern accords well with the overall theme of the prayer, which concerns the expiation of guilt from the community.

As in many societies, sexual transgressions in Weyéwa cause social and symbolic disorder. As Forth has pointed out, the Sumbanese represent such misdeeds in cosmological terms as a 'confusion of the inside and the outside' (1981:356). Such improprieties, he argues, are likened to '"wild" behaviour brought into the community which defiles the house and creates disorder within the group with which the house is associated' (1981:357). In Weyéwa, both incest and adultery are regarded as 'filthy' (*dírraka*) and hence polluting acts which threaten the stability of the community by causing 'confusion' (*káityo*; cf. Indonesian *kácau,* 'chaos').

While both 'incest' (*sála*) and 'adultery' (*sála* or *nkóku*) are regarded as polluting acts, different aspects of the consequences of these transgressions are emphasised. An incestuous union between a man and his sister, daughter, mother, or a natal member of his own clan is considered to have supernatural consequences, resulting in various misfortunes, from disease to crop failure. An adulterous liaison with the wife of a clan mate is also polluting, but much less severe in its religious consequences, requiring only a brief ceremony of purification. Adultery with the wife of a man of another clan is a more serious offence, not only disrupting the spiritual stability of the house of the cuckolded man, but requiring reconciliation between the two parties.

Among the Weyéwa, the chaos of the inside/outside violation is often represented by an alimentary idiom. The wrongful sexual act is metaphorically compared to the consumption or internalisation of a 'substance' which results in disorder and confusion. An important goal of the prayer is to externalise the guilt, to move it verbally *out* of the village up to the stars and moon.

Methods of data collection

Before discussing the prayer and its organisation, it might be well first to review the methods by which these data were collected, and the social context of the event in which it occurred.

In the course of over eighteen months of ethnographic fieldwork in the Weyéwa highlands, I observed, recorded, analysed and took part in a wide variety of ritual speech events, from rites of divination to marriage negotiations. These ceremonial gatherings are integral to the lively and ongoing tradition of religious practice and belief (*marápu*) still vitally maintained among this largely non-Christian, non-Islamic population of west Sumba. In every Weyéwa ritual performance 'prayer' (*bára*) is an essential feature. I observed more than a hundred occasions on which this central component of ritual was displayed, thirty-eight of which were taped by me and transcribed by native speakers of Weyéwa whom I had trained in transcription techniques. These assistants and I then checked the written text against the tape-recording, meanwhile eliciting commentary from the performers and other trained assistants on the various meanings of ritual speech words and phrases, the significance of which in many cases was not immediately apparent from the ordinary speech interpretations of the words.

The social setting of Mbulu Renda's prayer

This prayer was delivered at about 9 o'clock in the morning in the 'vestibule' of the house of Mbulu Mada, on the right-hand side, a portion of the house considered to have a privileged spiritual position associated with ancestral spirits and relics. Figure 1 shows the three main participants standing or sitting in the vestibule. The vaporous trail leading up to the stars and moon is the artist's image of the journey of the guilt as it is expelled from the village by the speaker's narration of the journey. Like

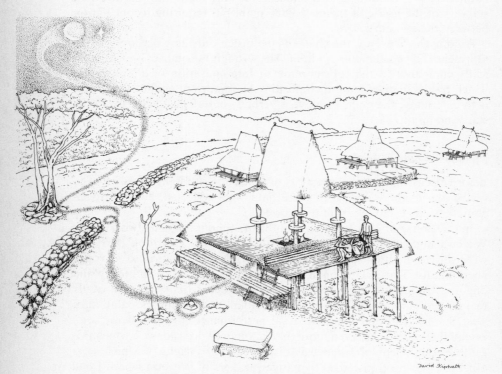

Figure 4.1. Expelling the guilt from the village

many prayers, the brief performance recorded in the text preceded a lengthy sequence of spectacular, all-night, ritual speech events, including 'divination' (*úrrata*) and 'placation rites' (*sáiso*) (see Kuipers 1982).

The situation for this prayer was an 'expiation' ceremony over the combined incest and adultery between Mbulu and his maternal uncle's second wife, Lyali. Technically, this was adultery, a liaison with the wife of a man of another patrilineal clan, a grave offence in Weyéwa. Ironically, it was because it also could be considered incest that bloodshed was avoided after their belated confessions. Apparently for the sake of reconciliation, the parties involved emphasised the importance of their prior kin connections; Lyali's agnatic link to Mbulu's clan and the affinal tie through Mbulu's mother's cuckolded brother. As such it was not regarded as a challenge to the jural authority of another clan over the reproductive rights to a female but, rather, a dangerously polluting act within a group of insiders, to be resolved behind closed doors.

Mbulu Renda was well qualified for the task of spokesman on the basis of his extraordinary and well-known skill in ritual oratory and other aspects of ritual practice, and his acquaintance and kinship affiliation (albeit somewhat distant) with the principals prior to the transgression and subsequent misfortune. Weyéwa say that, technically, anyone is capable of uttering a prayer, and most people do so at some point in their lives, although women and young children participate much less frequently in this activity than do older men. Within this latter category, however, there are certain particularly adept individuals who are renowned for their oratorical prowess and who are frequently called upon for their services to pray on behalf of others.

The structure of the text

The actual text of Mbulu Renda's prayer is provided in the reference text at the end of this paper. Since the graphic format of this text departs somewhat from the more standard styles of presentation of ritual speech for this region, a brief comment is in order. The presentation of this text has been ordered so as to take account graphically of various levels of structure: the 'scene', the 'stanza', the 'couplet' (or 'distich'), and the connective phrases between the couplets. Although the presence of couplets is well established for the eastern Indonesian area (Fox 1971, 1974, 1975, 1977), recognition of other units of ritual discourse is also important for a full contextual interpretation of Weyéwa ritual speech.

The three 'scenes' of the prayer, which have been labelled 'invocation', 'proposition' and 'resolution', exhibit unity of theme and temporal perspective. The thematic coherence of the scenes will be discussed in some detail. The temporal framework of Scene I, in which the offering is presented to the spirits, is established by the particle *ná'i*, 'to, at, into, towards'. This indicates proximate (not distant), future (not present), activity towards (not away from) a person (not an inanimate object). Time perspective in the second scene, in which a proposition is made relating past transgressions to present misfortunes, is established primarily by use of the particle *né'e*, 'then', which points to past, completed events, and by *ne ba hinna*, 'now', which refers to the present. The particle *ná'i* does not occur in Scene II, but reappears in Scene III, in which the guilt is carried out of the village *to* the stars and moon.

The boundaries of the scenes are signalled by shifts in topic, stylistic 'code-switching' and significant pauses. The 'code-switching' refers to the speaker's departure from strict 'couplet speech' to the use of what I call 'connective devices', phrases such as those on lines 299–301: *Mah! ne ba hinnangge, ka ku* ... ('well, now, so that I...'). Since Weyéwa spokesmen do not employ preformed chants or formulae, the boundaries between these segments of discourse are occasionally somewhat loose and not always easy to discover. However, such connective devices are often combined with prosodic features such as pauses (see Gumperz 1982:100–129) providing a clear signal of scene boundaries. In the text the separate 'scenes' are marked by Roman numerals.

Each scene can be further decomposed into breath-groups, which are distinguished by a falling intonational contour, and a thematic unity reflecting a relatively complete, sentence-like structure. Usually consisting of one or more couplets, these structures will be called, for lack of a better word, 'stanzas'. Distinguished in performance by a brief pause, these structures are graphically differentiated in the reference text by extra space between the lines.

The Weyéwa themselves consider couplets (*ngóbba*) to be the outstanding and distinctive feature of ritual speech. These conventional couplets in Weyéwa may take many shapes (see Kuipers 1982). They all, however, consist of traditionally paired lines of verse marked by rhythmic and semantic parallelism. In the reference text, couplets are graphically distinguished by indentation.

A difficulty in the transcription of couplets arises from the fact that these couplets are not just fixed paired lines: they are also extraordinarily productive units in which short verse lines are expanded with other traditional phrases to suit the speaker's intent. As a result, often the spoken lines of verse are longer than a written line text. For example, in the following lines, which refer to the process of invoking the spirits to receive the betel-quid offering, lines 1–3 and 4–6 are each part of a single line of Weyéwa verse, but in this treatment take up three text lines apiece. To show that, for instance, line 2 of this text does not constitute a new line of verse but is, rather, a continuation of the previous line, it is further indented.

Óruta kóki
  ta kalúnga
    ka ta mandí'i téppe
Wándorana wáwi
  ta marédda
    kái térrena pamáma

Gathered the monkeys
  in the field
    so that we can sit on the mat,
Summoned the pigs
  in the meadow
    so that you get the quid;

Analysis

These units – the scene, the stanza, the couplet, and connective devices – turned out to be useful not only when analysing how single lines fit into larger units of verbal behaviour but also in trying to understand the overall pattern of the linear organisation of the prayer as a whole. Scenes and stanzas merit special attention.

The structure of scenes exhibits a resemblance to the pattern of organisation of a social visit. The first scene concerns the invocation of the spirits, in which the deities are enjoined to accept an offering, and hear, acknowledge and further participate in the communication. The second scene provides a proposition, the real reason for the talk. The final scene consists of a resolution, in which something is done about the proposition.

How do we know that this three-scene sequence resembles the colloquial speech act of 'social visiting'? First of all, the Weyéwa say it is so. Although they do not explicitly recognise units such as the scene, they do refer to such prayers as *pamámana kúlla*, 'to exchange betel with the spirits'. Given the role of betel-chewing in Weyéwa social life, this is another way of saying 'visiting with the spirits'.

Another way of demonstrating the parallel is by comparing the structure of the two speech events. In everyday Weyéwa life, when one party has something 'weighty' (*mbóto*) to be discussed with another party, a social visit is in order. This routine rarely happens between close kin; it typically takes place only when there is some social distance among the parties. In these circumstances the communication begins with an 'offering', usually of the ingredients for a betel and areca nut chew. This may be accompanied by a transfer of gifts. It is followed by the actual main topic of talk: a petition, a proposal, or a confession. The visit ends with a final segment consisting of a conclusion, a resolution or action taken in response to the previous step.

These three phases of the event are bounded by linguistic and pragmatic acts. To take a hypothetical example, if a man wishes to make amends with another man over past disputes he may invite the person over to his house. On reaching the porch, the guest seats himself on a mat unrolled by the host. At this point the host offers the guest some betel, the quality of which reflects the emotion invested in the transaction. Sometimes he may accompany this with a gift of some kind, say cloth or a knife. He may offer it silently, but typically he will name the object being offered and refer to it with a deprecating metaphor, ostensibly to save the guest the embarrassment of feelings of obligation, saying 'take this old rag' (*dékke na karáttuka*). The main goal of this period is the transferral of goods and the establishment of communication between the two parties.

After some preliminary talk, and the obligatory period of exchange of betel characteristic of all Weyéwa social encounters (see also Conklin 1958), the host says explicitly *áppa pamái dénga* ('the reason for the visit'); for example, that he would like to apologise and to make up with his estranged friend. This marks the second scene of the process. The conclusion of the visit in this case would be some indication of acceptance or rejection on the part of the guest, perhaps by reciprocating in some way or by leaving in anger, depending on the situation. The point of the final scene is to respond in some way to the proposal, to take some action in relation to it.

What does all this have to do with the prayer? This tripartite organisation – consisting of what I have called the greeting or preliminary talk, followed by the 'reason for the visit', and then the final transaction – this sequence is reflected in the main themes of the three scenes of the prayer. The first scene is concerned with the invocation of, and the establishment of communication with, the spirit world. This is done by offering them *pamáma* ('betel quid', a deprecating metaphor for the 'animal offering'; lines 3–4, 8–9). In the second, proposition scene, the spokesman focuses on the nature of the transgression itself, describing it in terms of alimentary processes. In the third, resolution scene, the spokesman narrates what is being done about it: the sin is verbally escorted out of the village up to the stars and moon.

During the second scene, this entire in/out theme is repeated through the pragmatic activity of the main participants, Mbulu and Lyali, each of whom was given a coconut half-shell of bitter water which they somewhat reluctantly drank in, gargled and spewed out. The speaker refers to this activity in lines 257–276.

Like the initial sequence of a visit, the first scene of the prayer is mostly concerned with the provision and acceptance of the offering, and the establishment of communication between the participants. This is reflected in the theme of the couplets, having to do with the metalinguistic commentary on the nature of communicative relations between the ritual specialist and the spirit world. The reference text is rich in metaphor, not all of which can be explicated here. One prominent theme, however, is that of conveyance of speech.

Conveyance of speech

| 152 | *ka na bótina panéwena* | so that he brings his speech, |
| 153 | *ka na áilana kandáuke* | so that he conveys his talk; |

The theme of transferral also appears in this text as couplets in which the verbal, performative transfer of the offering is metaphorically compared to conveyance by boat and by horse (see lines 72–3).

Conveyance by boat and horse

| 72 | *paténa sóro bába* | conveyed by boat, |
| 73 | *a pandára bóti ngíndi* | brought by horse; |

One of the goals of transferral is the establishment of communication with the spirit world. The high percentage of quotative utterances, such as 'I say', 'you say', and so forth, accords well with this goal. Phrases like these are performative statements of who is speaking to whom. They help to highlight these networks by describing (and at once instantiating) the communicative relationships in the prayer. The point of this scene is to establish conversation, to engage the spirits in talk, to draw them in to the event.

The spokesman marks clearly the beginning of the second scene by bringing up, for the first time, the main topic of the discussion, the transgression, which he describes as incest. Incest, in this metaphorical representation, is a violation of the boundaries of inside and outside, expressed partly by the alimentary imagery of consumption. This alimentary theme is reflected in the use of the following traditional couplets:

Sexual transgression as the pollution of food

| 171 | *wé'e mángu nggéngge* | spiders in the water, |
| 172 | *rútta mángu ndábbo* | poison leaves in the pasture; |

This refers to wrongful sexual activity as pollution of the water source, poisoning of the food source of cattle and, indirectly, of humans (see also lines 211–212, 214–215, 295–298). Another recurring theme is:

Sexual transgression as obstructing alimentary process

173	*a kendénge*	which jams
174	*ru karáppe mánu*	a chicken bone [in the throat],
175	*a kalódana*	which sticks
176	*ru katékke ndára*	a horse skull bone [in the mouth];

This couplet refers to the bones caught in the throat (see also lines 201–206, 291–294).

Sexual transgression as improper consumption

271	*Ba wá'ikongge*	If there was
272	*ngá'a kála ngá'a*	food improperly eaten,
273	*wé'e kála énu*	water improperly drunk,

This refers to the consumption of tabooed or forbidden plants.

Retribution as cleansing alimentary process

274	*Ka na*	May [they]
275	*múmu*	gargle,
276	*parámo*	[and] wash;

This refers to the consumption of a substance which is both an emetic and a laxative (see also lines 266–267).

These preceding metaphors predominate in the second, proposition scene, in which the nature of the transgression is discussed. The beginning of the third scene is marked in part by the movement from alimentary imagery to the metaphor of the 'hunt' (*kalóla*), in which the hunting activity is represented as the pursuit of the transgression and the tracing of the steps of the sin out of the village.

Retribution as a hunt

301	*Ka ku*	So that I
302	*pandékedowangge lára*	walk the trail,
303	*Ka ku*	So that I
304	*pamánedowangge ínu*	follow the spoors;

In the final scene, beginning with line 299, the spokesman describes the process of guilt removal in graphic terms: Mbulu Renda uses the first person pronoun 'I' (*ku*), assuming the role of the Messenger Spirit who 'walks the trail//follows the spoor'. The altars at which offerings are placed in the course of this journey are represented as 'footprints' or 'tracks'. While these holy sites act as landmarks along the stages of the Messenger's journey, they also stand for many other things as well. They stand for the specific sins which caused the misfortunes; they stand for the misfortunes themselves (Lyali's fall, her father's death, the boy's sickness); and they are also the altars at which various verbally offered oblations are provided in retribution. Thus the 'trail' refers not only to the series of steps taken to right the wrongs, but to the sequence of misdeeds and transgressions which originally resulted in the tragedy. This hunting expedition is represented as a kind of journey of moral purification.

The imagery of the journey draws on the symbolism of the 'hunt' (*kalóla*). Just as a hunter with his dogs follows the spoors in an effort to capture the quarry, the spokesman traces the trail of misfortune and remedy which leads to the desired goals: the explanation of the misfortune and the provision of a remedy. Though at first the transgressions occurred as isolated events, disconnected in the minds of the actors, in this image they are vividly linked, not only as temporal stages of a hunting expedition but as the 'spoors' and 'tracks' which are indexically connected to their cause. Since hunting is a risky, emotionally charged enterprise among the Weyéwa, by appealing to this metaphor the spokesman condenses several meanings into a single intelligible framework.

With the hunting image, the underlying proposition that certain events are morally connected (as actions categorised as conceptually similar in some way) is overlaid with the notion of both temporal (before/after) and spatial (in front of/behind) connection. This fusing of imagery literally gives a direction, a kind of linearity, to what otherwise might be seen as disconnected events. It calls attention to the goal, the target, the quarry, rather than to the nature of the association between the events.

To summarise, the theme of the first scene is the establishment of communication with the spirits in an attempt to draw them 'in' to the house. This corresponds to the opening sequences of a social visit, in which the transferral of goods takes place and small talk prevails in order to establish communication. The second scene begins the main topic of discussion, that is, the topic of sexual transgression, which the speaker describes as a violation of the inside and outside, represented in alimentary terms. As in the social visit, it is in this second stage that one brings up the *reason* for the visit, the main proposition. In both the prayer and the social visit, the final scene represents some action taken in response to the proposition. In this prayer the final scene concerns the resolution of the problem of sexual transgression, by carrying the guilt out of the village.

The role of stanzas in the prayer

Regarding the analysis of the linear organisation of rituals, Tambiah has recently remarked that

> the classical framework in the anthropological study of rites in this mode is of course the tripartite scheme of Van Gennep (1909) – segregation, liminal period, and reaggregation – and Mauss's earlier scheme for sacrifice – entry, act and exit. (1979:140)

Tambiah cautions, however, against the uncritical use of this model for the interpretation of ritual events: 'This scheme, if employed mechanically, can mask certain perceptions.' For example, there are cases of

> rites of affliction which have internal recursive loops, and shifts in the media emphasized, and a combined pattern of progressions and reiterations, whose subtleties are not revealed by a prior

commitment to the tripartite strait-jacket as a point of departure. (1979:140)

As we have seen, the overall structure of Mbulu Renda's prayer offering does indeed seem to conform naturally with a tripartite sequence. However, at the level of stanzas, there does seem to be some internal repetition of the themes of previous and following scenes. Although each scene does indeed seem to have a clear temporal and thematic unity to it, it is as though sometimes the speaker gets off the track and refers to the preceding scene or the scene still to come. The invocation–proposition–resolution sequence repeats itself within the individual scenes of the prayer for emphasis, forming what Tambiah calls 'recursive loops'. It is interesting that this repetitive cycling of themes was also noted by Reichard (1944) to be a characteristic feature of Navaho prayer.

This repetitive patterning is reflected in Mbulu Renda's prayer. While most of the first scene is concerned with offering betel-quid and rice, not all of it is. For example, in the first scene of the prayer, the invocation, the spokesman repeats the offer of 'rice and betel-quid' to the ancestral spirits over and over (lines 1–6, 7–13, 23–27, 120–126), avoiding 'embarrassment' (*måkke*) when encountering holy, long-deceased ancestors by requesting that more intimate spirits verbally relay the offering to their elders on his behalf (lines 10–13, 14–22, 70–73, 89–93, 94–100, 101–108, 127–169). But he also hints at the actual proposition ('struggle') behind the prayer in lines 37–41, and alludes to its resolution (lines 42–44, 45–47, and especially lines 48–53, in which he says, essentially, that things are such that the transgression has been resolved to the point that it is in the spirits' lap, not ours). This hinting at the proposition is once again repeated in lines 54–61, and is followed by a discussion of Mbulu's attempted resolution in lines 62–69.

The beginning of the second scene was marked by a change of topic and a significant pause. In line 170, for the first time in the prayer, he begins to refer to what he considers to be 'the question': incest. This he describes in terms of the pollution of food. But immediately following this, in line 187, he has already returned to the theme of the invocation sequence – he invokes the spirits (that is, monkeys and pigs) to accept the quid. Although the speaker, Mbulu Renda, in this scene is clearly most interested in proposing that past incest is the reason for the present misfortune, he does so by repeatedly reiterating the invocation–proposition–resolution sequence.

The third scene makes less use of the repetition of the three-stage sequence. Except for the brief allusions to the offering (lines 382–386) and the transgression (lines 371–377), the scene is exclusively concerned with the journey of the sin out of the village and with straightening things out (lines 387–391).

A summary of the stanzas might be as follows:

I   1 1 1 1 1 2 2 3 3 3 3 1 2 3 1 1 1 1 1 1 1 1 1 1 1 1 1 1 1 1
II   2 1 1 1 3 2 2 2 3 3 3 1 1 1 1 2 3 3 2 2 2
III 3 3 3 3 3 3 3 3 3 3 3 3 3 3 2 1 3 3 3

The Roman numerals along the left hand side stand for the invocation (I), proposition (II), and resolution (III) scenes respectively, and each number to the right of it stands for the stanzas as they occurred in the text of that scene. The value of the number indicates whether the stanza concerns the invocation of the spirits (1), a proposition about the nature of the transgression (2) or a resolution to the problem (3).

As can be seen from this chart, the invocation scene contains essentially two repetitions of this tripartite sequence: a 122333 sequence, and a 123 pattern. Scene II, the proposition scene, also has two such repetitions, a 11322233 pattern (the fourth stanza of which does not precisely fit the mould), and a 1233 sequence. The third scene is the most uniform, with only a single brief 321 sequence, which could be seen as a reversal of the usual sequence.

While this chart somewhat oversimplifies the thematic complexity of the prayer by condensing its meanings into a 123 scheme, I believe it fairly represents the patterns of repetition in this speech event. The prayer is not an aimless, rambling stretch of verbal performance. The speaker follows a short pattern, a sequence which repeats throughout the prayer.

The overall similarity of the sequence in the prayer to the everyday colloquial speech act of social visiting provides persuasive evidence that what the speaker is trying to do with the prayer is something similar to that attempted on the social visit. He is trying to invoke the spiritual host's attention by providing an offering. In this way he establishes communication and then makes a request or states a proposition. Since this prayer is structured like a social visit, audience and speaker are thus predisposed to expect certain outcomes: that is, the proposal will be acted on in some way.

The fact that this sequence repeats itself not only in the overall structure of the prayer but within the individual scenes provides the prayer with a figure-like rhythm, beginning with two brief repetitions of the theme in Scene I, building intensity in Scene II with the more elaborate reiteration of the theme, and finally ending with a relatively consistent, untroubled characterisation of the resolution, in which things are presented as 'straightened out'.

Conclusion

The Weyéwa felt that this prayer was a success. The proper ritual procedure was carried out (*na déku náuta*, 'he followed the steps of the house ladder') and ritual conditions fulfilled, and exchanges of meat between the concerned parties could take place, soothing angry hearts. The mother's cuckolded brother, I noticed, received a sizeable portion of meat. This all undoubtedly helped facilitate re-establishment of social relationships between husband and wife, uncle and nephew. It is not my purpose here, however, to tackle the complicated question of the efficacy of the ritual.

The main purpose of this discussion has been to examine this prayer in the context of patterns of sociolinguistic behaviour in Weyéwa society. Examining the text in this way provides confirmation for 'unsuspected designs', such as scenes and stanzas, and helps us to understand, even anticipate, where the speaker is going with the prayer.

Another feature of this approach is its emphasis on shared, public and cultural forms, rather than relying solely on inferences about psychological structures. It examines the textual organisation not in terms of mentalistic, decision-making processes, nor in terms of individual capacities of memory and recall, but in terms of the shared patterns of communication observable within Weyéwa culture.

This prayer consists of shared symbols. But these symbols unfold according to a pattern which contributes to the prayer's significance. Analysing this text apart from the interactional pattern that guides its structure might have revealed an interesting monologue in which the use of vivid metaphorical images translates the particular sinful act into generalised shared conceptions of sexual transgression and its remedy. But this prayer is more than a soliloquy. The sequence exhibited by these metaphors corresponds well with the processes of interaction in a 'social visit'. It is as though the speaker draws a colloquial speech model for conversations and 'projects' it onto the ritual situation. It is interesting that other Sumbanese ritual speech acts, for example, 'divination' and 'placation', can also be related to their colloquial speech counterparts, in this case 'questioning' (*túwa*) and 'summoning' (*pamái*) respectively. Unlike what Goffman (1981) calls 'self-talk', which Weyéwa find embarrassing and indicative of mental illness, Weyéwa prayer is more like a turn at talk, a sequence of conversation.

The idiom of the 'social visit' accords well with the inside/outside dichotomy in the description of sexual transgression, since the guests are first invited 'in' to the house. In the prayer the spirits are drawn in to the conversation through the performative establishment of communicative relationships between the parties. In the visit, after the proposal is made, the conclusion is that the guests go 'out' of the house. In the prayer the departure scene coincides with the departure of wrongful acts from the life of the community, a departure which is verbally represented as a hunt. The successive reiteration of this three-part pattern within the scenes of the prayer itself builds and repeats these main themes.

Prayer is a central activity in the religious life of a community (see Fortes 1975), yet it is relatively rarely examined from an anthropological and linguistic point of view. As a parting challenge, I would venture to propose that in many of the ongoing ritual speech traditions in eastern Indonesia prayer is a significant element which can, upon inspection, be seen to be composed not only of units such as couplets but of larger intonational and thematic structures such as stanzas, and even scenes. When examined in the context of the sociolinguistic norms of those societies in which they occur, such units may provide clues as to the organization of ritual communication and ceremonial interaction.

Reference text

Mbulu Renda's Prayer

I

1	*Málla*	Well,
2	*Nénnati*	There by you
3	*dékke yása*	take the rice,
4	*mámana pamámangge*	chew this quid;
5	*yó'u, Málo*	you, Malo,
6	*yó'u, ínna Léda*	you, mother of Leda;
7	*Nénnati*	There by you
8	*yásangge*	[take] the rice,
9	*mámana pamáma*	chew the quid;
10	*Lúnggu lúmmukuni*	It is said by me: 'it is said by you'
11	*Nái*	To
12	*ínna,*	[your] mother,
13	*ámamu*	your father;
14	*Ka lúmmukuni ná'ingge*	So it is said by you to him
15	*A yánggu*	Who taught you
16	*tékki ngára*	to say [your] name,
17	*súma támo*	to utter [your] title;
18	*Myálo mónno Mbíli*	Myalo and Mbili:
19	*tandéi ndúwa palólo*	an extensive root,
20	*sadidi wólo ínna*	beside the creations of mother,
21	*lúwa sélu ándo*	replaced beet stalk,
22	*sangéra wólo áma*	next to the relics of father;

23	*Nénnati*	There by you
24	*yásangge*	[take] that rice,
25	*mámana pamáma*	chew that quid;
26	*Lúngguba*	It was said by me:
27	*Lúnggu tákka*	'It is truly said by me'.
28	*niádona*	[It is] they
29	*pakadéilo téru téko*	on whom the sword is hung,
30	*niádona*	[It is] there
31	*pakadánga sóro númbu*	where the spear is wedged;
32	*pawóti panéwe*	[to whom] speech is lifted,
33	*paáila kandáuke*	[to whom] talk is raised;
34	*Bahínna néwera*	If that is so around here
35	*pakanángi nóna*	what the dog-paddle swimming is for,
36	*pakále suma nggáda*	what the struggle is towards;
37	*Néwwe mále*	This night
38	*pasimbala tanáru*	[we] curse the sins,
39	*pakapéperuma tána*	[we] strike the earth;
40	*papalóle kámba káka*	we reel in white yarn,
41	*papamáne nggéngge rára*	we trail the red spiders;
42	*Tákka*	But,
43	*kúndila mawótingge–*	the hair is wrapped up in a bun,
44	*móto la masáilangge*	the cock's comb is erect;
45	*Néwera*	Here,
46	*wángungge wáwi*	[as the] base of the pig,
47	*pásangge kóki*	[as the] base for the monkey;
48	*Lúngguba hínnawe*	And it was said by me: 'it is so',
49	*Tákka néwwengge*	And so here,
50	*Hínna*	So
51	*Ka bábangge*	[It is] over;
52	*Néweti*	From here
53	*Ka ndá'iki*	It has departed.
54	*kau pandémangge*	so you receive [with] your hands,
55	*límma,*	[with] your hands,

56	*kau patúrungge*	so you incline
57	*bále*	your shoulders;
58	*Ne*	There
59	*pakapéperuma tána*	we strike the earth,
60	*Néwwe*	Here
61	*pasimbala tanáru*	we curse the sins;
62	*Hínagge nátti*	Thus it was said by him [guilty one]
63	*A*	Who is as a
64	*dúngga nda kandóteka*	lute which sings not,
65	*pówi nda kanyángika*	flute which plays not;
66	*a palólengge kámba káka*	who reeled in the white yarn,
67	*a mánggana panéwe*	who controls the speech,
68	*a pamánengge nggéngge rára*	who followed the red spider,
69	*a térrena kandáuke*	who holds the talk;
70	*Niákiwe kanyákka*	Thus it is that
71	*Néwwera*	Here,
72	*paténa sóro bába*	conveyed by boat,
73	*a pandára bóti ngíndi*	brought by horse;
74	*nggá'ika kau*	so that you
75	*bótiwe mbára inna*	bring it to mother,
76	*nggá'ika kau*	so that you
77	*áilangge mbára ámamu*	bring it to your father;
78	*ná'i a pótengge*	[to] him who twists
79	*túngga tána*	the mane of the land,
80	*ná'i a pamándongge*	[to] him who grips
81	*wábbo lókona*	the reins of the river;
82	*a póte púmu nggéso*	who twirls the handle of the cotton gin,
83	*a wíyo kámbu káduwe*	who ties the rope beneath the horns;
84	*Hínna*	So it is said,
85	*Kanyákka néwwera*	So that here,
86	*Nyákka*	So that
87	*kau pandémangge límma*	you receive with the hands,
88	*kau patúrungge bále*	you accept with your shoulders;
89	*Tákka*	But,

90	*wáta*	propped up
91	*papatúrukona lí'i*	on the basis of the word,
92	*áito*	extend out
93	*papadólakona lómma*	with the tongue;
94	*Ná'i ba wá'ikuni*	[To] him, if he is there,
95	*Ana Tawóra*	The Spiritual Messenger,
96	*Ana Karáki*	The Ghostly Envoy;
97	*ána lámu nggéngge*	child of myriad spider eggs,
98	*ána lámu táta*	child of the multitudinous birds;
99	*a paléradonda wáwi*	who disperses the pigs,
100	*a panóneka kabálla*	who scatters the grasshoppers;
101	*ka na*	so that
102	*wótinggu panéwe*	he brings you speech,
103	*ka na*	so that
104	*áilanggu kandáuke*	he brings you talk;
105	*tíddi*	to the side of
106	*wái manéra*	the *manera*-waters,
107	*ndónga*	amidst
108	*wái lapále*	the *lapale*-waters;
109	*Ná'i*	[To] him
110	*Ryángga pénde wíti*	Ryangga [who] can sing,
111	*Kyáze pénde púllu*	Kyasi [who] can speak;
112	*a púllu pakanikkingge*	who speaks to you with detail,
113	*a ngíki pakawólerangge*	who turns it around;
114	*ka na paténa*	so that he boats
115	*sóro bábangge*	across to the lap,
116	*mbára ínna*	to the mother;
117	*ná'ingge*	[to] them,
118	*nímbakuni ólumu*	them only,
119	*tadúkkibana tálla*	until we reach the gong [stage].
120	*Nénna yása*	[Take] the rice next to you
121	*pabótinggu panéwe*	to whom I bring my speech,
122	*paáilanggu kandáuke*	to whom I convey my talk;
123	*pakadíya tútu téra*	the barkcloth pounding board,
124	*pakápa láingo máte*	the potting clay;
125	*kandáwu patalíra*	the forest at [my] back,
126	*kambála pakadyátu*	the childbirth support cord;

127	*Lúmmuni ná'i*	It is said by you [to them]:
128	*Myálo*	'Myalo [name of ancestor]
129	*tandyúla wólo ngára*	who made a towering name;
130	*Myúta*	Myuta [name of ancestor]
131	*kasyása tánggu déndo*	the guardian of renown',
132	*ka téna*	so that [like] a ship
133	*páta nggíbilangge*	listing towards us
134	*lí'ina*	[is his] voice,
135	*ka na ndára*	so that [like] a horse
136	*páta móndelangge*	slipped before [us]
137	*lómma*	[is his] tongue;
138	*ka na bóti panéwe*	let him bring his speech
139	*mbára ínna*	to [his] mother,
140	*ka áilana kandáuke*	let him convey his talk
141	*mbára ámana*	to his father;
142	*a tállarana ró'ona*	[who] spread out his leaves,
143	*a wéwarana wúana*	[who] dispersed his fruit;
144	*a mángu sóra*	who has a personal spirit,
145	*a mángu pówo*	who has a personal ghost;
146	*a mángu pápa*	who has a pair,
147	*a mángu nggóba*	who has a [spiritual] counterpart;
148	*sóra*	personal spirit,
149	*pówona*	personal ghost;
150	*pápa*	pair,
151	*nggóbba*	counterpart;
152	*ka na bótina panéwena*	so that he brings his speech,
153	*ka na áilana kandáuke*	so that he conveys his talk;
154	*Ná'i*	[To] him
155	*ána céba tábbo líndaka*	who keeps the plates level,
156	*ána mbúru cána*	who goes into the yard,
157	*ána ryémba kóba kállu*	who tends the hanging cups,
158	*ána pénne úmma*	who goes into the house;
159	*Ka na bóti kandáuke*	So that he brings his talk,
160	*Ná'i ba wá'ini*	[To] him if he is there,
161	*ráta dángu nggéngge*	[him of] a thousand spiderlings,
162	*pókku ána ráwa*	myriads of mourning doves;
163	*lámbe a mbéleka*	the broad post-collar,
164	*parí'i a kaláda*	the great house-post;

165 *Nya*	He
166 *kóko*	is the throat [that]
167 *nda mbéingge*	does not like it,
168 *áte*	the liver [that]
169 *nda mbúsangge*	does not approve.

II

170 *Ba wá'ingge*	When there are
171 *wé'e mángu nggéngge*	spiders in the water,
172 *rútta mángu ndábbo*	poison leaves in the pasture;
173 *a kandénge*	which jams
174 *ru karáppe mánu*	a chicken bone [in the throat],
175 *a kalódana*	which sticks
176 *ru katékke ndára*	a horse skull bone [in the mouth];

177 *Wáli mónno*	And this has been
178 *Hínnakidongge*	Said
179 *Tákka híddi*	But they,
180 *álli pakambólo*	loinclothed little brothers,
181 *ána pakapóute*	headclothed little children;
182 *Tawóra Pínda Léti*	Spiritual Envoys,
183 *Karáki Pínda Námo*	Ghostly Messengers;
184 *Tanónggo Kawúku*	Personal Spirits,
185 *kaséde katáko*	skips along,
186 *pakóla matúwa*	holy force,

187 *Ne ba hínnawe*	And now
188 *Né'engge*	Then [they]
189 *Óruta kóki*	Gathered the monkeys
190 *ta kalúnga*	in the field
191 *ka ta mandí'i téppe*	so that we can sit on the mat,
192 *Wándorana wáwi*	Summoned pigs
193 *ta marédda*	in the meadow
194 *kai térrena pamáma*	so that you get the quid;
195 *Lúnggu ka lúmmu*	I declare so that you will say
196 *Wáli monno hínnakidongge*	It is so.

197 *Ka tákka*	But
198 *hítti patékki lóta lélu*	just now the yarn was spun,
199 *hítti panási wúnda kámba*	the cotton just combed;

200	*Hítti málenangge*	Last night
201	*Ne bána*	When
202	*kadénge ndúka búkku*	there was jammed in the throat
203	*rúwi mánu ínna*	the bone of the mother's chicken,
204	*Ne bána*	When
205	*kalóda ru*	[there was] stuck
206	*katékke ndárana*	skull bones of a horse;
207	*né'e a ndénga mátalodo*	then the sun was wrong,
208	*né'e a ndóku mátawulla*	then the moon was wrong;
209	*né'e a díraka pabába*	there was filth in the lap,
210	*né'e a ákita paléiro*	there was a curse close by;
211	*wé'e mángu nggéngge*	spiders in the water,
212	*rútta mángu ndábbo*	poison in the pasture;
213	*Né'e ba wá'indi*	Because there were
214	*wé'e mángu nggéngge*	spiders in the water,
215	*rútta mángu ndábbo*	poisons in the pasture;
216	*Tákka dádowangge*	But all right
217	*Ne ba hínna*	Now
218	*ka ku sísi*	'I clean
219	*pámba páredoangge*	my wet rice,
220	*ka ku wámmba*	I sweep my
221	*wélli úmmadowangge*	house foundation';
222	*Híddangge*	Is said by
223	*karére rai wóllana*	the offspring of the cucumber,
224	*Híddangge*	Is said by
225	*karóbbo rai úwana*	the offshoots of the potato;
226	*kána kákodowa*	may it depart:
227	*kangúdda áte lóko*	the garbage in the river bottom,
228	*kána kákodowa*	may it depart:
229	*kasómba áte lára*	the filth in midpath;
230	*Híddangge patékkida*	It is said by them these words of theirs
231	*Nyákka*	So that
232	*órutawu kóki*	[you] are gathered as monkeys
233	*ta kalúnga*	in the field,
234	*Nyákka*	So that

235	*wándorawu wáwi*	[you] are gathered as pigs
236	*ta marédda*	in the meadow;
237	*Ka ba mónno*	And now, and
238	*Hínnako*	If it is so,
239	*Ne ba hínnawe ne*	Right now,
240	*Ka málla!*	Well, then!
241	*Néwwengge kau*	Here, so that you
242	*Mandí'ina téppe ndéta*	Sit on the mat,
243	*Lúmmundi*	You say to them – the
244	*Tawóra Pínda Léti*	Spiritual Messengers,
245	*Karáki Pínda Námu*	Ghostly Envoy;
246	*Ka térrengge nékke*	Then take that over there
247	*patéteka úwe*	which erects the cane,
248	*pakónggola kaníki*	which lays down the candlenuts;
249	*Néwwe pawámmbo rábuka*	Here, we sweep out the ashes,
250	*Nggá'ika ka na*	In order that he
251	*mbúru néti ba wá'ingge*	settles here, if there is
252	*a diraka pabába*	filth in one's lap,
253	*Ka na*	So that he
254	*kákongge néti ba wá'ingge*	goes forth, if there is
255	*a ákita paléiro*	foulness in one's lap;
256	*Lúngguba hínnangge*	It was said by me: 'it is said by him'.
257	*Ne ba hínna*	Now,
258	*Nékke*	Over there,
259	*wé'e inna*	water of mother,
260	*wé'e áma*	water of father,
261	*wé'e nggósi*	water of the bottle,
262	*wé'e pénnga*	water of the dish,
263	*wé'e túaka*	pure water,
264	*wé'e wálu*	holy water,
265	*Kaa tórongge*	[May they] take it,
266	*Kaa múmurana*	[May they] gargle it,
267	*Kaa parámo*	[May they] wash their [hands];
268	*Náti ba wá'ini*	There they are,
269	*karére rai wólla*	offshoots of the cucumber,
270	*karóbbo rai úwa*	the offspring of the potato;

271	*Ba wá'ikongge*	If there was
272	*ngá'a kála ngá'a*	food improperly eaten,
273	*wé'e kála énu*	water improperly drunk,
274	*Ka na*	May [they]
275	*múmu,*	gargle,
276	*parámo*	[and] wash;

277	*Náti ba wá'i*	There, if there were
278	*pabénu*	[waters] drunk [improperly],
279	*pangá'a*	[foods] consumed [improperly];
280	*Ba wá'ini náti*	[And] if there is
281	*ána bánda*	some small animal,
282	*ána ránga*	some insignificant livestock;
283	*Ba wá'ini*	[And] if there are
284	*ána mánu*	some chicks,
285	*ána wáwi*	some piglets [eaten by mistake];

286	*Ne ba hínna*	Now
287	*ka ku tékke lóta lélu*	I wind in my yarn,
288	*Ne ba hínna*	Now
289	*ka ku nási wúnda kámba*	I clean my cotton;
290	*Ba*	If
291	*na kandéngekona*	there are jammed
292	*rúwi kawódu mánu ínna*	some bent chicken bones of mother,
293	*na kalódakona*	[if] there are stuck
294	*rúwi katékke ndára*	some skull bones of the horse;
295	*ba wá'ikongge*	if there are
296	*wé'e mángu nggéngge*	spiders in the water,
297	*ba wá'ikongge*	if there is
298	*rútta mángu ndábbo*	poison in the pasture;

III

299	*Mah!*	Well!
300	*Ne ba hínnangge*	Now,
301	*Ka ku*	So that I
302	*pandékedowangge lara*	walk the trail,
303	*Ka ku*	So that I
304	*pamánedowangge ínu*	follow the spoors;
305	*Lúnggu mónno hínnakido*	It is said by me: 'It is said by him',

306	*táru léirongge límma*	always extend your hands,
307	*byábangge kénga*	take on your lap;
308	*Tawóra Pínda Léti*	The Spiritual Messenger,
309	*Karáki Pínda Námu*	The Ghostly Envoy;
310	*bána wiwi papatúkkangge*	whose lips are commanded,
311	*bána áte pakambórongge*	whose heart is sealed;
312	*Ná'i*	[To] him:
313	*ána púllu*	child of speech,
314	*ána kandáuke*	child of talk;
315	*ána mbáni*	child of bravery;
316	*Ne ba hínnawe ne*	And now,
317	*Ka na mbúru ngíndiwe*	So that he descends
318	*Né'e*	Down there
319	*tómangge tíddi wái manéra*	by the *manera*-waters of
320	*tómangge ndónga wái lapále*	amidst the *lapale*-waters of
321	*ná'i wúdi papandénde*	the upright post,
322	*ná'i wátu papandénde*	the upright rock;
323	*ka na térrendi*	in order that he receive the
324	*táwila mabéla*	silver jewelry,
325	*ka na mándongge*	in order that he take the
326	*liwuta marángga*	golden ornament;
327	*ka na ténangge kóndo*	may they convey it by boat,
328	*ka na ndárangge ngíndi*	so that they bring it by horse;
329	*Ná'i*	[To] him
330	*a dáwa bínna kíkuna*	who guards the tail gate,
331	*a kándi bínna mángu*	who tends the nose gate,
	ngórana	
332	*Nggá'i*	Let him
333	*ka na wéiyana bínna*	open the door,
334	*ka na bówongge lára*	clear the road;
335	*ka na tómangge tambyáli*	so that he reaches
336	*bínna móne*	the male gate,
337	*ka na dúkkingge pú'u*	so that he arrives at
338	*káwango ndása*	the base of the banyan tree;
339	*Ka na patórona ná'i*	So that he might hand it on to
340	*tána papandíli*	the land that was moved,

341	*wátu papakái*	the rocks that were displaced;
342	*Nggá'i ka na*	So that he
343	*pandéke lára*	walks the path,
344	*pamánengge ínu*	follows the spoor;

345	*ka na padúkkina*	so that he brings it to
346	*ndónga wailapálena*	side of the *lapale*-waters of
347	*ka na patómana*	so that he brings it to
348	*tíddi waimanérana*	side of the *manera*-waters of:
349	*cára mánu lódo*	the cockspur of the sun,
350	*myóko mánu wúlla*	the bobbing-hen moon;

351	*ka na kabémbe íngi káka*	[and] cares for it in a white cloth,
352	*ka na karáwa wé'e kawálu*	treating it with holy water
353	*ná'i nyángo ólumu*	[to] him
354	*Ba wá'ini*	If it is there:
355	*kanggóula wúlla mále*	the evening star
356	*móto rámu rára*	with the red crown [Mars].

357	*Tákka nyáda*	But [it is] he
358	*a bílungge*	who carries [the message]
359	*béngge*	in his belt,
360	*a wúnggungge*	who carries [the message]
361	*límma*	in his hand;
362	*na mánu pakanékkengge*	[like] a pet chicken,
363	*na wáwi pakaráwangge*	[like] a pet piglet;
364	*Lúnggu mónno hínnakido*	It is said by me and it is so.

365	*Ne ba hínna yémmi*	Now, you
366	*Tawóra Pínda Léti*	Spiritual Messengers,
367	*Karáki Pínda Námu*	Ghostly Envoys;
368	*a pandékena lára*	who walk the path,
369	*a paléiro límma*	extending their hands;
370	*a pamánengge ínu*	who follow the spoors,
371	*Ba wá'ikongge*	If there is
372	*a dírraka pabába*	filth in the lap,
373	*a ákita paléiro*	foulness all about;
374	*a byábangge kénga*	held on the lap;

| 375 | *Ba wá'ikongge* | If there is |
| 376 | *a dírraka pabába* | filth in the lap, |

377	*a ákita paléiro*	foulness all about;
378	*úrutangge kédu*	chase the monkeys
379	*ta kalúnga*	in the field,
380	*wándorangge wáwi*	gather the pigs
381	*ta marédda*	in the meadow;
382	*Nákka mánu*	This here chicken,
383	*pawángge wáimu*	use it to stuff
384	*kéla kúrumu*	your waist belt,
385	*pakatánga wáimu*	use it to tie
386	*ngénge ngóramu*	your headcloth chinstrap;
387	*Ne ba hínna né'e*	And now
388	*ódonggai ndára*	the horse has straightened out,
389	*ngúngunggai téna*	the boat is headed forward;
390	*tíkinggai mbóro*	slit the *gewang* palm [leaf],
391	*wárenggai pónda*	slit the pandanus palm [leaf];
392	*léirongga límma*	extend your hands,
393	*byábangga kénga*	open your lap;
394	*Néna wékki ndéta*	There on their body
395	*Ka tá'ingge*	It shall be placed
396	*Tau!*	It is finished!

5

FASHIONED SPEECH, FULL COMMUNICATION: ASPECTS OF EASTERN SUMBANESE RITUAL LANGUAGE

GREGORY FORTH

The largest part of eastern Sumbanese ritual life consists of speeches conducted in a formal style which, following common usage, can be called a 'ritual language'. This paper has two principal aims: (1) to locate ritual language performances within the general scheme of eastern Sumbanese culture, paying particular attention to the value this idiom holds for members of this society, and (2) to review some of its most prominent formal features, concentrating especially on attributes which may prove to be of comparative interest. The data on which this paper is based are drawn from my own fieldwork carried out in the domain of Rindi. However, since eastern Sumba is both culturally and linguistically a largely homogeneous area, and because, with minor variations, the same ritual language tradition is found throughout this region, in what follows I shall for the most part refer to eastern Sumba, mentioning Rindi only where context requires.

General remarks

Eastern Sumbanese ritual language differs from ordinary discourse in several fundamental respects. Like similar and related traditions in other parts of Indonesia, it is most succinctly described in the phrase 'formal, formulaic, and parallelistic' (Fox 1971:215). Parallelism is evidenced by a prescribed pairing of words to form dyadic sets which appear as components of longer expressions, thus producing an overall pattern of paired lines or couplets. This principle affects both the semantics and syntax of ritual speech. Thus paired elements, which may provisionally be classified as comprising synonyms, various types of antithesis or 'synthetic' combinations, are usually morphologically identical and grammatically equivalent, and appear in corresponding positions within parallel lines.

Despite the overriding feature of dyadism, however, parallel terms and phrases compose a unity of reference in that they normally refer to single objects, actions, events, and concepts. The majority of individual terms employed in ritual language are ones also encountered in everyday speech, while a certain number are exclusive to the ritual idiom. Many of these special terms derive from other dialects, and when they occur they are paired with usually synonymous words taken from ordinary language.[1] A single term may in different contexts form dyadic sets with more than one other, but at any given time the limits of pairing are fixed by convention. This, then, is one respect in which ritual language can be called formulaic. In the eastern Sumbanese tradition, formulism is further manifest in that dyadic elements characteristically appear as components of a restricted range of parallel lines, while specific objects, events, and so on are expressed in a generally fixed form of words; thus the phraseology of this language displays a highly standardised character.[2] What is more, paired lines frequently occur in regular combination with a number of others, thus giving rise to longer passages which vary but little between different occasions of use. Hence, while single performances are not to be regarded as recitations of invariant texts, and in spite of the stylistic variation normally encountered between different speakers, given the ritual context it is very often possible to predict with some degree of accuracy the form and content of particular ritual language performances.

Although ritual language makes use of many of the same grammatical and morphological forms as ordinary language, in accordance with the requirements of parallelism and formulism not only does it exploit a somewhat limited range of these but further displays special attributes of its own. Instances of this include the use of nominal elements as verbs, the omission of affixes which in everyday discourse effect different forms of verbal roots with distinct senses, and the insertion of grammatical elements, such as prepositions, where according to the rules of ordinary speech it is not necessary to do so.[3]

As the foregoing observations suggest, eastern Sumbanese ritual language is a highly poetic and figurative style, being characterised by an extensive use of metaphor and oblique modes of expression. Even if one is thoroughly familiar with ordinary language, therefore, it is often impossible to determine the reference of ritual language expressions without recourse to native exegesis and a firm knowledge of eastern Sumbanese symbolism in general. Indeed, as I have noted elsewhere (1981:19), ritual language provides a rich source of material for the study of eastern Sumbanese symbolic thought, not least of all because parallelistic – or, more generally, dyadic – language coexists in this society with an elaborate system of dual symbolic classification which incorporates a dualistic cosmology.

The sociology of ritual language use

The two major, and by far the most frequent, occasions for ritual language use in eastern Sumba are *hamayangu*, speeches of invocation (or liturgies) addressed to the ancestors and other forms of divinity, and *luluku*, orations involved in transactions between affines and between other parties who, like wife-givers and wife-takers, are in context related as superior and inferior. *Hamayangu* are performed on a great variety of occasions, whenever it is necessary to make an appeal to or to propitiate spiritual beings; while *luluku* accompany all exchanges of prestations between affines (at marriages, betrothals, funerals, when making invitations, in the settlement of estrangements, in reconciliations, and so on) and exchanges of prestations, of the same sorts, between groups not related in any particular way, as for example when one clan provides another with a special cure or ritual service, or when compensation is given for transgression. Nowadays, *luluku* also take place when honoured guests, such as high-ranking government officials, are received with a gift and the slaughter of an animal. *Hamayangu* are performed by priests (*ama bokulu mahamayangu* or *mauratungu*),[4] while *luluku* are delivered by orators called *wunangu*, a word which also denotes the 'comb' on a weaving loom.[5]

Although it refers specifically to the oratorical speech of the *wunangu*, the term *luluku* can further be applied to ritual language in general. Consistent with this dual sense is the fact that invocatory and oratorical speech are in all formal respects identical. Moreover, whereas *hamayangu* denotes the totality of acts involved in communicating with spirits, *luluku* refers more particularly to the distinctive features of the speech style itself, which are equally characteristic of both invocations and orations. One indication of this is the apparent derivation of *luluku* from the partially synonymous word *lulu*, 'long, straight, continual, continuous', and 'thread, string, line' (see Kapita 1974:138). In this regard, then, *luluku* seems to focus on what might be described as the 'connectedness' of ritual speech, that is, the regular and required combination of elements governing its internal order, as well as the typical fluidity and fluency, and relative rapidity, of its utterance (see Forth 1981:19).[6]

To varying lesser degrees the typically parallelistic form of ritual language is also encountered in song, myth, and even ordinary discourse – particularly in discussions by older men concerning matters of customary and ritual importance. Yet in all these cases such parallel expressions as may occur are either the same or of the same type as ones found in orations and invocations, while, as regards ordinary speech, their occurrence appears simply to reflect the influence of ritual idioms on everyday discourse. In what follows, therefore, I shall concentrate upon invocation and oration as the major contexts of ritual speaking in eastern Sumba, employing 'ritual language' (or 'ritual speech') as a general term for the poetic style characteristic of both.

Eastern Sumbanese ritual speakers, the priests and orators, are always mature and very often elderly men. Although women too may formally employ ritual language, they do so only when performing songs, such as dirges and the chants which accompany the telling of certain types of traditional narratives; for in this society women are never engaged as orators or priests. What is more, although women and younger people may incidentally acquire some knowledge (apparently not inconsiderable in some instances) of invocatory and oratorical terms and phraseology, it is generally considered that only male speakers, after years of practice, can have a true command and proper understanding of the art. That ritual language is mostly the preserve of mature male functionaries is consistent with Rindi descriptions of invocatory and oratorical speech as *panii pandapingu tau dangu*, 'speech, language that is unknown to most [or the majority of] people' and *panii pandapingu anakedangu*, 'speech, language that is unknown to young persons'.

The role of priest or orator may be undertaken by any man with the requisite skill. Although knowledge of ritual language terminology and procedures may be passed on from father to son or from senior to junior agnates, it is mostly acquired simply by observing the practice of established speakers. In some instances, however, younger men may undergo what amounts to a period of apprenticeship while serving as assistants to more senior practitioners. In contrast to the generally ascriptive nature of status allocation in eastern Sumba, ritual speaking is an achieved, not an ascribed, function. It is therefore not restricted to members of any clan or social class, with the exception, in Rindi, of the nobility, who never themselves engage in ritual language performances but always employ persons of 'slave' (*ata*) or commoner rank to act on their behalf. Particular clans – in Rindi most notably those which serve as special ceremonial supporters (*tulaku paraingu*) of the ruling noble clan – are by tradition regarded as producing the most accomplished ritual speakers. Ideally, though, every clan should have at least one person able to act as priest or orator, and it is expected that the senior man of a local clan should be able to carry out priestly duties when necessary. But in spite of the fact that a great deal of eastern Sumbanese ritual life concerns single patriclans, it is by no means required that ritual language practitioners act only for their own clans. Indeed, persons belonging to other clans, mostly accomplished ritual speakers whose knowledge and ability are widely recognised, are frequently employed as orators or priests, and in some contexts, such as the execution of major rites and transactions with affines, this is actually preferred.[7]

One and the same man can perform the functions of both priest and orator. In fact, all orators except the most junior regularly conduct invocations in conjunction with oratorical exchanges, and some elderly orators engage in both sorts of tasks on a variety of occasions. Even so, in

Rindi there were a number of priests who never performed orations. In general, priests tend to be older than orators, and, indeed, are mostly elderly men. Since age, and particularly advanced age, is associated with spirituality in eastern Sumba, this difference is consistent with the fact that whereas orators function as intermediaries between groups of living persons, priests do so between mortal men and spiritual beings (see Forth 1981:168–170).[8]

It is worth pointing out that while expertise in ritual language is an admired quality in eastern Sumba, in this society such ability cannot secure for a practitioner any real advance in his social position, which is largely determined by such factors as age, lineal seniority, clan affiliation and, most importantly, social class membership. Thus, although an individual can gain respect and prestige through skill in ritual speaking, this does not in any significant way affect his formal social status. As regards temporal affairs at any rate, the prominent men in eastern Sumba are the nobles and higher-ranking commoners, who are also the wealthiest members of society, and not the orators and priests.

Another point which perhaps requires some emphasis is that ritual speakers are not mere functionaries but, being drawn mostly from the group of elders and ritual experts, are in addition the recognised repositories of all kinds of customary knowledge. This characterisation, however, applies more to priests than to orators, in part because the former are on the whole older men. In this regard it is interesting that in Rindi it was frequently said of orators that they are often not particularly knowledgeable of the 'meaning' or 'import' (*ihi*, generally 'content(s)') of the performances in which they are engaged, but only of 'the words'. As I shall discuss below, this idea seems to relate to a distinction between two types of knowledge. Nevertheless, some orators are certainly knowledgeable about more than the superficial aspects of ritual life and, indeed, are regularly consulted in a variety of customary matters.

The place of ritual language in eastern Sumbanese culture

A thorough analysis of the importance of ritual language in eastern Sumbanese culture would require a comprehensive investigation of the variety of words employed for 'language', 'speech', 'talking', and so on, and of ideas regarding the functions and significance of speech and sound in general – and of silence as well. Although I do not propose to undertake a study of this sort here, there are a number of points relating to these topics that will need to be considered, especially as they relate to native evaluations of ritual language. In what follows I shall refer mostly to Rindi.

While ritual speaking has an important place in social life, it should not be inferred from this that the Rindi value loquacity or that they are on the whole a talkative people. On the contrary, they can generally be described as reserved, reticent and taciturn, and moreover as secretive and unde-monstrative in their dealings with one another and with outsiders (see Forth 1981:21–22). As regards the way one should use speech, the Rindi in fact place a particular value on parsimony and I especially recall one occasion when this was explicitly revealed in the statement, amounting to a mild admonition, that if it is not absolutely necessary to say anything then it is better to remain silent.[9]

The Rindi also value caution in speech. One symptom of this is the concern they frequently express regarding what they call *panii ànga*, 'dis-orderly speech' or 'talking out of the top of one's head', and *kambàliku*, 'nonsense, drivel', or more to the point, 'lies, deceitful talk'. Indeed, one of my most enduring memories of fieldwork in Rindi is that of being constantly warned about people who were supposed to be guilty of those faults and the threat they posed to our investigations. In other ways as well, the Rindi reveal a rather acute awareness of the dangers of misun-derstanding inherent in language use. This attitude, then, suggests an evaluation of speech as a rather imperfect medium of communication, which in turn arguably relates to a tendency on their part to view social interaction generally as something difficult, demanding, and full of pit-falls.

Against this background one is better able to understand the particular value ritual language holds for the eastern Sumbanese. In its own lexicon the style is designated as *luluku pandoingu//peka pamangihingu*, which can be translated as 'speech that is fashioned [or created]//communication that is [made] dense [or compact, full]'. *Peka*, which appears here as the paired term of *luluku* (which, as indicated above, might be glossed as 'connected speech'), means 'to state, tell, explain, inform' (also 'to con-fess') and 'communication, statement, information'. Accordingly the en-tire expression can be used in either a nominal or a verbal sense. It should also be pointed out that *pandoingu*, which here qualifies *luluku* and is a form of *pandoi*, 'to make, create', might, somewhat more literally, be rendered as 'made, done finely', since it ultimately derives from *ndoi*, 'fine, beautiful, good' (see Kapita 1974:212, who further glosses *pandoi* as 'to repair, make good'). Indeed, if *luluku* is considered as a verb, then *pando-ingu* can be regarded as an instance of an adverbial construction which combines the affixes *pa-* and *-ngu* with a modifier – in this case *ndoi* – so that the entire phrase could then be taken to mean 'to speak [in the ritual style] well, finely', an interpretation which stresses the aesthetic quality of ritual language. With *pamangihingu*, the modifier of *peka*, on the other hand, the radical is *ihi* (or *ngihi*), 'content(s), full'; and this word, it is important to note, has the further sense of 'meaning' or 'import'.[10] In sum, therefore, the foregoing facts combine to suggest that, by contrast to ordinary speech, ritual language is conceived of as a form of communication which is specially and deliberately fashioned, and one that is especially articulate, concise, compact, and meaningful. This last attribute is further indicated by the frequent use in Rindi of the Bahasa Indonesia phrase *bahasa dalam*, 'deep, profound speech', to refer to utterances in ritual language.

Also relevant in the present context is the word *kajangu*, which denotes individual ritual language terms and phrases and, in its most general sense, means 'screen, partition, umbrella' and 'shelter, protection'. In this way, a term or phrase is described as the *kajangu* of that to which it refers; thus for example the expression *uma mandamobu//kaheli mandambata* 'house that does not rot//house-floor that does not break', is the *kajangu* for 'grave'. In a more specific application of the word, *kajangu* designates the usage whereby the names of two slaves are used, in speeches of invocation, to refer to a deceased nobleman; and it can also be applied to more mundane aliases or nicknames.

What is of particular interest here is the idea that the lexical components of ritual language shelter, screen off or disguise what they refer to. In one respect this might be thought to concern the characteristically figurative and abstruse quality of ritual phraseology: the fact that often a highly figurative term or phrase is used in place of the usual name of something. Yet not always is the reference of a ritual language expression obscure or difficult to understand; in fact, given the context of a particular speech, it is frequently quite transparent. Moreover, even where a figurative phrase is employed, the reference is usually known, and is in any case knowable in principle, and can be stated. It seems, therefore, that it may not be the simple reference of terms and phrases (*kajangu*) in ritual language – or at any rate not this alone – which is screened off or disguised, so much as the precise sense in which terms are appropriate to their denotata.

One advantage of this interpretation is that it clarifies the rather curious implication that a word can render obscure its referent. Yet there seems to be a middle course available here, namely that ritual language terminology reveals and conceals at one and the same time, that is to say, that it reveals, but only so much. This specification of *kajangu* strongly calls to mind Traube's description of Mambai ritual language as an idiom which employs 'complex linguistic ruses' and whose 'informing notion is always to conceal a deep religious truth', so that the 'words of a ritual chant are intended to veil, not to reveal' (1980: 291 n.1, 297).[11] In this connection Traube further remarks that Mambai chanters and priests constantly represent themselves as 'fools and babes' only mouthing 'the received uncomprehended words' passed down from the ancestors, while at the

This is merely tone of all symbolism.

same time implying that they too have true knowledge but will not impart it. Here as well there is a close similarity with eastern Sumbanese usage, as illustrated by the practice of experienced priests, who at the end of an invocation will describe themselves as having 'livers that are not yet broad//hearts that are not yet large' (*eti ndedi mbàlaru//puhu ndedi bokulu*), thereby alluding to their (supposedly) inferior knowledge, wisdom, and capability in contrast to men of former times (Forth 1981:170).

This brings us to eastern Sumbanese ideas about the relation between language and knowledge (*pingu*). In a way similar to the Mambai, for whom true knowledge resides in the 'stomach' (Traube 1980:298), the eastern Sumbanese distinguish a superior knowledge which resides in the 'liver' (*eti*) and which is inherent in the sense that it can only come with maturity and advanced age, from an inferior knowledge which is transferred in speech. Thus a person can be said to know something only because he has heard it from others, not because he knows it 'in his liver'. This relatively low estimation of knowledge acquired verbally is of course consistent with the aforementioned evaluation of language as an imperfect medium of communication and expression. Yet in this regard ritual language, by virtue of its formulaic nature, orderliness, and compactness, can be described as superior to ordinary speech, so that it is specially suited to the communication of such consequential and profound concerns as form the content of invocations and orations. Nevertheless, as the designation of the terminology of this language as *kajangu* would itself imply, it seems that even ritual language may not be able fully or adequately to convey 'knowledge of the liver'.

Since this superior type of knowledge can be regarded as a spiritual property, it seems relevant that eastern Sumbanese representations reveal an association between higher forms of divinity and silence. Thus in invocatory speech God is designated, among other ways, as 'the silent [and] still one//the obscure [and] dark one' (*na makandii makanawa//na makanjudingu makapàtangu*), while one expression that refers to a house consecrated to the first ancestor of a clan is 'silent [and] still house' (*uma makandii makanawa*). Similarly, matters of great religious and customary significance are described as *lii kanawa*, 'quiet matters', which may specify them not only as things that are not to be spoken of openly or carelessly but also, perhaps, as things which it is impossible fully to reveal through speech.

There is yet another way in which the word *kajangu* may be seen as pertaining to ritual language, and particularly to its use in invocations. In this setting, ritual language can be viewed as one of several necessary mediations facilitating communication between man and God, the highest form of divinity to whom the messages of invocatory performances are ultimately, though never directly, addressed. However, as I have shown elsewhere (Forth 1981:88–89), other mediating entities in this communication – such as the clan ancestors and other lesser forms of spirit – are represented in this same context as providing not only a connection but also a necessary separation, so that mankind is afforded protection from, among other things, the awful and tremendous power of God. This consideration, then, illuminates the sense of 'shelter, protection' contained in the word *kajangu*, so in this respect the invocatory use of ritual language may be said in part to afford protection to its users.[12] Here it is also relevant that an incorrect use of ritual language – or *njala hamayangu*, 'incorrect, erroneous invocation', as it is called – poses a threat to both the priest and the principal. Thus sickness, death, and other misfortune are commonly ascribed to failure to employ the proper form of words in addresses to spirit.

A Rindi priest performing an invocation at the river's edge (*hamayangu la ngamba luku//hingi wai*) on the occasion of a mother's first bath after childbirth

Of course, the foregoing is more relevant to the invocatory than to the oratorical use of ritual language. Nevertheless, the employment of this formal style is similarly an important factor in securing the separation and distance that is required between the two parties represented in oratorical performances. In the more general view, therefore, ritual language in eastern Sumba might be described as an idiom of indirectness.

Oration, invocation and exchange

Further understanding of the significance of ritual language in eastern Sumbanese culture requires closer attention to the two major types of performance in which it is employed, namely invocation and oration. I shall begin with oration.

As noted, oratorical speech is used in transactions between parties distinguished as superior and inferior, and most typically between groups related as wife-giver and wife-taker. On these occasions, which always involve an exchange of material valuables, the two groups do not confront one another directly but are represented by their respective orators. Oratorical speeches define the context and purpose of the (material) exchanges and serve to convey the wishes of the principals regarding the amount and quality of gifts to be exchanged. To some extent, though, the latter will usually have been decided upon in advance of the formal transactions. Thus orations more specifically provide a forum in which agreement between the two parties can be publicly secured and affirmed. In this respect orators will also, in an informal manner, convey messages between the two groups, both before the formal transactions and while they are in progress. Sometimes orations take place in the absence of one of the principals as, for example, when orators travel to other houses or villages to deliver invitations to affines. But at the major exchanges of prestations involved in marriages and funerals, for example, members of the two groups represented are always present. In this case the guest group, regardless of whether they are wife-givers or wife-takers, should sit on the front veranda of the house while the hosts remain at the back. The main negotiations between the two parties are then carried out by the orators inside the house itself, in the right front section of the building, which is also the area given over to invocations addressed to the clan ancestor and spirits of the dead. It should be mentioned, however, that this is something of an ideal arrangement and that when necessary, for example at funerals when a number of affinally related groups may need to be received at the same time, it can be modified in various ways.

During an engagement an orator is accompanied by an assistant or deputy called his *kandehangu,* 'foundation'. At the beginning and the end of a single speech, and in longer speeches at intermediate intervals as well, an orator will call out the name of his opposite number's deputy, who then answers with the phrase *jiaya*, 'that is it, correct', in order formally to acknowledge that he has heard and understood what has previously been said or to indicate that he is ready to receive a (further) communication. In this way, then, two orators never speak to one another directly. Since acknowledging the speech of the opposite orator, and carrying prestations that are to be transferred during the course of an oration, are the sole functions of a deputy, the role requires no special ability or experience and can be filled by any man. It is, however, often assigned to younger men who later go on to become orators; hence it may serve as a sort of apprenticeship.

Depending on the context of orations, the scale of the gift exchange, and the social standing of the two parties, oratorical performances in Rindi may involve, on either side, one or two pairs of orators and deputies. In illustrating the procedure followed on these occasions, I shall employ the example of orations where two pairs represent a given side, the arrangements for which are diagrammed in Figure 5.1.

The orators designated as A1 and B1 are called the *wunangu (ma)tanggu napa*, 'orators whose task is to wait, answer' (*napa* covers both meanings). These speakers are also described as *wunangu bokulu*, 'major orators', thus indicating their superiority to the other two orators (A2 and B2 in Figure 5.1), who are called the *wunangu (ma)tanggu laku*, 'orators whose task is to travel', or *wunangu (ma)tanggu paluangga-maingu*, 'orators who come and go'. I shall refer to these two types of speakers as stationary and mobile orators respectively.[13] Where only one orator (and a deputy) represents a given side, this speaker then combines the functions of stationary and mobile orator.

As their name implies, the stationary orators and their deputies remain on the two verandas. A typical performance, involving the transfer of a prestation, proceeds as follows (here assuming the transaction to be initiated by side A, occupying the front veranda). First, the stationary orator (A1) and his deputy sit facing the principal – that is, the group of principals usually led by a senior man who is himself not an orator, or at any rate in this capacity does not act as one – in order to discuss what needs to be said to the opposite side (B) and how any previous communication should be responded to.[14] This done, they turn 180 degrees to face the mobile orator (A2) and his deputy. The first orator (A1) then speaks to the second (A2),[15] formulating in the appropriate ritual language the message to be communicated, and transferring the prestations to be given over, to the opposite party (B). The mobile orator (A2) then repeats the message to the first speaker (A1) in order to show that he has understood its contents. With his deputy, who carries the prestation, this second speaker (A2) then ascends to the higher-lying interior floor of the house and, sitting facing his opposite number (B2), conveys the message he has been given, together with the prestation. The opposite mobile orator (B2) then repeats the message (to A2) and, this done, descends to the back veranda with the prestation and again repeats the message to his own stationary orator (B1), who in turn repeats it to B2 before communicating it to the principal (B). Since any prestation requires reciprocation, there then follows a formal reply and a counter-prestation, and here exactly the same procedure is followed as in conveying the original message.

It should be noted that each time a particular communication is repeated it is not exactly the same as the preceding speech. This is recognised by the speakers themselves, and indeed it is judged sufficient if only certain key lines are repeated. If this is not done the first orator will, just afterwards, informally point this out to the second. Moreover, in the repetition of a communication after it has been passed from one side to the other (for example, from A2 to B2), the second orator will include additional phrases indicating, for instance, that he cannot yet give a formal reply and that in order to do so he must first consult with his principal.

It is clear, therefore, that any single transaction – and exchanges between affines, for example when contracting a marriage, usually include a number of separate transactions (and hence prestations) – contains a good deal of repeated speech. The possible significance of this feature will be considered below. For the moment, however, it may be mentioned that the content of single speeches is further characterised by an internal repetition of key words, phrases and passages, and, in addition, that a recur-

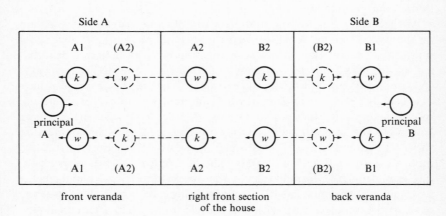

w = *wunangu* (orator)   A1, B1 stationary orators (and deputies)
k = *kandehangu* (deputy)   A2, B2 mobile orators (and deputies)

Figure 5.1. Disposition of speakers in oratorical performances

rence of the same terms within parallel lines is a conspicuous compositional feature of ritual language found in both oratorical and invocatory
speech.

Another aspect of oratorical performances that is worthy of note relates to the symbolism of even, or 'complete' (*nggànapu*) numbers, and
particularly the numbers four and eight, which in eastern Sumba figure as
symbols of completeness (see Forth 1981 *passim*). First of all, in the
procedures described above each side is represented by two pairs of orators and deputies, or four functionaries, making a total of four pairs or
eight individual functionaries in all. Of course, where only one pair acts
for a given side these totals are all reduced by one half. But this reduction
is entirely consistent with the symbolic equation in eastern Sumbanese
thought of numbers in the series two, four, eight and sixteen – an equation
which, moreover, indicates this form of numerical symbolism to be based
on a more fundamental dualism. Also, where two pairs of functionaries
are employed on either side, from the point of view of a single side the
communication of a message and its reply normally involves eight, or two
sets of four, segments of oratorical speech.[16] Referring again to Figure
5.1, this situation can be illustrated as follows:

$$
\left.
\begin{array}{llll}
\text{(i)} & \text{A1} & \rightarrow & \text{A2} \\
\text{(ii)} & \text{A2} & \rightarrow & \text{A1} \\
\text{(iii)} & \text{A2} & \rightarrow & \text{B2} \\
\text{(iv)} & \text{B2} & \rightarrow & \text{A2}
\end{array}
\right\} \text{ message transferred from A to B}
$$

$$
\left.
\begin{array}{llll}
\text{(v)} & \text{B2} & \rightarrow & \text{A2} \\
\text{(vi)} & \text{A2} & \rightarrow & \text{B2} \\
\text{(vii)} & \text{A2} & \rightarrow & \text{A1} \\
\text{(viii)} & \text{A1} & \rightarrow & \text{A2}
\end{array}
\right\} \text{ reply transferred from B to A}
$$

(This does not include the initial and final exchanges between the principals and their stationary orators but only oratorical speech which takes
place between pairs of orators and deputies.) The appearance of the numbers four and eight in this case results from the factor of repetition – both
direct repetition, where speech is, as it were, directly given back to the
previous speaker (as in exchanges (ii), (iv), (vi), and (viii) above), and
indirect repetition, where a repeated message is conveyed to a third party.
Therefore, with regard to the significance of even numbers in this society,
and especially the numerals four and eight, it may be supposed that one
purpose of this type of repetition – and the related factor of mediation – is
to render the communication of a message, and its reply, 'complete'.

We may now turn to the invocatory use of ritual language. In spite of
certain manifest differences, invocations (*hamayangu*) resemble oratorical
performance in several fundamental respects. The essential purpose of

invocation is to make a request or appeal to, and to propitiate, a spirit, and this always involves some sort of offering. As is consistent with the significance of the number four, the majority of invocations, and in particular those which include a sacrifice and food offering, comprise four named parts. Taking the example of invocatory speeches addressed to the clan ancestor, these are, in order of performance: (1) the *pingi hamayangu* (*pingi* is 'trunk, source', etc.), the main address in which the priest invites the ancestral spirit to descend and partake of a portion of betel and areca that is placed before him and, if a large animal (pig or buffalo) is to be slaughtered, dedicates this to the ancestor; (2) the *hamayangu manu*, which involves the dedication of a fowl (*manu*), or fowls if the rite also concerns additional spiritual entities (larger animals are never slaughtered except with one or more fowls); (3) the *hamayangu memi* (*memi* is 'to cook, cooked'), whereby the priest invites the spiritual addressee(s) to partake of an offering of cooked food and water; and (4) the *hamayangu pahàpa*, in which betel and areca (*pahàpa*) are again offered to the spirit or spirits. This sequence, it should be noted, parallels the formal reception of an honoured guest, who similarly is first offered betel and areca; then, after the slaughter of an animal, a cooked meal; and, finally, a further portion of betel and areca.

The three main features which invocations share with oratorical performances can be specified as repetition, mediation, and exchange. In the case of invocations, one form of repetition is evidenced by the fact that the three latter segments of an invocatory performance are for the most part abbreviated versions of the first (the *pingi hamayangu*), serving largely to reiterate specific points raised in the main address. In some ways this pattern seems comparable to the repetition of a message as it is passed between a number of orators, although in this latter instance such repetition is plainly a function of the factor of mediation – a connection which is not so clear in the case of invocation. In a different way, mediation also relates to another form of repetition encountered in both invocations and orations, that is, the recurrence of key phrases in any single segment of speech, since this phenomenon obviously increases the chances of essential portions of a message being correctly communicated. In fact, this consideration would appear to have relevance also for yet another type of repetition which, as noted, is characteristic of both the invocatory and the oratorical use of ritual language, namely the recurrence of the same terms in parallel lines.

In both major occasions of ritual language use in eastern Sumba, several levels of mediation, involving various sorts of substitution, can be distinguished. Thus, in oratorical performances orators act as intermediaries between the two principals, while in verbal exchanges between the orators themselves the speakers are represented by their deputies (*kande-*

hangu), so that it is always the latter and never the former who are directly addressed. And in performances where each principal is served by two pairs of orators and deputies, further mediation is of course provided by the fact that a message is transferred from one speaker to the other before being conveyed to the opposite side. In invocations, on the other hand, a priest acts as intermediary between a social group or individual – the beneficiary of the performance – and a spirit, while those spirits directly addressed by the priest (and especially the clan ancestors) are similarly regarded as intermediaries between man and God, the ultimate, though never the direct, addressee of all invocatory speech.

Communication with the world of spirit, however, further requires the mediation of a sacrificial fowl which, in the segment of an invocation called the *hamayangu manu*, is often spoken to thus:

Ronguwa na liinggu ba ninggau manu	Hear my voice you, fowl, who are here.
Ku-palikunggau lii	I use you to spread [extend, cast] the word(s),
Ku-pangàndinggau langu	I employ you to carry [send] the news.

Indeed, one might say that the fowl is the crucial mediator in this communication, since it is by way of the entrails (*ura*) of the bird, which reveal the will and disposition of the spirit invoked and thus serve as an augury, that the speech of the priest receives a reply.[17] Although the livers (*eti*) of larger animals, too, are similarly employed as auguries in this context, these animals are not represented as intermediaries in the same way as sacrificial fowls, but are mostly spoken of as a food offering. Even so, that the entrails of fowls and the livers of larger animals equally provide a means of communication between man and spirit calls to mind the aforementioned idea of a superior knowledge residing in the liver. In fact, as messages from spirit to man are communicated solely in this way and do not entail the relatively inferior medium of language, it might be supposed that such communication is superior to that which passes from man to spirit. Yet it should not be forgotten that the verbal style employed in both invocations and orations is a form of language that is superior to ordinary speech and, in so far as it may be said to take the place of the latter, can itself be regarded as forming another necessary level of mediation in these contexts.

Despite the prominence of mediation and repetition in invocatory and oratorical performances, however, the most fundamental and overriding feature of the two occasions of ritual language use is exchange, and more specifically the exchange of valuables (or values) of particular kinds. This aspect of orations is already clear from the fact that verbal exchanges between orators are always accompanied by an exchange of material goods. Indeed, in this respect it seems relevant to mention that the eastern Sumbanese word for 'language', *hilu*, also means '[to] change, exchange', thereby suggesting that, in this society, language might be conceived of as the paradigm of all forms of exchange, or at any rate as one of its most prominent instances.

Although there are obvious differences, invocation too involves an exchange, both of meanings and values. Thus, on the one hand, the speech of a priest is thought to be answered in the entrails and livers of sacrificial animals, while, on the other, material offerings to spirits are reciprocated in the sense that from any act of invocation (and therefore offering) specific benefits are expected to flow. Since gifts from man to spirit and from spirit to man are of manifestly different sorts, it is also relevant in this regard that prestations made to wife-givers and wife-takers (or, more generally, superiors and inferiors) also comprise valuables of opposite kinds and that, accordingly, these goods are similarly transferred in opposite directions. What is more, as I have noted elsewhere (Forth 1981:368–369), goods given to wife-givers (including bridewealth) are of the same type as certain valuables which are offered, or consecrated, to spirits.[18]

That exchange is the primary and essential feature of both invocations and oratorical performances thus goes some way towards explaining why these are the main settings for ritual language use in eastern Sumba. Evidence concerning comparable speech traditions in a variety of other societies makes it plain that ritual language characterised by parallelism is commonly employed in communicating with the world of spirit and in other situations of 'formalized interaction that call for a clear statement of shared premisses' (Fox 1975:128). Yet, not only is it clear that eastern Sumbanese ritual language is not exclusively a 'religious' or 'sacred' language, but by no means are all instances of 'formalized interaction' in this society occasions for the use of parallelistic speech. Since both invocation and oration involve communication between parties distinguished as superior and inferior, it might be supposed that hierarchy, and particularly the element of distance this normally entails, is a decisive criterion. But interaction between persons of lower rank and the nobility, for example, does not require the use of this verbal style, and neither does most intercourse between wife-givers and wife-takers – even though in these two instances a degree of formality, including the observance of other forms of verbal restriction, must always be maintained. What is both common and exclusive to invocation and oration, however, is a formalised exchange of values of prescribed kinds and regulated quantities. Thus, in eastern Sumba, ritual, or parallelistic, language can best be characterised as the verbal style that accompanies formal gift exchange. In this regard, the importance of ritual language is further underlined by the fact that performances in this idiom serve to articulate, and hence maintain, social and cosmological order: invocation in that it connects man and spirit, and oration as it is the vehicle for formal social interaction between wife-givers and wife-takers – in which respect it should be recalled that eastern Sumbanese society is governed by a system of asymmetric prescriptive alliance. In this latter connection it is also relevant that certain aspects of oratorical performances are explicitly conceived of in terms of a weaving analogy (*ngera tinungu*). As noted earlier, orators are called *wunangu*, a term which otherwise refers to the comb on a loom which separates the warp threads so as to facilitate the passage of the weft;[19] thus in this context the word evidently focuses upon the role of the orator as an intermediary. Moreover, in the lexicon of ritual language this particular metaphor is extended by the pairing of *wunangu* with *ngoda*, the name of a long wooden instrument placed next to the comb which is used to press down on the threads (see Kapita 1976b:228–229).[20] This analogy is especially interesting since in eastern Sumba the weaving of decorated textiles, which is carried out exclusively by women, is by far the most prominent and elaborate form of material art and, considering the uses to which decorated textiles are put, is also a major (and perhaps the major) contribution of women to ritual life. In contrast, parallelistic language is the highest expression of eastern Sumbanese verbal art, and as regards the major occasions of its use it is of course the preserve of men. Thus, while men and women are associated respectively with verbal and visual modes of expression (see Forth 1981:16, 19–20), to some extent the characteristic ceremonial forms of these are nevertheless represented with reference to a single image.

Formal features of ritual language

In the remainder of this paper I shall review a number of prominent formal features of eastern Sumbanese ritual language, referring mostly to the two texts given as Reference Texts 1 and 2. These texts, which exemplify invocatory and oratorical speech respectively, have been selected largely at random from a fairly extensive corpus I collected in Rindi, although my choice has been influenced by the fact that both are comparatively brief. While they are typical of their respective genres, therefore, neither text should be regarded as an especially good example. In addition, each text is presented here as it was performed on a single specific occasion, and no attempt has been made to 'correct' or 'improve' either in any way.

As mentioned earlier, the basic unit of eastern Sumbanese ritual language is the dyadic set. Dyadic sets may be either simple, comprising just two paired terms, or complex, each element then consisting of two or more terms which compose a single semantic entity. Longer paired expressions, or lines,[21] may comprise one, two, or three dyadic sets. Thus, for example, lines 2 and 3 of the oratorical text (Reference Text 2) – *jàka ta njara mera ndewa//jàka ta ahu mera ura*, 'as we are horses of equal spirit//as we are dogs of equal fortune' – contain two simple sets, namely *njara//ahu*, 'horse//dog', and *ndewa//ura*, 'spirit//fortune'. Two seems to be the most common number of dyadic sets, although lines with just one set often appear as well. I have yet to find lines containing four dyadic sets, and if they do occur they are certainly rare.[22]

Dyadic, or paired, elements can appear in either consecutive or alternate parallel lines (cf. Fox 1971:236), though the former is the more frequent arrangement. Another pattern which sometimes appears is where a given line is paired with the third following line. Using a and a_1, and b and b_1 to represent paired lines, and x and y to represent intervening lines (which may or may not themselves be paired), these three possibilities can be illustrated as follows:

(1)	(2)	(3)
a	a	a
a_1	b	x
b	a_1	y
b_1	b_1	a_1

Instances of the first pattern occur in lines 5–8 in Reference Text 1, instances of the second pattern occur in lines 29–32 of Reference Text 2, while instances of the third pattern occur in lines 1–4 of Reference Text 1 and in lines 10–13 and 11–14 of Reference Text 2.

The dyadic principle displayed in the pervasively parallelistic style of eastern Sumbanese ritual language is recognised by practitioners themselves in so far as they state that single components (terms, phrases, lines) should always appear with a 'partner', *papa*, a word which in its most general sense refers to one of two sides or one member of a pair.[23] Paired elements are also called *ndekilu*, which term is in this context synonymous with *papa*; thus components of dyadic sets are spoken of as being *papa-pangu* or *pandekilungu*, that is, mutually related as *papa* or *ndekilu*.[24] However, while, as noted earlier, certain single terms can in different speech contexts form dyadic sets with a number of others, by no means all words that appear in ritual language are paired, or have *papa* (or *ndekilu*). Indeed, only grammatical elements provisionally classifiable as verbs, nouns (including certain proper nouns, such as clan names, certain personal names and place names, and some numerical class words), adjectives, and adverbs regularly do so. Other elements (pronouns, articles, prepositions, and so on) thus do not form dyadic sets; and, although they may be repeated in parallel lines, in many cases such repetition is optional.

Furthermore, not all lines pair. A good number of unpaired lines, and unpaired expressions occurring within lines, consist of expressions such as *na nyuna ba tuna*, roughly translatable as 'now that being so' (see, for example, Reference Text 1, line 37), which function as connectives and thus serve to articulate segments of a single speech that concern distinct matters. In addition, the first and last lines of an oration are always unpaired, as is the last line of an invocatory address (which typically ends with the phrase 'you answer my voice [words]') and very often the first line as well. Many unpaired lines, however, must be accounted for in other ways. Excluding connective expressions and initial and final lines, in the two reference texts there is a total of thirteen unpaired lines. Of these, nine contain manifestly dyadic components, the majority of which appear in other contexts as paired terms in parallel lines. These dyadic elements are:

from Reference Text 1

ura tundu luku//wai maringu	rain that follows the course of the river//cool water	(line 9)
mànjaku//maringu	calm, still//cool	(line 38)
kiri//katiku	base//head	(line 39)
ratu/maràmba	religious leader//noble ruler	(lines 48, 91)
Ropa Nyali//Lada Mata		(line 59)
Hila Ndahi//Hila Baba	names of clan ancestors	(line 64)
Talu Namba//Karata Ende		(line 65)
Lai Lanjangu//Pala Kalinjaku	place name	(line 88)

from Reference Text 2

(ma)timbi//(ma)tara	[what is] thick//[what is] strong	(line 20)

Although unpaired, therefore, the lines in which the above terms appear can be regarded as being in accord with the basic dyadic structure of ritual language, and so complete in themselves. As Fox has noted with regard to Rotinese (1971: 239), examples of this sort show that parallel line structure is a secondary phenomenon which is derivative of composition based on dyadic sets.

Of the other unpaired lines in the two reference texts, one appears to reflect a simple failing on the part of the speaker. This concerns the expression *libungu lii*, 'to cast [out] the voice, words', which occurs as the main component of lines 45 and 68 in Reference Text 1, and which is normally paired with *wuangu pulu*, 'to give speech'. In contrast, the remaining unpaired lines, which all appear in Reference Text 2 (lines 15, 25,

28), each occur with their respective pairs earlier in the same text. Hence in these cases single lines might be understood as abbreviated forms of more elaborate expressions, the part then, as it were, standing for the whole.[25] Indeed, unpaired lines of this kind are so frequently encountered, especially, it seems, in oratorical speech, that they cannot be regarded as resulting from a lack of diligence or ability on the part of a speaker. Rather, they reflect a legitimate feature of ritual language usage.

In the eastern Sumbanese tradition, what may be called simple internal dyads, as exemplified by the pair *mànjaku//maringu* ('calm//cool') cited above, can be further combined with other simple dyads so as to compose series of four, six, and sometimes more terms (though always an even number). These single terms are then either simply conjoined, or separated only by articles, pronouns, simple connectives, and the like; in other words, by grammatical elements that do not pair. Although this pattern is not at all uncommon, no clear instances appear in the reference texts. But the following examples, taken from other texts I recorded in Rindi, will serve as representative illustrations:

(1)　*hiri//aha*　　　　　　to winnow//to polish
　　　ngilu//ngàmba　　　to blow [away]//to shake out[26]

(2)　*mbinu//nggànapu*　　full// complete
　　　talaru//ndàba　　　 finished [completed]//all [entire, whole]

(3)　*mbàraku//mbana*　　warm//hot
　　　puri//paita　　　　 sour [also bitter]//bitter
　　　mbàru//mangehi　　salty//burning [for example, of lime in the mouth]

(4)　*ura//hamangu*　　　[collective expression for]
　　　lunga//ranga　　　soul//spirit[27]
　　　ndewa//pahomba

In each of these combinations the constituent terms usually appear in the order outlined above, and for each of the component pairs (for example, *hiri//aha*) this order is invariable. As with two terms conjoined within a single line (for example, the pair *mànjaku//maringu* noted earlier), in all these examples the four or six elements together denote a unitary idea;[28] and it is possible to employ just the first two terms of the series without thereby affecting the meaning. This also applies to series comprising three pairs of words. In addition, with both examples of three-pair combinations cited above, the third pair is in fact included only occasionally.

With regard to establishing parallel line structure in these cases, it would appear most expedient to consider two conjoined terms as forming a single line. Examples (1) and (2) would then comprise two lines, and examples (3) and (4) three lines. In this way the first two instances might be regarded as examples of what Fox has called 'unrestricted double dyadic expressions' (1971: 240). However, it is important to note that with each of the instances given above there is little to indicate that the first and second elements of one line respectively form dyadic sets with the first and second elements of the following line (cf. Fox 1971:240). Thus, taking the first two lines of example (3) as an illustration, *mbàraku* ('warm') does not appear to pair specifically with *puri* ('sour'), and neither does *mbana* ('hot') with *paita* ('bitter'). Rather, it seems that in cases of this type two conjoined terms occurring within a single line (for example, *mbàraku* and *mbana*) must be treated as a unity which is then paired with the two terms of the succeeding line considered as a similar unity.

With examples (3) and (4) above, we are, of course, apparently left with a third, unpaired line. Yet it is abundantly clear that in each of these instances this line belongs with the two which precede it. Therefore it seems that this sort of pattern should be regarded as a distinct and special kind of exception to the general pairing of lines which is characteristic of eastern Sumbanese ritual language.

The foregoing considerations are equally relevant to the analysis of another pattern which occurs in invocations, whereby the names of certain plants, for example, are grouped in fixed dyads and then uttered in succession so as to produce series of two or, more usually, four dyads, or four or eight individual names. But it is not only single words that can combine to form configurations of these sorts; for one also finds serial combinations, as they may be described, where the component elements each comprise two terms which together compose a semantic whole. One example of this is the common expression *kuru uma/padua kaheli//njonga tuluru/eti aü*, 'interior of the house/centre of the house-floor// space between the hearth-stones/liver of the hearth'. Although 'house' (*uma*) and 'house-floor' (*kaheli*) appear as parallel terms within paired lines in a variety of other ritual language contexts (see, for example, Reference Text 2, lines 29–31), in the present case 'interior of the house' (*kuru uma*) is more readily understandable as a single unit, and likewise 'centre of the house-floor' 'space between the hearth-stones', and 'liver of the hearth'. Thus the entire expression is best construed as forming two parallel lines which each comprise two conjoined elements (though these each consist of two single terms), as with the examples of combinations of four single terms noted above.

Since in the case just described we are at one level dealing with single terms that cannot be analytically separated, this may be considered an instance of what Fox has termed an 'idiomatic double dyadic expression' (1971:240). However, in eastern Sumbanese ritual language there also occur a few instances of combinations of elements which, while they can broadly be regarded as idiomatic, appear as components of single, unpaired lines. One instance of this is the previously mentioned expression *ura tundu luku*//*wai maringu*, 'rain that follows the course of the river// cool water', which is a formulaic reference to the heavy rains of the early part of the wet season (see Forth 1983). In some respects it might be thought that here *ura* ('rain') forms a dyadic set with *wai* ('water'), and similarly *tundu luku* ('that follows the course of the river') with *maringu* ('cool'), especially since 'following the course of the river' is for the eastern Sumbanese essential to the symbolic property of 'coolness' in this context. Yet the fact is that each of these two phrases conveys a unitary sense which is lost when their individual elements are treated in isolation. Thus, for one thing, *wai maringu* embodies a variety of meanings which are not adequately conveyed by the translation 'cool water' (see Forth 1981:98–100). For another, *ura* and *wai* do not figure as a pair in other ritual language expressions, and neither do *tundu luku* and *maringu*. Hence, for these reasons and because the two entire phrases are consistently conjoined as in line 9 of Reference Text 1, their employment here is formally equivalent, for example, to that of *mbàraku* ('warm') and *mbana* ('hot'). In other words, they are best regarded as components of one expression which can be treated as a single, unpaired line.

In the two reference texts there are also a number of instances of idiomatic combinations which, in contrast, do occur as dyadic elements of parallel lines and therefore more clearly conform to the analytical class defined by Fox (see, for example, Reference Text 1, lines 5–6, 22–23, 76–77, 83–84, 85–86; and Reference Text 2, lines 17–19).

Most of the compositional features so far outlined represent exceptions (or partial exceptions) to the most general form of eastern Sumbanese ritual language, that is, the production of parallel lines from simple dyadic sets. However, there is another common phenomenon that may be regarded as being at variance with the rule of parallelism, which we have yet to consider: namely, the repetition of elements in paired lines.

In the eastern Sumbanese tradition, repeated elements, including a good many which have semantic value, are encountered in the majority of lines containing just one or two parallel elements and in many which contain three. Using x and y for semantic elements which repeat, and a, a_1, b, and b_1 for paired elements, several examples of repetition occurring within parallel lines taken from the two sample texts can be illustrated as follows:

(1)   a   x   // a_1 x
      eti tana   //*puhu tana*
      liver of the earth   //heart of the earth
      (Reference Text 1, lines 49–50)

(2) x   a   // x a_1
hupu mahanggula //*hupu mahanganji*
ultimate ruler   //ultimate prince
(Reference Text 1, lines 12–13)

(3) a   x   b   //a_1 x b_1
njara mera ndewa   //*ahu mera ura*
horses of equal spirit //dogs of equal fortune
(Reference Text 2, lines 2–3)

(4) x   a   b   x a_1 b_1
lua la uma mandamobu   //*lua la kaheli mandambata*
to go to the house that does not rot //to go to the house-floor
that does not break

(Reference Text 2, lines 29–31)

(5) x   y   a   //x   y a_1
patu ngia marara   //*patu ngia mabara*
four portions of gold//four portions of silver
(Reference Text 1, lines 2–3)

Considering only lines comprising a total of three elements that are paired or repeated, there are, logically, three further possibilities:

a   x   y//a_1 x   y
a   b   x//a_1 b_1 x
x   a   y//x a_1 y

No instances of these, however, appear in the sample texts, and while examples of the first (a x y//a_1 x y) can be found elsewhere, this pattern seems to be uncommon. Moreover, at the present stage of my investigations into eastern Sumbanese ritual language I have yet to encounter instances of the other two configurations. In these respects, then, it may tentatively be observed that, in combinations of one or two parallel elements with one or two repeated terms, the former seem to appear rather more frequently in initial and/or final positions than in a medial position. As yet, though, it is unclear what significance might be attached to this observation.[29] In lines containing both parallel and repeated terms, the maximum number of repeated elements appears to be two. Lines composed entirely of repeated terms occurring in paired positions are rare, though one instance is found in Reference Text 2 (lines 9–12).

It is important to note that, while some repeated terms never pair, many do form dyadic sets in other contexts. Thus, taking only the examples cited above, *tana*, 'earth, land, soil, country, ground', etc., which is repeated in lines 49–50 of Reference Text 1, forms dyadic sets with *wai*, 'water', *rumba*, 'grass, weeds', and *pindu*, 'gate' elsewhere in the same text (see lines 53–54, 57–58, and 87–89), while in other texts it frequently appears as the pair of a variety of other terms, including *luku*, 'river', *awangu*, 'sky', *paraingu*, 'chief village, domain', *ai*, 'wood, tree', and *watu*, 'stone'. Similarly, *mera*, 'equal', which is repeated in lines 2–3 of Reference Text 2, pairs in other places with *hama*, 'same' (see Reference Text 2, lines 7–8).

It seems, then, that in cases such as these repetition must be regarded as a deliberate compositional device rather than as a simple reflection of the inherent limits of pairing in respect of single lexical elements. In this regard it is also worth noting that the appearance of the same element in different dyadic sets, and as a repeated term, can involve different senses of the word in question (cf. Fox 1971:232, 1975:110). Thus, with *tana* ('earth', etc.), where this term is repeated, as in the example noted above, it is the earth as a whole, as a source and sustainer of life and as a spiritual as well as a material entity, which is specifically and exclusively referred to, while where *tana* is paired with *rumba* ('grass, weeds') and *pindu* ('gate'), the word focuses more on the senses of 'land' (or a particular area of land) and 'soil'. On the other hand, when *tana* forms a dyadic set with *wai*, 'water' (as in the expression *katiku tana//katiku mata wai*, 'head of the earth//source of the water(s)'; the second instance of *katiku*, 'head', is optional here), the two terms modify respectively the paired elements *katiku* ('head') and *mata* ('eye, source', etc.), both of which can express the idea of a beginning or point of origin (see Forth 1981:69 n.22). Hence in this context the reference is not to the earth in its entirety but to particular, analogous, and cosmologically significant aspects of earth (or 'the earth') and water. In analysing the variety of dyadic connections a single term can sustain, that is its semantic range (see Fox 1971:245), therefore, it would appear most useful in cases of this sort to consider repetition as a pairing of an element with itself (cf. Fox 1975:116).

This is not to claim, however, that these considerations are equally relevant to the repetition of all words that otherwise pair. Indeed, in some instances it may be supposed that repetition serves more as a sort of focusing device, to set off or highlight either the repeated term or paired terms occurring in the same lines. This interpretation seems to have some applicability, for example, in the case of the phrases *njara mera ndewa//ahu mera ura*, 'horses of equal spirit//dogs of equal fortune', since the repeated term *mera*, 'equal' (and, more generally, the idea of equality) appears in this ritual context to be, semantically, the most essential element. Another factor which undoubtedly has some bearing on the incidence of repeated terms is differences in ability or standard of performance of different speakers, or indeed of the same speaker on different occasions. One apparent instance of this is the repetition of *toma*, 'to reach', in the lines *tomanggunya na tula pakajanga//tomanggunya na rehi pakawuku,* 'I reach the notched support//I reach the knotted time' (Reference Text 1, lines 5–6), since normally, in this same context, *toma* is paired with *dehi(ngu)*, 'to come to, arrive at' (*dehi* also means 'exact(ly), precise(ly)').

Concluding remarks

This paper is intended as a general introduction to eastern Sumbanese ritual language, and I have attempted to cover several diverse aspects of this speech tradition. As regards form, however, its defining feature is, of course, parallelism, so it is parallelism which must be the focus of any comparison with other, related traditions. In concluding, then, I shall confine my remarks to the connection between parallelism and another prominent, and in some ways similar, compositional feature of eastern Sumbanese ritual language: namely, repetition within paired lines as described above.

The importance of viewing parallelism in relation to this sort of repetition has recently been shown by Fox (1977:73–74), who has suggested that it may be possible to construct a scale of complexity for different ritual languages on the basis of the extent to which these two features occur. Of the various instances he reviews, the one which displays the greatest overall reliance on parallelism is Rotinese ritual language. In this regard, judging from comparative data provided by Fox, both in that paper and elsewhere (1971, 1975), eastern Sumbanese appears on the whole to be rather less parallelistic than Rotinese and therefore more dependent on repetition, while at the same time rather more consistently parallelistic than the other traditions, from various parts of the world, which Fox cites (1977:74–77).[30]

As Fox points out in the same paper (1977:73), parallelism differs from repetition in that it involves a differentiation of elements, while the two features resemble one another in that both involve an identification of elements. As far as eastern Sumbanese ritual language is concerned, this similarity between parallelism and repetition is in fact suggested by native ideas regarding the purpose of parallelism. Earlier I noted that one apparent function of the repetition of terms within paired lines is to ensure the correct communication of a message. Unfortunately, I cannot say whether this aspect of the phenomenon is recognised by the eastern Sumbanese themselves since I never thought to ask what its purpose might be (or, indeed, why some terms are, in some contexts, paired while others are not). On the other hand, though, just such an explanation was given for parallelism. Thus, I was told that terms and phrases are regularly paired in ritual language so that if an addressee does not take the meaning of one element its pair will make good the deficiency (Forth 1981:19). This statement reveals a rather pragmatic concern for the effectiveness of ritual speech in exchanges between two parties, and in this regard it seems significant that ritual language is mostly employed in eastern Sumba to convey information, or messages, the correct communication of which is seen to have important practical consequences.

It seems reasonable, therefore, to suppose that parallelism and repetition may subserve common ends.[32] But there is an essential difference to be noted here, for, while repetition can facilitate correct communication where one of two repeated terms is not received by the addressee, the native rationalisation for parallelism seemed to refer not so much to this possibility as to that of a term being received but not understood, its paired term then serving to clarify its meaning. Thus, whereas in the first situation what is crucial to correct communication is identification, in the second it is, on the contrary, differentiation. In other words, although that repetition and parallelism can be seen to subserve the same general function in ritual language communication they would nevertheless appear to do so in different ways.

Considered in this light, the native explanation for parallelism appears to present a problem; for although in the above respect differentiation is evidently the essential property of parallelism, identification seems still to be entailed in the idea that one term can compensate for, or clarify, another. Indeed, as it stands, the statement might be taken as suggesting that, though distinct, paired terms are essentially synonymous. Yet the members of many such dyads are in fact related by various forms of antithesis, while others cannot easily be accommodated to either of these two logical classes. How, then, can the meaning of a term be clarified, for example, by one that is opposed to it in meaning? I do not propose to attempt a complete answer to this question here – not least because it touches upon the thorny issue of synonymy. Suffice it to say, however, that a solution might be found in the fact that, as other native statements suggest (see Forth 1981:19, 415–416; and note 24 of this paper), paired terms, regardless of their apparent logical connection, can in context further be regarded as complementary components of a single semantic unity. Therefore, by virtue of this latter kind of relation – which of course derives from the fact that ritual language pairings are fixed by tradition – by receiving one element it would be possible to understand by it the whole of which it forms a part.[33] As further support for this idea I would add that certain paired terms in eastern Sumbanese which otherwise have manifestly opposed meanings (or at any rate ones that are clearly not synonymous) can nevertheless express a single idea (see Forth 1981:41 n.27, 67, 69). These considerations thus indicate the inadequacy of such categories as 'synonymy' and 'antonymy' in the analysis of ritual language pairings. But to pursue this matter any further here would take us deeper into the semantic structure of eastern Sumbanese ritual language; and this is a topic which is best left for separate treatment elsewhere.

Reference text 1

Invocation

The rite of which the following example of invocatory speech forms part is called *pakalokangu kawàdaku la katoda bungguru*, 'to arrange pieces of metal at the communal altar', and is one of an annual series of rites of renewal collectively known as *pamangu katoda*, 'feast of the altars'. The altar referred to here is located in a central position within a complex of fields, and the rite is principally addressed to the spiritual presence of this place, called the 'communal mother and father' (or 'mother and father who are united, gathered together'), *ina bungguru//ama bungguru*. In this segment of the rite offerings of pieces of gold and silver, betel and areca, and a fowl are dedicated to this spiritual presence, and the general purpose of the procedure is to ensure that the 'communal mother and father' will continue to care for the fields and the crops. Other spiritual entities mentioned in the text include the ancestor of the *mangu tanangu* ('lord of the land') clan, who is named Ropa Nyali-Lada Mata, and the ancestors of the two most prominent clans that have fields in this agricultural complex, Umbu Hila Ndahi-Hila Bana (clan Kanatangu) and Talu Namba-Karata Ende (clan Luku Walu).

1	*Nanjaka da àmahu padatu*	There are the cut-up pieces of metal,
2	*Patu ngia marara*	Four portions of gold,
3	*Patu ngia mabara*	Four portions of silver.
4	*Nanjaka da pahàpa pakanata*	There are the encircling [pieces of] betel and areca.
5	*Tomanggunya na tula pakajanga*	I reach the notched support,
6	*Tomanggunya na rehi pakawuku*	I reach the knotted time,
7	*Tomanggunyaka na kanduruku handàkangu*	I have reached the first thunder,
8	*Na katuburu panjalangu*	The regular turbidity,
9	*Tàkananyaka na ura tundu luku-wai maringu*	The rain that follows the course of the river, the cool water, has arrived.
10	*E kanuka budi ina bungguru*	Ah [now it] must concern the communal mother,
11	*La ama bungguru*	The communal father,

12	*Na hupu mahanggula*	The ultimate ruler,
13	*Na hupu mahanganji*	The ultimate prince,
14	*La papangga bei*	At the place where one walks creeping,
15	*Laku nyakungu*	[At the place where] one goes bowing.
16	*Taï àmbu mbulangu*	In future do not forget,
17	*Àmbu marombangu wàna-du*	Do not neglect, it is said,
18	*Na hupu lii tura*	The ultimate promise,
19	*Na hupu lii njanji*	The ultimate compact.
20	*Àmbu mbula*	Do not forget,
21	*Àmbu marombanya*	Do not neglect,
22	*Na hupu lii lakunda*	The first winding on of the thread,
23	*Na hupu lii lawàdi*	The first tying of the warp,
24	*Na kangura winu koka*	The bud of the stirring [?] areca,
25	*Na kameli kuta hàmu*	The sprout of the good [original] betel,
26	*Da kuluru malundungu*	The rolled-up offerings which fulfil,
27	*Da huluku matoma*	The wound-up offerings which suffice.
28	*Ku aha wànya na polana*	With this I polish the stems,
29	*Ku hemi wànya na runa*	With this I wipe off the leaves,
30	*Ka peku mbukutu na runa*	So that the leaves will be dense,
31	*Ka peku karanggungu na nggaina*	So that the bunches [of fruit] will be packed,
32	*Na wataru kawunga wua*	[On] the maize that first bears cobs,
33	*Na uhu kawunga wili*	The rice that first bears ears,
34	*Ka peku liina na kapuka rumba raïngu*	So that there may be profit in the tips of the grass that are laboured over,
35	*Na kapuka rumba haka*	The tips of the grass that rise up [are high].
36	*Ka wànggunyaka budi wànggu-du*	Thus must I indeed speak.
37	*Na nyuna ba tuna*	Now, that being so,
38	*Mànjaku maringu aru-wa*	[Make] calm and cool
39	*Na pajaranggu la kiri la katiku*	What I have spread apart [planted] at the foot [and] at the head [of the field].
40	*Dulungu da amuna*	Let the roots stretch downwards,

41	*Tabonga da kahulukuna*	Let the shoots unfurl.
42	*Ka wànggunyaka budi wànggu-du*	Thus must I indeed speak
43	*La ina bungguru*	To the communal mother,
44	*La ama bungguru*	To the communal father,
45	*Libu àrunya lii*	Pray cast out the voice [words]
46	*La malinjaku babana*	To the one with a smooth lap,
47	*La malàmbi homuna*	To the soft suckler,
48	*Tana ratu maràmba*	The earth [that is] the religious leader and noble ruler,
49	*Eti tana*	[To] the liver of the earth,
50	*La puhu tana*	To the heart of the earth,
51	*Hamana la kiri awangu*	And to the base of the sky,
52	*Mata lodu*	The source of the sun,
53	*Hamana la katiku tana*	And to the head of the earth,
54	*La katiku mata wai*	The head [that is] the source of the water(s).
55	*Ka wànggunyaka budi wànggu-du ka ni*	Thus must I indeed speak here.
56	*Hinggilu mahaniina*	There remains a separate matter,
57	*Na matanangu haupu*	The one who holds each handful of earth,
58	*Na marumbangu hawàla*	The one who holds each blade of grass,
59	*Na mandapuna i Ropa Nyali-Lada i Mata*	[The one who is] Ropa Nyali-Lada Mata,
60	*Pamera lii*	Be equal in voice,
61	*Pahama pulu-ka*	Be the same in speech
62	*Da makaraba tana ngangu*	[With] those who use the land as eating vessels,
63	*Da makaraba tana ngunungu*	Those who use the land as drinking vessels,
64	*Mandapuna i Umbu Hila Ndahi-Hila Baba*	[The one who is] Umbu Hila Ndahi-Hila Baba,
65	*Hamana i Talu Namba-Karata Ende*	And Talu Namba-Karata Ende.
66	*Jiaduyaka nàhu hi ku toma-ha ngaru*	Now indeed I contact them with the mouth,
67	*Hi ku kela-ha làma*	I reach them with the tongue,
68	*Ka peku libu-nda lii*	So that we may cast out the voice [words]
69	*La malinjaku babana*	To the one with a smooth lap,
70	*La malàmbi homuna*	To the soft suckler.

71	*Na nyuna ba tuna*	Now, that being so,
72	*Na tara liinda*	The sharpness of our voice,
73	*Na ruru pekanda*	The cut of our words,
74	*Jàka tuba*	If [it is] right,
75	*Jàka deninguna*	If it is correct,
76	*Nilua pàku taï na kajowa tanda*	Here in a moment [there will be] the prominent sign,
77	*Na pakiku kurangu*	The [one with a] shrimp-like tail.
78	*Wuangu-ka manu mbànitu panggoharungu*	Provide a fowl that is taut [and] close together,[34]
79	*Mbàlaru parungu*	That is broad and cries out.
80	*Ka wànggunyaka budi wànggu-du*	Thus must I indeed speak.
81	*Na nyuna ba tuna*	Now, that being so,
82	*Jàka nda tuna*	If it is not as it should be,
83	*Na wunjilu kawanana*	Its winding [to the] right [correctly],
84	*Na hepilu kajàngana*	Its loading up compactly,
85	*Nyuda-ka da palitingu rehi*	It is they who will [place the] tread on the line,
86	*Da paàpangu-ka pupu*	They will cause the sign to be grasped,
87	*Na makawunga tura tana*	Those who first tilled the earth [soil]
88	*Lai Lanjangu-Pala Kalinjaku*	At Lai Lanjangu-Pala Kalinjaku,
89	*Na makawunga laka pindu*	Those who first erected the gate,
90	*Mandapu pera dàngu-danya*	They are sitting together with
91	*Tana ratu maràmba*	The earth [that is] the religious leader and noble ruler,
92	*Eti tana*	[At] the liver of the earth,
93	*La puhu tana*	At the heart of the earth.
94	*Ka wànggunyaka budi wànggu-du*	Thus must I indeed speak.
95	*Nda na dangu-a na diha*	The thoughts are not many,
96	*Nda na woru-a na peka*	The words are not expansive,
97	*Kau hemaka na liinggu*	You answer my voice [words].

Reference text 2

Oration

The selection of the following short segment of oratorical speech, to serve as an example of this genre, has been in some measure influenced by the sentimental value it holds for my wife and myself. It was performed on our behalf at the first funeral we attended in Rindi, in May 1975. The deceased was a man of the clan Ananggela (in ritual language called Haparuna Ananggela-Palarangu Haumama), and the speech accompanied the presentation of a pig for slaughter and a metal pendant and chain, given to us in exchange for a cloth which we had earlier presented to the bereaved. (On this occasion, then, we were, in effect, received by Ananggela as wife-givers.) The name Hingitana is that of the 'deputy' (*kandehangu*) of the speaker who represented us in this matter, and we were referred to as *ina jawa bara//ama kopani*, 'white foreign mother//father of the Company' (a reference to the former Dutch East India Company), which is the usual way of designating foreigners, and especially Europeans, in ritual language.

As with the example of invocatory speech given in Reference Text 1, much of the language employed here is clearly rather figurative, and it would require a good deal of exegesis to render the precise meanings of many passages. It may, however, be worth noting that the expressions which appear in lines 20–22, 26–27, and 33–34 refer to the subsequent act of dedicating and sacrificing the pig presented to us, as a means of informing the clan ancestor of this transaction and securing his blessing and protection.

1	*Mu patinginya Hingitana*	You listen to it, Hingitana,
2	*Lànga tàka nàhu jàka ta njara mera ndewa*	Most definitely now, as [if] we are horses of equal spirit [destiny],
3	*Jàka ta ahu mera ura*	As [if] we are dogs of equal fortune [soul].
4	*A na nyuna ba tuna*	Ah, then, that being so,
5	*Ninyaka na àmahu hawàlangu*	Here is the one length of metal [chain],
6	*Na mamuli hau*	The one metal pendant.
7	*Duna ka peku pamera mera-a-nda la lima*	This so that our hands will be equal,
8	*Duna ka peku pahama hama-a-nda la ngaru*	This so that our mouths will be the same.
9	*Màla jàka wànggu-ka nàhu*	Let [it be] as I say now,
10	*Ba ku kaüya la ngaru*	When I tear it with the mouth,
11	*Duku mandapunggu Haparuna Ananggela*	I [who am] Haparuna Ananggela,
12	*Jàka wànggu-ka nàhu*	As I say now,
13	*Ba ku datuya la lima*	When I slice it with the hand,
14	*Duku mandapunggu-ka Palarangu Haumama*	I [who am] Palarangu Haumama.
15	*A la mamuli hau*	Ah, with the one pendant,

16	*Hi njara mera ndewa-i-ndanyaka nàhu*	Thus we are [in this way] horses of equal spirit,
17	*Ba ta punangu wai mata*	When we have something in our eyes that makes us cry,
18	*Hi ahu mera ura-i-ndanyaka nàhu*	Thus we are [in this way] dogs of equal fortune,
19	*Ba ta hangginangu wai wira*	When we choke on nasal mucus.
20	*Màta-a ka ta karahangu-a matimbi matara*	Let us place ourselves beside what is thick and what is strong,
21	*Màta ka na utu-a-nda kajangu matimbi*	So that there may be sewn for us a thick screen,
22	*Ka na punggu-a-nda maü maparungu*	So that there may be cut [and constructed] for us a broad shelter.
23	*Na ina jawa bara una*	The white foreign mother,
24	*Na ama kopani*	The father of the company,
25	*Ba ta njara mera ndewa duka*	As we are indeed horses of equal spirit,
26	*La hulukungu lii wàmunya*	To the dedication of the speech, you say to him,
27	*La pangatungu pingu*	To the conveying of the knowledge,
28	*Ba pamerandanyaka la lima*	As our hands are equal.
29	*Luananyaka la uma mandamobu duna*	He [the deceased] has gone to the house which does not rot,
30	*Na papameranda la lima*	The one who has made our hands equal,
31	*Hi luananyaka la kaheli mandambata*	He [the deceased] has gone to the house-floor which does not break,
32	*Na papahamanda la ngaru*	The one who has made our mouths the same.
33	*Ngeri wàmu ka ta pangatungu pingu*	You state carefully, so that we may convey the knowledge,
34	*Ngeri wàmu ka ta hulukungu lii*	You state carefully, so that we may dedicate the speech.
35	*Wàna hiana dumu Hingitana*	It is said to you there, Hingitana.

6

MANU KAMA'S ROAD, TEPA NILU'S PATH: THEME, NARRATIVE, AND FORMULA IN ROTINESE RITUAL LANGUAGE

JAMES J. FOX

This paper provides a reading of the translation of a single text in Rotinese ritual language. I have chosen this text for a variety of reasons, but, in particular, because it offers a glimpse of the world created through the cultural imagination of the Rotinese. The underlying assumptions, conventional expressions, and complex philosophy of life that give coherence to this poetic world cannot all be explicated in this paper. My intention is simply to examine the text selectively at various levels from its metaphysical allegory to the minutiae of the formulae embodied in it. As such, this reading may provide something of an introduction to the possibilities of this form of poetry.

Introduction to the historical text

In 1911 the renowned Dutch linguist, J.C.G. Jonker, published the text of a long Rotinese ritual chant. He added this single chant to his collection of Rotinese texts as an 'example of poetic style' which he recognised was characterised by 'sustained parallelism'. But instead of translating the chant, which he implied was 'obscure', he merely provided a series of notes to it with a translation of the ordinary language paraphrase that accompanied the text (Jonker 1911:97–102, 130–135).[1] In 1913 Jonker published another collection of texts in a variety of Rotinese dialects and, in 1915, his massive Rotinese grammar, but he never again gave further consideration to the chant, and so it has remained the only untranslated portion of his vast corpus of Rotinese material.

Far from being 'obscure', this untranslated text, entitled *Ana-Ma Manu Kama ma Falu-Ina Tepa Nilu*, is a clear, superbly structured example of Rotinese ritual language. It is a funeral chant that belongs to the broad class of chants for *ana-mak ma falu-ina*, 'orphans and widows'. In all probability it was gathered in 1900 when Jonker visited the Timor area, or shortly thereafter, when he had returned to Makassar but continued to correspond with and receive written textual material from various local

Rotinese informants.[2] This makes the *Manu Kama ma Tepa Nilu* chant the oldest ritual text available for comparison with present forms of ritual language.

My first purpose in this paper is to provide a translation of the *Manu Kama ma Tepa Nilu* text. But rather than simply translate the words of the text, I would like to offer some explanation of the basic ideas expressed in it, since these ideas embody concepts that are fundamental to a Rotinese philosophy of life. At a more technical level, I wish to make comparisons between forms in this chant and those in current use in Roti, and thereby begin to explicate how the conventions of canonical parallelism interact with the syntactic requirements of an oral poetry to produce stylised phrases and formulae.

This paper comprises three parts. I begin, in Part I, with a personal preface to the text, describing its importance to my own field research on ritual language. I then examine the fundamental idea in the text, the concept of 'orphan and widow', and, with this as background, give an outline summary and brief exegesis of the text itself. In Part II, I discuss the formal structure of Rotinese ritual language and, to illustrate continuity in the language, I compare examples from the text with excerpts from compositions by contemporary oral poets, focusing specifically on formulae used to mark episodes and advance chant narration.[3] I conclude this discussion with various remarks on oral intercommunication, narrative structure, and verbal authority in Rotinese poetry. Finally, in Part III, I provide a complete translation of the *Manu Kama ma Tepa Nilu* text. The translation of this text effectively completes the Jonker corpus of Rotinese texts, and is offered in homage to a Leiden scholar of great stature on whose work I have relied from the beginning of my research on eastern Indonesia.

I

Preface to the text

On my first trip to Roti in 1965, I took with me a copy of Jonker's *Rottineesche Teksten*, which contained the untranslated text of *Manu Kama ma Tepa Nilu*. In the early stages of my fieldwork, as I was attempting to formulate a direction to my research, I was assisted by two poets: Peu Malesi, who would visit me occasionally in the hamlet of Ufa Len where I lived; and Stefanus Adulanu, 'Old Meno' as he was called, the ritual 'Head of the Earth' in Termanu, whom I visited in the nearby hamlet of Ola Lain.

Peu Malesi was the first poet from whom I was able to record a lengthy chant, and it took me several weeks of intermittent work to manage to transcribe, translate, and comprehend what he had recited for me. A school teacher, J. Pello, assisted me with the transcription, while Meno and two elders from Ufa Len, Mias Kiuk and Nggi Muloko, helped in the slow, line-by-line translation and exegesis of the transcribed text. At the time I had virtually no grasp of the Rotinese language, no idea of the structure of ritual language, and no clear sense of what I was doing other than responding to what the Rotinese themselves insisted was the most important thing for me to do. During this period Meno willingly answered my questions, and allowed me to accompany him when he attended the local court where he and other clan elders heard and judged disputes, but at no time, despite several promises, did he recite for me a chant of his own. As he explained to me later, he was uncertain of my intentions and seriousness and was waiting to see how I proceeded.

When, eventually, I reached the point of understanding the Malesi chant and had begun to make sense of its structure, I realised that the *Manu Kama ma Tepa Nilu* text had much the same structure and, from the little that I could make out, was obviously of ritual importance. I therefore resolved to translate it. As a start, without any prior explanation of

Rotinese chanters doing *bapa* – chanting to the beat of the drum – at a mortuary ceremony in honour of the deceased Head of the Earth from Termanu, S. Adulanu

its origin, I simply read it, as carefully as I could, to Mias Kiuk and Nggi Muloko. They were indeed impressed but, to my surprise, they assumed it was another chant that I had recorded from Peu Malesi. The language of the text was such that, without being alerted, their assumption was that it was a contemporary specimen of ritual language. Only when I explained the background to the text were they able to point to expressions that they felt were no longer commonly used by chanters.

After working on the text for some time, I offered to read it to Meno, but he instead proposed that I read it before all the assembled elders at the end of a court session. Without my fully realising it, he was arranging my first public performance as a chanter. With a suitable preface about how I was bringing back to Roti a chant that had been taken down and safe-guarded in Holland for generations, my performance, even though it only involved reading a text, was sufficient to establish some credibility to my endeavours and allow me to enter into an exchange of chants among the poets of Termanu. From then on, Meno and other poets were willing and indeed eager to allow me to record them.

The *Manu Kama ma Tepa Nilu* chant initiated a dialogue in another sense. Chanters regularly respond to other chanters by interpolating passages in their performances that allude to previous performances. In my case, even after having translated *Manu Kama ma Tepa Nilu*, its meaning remained elusive. On Roti there are mortuary chants intended to fit all appropriate social categories of deceased persons: nobles or commoners, rich or poor, those who die old or those who die unmarried; but the most general of all are 'orphan and widow' chants, of which there are many, that can be adapted to suit almost any mortuary occasion. *Manu Kama ma Tepa Nilu* belongs to this general class of chants. One of my difficulties, however, in discussions with Meno, was in understanding the significance the Rotinese attach to the concept of 'orphan and widow'. And it was in answer to my questioning on this subject, months later, that Meno interpolated a passage in his recitation of the chant *Lilo Tola ma Koli Lusi* that alluded to my queries about *Manu Kama ma Tepa Nilu*. This passage was the first of many dialogue exchanges conducted in ritual language as part of the process of my learning the language and its significance.

As in all skilful interpolations, it is difficult – and to some extent arbitrary – to designate where in the *Lilo Tola ma Koli Lusi* chant the interpolated passage begins or ends. Here I quote sixteen lines that are clearly the most pertinent part of Meno's reply:

Se ana-mak?	Who is an orphan?
Na basang-ngita ana-mak	All of us are orphans.
Ma se falu-ina?	And who is a widow?
Na basang-ngita falu-ina	All of us are widows.

Fo la-fada lae	They speak of
Manu Kama dala Dain	Manu Kama's road to Dain
Ma Tepa Nilu eno Selan	And Tepa Nilu's path to Selan.
Na basang-ngita ta enon	All of us have not his path
Ma basang-ngita ta dalan	And all of us have not his road.
Sosoa-na nai dae bafak kia nde bena	This means that on this earth, then,
Ana-mak mesan-mesan	Each person is an orphan
Ma falu-ina mesan-mesan	And each person is a widow.
De mana-sapeo nggeok	Those who wear black hats
Do mana-kuei modok ko	Or those who wear green slippers,
Se ana-ma sila boe	They will be orphans too
Ma falu-ina sila boe	And they will be widows too.

Meno's reply contains three elements that point to an understanding of the *Manu Kama ma Tepa Nilu* text and its underlying philosophy. First, Meno makes explicit the basic Rotinese conception of widowhood and orphanhood as a metaphor symbolising a universal human condition. Then, in alluding to 'Manu Kama's road to Dain//Tepa Nilu's path to Selan', he refers to various courses of human life, all of which imply mortality. And from this follows his third point that since mortality is the fundamental cause of the condition of widowhood and orphanhood, it is at the same time the obliterator of all social distinctions of class or origin. The phrase 'Those who wear black hats//Those who wear green slippers' is an old formulaic designation for the Dutch. (This phrase probably dates from the period of the Dutch East India Company, 'black' and 'green' being the symbolic colours of the north and west quadrants from which the Company was considered to have originated.) Powerful Europeans, like all others, are reduced to widowhood and orphanhood. Hence, despite differences in life course and origin, there are ultimately no differences in the human condition. Meno's reply is thus a highly condensed statement of various closely related notions. From the several points he makes can be derived other notions that are equally important to an understanding of the concept of widow and orphan, and it is these notions I propose to examine in greater detail as prelude to a consideration of the *Manu Kama ma Tepa Nilu* text.

The concept of widow and orphan

The concept of widow and orphan is a multiplex notion whose basis is to be found in the context of the funeral ceremony. On Roti, death's disruption is regarded as affecting primarily the close relatives of the deceased, particularly brothers and sisters, parents, descendants, and spouse. These relatives are the 'bereaved' (*mana-faluk*). They are responsible for providing the funeral feast, but must themselves fast until after the burial. Women among the bereaved are expected to bewail the deceased. Maternal relatives, on the other hand, who are invited to feast, are paid to perform ritual services at the funeral; they are supposed to cleanse the bereaved on the day after the burial and provide the foods that break their fast.

In ritual language the bereaved are referred to as 'orphans and widows' (*ana-mak ma falu-inak*), and their condition is described as *ma-salak ma ma-singok*. The full formula for the bereaved is *ana mak ma-salak ma falu-ina ma-singok*. The Rotinese word *sala(k)* embraces many of the related senses of its Indonesian cognate *salah*, 'error, mistake, fault, guilt, wrong', and has become, for Christian Rotinese, the word for 'sin'. *Sala(k)* may refer, however, both to actions that were done intentionally and those that have occurred by accident, and in many contexts merely implies that something is 'out of place', or simply 'displaced'. *Singo(k)*, the term with which *sala(k)* is paired, has a similar sense. It refers to something that is 'off-course, deviant, or divergent' – something that has missed its target, or strayed from its set path. Since the Rotinese conceive of an ideal order which is manifest only in the heavenly spheres, all of human life is condemned to disorder and imperfection. Death is merely the most prominent occasion at which the human condition is made evident.

Given this understanding, the metaphor of widow and orphan can be used in numerous contexts. In situations of dependency, and particularly in making requests for assistance, the subordinate party identifies his position as that of orphan and widow. Such a position is one of distress and requires compassion:

Te au ana-ma ma-salak	I am an orphan displaced
Ma au falu-ina ma-singok	And I am a widow astray,
De au ana mak loe-loe	I am a humble orphan
Ma au falu inak dae-dae	And I am a lowly widow.

The hope is expressed that the superior party will be generous and unstinting:

Fo ela neka lama-kako bafa	Let the rice basket overflow its brim
Na dai ana-ma leo	To be enough for a clan of orphans,
Ma bou lama-lua fude	And let the lontar jar froth over
Na ndule falu-ina ingu	To be sufficient for a lineage of widows.

Previously, the orphan and widow metaphor was used to characterise the relationship of all subjects to the Lord of their domain. The same metaphor can still be used to describe the relationship of dependants to patrons within their clan or lineage. This short petition given to me by Meno is a good example of the imagery used in making requests. The images are characteristically Rotinese: the cooking of lontar palm syrup and the cutting of leaves and leaf, stalks from the palm. The concluding image of a dense forest with branches touching one another is a common botanic metaphor for order and harmony in society.

Lena-lena ngala lemin	All you great ones,
Lesi-lesi ngala lemin	All you superior ones,
Sadi mafandendelek	Do remember this,
Sadi masanenedak	Do bear this in mind:
Fo ana-ma tua fude	Save the froth of the cooking syrup for the orphans
Ma falu-ina beba langa la	And the heads of the palm leaf-stalks for the widows.
Tua fude dua kako na	When the froth spills over twice,
Kako kao mala sila	Scoop it up for them,
Ma beba langa telu te na	And when the stalk's head droops thrice,
Te tenga mala sila	Lop it off for them,
Fo ela-ana-ma bei tema	So the orphans may remain intact
Ma falu-ina bei tetu	And the widows stand upright,
Fo leo tema toe-ao lasin na	Intact like a dense forest,
Teman losa don na	Intact for a course of time,
Ma tetu lelei nulan na	And upright like a thick wood,
Tetun nduku nete na	Upright for an age.

Using more elaborate metaphors, a patron may be compared to a shepherd who tends a 'herd' of orphans and a 'flock' of widows, or to a great tree around which orphans gather and widows circle. Two examples of this kind of imagery, both taken from the same chant, *Ndi Lonama ma Laki Elokama*, which I recorded from the poet Stefanus Amalo in 1966, may serve as illustration. The first utilises the image of the herdsman:

Te hu touk Ndi Lonama	The man, Ndi Lonama,
Ma ta'ek Laki Elokama	And the boy, Laki Elokama,
Tou ma-bote biik	Is a man with flocks of goats
Ma ta'e ma-tena kapak	And is a boy with herds of water buffalo.
De basa fai-kala	On all the days
Ma nou ledo-kala	And every sunrise
Ana tada mamao bote	He separates the flock in groups
Ma ana lilo bobongo tena	And forms the herd in circles,

Na neui te tada tenan	Bringing his herd-separating spear
Ma neni tafa lilo bote-na	And bringing his flock-forming sword,
Fo te nade Kafe Lasi	His spear named Kafe Lasi
Ma tafa nade Seu Nula	And his sword named Seu Nula.
Fo ana loe tafa neu be na	Where he lowers his sword,
Bote hae neu ndia	The flock stops there,
Ma te'e te neu be na	And where he rests his spear,
Tena lu'u neu ndia	The herd lies down at that place.
Fo tena ta neu luu	It is not the herd that lies down
Ma bote ta neu hae	And not the flock that stops,
Te ana-mak-kala hae	But it is orphans who stop
Ma falu-ina-la lu'u	And widows who lie down.

The second example is contained in the instructions of the dying Ndi Lonama//Laki Elokama. (Because of the rules of parallelism, all chant characters – as indeed all places – have double names; by convention I refer to these characters in the singular but by their double name.) Thus Ndi Lonama//Laki Elokama instructs his family to continue his practice of caring for orphans and widows:

De tati mala bau ndanan	Cut and take a branch from the *bau* tree,
Ma aso mala tui baen	Slice and take a limb from the *tui* tree
Fo tane neu dano Hela	To plant at the lake Hela
Ma sele neu le Kosi	And to sow at the river Kosi
Fo ela okan-na lalae	That its roots may creep forth
Ma samun-na ndondolo	And its tendrils may twine
Fo ela poek-kala leu tain	For shrimp to cling to
Ma nik-kala leu feon	And crabs to circle round;
Fo poek ta leu tain	It is not shrimp that cling there
Te ana-mak leu tain	But orphans who cling there,
Ma nik ta leu feon	And it is not crabs that circle round
Te falu-ina leu feon	But widows who circle round.

In virtually all widow and orphan chants, emphasis is placed on the wanderings of the orphan and widow – the quest of the displaced for sustenance, support, and a proper abode. Thus, for example, in a chant by Meno that relates the death of the chant-character Lusi Topo Lani//Tola Tae Ama, his widow, Bisa Oli//Ole Masi, is left to care for his orphan, Lilo Tola//Koli Lusi. Much of this chant is taken up with the search by the widow to find food to raise her orphan child. Her need prompts her to seek 'the early millet harvest//the first lontar yields' in the domain of Medi do Ndule, and her request, as she journeys, is as follows:

Na kedi fe au dok	Cut for me a leaf
Ma dui fe au bifak	And strip for me a leaf-stalk,
Fo au ane neu lapa eik	That I may plait sandals for [my] feet
Ma au sika neu sidi su'uk	And I may open out a cover for [my] breast,
Fo au la'o unik ledo Medi	For I walk toward Medi's sun
Ma au lope unik fai Ndule	And I head for Ndule's day.

In the Christian reinterpretation of traditional cultural themes, this quest is regarded as a kind of pilgrim's progress – mankind's journey to a heavenly home. The general structure of orphan and widow chants, as will be evident from the *Manu Kama ma Tepa Nilu* chant, lends itself to a variety of similar allegorical interpretations. There is a commonality between the narrative structure of these chants and the Rotinese conception of the course of human life.

Outline of the Manu Kama ma Tepa Nilu text

The text of *Manu Kama ma Tepa Nilu* runs to 334 lines and can be divided into five main episodes. Episode 1 (lines 1 to 34) begins with the marriage of the woman Silu Lilo//Huka Besi with the man Kama Lai Ledo//Nilu Neo Bulan, and the birth and early childhood of Manu Kama//Tepa Nilu (henceforth MK//TN). All chant characters have dual names and MK//TN takes the second portion of his name (Kama//Nilu) from that of his father Kama Lai Ledo//Nilu Neo Bulan. His father's name includes the names Ledo//Bulan, 'Sun'//'Moon', which signify a high heavenly origin. Recognition of this 'origin' is essential to appreciate what happens in later episodes when MK//TN is not given the respect he deserves.

Episode 1 continues in describing first the death of MK//TN's father and then of his mother. This leaves MK//TN as an orphan and widow. Since in ritual language 'father' pairs with 'mother's brother' and 'mother' pairs with 'father's sister', being an orphan and widow is described as lacking all of these important relatives. The episode ends, as do subsequent episodes, leaving MK//TN with tears streaming from his eyes and snot running from his nose. This is portrayed with elaborate botanic imagery:

31	*De lu ko boa na'u*	Tears like *bidara* fruit in the grass,
32	*Ma pinu kaitio telan*	Snot like *kaitio* [-leaves] in the underbrush,

33	*Lama-noma oba-tula*	They pour like juice from a tapped *gewang*
34	*Do lama-titi ate lasi*	And flow like sap from an old *ate.*

Episode 2 (lines 35 to 98) describes MK//TN's encounter with the woman Bula Pe//Mapo Tena, who finds him weeping and takes him in as his mother and aunt:

45	*Bo ana-ma Manu Kama*	Oh, orphan Manu Kama,
46	*Do bo falu-ina Tepa Nilu*	Oh, widow Tepa Nilu,
47	*Mai, te Silu Lilok nde au*	Come, Silu Lilok am I
48	*Do Huka Besik nde au*	Or Huka Besik am I.
49	*Boe ma ta nae Bula Pe*	So do not say Bula Pe
50	*Te nae Silu Lilok*	But say Silu Lilok,
51	*Ma ta nae Mapo Tena*	And do not say Mapo Tena
52	*Te nae Huka Besik*	But say Huka Besik.

Then one day at dawn MK//TN hears the 'soft voices and gentle songs' of 'blackbirds and green parrots' (*koa*//*nggia*). In Rotinese poetry blackbird and parrot is the conventional metaphor for a young attractive girl. And, as these blackbirds and parrots approach MK//TN,

61	*Boe ma ala kako dodoe hala-nala*	They sing with soft voices
62	*Ma ala hele memese dasi-nala*	And they warble with gentle songs.
63	*De ala kako-lala Manu Kama dalen*	They sing to Manu Kama's heart
64	*Ma hele-lala Tepa Nilu tein*	And warble to Tepa Nilu's inner being.

At this, MK//TN wakes Bula Pe//Mapo Tena and asks her:

77	*Mu asa fe-ng-au koa halak*	Go buy for me the blackbird's voice
78	*Do tadi fe-ng-au nggia dasik*	Or get for me the green parrot's whistle
79	*Fo ela au a-hala nggia halak*	So that I may make voice to the black bird's voice
80	*Ma au a-dasi koa dasik*	And I may sing to the green parrot's song.
81	*Fo sama leo inang boe*	That you may be just like my mother
82	*Do deta leo te'ong boe*	Or that you may be similar to my aunt.

In the conventions of the poetry, this is a request that Bula Pe//Mapo Tena provide the bridewealth, consisting of water-buffalo and gold, to allow MK//TN to marry. In reply, Bula Pe//Mapo Tena says that she has nothing of value except her person, which she offers in the place of proper bridewealth:

83	*Mu bola inam leo kapa*	Go, tie your mother like a water buffalo,
84	*Fo leo-leo leo kapa*	Circling round like a water-buffalo,
85	*Ma mu tai te'om leo lilo*	And go weigh your aunt like gold,
86	*Fo benu-benu leo lilo*	Balanced gently like gold,
87	*Te au ina ndeli-lima-ku'u-tak*	For I am a woman without a ring on her finger
88	*Ma au feto liti-ei-tak*	And I am a girl without copper on her legs.

On hearing this answer, MK//TN feels the 'heart's regret of an orphan and the inner grief of a widow'. He takes up his father's bow and his uncle's blowpipe and leaves, with tears running down his cheeks and snot falling from his nose. 'Bow and blowpipe' – material objects that have long since disappeared from use on Roti – are significant in poetry as the principal objects with which young men 'hunt' blackbirds and green parrots.

Episode 3 (lines 99 to 176) repeats and elaborates similar events to those in Episode 2. This time MK//TN meets the woman Lide Muda//Adi Sole, to whom he reveals his plight and elaborates on his sorry condition:

111	*Au ana-ma Manu Kama*	I am the orphan Manu Kama
112	*Ma au falu-ina Tepa Nilu*	And I am the widow Tepa Nilu,
113	*Au a-ina ingu inan*	I have, as mother, the land of my mother,
114	*Ma au a-te'o leo te'on*	And I have, as aunt, the clan of my aunt.
115	*Ala hopo kedok Manu Kama*	Gruffly they mix lontar syrup for Manu Kama,
116	*Ma ala sode odak Tepa Nilu*	Sourly they serve rice to Tepa Nilu,
117	*Ala lo tuluk Tepa Nilu*	They offer things with a shove to Tepa Nilu
118	*Ma ala sipo le'ak Manu Kama*	And they take things with a tug from Manu Kama.
119	*Au ana-ma dai-lena-ng*	My orphaned state is increased,
120	*De au ana-ma-ng boe mai*	I am more an orphan than ever,

121 *Ma au falu-ina tolesi-ng*   My widowed state is made
                                         greater,
122 *Au falu-ina-ng boe mai*   I am more a widow than ever.

Lide Muda//Adi Sole offers to take him in, saying:

124 *Bo Manu Kama-e*   Oh, Manu Kama,
125 *Mai uma-t-ala uma leon*   Come to our house,
127 *Bo Tepa Nilu-e*   Oh, Tepa Nilu,
128 *Mai lo-t-ala lo leon*   Come to our home,
129 *Te au leo inam Silu Lilo boe*   For I will be like your mother,
                                         Silu Lilo,
130 *Ma au leo te'om Huka Besik*   And I will be like your aunt,
     boe!   Huka Besik!

MK//TN settles in and is properly served with rice and millet. He calls
Lide Muda//Adi Sole 'his mother of birth and his true aunt'.

    But again at dawn come the soft voices and gentle songs of the
blackbirds and parrots, and again he wakes his new-found mother and
aunt and requests bridewealth with which to marry:

153 *Bo ina-ng-o-ne*   Oh, my mother,
154 *Do bo te'o-ng-o-ne*   Oh, my aunt,
155 *Fo'a fanu mapa-deik*   Wake and stand up,
156 *Ma lelo afe manga-tuk!*   Come awake and sit up!
157 *Te siluk nai dulu so*   Morning is in the east
158 *Ma hu'ak nai langa so*   And dawn is at the head.
159 *Buluk-a bei Manu Kama inan*   If you are Manu Kama's mother
160 *Do buluk-a bei Tepa Nilu te'on*   Or if you are Tepa Nilu's aunt,
161 *Mu asa fe-ng-au koa*   Go buy for me a blackbird
162 *Ma mu tadi fe-ng-au nggia!*   And go get for me a green
                                         parrot!
163 *Te au ae [d]o Silu Lilok*   So I may call you Silu Lilok
164 *Ma au ae [d]o Huka Besik*   And I may call you Huka Besik

    But Lide Mudak//Adi Sole replies in the same way as Bula Pe//Mapo
Tena:

167 *Au ina ndeli-lima (-ku'u)-tak*   I am a woman without a ring on
                                         her finger
168 *Ma au feto liti-ei-tak*   And I am a girl without copper
                                         on her legs.

So, once more, with snot and tears, MK//TN sets off on his quest.

169 *Boe ma ana-ma Manu Kama*   So the orphan Manu Kama
170 *Le'a-na kou-koa-n*   Grabs his blackbird-hunting bow

171	*Ma falu-ina Tepa Nilu*	And the widow Tepa Nilu
172	*Nole-na fupu-nggia-n*	Snatches his parrot-hunting blowpipe.
173	*De neu tunga sanga ina bongin*	He goes in search of a mother of birth
174	*Ma neu afi sanga te'o te'en*	And goes to look for a true aunt.
175	*Na te lu dua tunga enok*	Two tears fall along the path
176	*Ma pinu telu tunga dalak*	And three drops of snot fall along the road.

Episode 4 (lines 177 to 232) describes MK//TN's next encounter with a woman, Lo Luli//Kala Palu, who offers to adopt him. This time, late at night, MK//TN hears the sound of drum and gongs, 'the resounding buffalo-skin drum and the booming goat-skin beat', and he is told the Sun and Moon are giving a feast at Rainbow Crossing and Thunder Round. MK//TN asks Lo Luli//Kala Palu to lead him to the celebration and there he is recognised by the Sun and Moon. Instead of being served properly, however, MK//TN is insulted:

215	*Boe ma la-lelak Manu Kama*	They recognise Manu Kama
216	*Ma la-lelak Tepa Nilu*	And they recognise Tepa Nilu,
217	*De ala ko'o fe Manu Kama nesuk*	They pick up a rice pestle for Manu Kama
218	*De lae [do] kana*	And they call it a small table,
219	*Ma ala keko fe Tepa Nilu batu*	And they push over a rock for Tepa Nilu
220	*De lae [do] kandela*	And they call it a chair.
221	*De malole-a so*	This was good
222	*Do mandak-a so*	And this was proper.
223	*Te boe ma ala ke te'i*	But then they cut and divide the meat
224	*Ma ala sode ndui*	And they spoon and scoop food,
225	*De ala fe Tepa Nilu betek*	They give Tepa Nilu millet
226	*Ma ala fe-n neu lu'ak*	And they give it to him in a rice basket,
227	*Ma fe Manu Kama bak*	They give Manu Kama lung
228	*Ma ala fe-n neu lokak*	And they give it to him in a meat bowl.
229	*Boe ma Manu Kama nasa-kedu*	So Manu Kama begins to sob
230	*Ma Tepa Nilu nama-tani*	And Tepa Nilu begins to cry.
231	*Boe ma ana fo'a fanu de la'o*	He gets up and leaves
232	*Ma ana lelo afe de lope*	And he stands up and goes.

This puts an end to this episode and MK//TN continues his search.

Episode 5 (lines 233 to 334), with which the chant concludes, is the longest and most complex segment of the poem. This time MK//TN meets the woman Kona Kek//Leli Deak and together they go to live in Lini Oe//Kene Mo. MK//TN, who has, by this time, become an able-bodied young man, begins to do work for his new mother and aunt, tapping lontar palms and working in the fields:

245	*Ana pale mane fe inan*	He taps male lontars for his mother
246	*Ma lenu feto fe te'on*	And saps female lontars for his aunt,
247	*Fe te'on Kona Kek*	To give to his aunt Kona Kek
248	*Ma fe inan Leli Deak*	And give to his mother Leli Deak.
249	*Neu lele bina fe inan*	He goes to clear dry fields for his mother
250	*Ma seku ndenu fe te'on*	And he prepares gardens for his aunt.

While MK//TN is working in a distant field, a ship appears and Kona Kek// Leli Deak, who sees it, goes to ask:

261	*Baluk se balu-n-o?*	This ship, whose ship is it?
262	*Ma tonak se tona-n-o?*	And this perahu, whose perahu is it?
263	*Balum fua loba Selak*	[If] your ship carries *loba*-bark from Selak,
264	*Tonam ifa lani Daik*	[If] your perahu bears *lani*-medicine from Daik,
265	*Na au asa ala fa dei*	Then, I'll buy a little
266	*Do au tadi ala fa dei!*	And I'll get a little!

The perahu's captain, Bui Kume//Lo Lengo, invites Kona Kek//Leli Deak on board, saying:

267	*Au Buik balu-na ia*	I, Buik, own this ship
268	*Do au Lok tona-na ia*	Or I, Lok, own this perahu.
269	*Lolek sio lai lain*	Nine fine things are on board
270	*Ma ladak falu lai ata*	And eight delightful things are on top.
271	*Laba kae mai lain*	Mount and climb, come on board,
272	*Ma tinga hene mai ata*	And step and ascend, come on top.
273	*Fo dale be na asa*	What pleases you, buy it,
274	*Ma pela be na peda-n!*	And what displeases you, put it back!

While Kona Kek//Leli Deak is on board and is busy rummaging through the goods on the ship, Bui Kume//Lo Lengu sets sail for Sela//Dai. Thus, when MK//TN returns home at the end of the day, he is told that his mother and aunt have been carried away and are now on Sela//Dai. On hearing this, MK//TN climbs into a 'pig's feeding trough and giant-clam shell' and sets off in search of his mother and aunt on Sela Sule//Dai Laka:

307	*Boe ma ana-ma Manu Kama*	So the orphan Manu Kama
308	*Ma falu-ina Tepa Nilu*	And the widow Tepa Nilu
309	*Hela hako hani bafin*	Pulls a pig's feeding trough
310	*Ma le'a kima lou metin*	And tugs the tide's giant-clam shell.
311	*Ana sa'e kima lou metin*	He perches upon the tide's clam shell
312	*Ma ana tai hako hani bafin*	And nestles in the pig's feeding trough.
313	*De ana tunga inan Kona Kek*	He searches for his mother, Kona Kek,
314	*Ma ana afi te'on Leli Deak*	And he looks for his aunt, Leli Deak,
315	*De leo Sela Sule neu*	And goes to Sela Sule
316	*Ma leo Dai Laka neu*	And goes to Dai Laka,
317	*Neu de nita inan Kona Kek*	Goes and sees his mother, Kona Kek,
318	*Ma nita te'on Leli Deak*	And sees his aunt, Leli Deak,
319	*Nai Sela Sule*	On Sela Sule
320	*Do nai Dai Laka*	Or on Dai Laka.

After having reached Sela//Dai, MK//TN rests for a while and then tells Bui Kume//Lo Lengu to take a message back to the lords and headmen of Lini Oe//Kene Mo from whence he has come. It is with this message that the chant ends:

323	*Bo Bui Kume-e*	Oh, Bui Kume,
324	*Do bo Lo Lengu-e*	Oh, Lo Lengu,
325	*Mai leo Lini Oe mu*	When you go back to Lini Oe
326	*Do leo Kene Mo mu*	Or go back to Kene Mo,
327	*Mu ma-fada lena Lini-la*	Go and tell the lords of Lini
328	*Do ma-fada lesi Kene-la*	Or tell the headmen of Kene,
329	*Mae: sek-o make-nilu neo-la*	Say: Come and see me
330	*Tasi-oe pepesi-la*	Where the water of the sea strikes the land.
331	*Dae lai Dain boe*	There is a homeland on Dain too

332	*Ma oe lai Selan boe*	And there is native-water on Selan too.
333	*De au lo-ai kada Selan*	My tomb-house will be on Selan
334	*Ma au late-dae kada Dain*	And my earthen-grave will be on Dain.

This final message announces an end to the quest. As in other similar chants, the orphan and widow find a home, but this home is 'a tomb-house and earthen-grave'. The message confirms the deep allegorical sense in which the chant is intended to be taken and reinforces its appropriateness to a funeral setting.

In Rotinese mortuary rituals the coffin is described as a 'ship' and burial involves the launching of this ship of the dead on its voyage to the other world. Meno, in his response to my questions about this chant, referred to 'Manu Kama's road to Dain//Tepa Nilu's path to Selan'.[4] The context of this reference makes it clear that he interprets MK//TN's journey as a passage to the grave, and that though each person's journey is different, the end is the same for all. This is the Rotinese equivalent of the medieval *memento mori* – the ultimate qualification on all human endeavour.

II

A formal description of Rotinese ritual language

Rotinese ritual language is based on a variety of cultural conventions. To understand the language and to facilitate comparisons with other languages that utilise some form of parallelism, it is essential to specify these cultural conventions as precisely as possible. For this reason, in previous publications (Fox 1971, 1974, 1975, 1977) I have attempted to fashion a formal terminology to describe the language. Here I wish to review briefly my description of ritual language and indicate how far my present studies have carried me.

Rotinese ritual language is characterised by a strict canonical parallelism. This means, in effect, that apart from a small number of unpaired forms – pronouns, connectives, 'prepositional' and a few other invariant elements (see Fox 1971:254, 255) – all elements must be paired. In formal terminology each individual element must form part of a 'dyadic set'. In composition dyadic sets produce parallel lines whose overwhelmingly most common poetic form is the couplet, though other serial arrangements of lines are entirely acceptable and are often considered as evidence of a greater mastery of the language. The elements that compose any particular dyadic set should, in their parallel lines (or occasionally in the two halves of a single line), correspond exactly in position and as far as possible in morphological structure. Paired elements often have the same number of syllables but, as far as I can determine, this is not a requirement. Hence parallel lines may be, and frequently are, of different syllable lengths. Lines may vary from seven to eleven syllables, with the majority hovering around the eight- or nine-syllable mark.

On the basis of a systematic study of the lexicon of Rotinese ritual language comprising approximately one-third of my present corpus of texts (Fox 1972a, 1972b), it is possible to specify in some detail the linkages among elements of the language. Any element that forms a dyadic set with another element is said to be 'linked' to that element, and the number of an element's links constitute its 'range'. An element that forms a set with only one other element has a 'range of one', whereas an element that forms sets with various other elements has a range equal to the number of its links.[5] Thus, for example, on the basis of all texts that I have so far translated and analysed, the word *nade(k)*, the generic word for 'name', only forms a set with the specific word for 'ancestral name', *tamo(k)*. Because of this single link, its range is one. Similarly, the word *nafi(k)* 'sea cucumber', only forms a set with *sisi(k)*, 'mollusc'; hence its range is also one. By contrast, the word *dae*, meaning 'earth, land, low, below', has links with eleven other elements, as do *ai*, meaning 'plant, tree, wood', and *tua*, the word for the lontar palm and its products. All these elements have a range of eleven.

From this point of view, linkages (and the semantic associations they imply) are more important than the dyadic sets themselves, since, on their own, individual dyadic sets tend to obscure more complex interrelations. It is critical to focus on linkages because the elements that form any one dyadic set may have a very different range of linkages. Thus, for example, the word *meo*, 'cat', has a range of one since it only links with *kue*, 'civet-cat', whereas *kue* has a range of four, linking not only with *meo* but also with *kode*, 'monkey', *bafi*, 'pig', and *fani*, 'bee'. Similarly, *asu*, the word for 'dog' that occurs only in ritual language, links with *busa*, the ordinary language word for 'dog'; *busa*, in turn, links as well with *manu*, 'chicken', and with other elements that form compound or complex dyadic expressions.

In the present dictionary of ritual language (Fox 1972b), which consists of just under 1400 lexical elements, every element can be identified precisely in terms of its specific linkages. By conservative enumeration that disregards all names and compound forms, 46 per cent of all elements link with only one other element. Were compounds treated as single forms, this percentage would rise considerably, to well over 60 per cent of the lexicon. In practice this means that a Rotinese poet must know in remarkable detail exactly which words form obligatory sets: that *kedu*, 'to sob', can only pair with *tani*, 'to cry'; or that *nitu*, 'spirit', can only pair with *mula*, 'ghost'. On the other hand, a substantial portion of the lexicon has a range greater than one, thus allowing the poet some flexibility in composition. Yet only a small proportion of these elements – thirty-three in the present dictionary – have a range greater than five. These multiple-linkage elements which include various words for directional orientation, words for 'earth', 'water', 'rock', and 'tree', plant-parts, body-parts, and verbs for expressing position or balance, may be considered to form a core of primary symbols in the ritual language (Fox 1975).

Graph procedures are eminently suited to represent the formal semantic associations among elements with multiple linkages (see Fox 1974:77–79, 1975:121–124), and it is possible to speculate that as the dictionary of ritual language develops it may yield one or two large networks that would encompass as much as half of the lexicon, leaving perhaps the other half as a particularistic array of single-linked elements. This would provide a more precise understanding of one aspect of the canonical structure of Rotinese ritual language.

Rotinese ritual language is, however, 'canonical' in another sense. In the terminology of Roman Jakobson, who devoted considerable attention to the study of parallelism (Fox 1977), the required lexical pairing of semantic elements and the network of associations that underlie this pairing represents a canonical ordering of the paradigmatic or 'metaphoric pole' of language (Jakobson and Halle 1956:76–82). Strictly speaking, parallelism refers to this patterning base on 'positional similarity'. But Rotinese ritual language is also remarkably well ordered along the syntagmatic, or what Jakobson called the 'metonymic pole' of language. In other words, phrases and lines in ritual language are frequently composed of recognisable formulae which, because of the strict requirements of parallelism, become redoubled in parallel formulae. Thus, a considerable portion of Rotinese ritual language consists of couplets and even longer sequences that are formulaic in both a paradigmatic and a syntagmatic sense.

Within a large corpus of textual materials the importance of these formulae becomes increasingly evident. Most poets – indeed all poets from whom I have been able to elicit a sufficient corpus on which to base a judgement – rely on what may be called, somewhat redundantly, 'standard' formulae, to which they may add some minor individual embellishment to distinguish their usage from that of other poets.[6] Thus individual poets develop their own personal 'style' in relation to certain 'standard' forms of their dialect area. Variations in formulae occur because personal style is regarded as important; yet within the general radius of any particular dialect area rival poets are expected to gather on ritual occasion to take turns in leading a chorus of fellow chanters. This requires poets to 'attune' themselves to one another and to 'play' with variations on their personal patterns of expression.

The interaction of the formulaic features of ritual language with the rules of parallel composition creates further complexity. Since approximately 50 per cent of the lexicon consists of elements that may pair with more than one other element, it is possible and indeed common for a formulaic line to couple with two (or more) variant, yet equally formulaic, lines. Individual poets on their own tend to settle on a single pattern for their couplets, but, in the company of other poets, they may alter their set patterns to suit the occasion.

To define and demonstrate what is in fact 'formulaic' in Rotinese ritual language is a difficult task requiring a large and varied corpus and, equally important, a historical perspective. It is in this respect that the Jonker text is crucial, since it may reasonably be considered to represent the standard pattern of ritual language at the turn of the century. I therefore propose to examine selected formulae in the text and compare them with formulae from various chants I have gathered since 1965.

The continuity of formulae in ritual language

In some sense, all of ritual language is formulaic. Certain formulae, however, occur repeatedly not simply as couplets but as a patterned sequence of lines. Invariably these sequences mark the beginning of a chant and episodes within it. More exactly, they punctuate a narrative sequence which, though strictly patterned, may have recourse to less obvious formulaic devices. Elsewhere I have referred to these formulae as 'formulaic chains' and developed a simple notation that could be used to generate a beginning for any mortuary chant (Fox 1971:244–245).

Because of the patterning of ritual language, it would be a relatively simple exercise to develop similar notational schemes for other formulaic chains – as indeed it is possible to devise a notational description for any sequence in ritual language. To indulge in such exercises, however, would be to overlook a crucial feature of ritual language composition, namely, that certain sequences occur frequently and are, as it were, the basic stock-in-trade of all poets in a particular dialect area. These sequences – to adopt another metaphor – are the reliable sub-routines of a poet's program, whereas other sequences may be highly individual in their compositional phrasing.

A crucial step toward understanding the 'formulaic' is to recognise the degree of difference in composition among the various sequences of a chant. This can only be done by the comparison of a large body of texts from different contemporary poets or by the comparison of historical texts with contemporary ones. Each procedure provides its own view of the nature of composition. Since *Manu Kama ma Tepa Nilu* is the only text that offers the possibility of historical comparison, I would like to devote my attention to a careful examination of some of the formulaic sequences whose continuity with contemporary forms makes them of particular interest. Specifically, I consider five examples of formulaic sequences in the text, some of which occur more than once. Comparisons, internally as well as with contemporary examples, are intended to highlight the way in which these sequences serve as recognisable narrative markers.

Genealogical introduction

The first twenty-four lines of *Manu Kama ma Tepa Nilu* are entirely composed of common formulae. The beginning of most mortuary chants relies on an opening sequence that provides the genealogical and connubial affiliations of the chief chant character. In some chants, this may cover two or more generations. For purposes of identification, this might be called a 'Genealogical Introduction' sequence. Ostensibly this sequence describes the marriage and birth of the chief chant character. What is critical, however, to a Rotinese audience is the information conveyed about this character by the succession of names. In MK//TN's case, his heavenly origins are revealed by the addition of the words for Sun and Moon as part of his father's name. As comparative illustration, the first eight lines of the text may be compared with the first eight lines of the chant, *Ndi Lonama ma Laki Elokama*, by S. Amalo (Fox 1972a:34–43).

	Manu Kama ma Tepa Nilu	
1	*Soku-lala Silu Lilo*	They lift Silu Lilo
2	*Ma lali-lala Huka Besi*	And they carry Huka Besi.
3	*Lelete neu sao*	She bridges the path to marry
4	*Do fifino neu tu*	Or joins the way to wed,
5	*Sao Kama Lai Ledo*	To marry Kama Lai of the Sun
6	*Do tu Nilu Neo Bulan*	Or to wed Nilu Neo of the Moon.
7	*De bongi-nala Tepa Nilu*	She gives birth to Tepa Nilu
8	*Ma lae-nala Manu Kama*	And brings forth Manu Kama.

Ndi Lonama ma Laki Elokama	
Soku Lisu Lasu Lonak	They lift Lisu Lasu Lonak
Ma lali Dela Musu Asuk	And they transfer Dela Musu Asuk.
De lelete neu sao	She bridges the path to marry
Ma fifino neu tu	And she joins the way to wed.
De ana tu Ndi Lonama	She weds Ndi Lonama

Ma sao Laki Elokama	And she marries Laki Elokama.
Boe ma ana bongi-na Solu Ndi	She gives birth to Solu Ndi
Ma ana lae-na Luli Laki	And she brings forth Luli Laki.

A trivial difference is in the use of verbal suffixes which indicate whether the subject and/or object of the verb is singular or plural. In ritual language this distinction is regarded as irrelevant since, as Rotinese explain, 'singulars' are always phrased as 'duals'. Another minor difference is in the sequencing of the verbs 'to marry': *sao//tu*. The *Manu Kama ma Tepa Nilu* text first uses *sao*, then *tu*, whereas S. Amalo reverses this order, using *tu*, then *sao*. Both, however, use the same formulae: *lelete neu sao//fifino neu tu*. This appears to be a relatively stable formulae in that *tu* and *sao* are not reversed (*lelete neu tu//fifino neu sao**), though there is nothing in the rules of the language, except common usage, to exclude such a phrasing. Nor is this the only formula that relies on the dyadic set of *lelete//fifino*. Thus, for example, the chanter, Seu Bai (Elia Pellondou) in the origin chant for *Sua Lai ma Batu Hu* uses the following formula:

Ana tao lelete batu	He makes a stone bridge
Ma ana tao fifino dae	And he makes an earthen path.
De ana tu inak-ka Soe Leli	Then he weds the woman, Soe Leli,
Ma sao fetok-ka Pinga Pasa	And marries the girl, Pinga Pasa.

It is also worth noting that there are less elaborate opening sequences. Meno, for example, commonly used a simpler sequence that substituted the verb *ifa*, which means 'to carry by cradling', for the verb *lali*, which has the sense of 'shifting' or 'transferring'. Both verbs can be used to refer to the bridal procession by which a woman is physically carried or led (see photograph, Fox 1980b:103) to her husband's house. An example of this is taken from the chant *Lilo Tola ma Koli Lusi* by Meno (Fox 1972a:85–97):

Ala soku-la Ole Masi	They lift Ole Masi
Ma ala ifa-la Bisa Oli	And they cradle Bisa Oli.
De ana tu Lusi Topu Lani	She marries Lusi Topu Lani
Ma ana sao Tola Tae Ama	And she weds Tola Tae Ama.
De bongi-na Lilo Tola	She gives birth to Lilo Tola
Ma ana lae-na Koli Lusi	And she brings forth Koli Lusi.

Death and abandonment

What might be termed a 'Death and Abandonment' sequence occurs twice in the text. Lines 13 to 16 recount the death of MK//TN's father and lines 21 to 24 repeat this sequence, with only a slight variation, in recounting the death of MK//TN's mother. As an episode ending, this sequence occurs in virtually all mortuary chants. As an example it is possible to compare lines from *Manu Kama ma Tepa Nilu* with those from the chant *Lilo Tola ma Koli Lusi*, in which Meno has given a slightly different embellishment to this formula.

	Manu Kama ma Tepa Nilu	
13	*Te hu Kama Lai Ledo lalo*	But Kama Lai of the Sun dies
14	*Ma Nilu Neo Bulan sapu*	And Nilu Neo of the Moon perishes.
15	*De sapu ela Manu Kama*	He dies leaving Manu Kama
16	*Ma lalo ela Tepa Nilu*	And he perishes leaving Tepa Nilu,
17	*Ela Tepa Nilu no inan*	Leaving Tepa Nilu with his mother
18	*Ma ela Manu Kama no te'on*	And leaving Manu Kama with his aunt [FZ].

Lilo Tola ma Koli Lusi	
Boe ma Lusi Topu Lani sapu	So Lusi Topu Lani dies
Ma Tola Tae Ama lalo	And Tola Tae Ama perishes.
Ana sapu ela Koli Lusi	He dies leaving Koli Lusi
Nanga-tu no te'on	To sit with his aunt [FZ]
Ma lalo ela Lilo Tola	And he perishes leaving Lilo
Nasa-lai no inan	To lean upon his mother.

The first twenty-four lines of the *Manu Kama ma Tepa Nilu* text are remarkable for their sustained and repeated use of common formulae. Two Death and Abandonment sequences are deftly linked to a Genealogical Introduction by the use of what is probably the single most common episode-ending formula in ritual language: the couplet *De malole-a so//Do mandak-a so* 'This was good or this was proper', which occurs in lines 11 and 12 and again in lines 19 and 20. Between the Genealogical Introduction and the death of MK//TN's father only a single formulaic couplet is inserted as reference to MK//TN's childhood. In many mortuary chants this can be a subject for considerable elaboration.

The composition of these first twenty-four lines can be analysed in terms of the following formulae: (1) Genealogical Introduction (lines 1–8); (2) Childhood Couplet (lines 9–10); (3) Good and Proper Couplet (lines 11–12); (4) Death and Abandonment Sequence (lines 13–18); (5) Good and Proper Couplet (lines 19–20); and (6) Death and Abandonment Sequence (lines 21–24). The theme of 'orphan and widow' is then announced and the chant proceeds to a set of formulae that initiate the second episode in MK//TN's life's journey.

Grief and the tearful encounter

Various expressions of grief mark transitions in the *Manu Kama ma Tepa Nilu* text. At six different junctures in the text MK//TN is described as crying, usually with tears and snot running down his face (lines 31–34, 40–42, 97–98, 175–176, 183–186, 229–230). By the conventions of parallelism, *lu* ('tears') and *pinu* ('snot') form an obligatory dyadic set, whereas *idu* ('nose') may form a set with either *mata* ('eye') or *nasu* ('cheek'). Similarly the verbs *-sasi//-tuda* ('to overflow, pour down, drop down') and the verbs, *-kedu//-tani*, ('to cry, weep, sob') also form pairs. All of the various descriptions of crying in the text use one or more of these sets, yet each is different and each expression varies.

Thus, the first of these expressions, which I have already noted, involves elaborate botanic comparisons to a number of sap- and juice-yielding plants. Other of these expressions, however, conform to a recognisable formulae. Thus, for example, when MK//TN leaves the woman Silu Lilo//Huka Besi, the following lines occur embedded in a set of other formulae:

97	*Nate lu lama-sasi nasu*	But tears pour down his cheeks
98	*Ma pinu lama-tuda idu*	And snot falls from his nose.

These lines may be compared, for example, to lines in any of a number of compositions: *Suti Solo no Bina Bane* by the blind chanter of Baa, L. Manoeain, or *Meda Manu ma Lilo Losi* by Meno.

Suti Solo no Bina Bane

Ala mai nda Bina Bane no Suti Solo	They meet Bina Bane and Suti Solo,
Pinu lama-tuda idu	Snot falls from his nose
Ma lu lama-sasi mata	And tears pour from his eyes.

Meda Manu ma Lilo Losi

De inan leo Ona Ba'a	Her mother like Ona Baa,
Pinu lama-tuda idu	Snot falls from her nose,
Ma te'on leo Lusi Lele	And her aunt like Lusi Lele,
Lu lama-sasi mata	Tears pour from her eyes.

The only difference in the contemporary examples is the use of eye (*mata*) instead of cheek (*nasu*).

Similar comparisons can be made in regard to the formula for sobbing and crying. Thus, when MK//TN is served meat improperly at the heavenly feast, the following lines occur as MK//TN prepares to leave:

229 *Boe ma Manu Kama nasa-kedu*   So Manu Kama begins to sob
230 *Ma Tepa Nilu nama-tani*   And Tepa Nilu begins to cry.

In the version of *Suti Solo ma Bina Bane* by Meno, similar lines occur at different junctures:

Suti Solo ma Bina Bane I

Te hu Suti bei name-tane   But Suti continues to cry
Ma Bina bei name-kedu   And Bina continues to sob.

Suti Solo ma Bina Bane II

Bina boe nasa-kedu   Bina thus begins to sob
Ma Suti boe name-tani   And Suti thus begins to weep.

Again in a chant *Doli Mo ma Lutu Mala* that reveals the origin of rice and millet, Meno has utilised the same formula, repeating in an entirely different context the theme of the quest in *Manu Kama ma Tepa Nilu*:

Doli Mo ma Lutu Mala

Doli Mo nasa-kedu   Doli Mo begins to sob
Ma Lutu Mala nama-tani   And Lutu Mala begins to weep,
Fo nasa-kedu sanga inan   Sobbing for his mother
Ma nama-tani sanga te'on   And crying for his aunt.

The fact is, however, that these various expressions of crying and weeping do not, on their own, qualify as formulaic sequences. At most they involve the use of only a couple of dyadic sets. Yet they invariably serve as transition markers indicating the end of an episode or event and the beginning of another. In the chant *Suti Solo ma Bina Bane* they mark each stage of an extended dialogue; in *Doli Mo ma Lutu Mala* they mark the first encounter with the seeds of rice and millet. Thus in these and other chants, including *Manu Kama ma Tepa Nilu*, they are themselves only part of a longer formulaic sequence. One version of this sequence could be described as the 'Tearful Encounter' sequence. It is possible to compare three examples of this in *Manu Kama ma Tepa Nilu:*

Tearful Encounter I

97   *Nate lu lama-sasi nasu*   But tears pour down his cheeks
98   *Ma pinu lama-tuda idu*   And snot falls from his nose.
99   *Boe ma lima leu la-nda*   Then arms go to meet
100 *Do langa leu la-tongo*   Or heads go to encounter
101 *Inak dua esa nade Lide Muda* Two women, one named Lide
                                    Muda
102 *Ma esa nade Adi Sole*   And one named Adi Sole.

Tearful Encounter II

175	*Nate lu dua tunga enok*	Two tears fall along the path
176	*Ma pinu telu tunga dalak*	And three drops of snot fall along the road,
177	*Boe ma langa leu la-tongo*	Then heads go to encounter
178	*Ma lima leu la-nda*	And arms go to meet
179	*Inak esa nade Lo Luli*	A woman named Lo Luli
180	*Ma fetok esa nade Kala Palu*	And a girl named Kala Palu.

Tearful Encounter III

229	*Boe ma Manu Kama nasa-kedu*	So Manu Kama begins to sob
230	*Ma Tepa Nilu nama-tani*	And Tepa Nilu begins to cry,
	... ...	... ...
233	*Boe ma lima leu la-nda*	Then arms go to meet
234	*Ma langa leu la-tongo*	And heads go to encounter,
235	*Mai tongo Leli Deak*	Come to encounter Leli Deak
236	*Do mai nda Kona Kek*	Or come to meet Kona Kek.

In these tearful encounters the women who meet MK//TN are able to strike up a dialogue and inquire about his condition and destination. These sequences can be compared with the extended sequence in *Suti Solo no Bina Bane* by L. Manoeain in which Suti Solo//Bina Bane encounters the women of Timor:

Boe ma ina Helok-ka mai nda duas	The Helok woman comes to meet the two
Ma fetok Sonobai mai tongo duas-sa	And the Sonobai girl comes to encounter the two.
Lu la-sasi mata	Tears pour from their eyes,
Ma pinu la-tuda idu	Snot falls from their nose.
Boe ma lae:	So they say:
Sala hata leo hata	What wrong like this
Ma singo hata leo hatak	And what mistake like this,
De ei pinu idu	This snot from your nose
Ma lu mata?	And these tears from your eyes?

As always, the tearful encounter dramatically refocuses on the condition of the orphan and widow.

Desire and the dawn encounter

Besides these tearful encounters, however, there is another set of 'encounters' in *Manu Kama ma Tepa Nilu*. We may call these 'Dawn Encounters'. In these encounters (lines 53–60, 137–146) green parrots and blackbirds come to sing to MK//TN. By the conventions of Rotinese poetry these birds are the iconic representation of sexually attractive women and their most alluring songs are always heard at dawn.

The two encounters are virtually identical (lines 53–54 = 137–138, 55–60 = 141–150); the only difference is the addition of two lines describing the colour of the dawn in the second encounter (lines 39–40). The shorter of these two passages is as follows:

53	*Boe ma faik esa ma-uni*	Then on one certain day
54	*Ma ledok dua ma-tee*	And at a particular time
55	*Siluk ana mai dulu*	Morning comes to the east
56	*Ma huak ana mai langa*	And dawn comes to the head.
57	*Boe ma koa bei timu dulu-la*	Blackbirds are still in the dawning east,
58	*Ala meli ei de ala mai;*	They lift their legs, they come.
59	*Ma nggia bei sepe langa-la*	And the green parrots are still at the reddening head,
60	*Ala la lida de ala mai*	They flap their wings, they come.

These lines merely set the scene for the birds' song. They are of interest, however, because they consist of common formulaic sequences and express crucial symbolic conventions about space and time. The first two lines, for example, contain one of the most recurrent episode-initiating formulae in Rotinese poetry. The following literal translation gives an idea of the specific dyadic sets that make up this formula:

Boe ma faik esa ma-uni	Then day one certain
Ma ledo dua ma-te′e	And sun two true

The sequence links the words for 'day' and 'sun', the numerals 'one' and 'two', and terms that assert 'specificity' and 'truth'. With some variation, the formula is a recognisable part of the repertoire of all the poets I have recorded. For example, the poet S. Amalo, and the poetess L. Adulilo use the following variant: *Faik esa ma-nunin ma ledo dua ma-teben* (*manunin* is an alternate form for *ma-unin* and *matee* for *ma-teben*). This usage is generally accepted as standard. On the other hand, both Meno and Seu Bai, who learned from him, use the variant *Faik esa ma-nunin ma ledok esa mateben*. The repetition of the numeral *esa*, meaning 'one', is an obvious imperfect parallelism and, as far as I can determine, used specifically by these two poets as a distinctive key signature to their compositions.

The second formula in these lines may be translated literally as follows:

Siluk ana mai dulu	Morning, it comes east,
Ma hu′ak ana mai langa	And dawn, it comes head.

The dyadic set, *dulu*//*langa*, which links 'east' and 'head', is one of several dyadic co-ordinates that structure Rotinese symbolic space. Other sets

link 'west' and 'tail', 'north' and 'left', and 'south' and 'right', thus representing the island in the image of an outstretched creature which is variously
conceived of as a crocodile, a buffalo, or a man (see Fox 1973:356–358). In
this symbolic structure the east, as the source of the dawn and of the renewal
of life, constitutes a privileged direction, and dawn encounters are potentially
auspicious in contrast to midnight encounters, which are generally dangerous and inauspicious. Dawn encounters and midnight encounters are both
standard poetic situations.[7] And there is even what might be called the 'False
Dawn Encounter' in which a chant character misjudges the time by mistak-
ing the dead of night for the early morning and so rises to meet his or her
doom. Thus, in the poem *Meda Manu ma Lilo Losi* by Meno, two chant
characters enter into a dialogue about the dawn:

Meda Manu//Lilo Losi says:

Te busa-a na-hou	For the dog has barked
De siluk lai dulu so	So daylight is in the east,
Ma manu-a kokoa	And the cock has crowed
De hu'ak lai langa so	So dawn is at the head.

Her mother, Lusi Lele//Ona Baa, replies:

Te siluk bei Ta dulu	Daylight is not yet in the east
Ma hu'ak bei ta langa	And dawn is not yet at the head.
Besak-ka bolo-do neu dua	Now night is at its height
Ma fati-lada neu telu	And dark is at its peak.

In the end, Meda Manu//Lilo Losi disregards her mother's advice and
leaves the house, only to be attacked by wandering spirits.

Tomb guarding and planting

As a final example of the use of formulae to mark transitions in narrative
structure, we may consider the way in which the *Manu Kama ma Tepa
Nilu* text concludes. Unlike the elaborate formulaic sequences that were
strung together at the beginning, the chant ends with a simple couplet:

333 *De au lo-ai kada Selan*	My tomb-house will be on Selan,
334 *Ma au late-dae kada Dain*	And my earthen-grave will be on Dain.

The reference here is to the wooden structure resembling a house that
Rotinese once commonly built over the grave to form a kind of tomb.
This ending is thus appropriate to a mortuary chant, but the use of this
single couplet, on its own, gives no indication of the fact that in other
mortuary chants similar couplets are generally part of longer, more elaborate formulaic sequences. At best this couplet may be considered as a
truncated evocation of these other sequences.

Two variant sequences, both commonly employed in mortuary chants, can be distinguished. One might be called the 'Tomb Guarding' variant; the other the 'Tomb Planting' variant. A short example of 'Tomb Guarding' can be taken from the poem *Pau Balo ma Bola Lungi* by S. Amalo. In this poem a bereaved daughter, Liu Pota//Menge Solu, watches over the tomb of her father:

Pota Popo sapu	Pota Popo perished
Ma Solu Oebau lalo	And Solu Oebau died.
De au anga-tu late-dae	Thus I sit upon an earthen-grave
Ma au asa-lai lo-ai	And I lean upon a tomb-house.

In this way, Liu Pota//Menge Solu is able to refuse Pau Balo and Bola Lungi's overtures and he must go off in search of another woman. As an example of 'Tomb Planting', the final sequence of the poem *Kea Lenga ma Lona Bala* by Seu Bai may be cited. The Ndaonese chant character *Kea Lenga//Lona Bala*, whose wife has died while he is away, sends a coconut and areca nut back to Ndao to be planted at his wife's grave. The poem concludes with these words:

Fo ela na la-boa langan	Let the coconut grow fruit at her head
Ma ela pua la-nggi ein	And let the areca nut sprout flower stalks at her feet,
Fo ela au falik leo Ndao u	So that when I return to Ndao
Na au lelu u late-dae	I may go to look upon her earthen-grave
Ma au tulek leo Folo u	And when I go back to Folo
Na au lipe u lo-ai	I may stare upon her tomb-house.

Concluding remarks

I proposed this paper as an introduction to the possibilities of Rotinese poetry. Only in analysing a long poem do various of these possibilities become evident. Although I have focused on a single text, I have tried to indicate some of the strategic levels at which this poetry can be read. In conclusion I would like to comment on the text in terms of three features of the poetry. These relate to oral intercommunication, narrative structure, and verbal authority.

The fact that the *Manu Kama ma Tepa Nilu* text was originally gathered at the beginning of the twentieth century did not prevent it from being taken up immediately as part of an ongoing dialogue among contemporary poet-chanters in Termanu. Meno responded to my public rendering and to my questions about the text by inserting comments in his own compositions. This is how chanters communicate with one another. Any chant can, and often does, relate to a variety of other chants – sometimes by the briefest of passing allusions (the change of a single word, for example, to imitate another chanter's style) and, at other times, by taking up a theme and elaborating on it. All of this is part of a dense web of oral intercommunication, much of which is so specific that it is difficult to recover outside the immediate context of a particular performance. Ritual gatherings were – and to a lesser extent still are – the occasions where chanters would gather to vie with one another in performance. This basic aspect of social life provides the means of maintaining oral intercommunication and collective textual elaboration.

The formulaic structures of *Manu Kama ma Tepa Nilu* serve to facilitate this oral intercommunication. My argument in the paper has been that although Rotinese poetry is virtually all 'formulaic', certain formulaic sequences are distinguishable as markers at the beginnings and ends of episodes. These routine sequences are remarkably similar among all poets and stand out as such in contrast to the subtler composition of other lines. The fact that the *Manu Kama ma Tepa Nilu* text was mistaken for a contemporary chant by several Rotinese was due in large part, I suspect, to the prominence of these formulaic markers throughout its narrative structure.

The narrative structure of *Manu Kama ma Tepa Nilu* is similar in form to the structures that articulate virtually all long Rotinese chants. These chants invariably recount a tale of some sort and a high proportion of them feature a journey. Here there is a coincidence between a formal narrative order and an image of the course of life. In the predominant Rotinese view, enhanced as it is with ideas from Christianity, life is conceived of as a successive movement, consisting of a series of transformations, leading to an eventual end. This progressive development from an initial base – a process that can also be represented by various botanic metaphors – is not conceived of as turning back upon itself or as ending in a cyclical return. Instead it is articulated as an ordered sequence with a clear beginning and a definite end. Such sequences are of common occurrence throughout Rotinese culture and constitute what I would argue are a privileged image in the overall structuring of Rotinese cultural conceptions.[8]

This privileged status of the ordered sequence contributes to the authority with which certain texts are endowed. Although ritual language can be used in any situation of formal interaction, there are only two occasions for which there exist established canonical poems: celebrations of origin and celebrations of conclusion. Similarly, there are only two kinds of canonical poems: origin chants and mortuary chants. Origin chants bless the beginnings of specific activities. They recount the founding of these activities and the acquisition of the essential objects with which they are associated: the origin of fire and of tools, and the building of the first house; the origin of the first seeds of rice and millet and their transmission and planting; the origin of coloured dyes, of weaving, and the creation of cloth. By contrast, mortuary chants recount the demise of an individual, but do so by comparing the individual to a character whose life course follows a definite pattern.

The formulaic utterances of ritual language are regarded as ancestral wisdom. A chanter is thus the medium of an authoritative cultural voice which speaks decisively at the beginnings and ends of sequences that define an order to life itself.

III

Reference text

Ana-Ma Manu Kama ma Falu-Ina Tepa Nilu

1	*Soku-lala Silu Lilo*	They lift Silu Lilo
2	*Ma lali-lala Huka Besi*	And they carry Huka Besi.
3	*Lelete neu sao*	She bridges the path to marry
4	*Do fifino neu tu*	Or joins the way to wed,
5	*Sao Kama Lai Ledo*	To marry Kama Lai of the Sun
6	*Do tu Nilu Neo Bulan*	Or to wed Nilu Neo of the Moon.
7	*De bongi-nala Tepa Nilu*	She gives birth to Tepa Nilu
8	*Ma lae-nala Manu Kama*	And brings forth Manu Kama.
9	*De na-lelak fiti fulik*	He learns to play with *fulik* marbles
10	*Ma na-lelak selo so'ek*	And learns to spear the coconut shell.
11	*De malole-a so*	This was good
12	*Do mandak-a so*	Or this was proper.
13	*Te hu Kama Lai Ledo lalo*	But Kama Lai of the Sun dies
14	*Ma Nilu Neo Bulan sapu*	And Nilu Neo of the Moon perishes.
15	*De sapu ela Manu Kama*	He dies leaving Manu Kama
16	*Ma lalo ela Tepa Nilu*	And he perishes leaving Tepa Nilu,
17	*Ela Tepa Nilu no inan*	Leaving Tepa Nilu with his mother
18	*Ma ela Manu Kama no te'on*	And leaving Manu Kama with his aunt [FZ]

19	*De malole-a so*	This was good
20	*Do mandak-a so*	Or this was proper.
21	*Te hu neu ma Silu Lilo ana lalo*	But then Silu Lilo, she dies,
22	*Ma Huka Besi ana sapu*	And Huka Besi, she perishes.
23	*De sapu ela Manu Kama*	She dies leaving Manu Kama
24	*Ma lalo ela Tepa Nilu*	And she perishes leaving Tepa Nilu.
25	*De ana-ma Manu Kama*	An orphan is Manu Kama
26	*Ma falu-ina Tepa Nilu*	And a widow is Tepa Nilu.
27	*Ana sala ama-na bai*	He lacks a father too,
28	*Ma singo ina-na bai*	He misses a mother too,
29	*Sala to'o-na bai*	Lacks a mother's brother too,
30	*Ma singo te'o-na bai*	And misses a father's sister too.
31	*De lu ko boa na'u*	Tears like *bidara* fruit in the grass,
32	*Ma pinu kaitio telan*	Snot like *kaitio*[-leaves] in the underbrush,
33	*Lama-noma oba-tula*	They pour like juice from a tapped *gewang*
34	*Do lama-titi ate lasi*	And flow like sap from an old *ate.*
35	*Boe ma inak ia Bula Pe*	Then the woman Bula Pe
36	*Ma fetok ia Mapo Tena*	And the girl Mapo Tena
37	*Lelu naka-nae nita-n*	Looks and stares at him,
38	*Ma lipe nala-mula nita-n*	Gazes and inspects him,
39	*De ana-ma Manu Kama*	The orphan Manu Kama,
40	*Lu dua-o dua*	Tears falling two by two,
41	*Ma falu-ina Tepa Nilu*	The widow Tepa Nilu,
42	*Pinu telu-o telu*	Snot running three by three.
43	*Boe ma na-lo lelena*	So she calls out loudly
44	*Ma na-nggou ngganggali*	And she shouts out clearly.
45	*Nae: bo ana-ma Manu Kama*	She says: Oh, orphan Manu Kama,
46	*Do bo falu-ina Tepa Nilu*	Oh, widow Tepa Nilu,
47	*Mai, te Silu Lilok nde au*	Come, Silu Lilok am I
48	*Do Huka Besik nde au*	Or Huka Besik am I.
49	*Boe ma ta nae Bula Pe*	Do not say Bula Pe
50	*Te nae Silu Lilok*	But say Silu Lilok,
51	*Ma ta nae Mapo Tena*	And do not say Mapo Tena
52	*Te nae Huka Besik*	But say Huka Besik.
53	*Boe ma faik esa ma-uni*	Then on one certain day
54	*Ma ledok dua ma-tee*	And at a particular time

55	*Siluk ana mai dulu*	Morning comes to the east
56	*Ma hu'ak ana mai langa*	And dawn comes to the head.
57	*Boe ma koa bei timu dulu-la*	Blackbirds are still in the dawning east,
58	*Ala meli ei de ala mai*	They lift their legs, they come.
59	*Ma nggia bei sepe langa-la*	And the green parrots are still at the reddening head,
60	*Ala la lida de ala mai*	They flap their wings, they come.
61	*Mai boe ma ala kako dodoe hala-n-ala*	Then, they sing with soft voices
62	*Ma ala hele memese dasi-n-ala*	And they warble with gentle songs.
63	*De ala kako-lala Manu Kama dalen*	They sing to Manu Kama's heart
64	*Ma hele-lala Tepa Nilu tein*	And warble to Tepa Nilu's inner being.
65	*Boe ma ana-ma Manu Kama*	The orphan Manu Kama
66	*Ma falu-ina Tepa Nilu*	And the widow Tepa Nilu,
67	*Ana fafae neu inan*	He wakes his mother
68	*Ma o'ofe neu te'on*	And shakes his aunt,
69	*Ma nae: bo ina-ng-o-ne*	And says: Oh, my mother,
70	*Do bo te'o-ng-o-ne*	Oh, my aunt,
71	*Fo'a fanu mapa-deik*	Wake and stand up,
72	*De lelo afe manga-tuk*	Come awake and sit up,
73	*Te siluk nai dulu so*	Morning is in the east
74	*Ma hu'ak nai langa so*	And dawn is at the head.
75	*Buluk-a ma-dalek nai o*	Now have a heart
76	*Do ma-teik nai o*	And be concerned [have a stomach].
77	*Mu asa fe-ng-au koa halak*	Go buy for me the blackbird's voice
78	*Do tadi fe-ng-au nggia dasik*	Or get for me the green parrot's whistle
79	*Fo ela au a-hala nggia halak*	So that I may make voice to the blackbird's voice
80	*Ma au a-dasi koa dasik*	And I may sing to the green parrot's song
81	*Fo sama leo inang boe*	That you may be just like my mother
82	*Do deta leo te'ong boe*	Or that you may be similar to my aunt.
83	*Boe ma nae: mu bola inam leo kapa*	Then she says: Go, tie your mother like a water-buffalo,

84	*Fo leo-leo leo kapa*	Circling round like a water-buffalo,
85	*Ma mu tai te'om leo lilo*	And go weigh your aunt like gold,
86	*Fo benu-benu leo lilo*	Balanced gently like gold,
87	*Te au ina ndeli-lima-ku'u-tak*	For I am a woman without a ring on her finger
88	*Ma au feto liti-ei-tak*	And I am a girl without copper on her legs.
89	*Boe ma ana-ma Manu Kama*	So the orphan Manu Kama
90	*Ma falu-ina Tepa Nilu*	And the widow Tepa Nilu,
91	*Ana sale dale-ana-ma-na*	He has the heart's regret of an orphan
92	*Ma ana tuka tei falu-ina-na*	And has the inner grief of a widow.
93	*Besak-a le'a-na aman kou-na*	Now he grabs his father's bow
94	*Ma nole-na to'on fupu-na*	And snatches his uncle's blowpipe.
95	*De ana lope no hu'a-langak*	He goes, swinging his arms, with dawn at the head,
96	*Ma ana la'o no silu-duluk*	And he goes, lifting his legs, with morning in the east,
97	*Na te lu lama-sasi nasu*	But tears pour down his cheeks
98	*Ma pinu lama-tuda idu.*	And snot falls from his nose.
99	*Boe ma lima leu la-nda*	Then arms go to meet
100	*Do langa leu la-tongo*	Or heads go to encounter
101	*Inak dua esa nade Lide Muda*	Two women, one named Lide Muda
102	*Ma esa nade Adi Sole*	And one named Adi Sole.
103	*De Lide Mudak na-nggou*	Lide Muda shouts out.
104	*Nae: bo Manu Kama-e*	She says: Oh, Manu Kama,
105	*Leo dae be mu?*	To what land are you going?
106	*Ma Adi Sole na-lo*	And Adi Sole calls out.
107	*Nae: bo Tepa Nilu-e*	She says: Oh, Tepa Nilu,
108	*Leo oe be mu?*	To what water are you going?
109	*Ma nae: aue! o Lide Mudak*	And he says: Aue! Oh, Lide Mudak,
110	*Do o Adi Sole!*	Oh, Adi Sole!
111	*Au ana-ma Manu Kama*	I am the orphan Manu Kama
112	*Ma au falu-ina Tepa Nilu*	And I am the widow Tepa Nilu.
113	*Au a-ina ingu inan*	I have, as mother, the land of my mother,

114	*Ma au a-te'o leo te'on*	And I have, as aunt, the clan of my aunt.
115	*Ala hopo kedok Manu Kama*	Gruffly they mix lontar syrup for Manu Kama,
116	*Ma ala sode odak Tepa Nilu*	Sourly they serve rice to Tepa Nilu.
117	*Ala lo tuluk Tepa Nilu*	They offer things with a shove to Tepa Nilu,
118	*Ma ala sipo le'ak Manu Kama*	They take things with a tug from Manu Kama,
119	*Au ana-ma dai-lena-ng*	My orphaned state is increased,
120	*De au ana-ma-ng boe mai*	I am more an orphan than ever,
121	*Ma au falu-ina tolesi-ng*	My widowed state is made greater,
122	*Au falu-ina-ng boe mai*	I am more a widow than ever.
123	*Boe ma inak ia Lide Mudak nae:*	So this woman Lide Mudak says:
124	*Bo Manu Kama-e*	Oh, Manu Kama,
125	*Mai uma-t-ala uma leon!*	Come to our house!
126	*Ma fetok ia Adi Sole nae:*	And the girl Adi Sole says:
127	*Bo Tepa Nilu-e*	Oh, Tepa Nilu,
128	*Mai lo-t-ala lo leon*	Come to our home,
129	*Te au leo inam Silu Lilo boe*	For I will be like your mother Silu Lilo,
130	*Ma au leo te'om Huka Besik boe!*	And I will be like your aunt Huka Besik!
131	*Hu ndia de ala dengu doli Manu Kama*	Therefore they pound rice for Manu Kama
132	*De ala hao hade Manu Kama*	And they serve rice to Manu Kama.
133	*Hu ndia de ala tutu lutu Tepa Nilu*	Therefore they beat millet for Tepa Nilu
134	*De ala fati bete Tepa Nilu*	And they offer millet to Tepa Nilu.
135	*Boe ma nae do ina bongin*	So he calls her his mother of birth
136	*Ma nae do te'o teen*	And he calls her his true aunt.
137	*Boe ma faik esa ma-uni*	Then on one definite day
138	*Ma ledok dua ma-tee*	And at a certain time,
139	*Pila poe-oe-na-n*	Red as a shrimp in water
140	*Ma modo masala-na-n*	And yet still green,
141	*Siluk ana mai dulu*	Morning comes to the east,
142	*Ma hu'ak ana mai langa*	Dawn comes to the head.

143	*Boe ma koa bei timu-dulu-la*	Blackbirds are still in the dawning east,
144	*Ala meli ei de ala mai*	They lift their legs, they come.
145	*Ma nggia bei sepe-langa-la*	And green parrots are still at the reddening head,
146	*Ala la lida de ala mai*	They flap their wings, they come.
147	*Mai boe ma ala kako dodoe hala-n-ala*	There, they sing with soft voices
148	*Ma ala hele memese dasi-n-ala*	And they warble with gentle songs,
149	*De ala kako-lala Manu Kama dalen*	They sing to Manu Kama's heart,
150	*Ma hele-lala Tepa Nilu tein*	They warble to Tepa Nilu's inner being.
151	*Boe ma Manu Kama fafae Lide Mudak*	Then Manu Kama wakes Lide Mudak
152	*Ma Tepa Nilu o'ofe Adi Sole*	And Tepa Nilu shakes Adi Sole.
153	*Nae: bo ina-ng-o-ne*	He says: Oh, my mother,
154	*Do bo te'o-ng-o-ne*	Oh, my aunt,
155	*Fo'a fanu mapa-deik*	Wake and stand up,
156	*Ma lelo afe manga-tuk!*	Come awake and sit up!
157	*Te siluk nai dulu so*	Morning is in the east
158	*Ma hu'ak nai langa so*	And dawn is at the head.
159	*Buluk-a bei Manu Kama inan*	If you are Manu Kama's mother
160	*Do buluk-a bei Tepa Nilu te'on*	Or if you are Tepa Nilu's aunt,
161	*Mu asa fe-ng-au koa*	Go buy for me a blackbird
162	*Ma mu tadi fe-ng-au nggia*	And go get for me a green parrot,
163	*Te au ae [d]o Silu Lilok*	So I may call you Silu Lilok,
164	*Ma au ae [d]o Huka Besik*	And I may call you Huka Besik.
165	*Boe ma inak ia Lide Mudak*	So this woman Lide Mudak
166	*Ma fetok ia Adi Sole nata ma nae:*	And this girl Adi Sole answers and says:
167	*Au ina ndeli-lima [-ku'u]-tak*	I am a woman without a ring on her finger
168	*Ma au feto liti-ei-tak*	And I am a girl without copper on her legs.
169	*Boe ma ana-ma Manu Kama*	So the orphan Manu Kama
170	*Le'a-na kou-koa-n*	Grabs his blackbird-hunting bow
171	*Ma falu-ina Tepa Nilu*	And the widow Tepa Nilu
172	*Nole-na fupu-nggia-n*	Snatches his parrot-hunting blowpipe.

173	*De neu tunga sanga ina bongin*	He goes in search of a mother of birth
174	*Ma neu afi sanga te'o te'en*	And goes to look for a true aunt.
175	*Na te lu dua tunga enok*	Two tears fall along the path
176	*Ma pinu telu tunga dalak*	And three drops of snot fall along the road.
177	*Boe ma langa leu la-tongo*	Then heads go to encounter
178	*Ma lima leu la-nda*	And arms go to meet
179	*Inak esa nade Lo Luli*	A woman named Lo Luli
180	*Ma fetok esa nade Kala Palu*	And a girl named Kala Palu.
181	*Nae: bo Manu Kama-e*	She says: Oh, Manu Kama,
182	*Do bo Tepa Nilu-e*	Oh, Tepa Nilu,
183	*O lu-mata leo hatak*	Why the tears from your eyes
184	*Do o pinu-idu leo hatak?*	Or why the snot from your nose?
185	*Boe ma nae: au lu mata sanga inang*	So he says: The tears in my eyes seek my mother
186	*Ma au pinu idu afi te'ong*	And the snot of my nose looks for my aunt,
187	*Sanga inang Silu Lilok*	Seeks my mother Silu Lilok
188	*Ma afi te'ong Huka Besik*	And looks for my aunt Huka Besik.
189	*Ma nae: ata uma-t-ala uma leon*	And she says: Our home, come to our home
190	*Ma ata lo-t-ala lo leon!*	And our house, come to our house!
191	*Te au sama leo inam boe*	For I will be like your mother
192	*Ma deta leo te'om boe*	And I will be similar to your aunt.
193	*Bolok-ala tao do*	Late in the evening,
194	*Ma fatik-ala tao lada*	In the middle of the night,
195	*Boe ma lama-nene lololo*	They constantly listen to,
196	*Ma lama-nia ndanda*	They continually hear,
197	*Labu kapa behoe*	The resounding buffalo-skin drum
198	*Ma dele bi'i bendena*	And the booming goat-skin beat.
199	*Boe ma na-tane neu inan*	So he asks his mother
200	*Ma teteni neu te'on nae:*	And questions his aunt, saying:
201	*Labu sila leme be mai*	The drums come from where
202	*Ma meko sila leme be mai?*	And the gongs come from where?
203	*Ma nae: leme Elu Ladi mai*	And she says: From Rainbow Crossing
204	*Do leme Tata Feo mai*	Or from Thundering Round,
205	*Te Bulan ana tati hani*	For the Moon kills his animals

206	*Ma Ledo ana soe usu*	And the Sun slaughters his stock.
207	*Nae: na la'o le'a au dei*	He says: Lift your legs, carry me then,
208	*Ma lope nuni au dei*	And move your arms, lead me then.
209	*Fo meko teu taka-neni*	Let us go and see the gongs
210	*Ma labu teu ta-nilu*	And let us go and observe the drums.
211	*Boe ma leo Elu Ladi leu*	So they go to Rainbow Crossing
212	*Ma leo Tata Feo leu*	And they go to Thundering Round.
213	*Leu te Bulan ana tao feta*	They go, for the Moon gives a feast
214	*Ma Ledo ana tao dote*	And the Sun has a celebration.
215	*Boe ma la-lelak Manu Kama*	They recognise Manu Kama
216	*Ma la-lelak Tepa Nilu*	And they recognise Tepa Nilu.
217	*De ala ko'o fe Manu Kama nesuk*	They pick up a rice mortar for Manu Kama
218	*De lae [do] kana*	And they call it a small table
219	*Ma ala keko fe Tepa Nilu batu*	And they push over a rock for Tepa Nilu
220	*De lae [do] kandela*	And they call it a chair.
221	*De malole-a so*	This was good,
222	*Do mandak-a so*	And this was proper.
223	*Te boe ma ala ke te'i*	But then they cut and divide the meat
224	*Ma ala sode ndui*	And they spoon and scoop food.
225	*De ala fe Tepa Nilu betek*	They give Tepa Nilu millet
226	*Ma ala fe-n neu lu'ak*	And they give it to him in a rice basket,
227	*Ma fe Manu Kama bak*	They give Manu Kama lung
228	*Ma ala fe-n neu lokak*	And they give it to him in a meat bowl.
229	*Boe ma Manu Kama nasa-kedu*	So Manu Kama begins to sob
230	*Ma Tepa Nilu nama-tani*	And Tepa Nilu begins to cry.
231	*Boe ma ana fo'a fanu de la'o*	He gets up and leaves
232	*Ma ana lelo afe de lope*	And he stands up and goes.
233	*Boe ma lima leu la-nda*	Arms go to meet
234	*Ma langa leu la-tongo*	And heads go to encounter,
235	*Mai tongo Leli Deak*	Come to encounter Leli Deak
236	*Do mai nda Kona Kek*	Or come to meet Kona Kek.
237	*De na-ina Leli Deak*	Then he has a mother Leli Deak

238	*Ma na-te'o Kona Kek*	And he has an aunt Kona Kek.
239	*De noke nae Silu Lilok*	He asks to call her Silu Lilok
240	*Ma hule nae Huka Besik*	And he requests to call her Huka Besik,
241	*Te bei Lini Oe bobongin*	For she is still in Lini Oe's birth group
242	*Ma bei Kene Mo lalaen*	And she is still in Kene Mo's descent group.
243	*Boe ma ala leo Lini Oe leu*	So they go to Lini Oe
244	*Do leo Kene Mo leu*	Or they go to Kene Mo.
245	*Ana pale mane fe inan*	He taps male lontars for his mother
246	*Ma lenu feto fe te'on*	And saps female lontars for his aunt,
247	*Fe te'on Kona Kek*	To give to his aunt Kona Kek
248	*Ma fe inan Leli Deak*	And give to his mother Leli Deak.
249	*Neu lele bina fe inan*	He goes to clear dry fields for his mother
250	*Ma seku ndenu fe te'on*	And he prepares gardens for his aunt.
251	*Ana-ma Manu Kama*	The orphan Manu Kama
252	*Falu-ina Tepa Nilu*	And the widow Tepa Nilu
253	*Nala neu lele bina*	Goes to clear dry fields
254	*Ma nita neu seku ndenu*	And goes to prepare gardens
255	*Nai tadu-hade dea*	At a distant rice village
256	*Ma nai nggolo-bete dea*	And a distant millet spot.
257	*Boe ma Buik tona-na toda*	Then Buik's ship appears
258	*Ma Lok balu-na sou*	And Lok's perahu becomes visible.
259	*De Leli Deak lipe nita-n*	Leli Deak looks and sees it
260	*Ma Kona Kek lelu hapu-n*	And Kona Kek stares and discovers it.
261	*Boe ma nae: baluk se balu-n-o?*	She says: This ship, whose ship is it?
262	*Ma tonak se tona-n-o?*	And this perahu, whose perahu is it?
263	*Balum fua loba Selak*	[If] your ship carries *loba*-bark from Selak,
264	*Tonam ifa lani Daik*	[If] your perahu bears *lani*-medicine from Daik,
265	*Na au asa ala fa dei*	Then, I'll buy a little
266	*Do au tadi ala fa dei!*	And I'll get a little!

267	*Nae: au Buik balu-na ia*	He says: I, Buik, own this ship
268	*Do au Lok tona-na ia*	Or I, Lok, own this perahu.
269	*Lolek sio lai lain*	Nine fine things are on board
270	*Ma ladak falu lai ata*	And eight delightful things are on top.
271	*Laba kae mai lain*	Mount and climb, come on board,
272	*Ma tinga hene mai ata*	And step and ascend, come on top.
273	*Fo dale be na asa*	What pleases you, buy it,
274	*Ma pela be na peda-n!*	And what displeases you, put it back!
275	*De inak ia Kona Kek*	This woman Kona Kek
276	*Ma fetok ia Leli Deak*	And this girl Leli Deak
277	*Tinga hene neu lain*	Steps and ascends on board,
278	*Do laba kae neu ata*	Mounts and climbs on top.
279	*Mai de peda esa nggao esa*	There, she puts one thing back, takes another,
280	*Ma hoi esa nggali esa*	And picks up one thing, throws another back.
281	*Sek-o inak ia Bui Kume*	Indeed, this woman is for Bui Kume
282	*Ma fetok ia Lo Lengu*	And this girl is for Lo Lengu,
283	*Ina malei selak*	A woman to increase the cargo
284	*Ma feto ma lalo banak*	And a girl to add to the load.
285	*Boe ma ala kale kola dua-dua*	So they shake the oar-rings two by two,
286	*De ala la'o*	They leave,
287	*Ma ala hela tuku telu-telu*	And they pull the oars three by three,
288	*De ala leu*	They go,
289	*Leko la Selan leu*	Turning the sail toward Sela
290	*Do pale uli Dain leu*	Or guiding the rudder toward Dai.
291	*Boe te ana-ma Manu Kama*	So the orphan Manu Kama
292	*Ma falu-ina Tepa Nilu*	And the widow Tepa Nilu
293	*Ledo neu hulu manun*	At the time of sun for gathering chicken
294	*Ma fai neu hani bafin*	And at the time of day for feeding pigs,
295	*Ma ana seku ndenu lolo-fali*	[And] he returns from preparing gardens

296	*Ma ana lele bina diku-dua*	And he comes back from clearing fields.
297	*De uma nala uma mai*	He reaches his home
298	*Ma lo nala lo mai*	And reaches his house.
299	*Mai boe ma inak-a Lide Mudak*	There the woman Lide Mudak
300	*Do fetok-ia Adi Sole nafada nae:*	Or the girl Adi Sole speaks, saying:
301	*Inam nai Selan so*	Your mother is on Sela
302	*Do te'om nai Dain so*	And your aunt is on Dai,
303	*Sela mana-babi boa-la*	Sela concealed behind great *boa* trees
304	*Ma Dai mana-hapa piko-la*	And Dai covered by great *piko* trees.
305	*Fua leni-n ana so*	They have carried her away
306	*Ma ifa leni-n ana so*	And have cradled her away.
307	*Boe ma ana-ma Manu Kama*	So the orphan Manu Kama
308	*Ma falu-ina Tepa Nilu*	And the widow Tepa Nilu
309	*Hela hako hani bafin*	Pulls a pig's feeding trough
310	*Ma le'a kima lou metin*	And tugs the tide's giant-clam shell.
311	*Ana sa'e kima lou metin*	He perches upon the tide's clam shell
312	*Ma ana tai hako hani bafin*	And nestles in the pig's feeding trough.
313	*De ana tunga inan Kona Kek*	He searches for his mother Kona Kek
314	*Ma ana afi te'on Leli Deak*	And he looks for his aunt Leli Deak
315	*De leo Sela Sule neu*	And goes to Sela Sule
316	*Ma leo Dai Laka neu*	And goes to Dai Laka,
317	*Neu de nita inan Kona Kek*	Goes and sees his mother Kona Kek
318	*Ma nita te'on Leli Deak*	And sees his aunt Leli Deak
319	*Nai Sela Sule*	On Sela Sule
320	*Do nai Dai Laka*	Or on Dai Laka.
321	*Ana sungu Dain fai dua*	He sleeps on Dai for two days
322	*Do ana pe'uk Selan ledok telu*	And he rests on Sela for three days [suns].
323	*Boe ma nae: bo Bui Kume-e*	Then he says: Oh, Bui Kume,
324	*Do bo Lo Lengu-e*	Oh, Lo Lengu,
325	*Mai leo Lini Oe mu*	When you go back to Lini Oe
326	*Do leo Kene Mo mu*	Or go back to Kene Mo,

327	*Mu ma-fada lena Lini-la*	Go and tell the lords of Lini
328	*Do ma-fada lesi Kene-la*	Or tell the headmen of Kene,
329	*Mae: sek-o maka-nilu neo-la*	Say: Come and see me
330	*Tasi-oe pepesi-la*	Where the water of the sea strikes the land.
331	*Dae lai Dain boe*	There is a homeland on Dain too
332	*Ma oe lai Selan boe*	And there is native-water on Selan too.
333	*De au lo-ai kada Selan*	My tomb-house will be on Selan
334	*Ma au late-dae kada Dain*	And my earthen-grave will be on Dain.

7

THE CASE OF THE PURLOINED STATUES: THE POWER OF WORDS AMONG THE LIONESE

ERIKO AOKI

Introduction

This paper deals with problems concerning the efficacy of ritual language.[1] These problems will be investigated in relation to a specific case of stolen communal heirlooms which occurred during the period of my field research in 1983.[2]

In dealing with these problems, we should distinguish two aspects of the efficacy of ritual language: the power of words which are believed to bring to realisation what is intended, and the effectiveness of words in appealing to the imagination.

Like other peoples in central Flores,[3] the Lionese people have a strong belief in the power of words. They insist that curses can kill, discourage, or cause misfortune to persons who are antagonistic to them, and that spells can protect them from misfortune.

Although the thieves who stole the heirlooms were repeatedly cursed in ritual language, they did not seem to die, nor did they reveal themselves, nor return the heirlooms. How could the inefficacy of these curses, then, be reconciled with Lionese belief in the power of words and their confidence in the effectiveness of words?

By interpreting the phrases in the ritual speeches presented in the course of events prompted by the disappearance of the heirlooms, I hope to make clear the Lionese concept of their society and the social role of ritual language. Furthermore, on the basis of this analysis of specific examples of Lionese ritual language, I would like to comment on the general significance of the study of ritual language. And then, by exploring the explanation for the failure of the curse, I would like to elucidate the Lionese theory of the power of words.

The Lionese people

The Lionese population numbers approximately 130,000.[4] The data I use in this paper come from a village which is located on a mountain in the central part of the Lionese-speaking area. The Lionese language belongs to the Bima–Sumba language group and may be considered a dialect of the Endenese language.[5] The Lionese-speaking area borders on the Endenese to the west, the Sikkanese to the east, the Flores Sea to the north, and the Savu Sea to the south. Significant dialectal variation is found, especially between western Lio and eastern Lio. The language spoken in the village in which I stayed is classified as a western dialect (see Greuter 1946).

The present usage of the term *lio* as an ethnic designation owes much to the history of administration in the area. Before contact with the Dutch, there were no kingdoms or encompassing authority over the area. The rajas, 'administrative rulers', were first certified by the Dutch in 1917: the Raja of Ndona in the western Lionese area, and the Raja of Tanah Kunu Lima in the eastern Lionese area. In 1924 these two *kerajaans* were reorganised into one *kerajaan* under the name Kerajaan Lio (van Suchtelen 1921:85–6; Winokan 1960:6).

Although the reason for the adoption of the word *lio* for the administrative area is not known, this word has several indigenous meanings. According to some informants, this word came from the name of a place called Nua Lio Boto on the north coast; other informants told me that it had been adopted from an ancestor's name. But no one could give any further explanation about the significance of the place or the ancestor. In general usage, by contrast with the word *ndu'a*, *lio* refers to a region nearer to the south coast. The central mountainous region is referred to as *ndu'a* in contrast to the southern coastal region, but in contrast to the northern coastal region it is called *lio*. In this daily context, *'ata lio*, 'the people in the *lio* area', means the people who live nearer to the south coast.

People still remember a song about the Raja of Lio, which is sung with a Westernised melody.

'Ema kami	Our father,
Waké raja	The approved raja,
'Ata ngga'é	The supreme man,
Ria tana	The greatness on the earth,
'O mera Wolo Waru mena	Who lives in Wolo Waru[6] in the east,
Nua puu	Nua Puu,[7]
Tana Lio	The Lionese land.

We can presume that this song was made for the purpose of asserting the Raja's authority over the area, and it is conceivable that this song contributed to a sense of Lionese identity.

Ritual language is characteristic of Lionese culture, as it is of the cultures of other peoples in eastern Indonesia. There are many genres in Lionese ritual language which are characterised by parallelism, euphemism, and metaphorical expression. Lionese ritual language can be called traditional because knowledge of ritual language is usually thought to be handed down from generation to generation and there are many canonical expressions to be learned. But the rules concerning dyadic sets are not as strict as, for example, in Rotinese ritual language (see Fox 1971:230). The Lionese people appreciate the creativity of the performers in using new expressions in ritual language. A Lionese proverb states, *'ola mbé'o no'o du'a du'a*. This adage means that each person can have his own knowledge, in other words, that one person's knowledge is probably different from another's. The ways of acquiring knowledge that render it powerful are secretive. Such knowledge is given not by human beings but by mysterious beings. It can be said that Lionese ritual language tends towards diversity, which makes Lionese ritual language vivid, impressive, and disputable as well.

Social background

The place where I stayed was in the domain of a traditional village, a *nua*, located in the centre of the Lionese area. A *nua* (which I translate as 'village') is regarded as a permanent place of residence. Houses outside the *nua* are regarded as temporary huts in fields, even if people live there for long periods of time. A village has its ritual domain and is ritually autonomous. There is one set of altar stones, *tubu musu*, in the ritual courtyard, *koja kanga*, at the centre of a village and these are the only altar stones and ritual courtyard in the domain. The authority over the domain is concentrated in the village and in its body of priests.

The village where I did my research stands on a foundation about two metres high and is composed of thirteen named houses surrounding the altar stones, the ritual courtyard and the temporary ritual hut, *kuwu*, beside them. A middle-aged priest remembers that when he was a little child there used to be a proper ritual hut, *keda*, more named houses, and other houses located on the periphery, each of which was secondary to one of the named houses. Since fires burned down the village several times, only thirteen named houses and a temporary ritual hut have been rebuilt. There are settlements composed of clusters of houses adjacent to the village. These settlements used to be larger and more populated. Up until the last three or four decades most of the villagers resided in the village or in the adjoining settlements. The village was a place not only for rituals but for everyday life.

The villagers now number 2500.[8] Since wet rice cultivation became prevalent in the 1960s, most of them have left the village and the adjoining settlements to reside near the wet rice fields in the lowlands of the domain. This process of shifting residence has been accelerated by the fact that the main road, which makes transportation easier, runs through the low-lands. At present only a few people live in the village. Almost all the villagers remain settled in the lowlands and spend most of their time taking care of the twice-yearly crops of wet rice; they go back to the village to attend rituals once or twice a year.

There are forty-four priests (*mosa laki*) in the village, and they form a body which has the collective right to conduct rituals and control the ritual domain. From a cosmological point of view, the number of priests should be seven. Through historical events, the number has increased. Since there is a Lionese principle that past affairs should not be brought up, how the position of a certain priest was established is usually kept secret. Each priest has the right to at least one ritual role. There is a difference in the importance of each ritual role and on the basis of these differences the priests are thought to be organised hierarchically. But, at the same time, their statuses are regarded as equal, since each should respect the ritual right of the others regardless of the differences in impor-tance. Two priests, in particular, have positions of considerable ritual importance. One is called *mosa laki pu'u*, the 'origin priest' (*mosa laki*, 'priests'; *pu'u*, 'trunk, origin'), and the other is called *mosa laki ria béwa* or simply *ria béwa*, the 'great priest' (*ria*, 'big, great'; *béwa*, 'long, high, deep'). The 'origin priest' plays a most important role and the 'great priest' assists him on ritual occasions. Sowing is prohibited until the 'origin priest' sows ceremonially after an annual ritual called the 'great ritual', *nggua ria*, the most important calendrical rite in the village. The 'great ritual' is one of the few occasions on which the villagers stay to-gether in the village for several days and the feeling of belonging to the village is expressed.

Because of the recent penetration of Christianity, the villagers stop working on Sundays to see each other in a little chapel located in each congregational area, instead of spending days and nights together on frequent ritual occasions in the centre of the village, as former generations did.

The villagers themselves recognise that there are two opposed factions among them. These factions originated a decade ago in a conflict which occurred when the villagers became involved in a dispute between two other nearby villages. This dispute, which was over land, led to a lawsuit, which was dealt with at the district government office. On that occasion some priests from the village where I was living, including the 'origin priest', had supported one of the contending villages, while other priests had supported the second. These opposing priests sued the 'origin priest' because he had opened the sacred box and taken out some ritual objects to show as evidence at the government district office, though it was prohibited to open the box without agreement of all the priests. The 'origin priest' was imprisoned for about six months.

The statues

The communal heirlooms which disappeared were two statues, representing a man and a woman, called *'amé naka* and *'iné naju* (*amé*, 'father', term of address to a man or boy; *naka*, 'to steal','jack-fruit'; *'iné*, 'mother', term of address to a woman or girl; *naju = poi naju*, a kind of grasshopper). The names evoke several folk etymologies but there is no commonly shared interpretation.

The statues play no part in any myth, nor does any legend tell of their origin. I was told one brief folk tale concerning them.

> There were two wild pigs, a boar and his sister. The boar's name was Méra Pano and his sister's name was Jéngo Wolé. One day they ran out of chillies. Jéngo Wolé said, 'We've run out of chillies. What shall we do?' 'There are chillies in the valley over there,' said Méra Pano, while he had already set a trap there. Jéngo Wolé went there to pick chillies and was caught in the trap. Then Méra Pano came. Though she asked him to release her from the trap, he did not help her, but raped her there, saying, 'I must do it anyway.' Méra Pano and Jéngo Wolé are *'amé naka 'iné naju.*[9]

Compared with the altar stones, the statues are ritually peripheral, though they do have a certain ritual importance; for example, in the 'great ritual', *nggua ria*, offerings must be made to them at the last stage of the ritual.

The statues are categorised as 'magical objects', *raju*, which give spiritual power or luck to the individuals who happen to be selected by them. But the statues can inflict harm on others. They can cause disease, barrenness, death, or misfortune. It is said that women or children without clothes should not see them, because the statues might tickle their sides to make them sick, so sick that they might die.

The statues are objects of worship. But hardly any of the villagers have ever seen them, even though they had been kept in a small hut located on the way into the village. Offerings on the occasion of the 'great ritual', *nggua ria*, had been conducted by only three specific priests from among the forty-four in the village; most of the priests had therefore never seen the statues either, or, if they had, had only seen them once or twice. The villagers differ in their opinions as to the ritual importance of the statues and as to the ritual rights concerning them. The statues appeared old. The villagers did not estimate how old they were, but believed that they had been passed down from ancestor to ancestor for an unimaginably long time. Some suggested that they were the images of the first ancestors. Others said that they were really old, but not as old as the age of the first ancestors.

According to one informant, a pair of phrases *ine pu'u puu//'amé kamu lema* 'Mother of the old trunk//Father of the deep root' alludes to the statues, *'amé naka 'iné naju*, and another phrase *'iné ria//fai ngga'é*, 'Great Mother//Divine Wife', alludes to the female statue, *'iné naju*. The villagers were generally proud of the antiquity of the statues, which they thought proved that the village was very old. This evaluation consequently assured their prestige in regard to other villages.

Because of the statues' magical power, which was usually destructive, the villagers feared these statues very much and had avoided contact with them for such a long time that these figures did not seem to have become part of the villagers' life. But after their disappearance, the statues suddenly moved into the centre of the villagers' world.

The sequence of events

The disappearance of the statues

The villagers do not know the precise date of the statues' disappearance. One day in August 1983 a villager happened to discover that one of the wall planks of the hut in which the statues had been kept was out of place. Since the circumstances of this discovery were not publicly explained and were never discussed openly, the villagers remained puzzled about the discovery. The case was further complicated by the fact that this man kept silent for several days after the discovery, which caused other villagers to suspect him. He told of his discovery to one of the priests supposed to have ritual rights to the statues. The discoverer and the priest went to look into the hut and realised that the statues had disappeared. The last time the priest, who happened to be a teacher at a local elementary school, had seen them was in the middle of June 1983; on that occasion he had offered to them several baskets which the school children in his class had made. This act was vaguely criticised later as being wrong, since it confused daily matters and traditional matters to such an extent that it might have occasioned the statues to leave the village. Since that time, nobody had seen the statues nor had even paid attention to the hut, although a considerable number of people had passed by. The discoverer and the priest found there several clues pointing to theft. Soon after the news spread that the statues had been stolen, the priests and their followers went up to the village to deal with the matter. A priest made the following utterance in ritual language:

Text 1

1	*Kita mai 'iwa nara ngai*	We came here not because of our personal desire,
2	*Kita sé'a 'iwa 'uku lubu*	We arrived here not because of our personal judgement,
3	*Taa kita mai pu'u ria pai*	But we came here because the great origin called,
4	*Kita sé'a tolo béwa niu*	We arrived here because the high heaven summoned.
5	*Bou tebo laki*	Gather the bodies of the priests,
6	*Mondo loo 'ongga*	Summon the trunks of the priests.
7	*Kaa kita repa soko soro*	We eat rice, conversing,
8	*Sepa kita ndari ndé'o*	We relish vegetables, singing,
9	*Kéa kaa*	Eating noisily,
10	*Ghiju minu*	Drinking busily,
11	*Pu'u 'iné bopa*	Because Mother disappeared,
12	*'Amé melé*	Father vanished.
13	*Bopa rewa kobé rua telu*	Two or three nights have already passed since the disappearance,
14	*Melé rewa leja sutu lima*	Four or five days have already passed after vanishing.
15	*Gaé kita péré mbé'o*	Let us search for them to know,
16	*Pita kita péré téi*	Let us look for them to discover,
17	*Nduu nduu kita péré dubu*	Trace, trace them to attain,
18	*Leti leti kita péré deki*	Follow, follow them to reach.
19	*'Iné sii nggoro fi'i joo*	Mother, since the raft slid down,
20	*'Ema sii kala nopo néta*	Father, since the *néta*-wood[10] crawled down,
21	*Sii poi nosi*	Since *poi*-grasshoppers showed it,
22	*Nombi péra*	*Nombi*-grasshoppers taught it.

The village suddenly became extraordinarily active. A pig was slaughtered to serve to the priests while they were discussing the matter. A priest volunteered to intone chants called *nangi tana watu*, 'mourning on land and stones', sitting at the altar stones all day and night to invoke the spirits, and the ancestors, to punish the persons who had stolen the statues.

One priest played the role of chairman at the priests' conference. This role is traditionally called *késo besi//rero mbelo*, 'who steps on things to be smashed//who places weight on things to be bent'. He was selected as *késo besi//rero mbelo* because, the previous year, he had presented himself, in a more or less arbitrary way, to the government officers who had visited the village. Since this kind of conference had not been held for a long time, they seemed to have forgotten how to discuss the solution of a village-wide problem. Many spoke in broken Indonesian instead of Lionese ritual language. At last it was decided to consult a few famous diviners from outside the village and to ask the district police for their help as well.

Rumours

While the conference and the feast were being held in the village, many rumours circulated among the villagers. On the basis of the diviners' information, the evidence left by the thieves, and various people's dreams, the villagers were sure that people from their own village had committed the theft. They suspected each other. Many of these suspicions reflected the split between the two factions in the village. For example, while a rumour spread that a particular villager involved in one faction had stolen the statues to pass on to a stranger who had stayed with him just prior to the statues' disappearance, another rumour arose that my main informant, who was loosely involved in the other faction, had invisibly taken the statues in a 'mysterious-scientific' way unknown to the villagers but known only to the Japanese, in order to give the statues to the Japanese woman. Most suspicions, however, were not sufficiently well founded to influence any collective decision.

One day, early in the morning, while they were busy gossiping, one of the villagers was found lying still on a road as if he were dead. As soon as he got up, he shouted that *'amé naka 'iné naju* were crushing him and began to accuse two villagers as the primary culprits, saying that they told him to steal the statues to deliver to them. This man, the accused men, and a few other witnesses were investigated by the district police. The accused men insisted that the man was lying. No evidence was found. After several days the accuser withdrew his former statement; then, several days later, he asserted it again.

All the priests were once more summoned to the village to settle the dispute. After sitting, eating, and drinking together, for a few days, they decided to subject the accuser and the accused to a traditional ordeal, to which they expressed their willing agreement. It was also decided that after the ordeal, since there was no further action that the priests could take, the matter should be turned over to the police. A priest described the sequence of events as follows:

Text 2

| 1 | *Siku méko* | The moving elbow, |
| 2 | *Lima lama* | The quick hand, |

3	*Boo lobo*	Bursting sprout,
4	*Suga nuwa*	Spurting fecundity,
5	*Ngai 'até nara*	Because of the desiring liver,
6	*Lura bhoo*	The gushing saliva,
7	*Kai naka*	He stole.
8	*Taa*	But,
9	*Demi 'ana 'ina*	If this child
10	*Ngéé leka tuba 'iné*	Was born from the abdomen of Mother,
11	*Beka leka kambu 'amé*	Was generated from the belly of Father,
12	*'Iné ghaa*	Mother here
13	*'Iwa séghu no'o téké kéu*	Will never push him back with the wrist,
14	*'Iwa tibha no'o longgo lima*	Will never shake him off with the back of the hand.
15	*Ngeta 'ana mai wola*	In order that the child comes back,
16	*Sé'a walo*	Returns again,
17	*Ngguju si lo'o lo'o*	Whisper in a very faint voice,
18	*Ngao si dhengo dhengo*	Speak in a very low voice,
19	*Ghalé watu ma'é wa'u*	So as not to go out on the stones down there,
20	*Ghalé tana ma'é mbana*	So as not to walk out on the earth down there.
21	*Taa*	But,
22	*'Ata laki ghaa mera rewa*	The priests here have sat down,
23	*Leja rua telu*	For two or three days,
24	*Kobé sutu lima*	Four or five nights.
25	*Deki*	Then,
26	*'Ata laki su'u su'u 'iwa sélé kolo*	The priests carried it on their head without leaning,
27	*Wangga wangga 'iwa mbénga wara*	Carried it on their shoulder without averting.
28	*'Iné ghé napa napa pémé rewa*	Mother has waited and looked forward,
29	*Kobé rua telu*	For two or three nights,
30	*Leja sutu lima*	Four or five days,
31	*'Ana ngangé wé'é réwo*	The child has not come close.
32	*Wa'u si ghalé watu*	Let us go out on the stones down there,
33	*Wa'u si ghalé tana*	Let us walk out on the earth down there.

34	*'Iné wai joka*	Mother will throw him away,
35	*Leka 'ata mangu lau*	To the people of the mast down there,
36	*Leka 'ata laja ghawa*	To the people of the sail down there,
37	*Leka tua 'aé*	To the foreign authorities,
38	*Joka leka pemerinta.*	Will throw him away to the government.

Another priest described the whole sequence of events in ritual language, suggesting that it was still preferable that the case should be settled in the traditional way:

Text 3

1	*Kau ghéo leka téké kéu*	If you turned at the wrist,
2	*Dau ngguju dhengo*	You must whisper in a low voice.
3	*Lema mera mai*	Only yesterday,
4	*Mera bhondo la'é ngodo godo*	When many people sat but had not felt tired yet,
5	*Ngangé ngguju lo'o*	You did not want to whisper in a faint voice.
6	*Wengi rua*	The day before yesterday,
7	*La'é mera ngara paka*	When people had not felt stiff yet,
8	*Ngangé ngao dhengo*	You did not want to speak in a low voice.
9	*Mera néa ngodo godo*	After having sat long to feel tired,
10	*Lowa tani tuka*	Enduring hunger in the stomach,
11	*Kau ngguju lo'o*	If you whisper in a faint voice,
12	*Moa siké foko*	Bearing thirst in the throat,
13	*Kau ngao dhengo*	You speak in a low voice.
14	*Naa*	Then,
15	*Ria leka tuka kau*	You will have a swollen stomach,
16	*Roo leka foko kau*	You will have a sore throat,
17	*Niku leka buku siku*	You bent at the elbow,
18	*Ghéo leka téké kéu*	You turned at the wrist,
19	*Ria leka tuka*	You will have a swollen stomach,
20	*Roo leka foko*	You will have a sore throat.
21	*Mera mai*	Yesterday,
22	*Bou leka tubu toko bhondo ma'é lo'o*	Many people gathered at the sacred stones, never diminished,

23	*Lélé dowa*	All heard,
24	*'Ina mondo ghaa fi'i kanga*	Attended here at the ritual centre,
25	*Mondo bhaka 'ata fai 'ata kaki*	All the women and the men attended,
26	*Mondo bhaka*	All attended.
27	*Niku leka buku siku*	You bent at the elbow.
28	*Ngguju lo'o wola na*	Whisper back in a faint voice,
29	*Lowa téké tuka*	Since people are enduring hunger in the stomach.
30	*Ngao lo'o walo na*	Speak again in a faint voice,
31	*Moa siké foko*	Since people are bearing thirst in the throat,
32	*Duu rewa ngodo godo*	People have sat long enough to become tired.
33	*Mera mai*	Yesterday,
34	*Koré ngangé mboré*	You did not want to dig into our ears,
35	*Wiwi dowa*	All talked.
36	*Ngéé leka tuka*	If you were generated from the abdomen,
37	*Koré mboré*	Dig into our ears,
38	*Ngao lo'o lo'o ghélé wawo bu'u*	Speak in a very faint voice at the hearth,
39	*Ngguju dhengo dhengo ghélé lata loro*	Whisper in a very low voice at the front floor.
40	*Watu ma'é wa'u*	Do not go out on the stones,
41	*Tana ma'é mbana*	Do not walk out on the earth.
42	*Demi mbana ghalé tana*	If you walked out on the earth,
43	*'Ata riwu réwo*	Thousands of others would know,
44	*Nitu lédo*	*Nitu*-spirits would make you lose your way.
45	*Tika ghalé watu*	If you stepped on the stones,
46	*'Ata ngasu pésa*	Hundreds of outsiders would know,
47	*Pa'i pénggo*	*Pa'i*-spirits would bend your way,
48	*Pa'i lai lowo*	*Pa'i*-spirits who walk along rivers,
49	*Juu léta wolo*	*Juu*-spirits who walk on ridges.[11]

50	*Ho'o ngéré béré 'oro*	They said yes like chorusing streams,
51	*Pusu tuu ghéa tubu toko*	That your heart should be brought to the altar stones,
52	*Wiwi dowa*	All talked,
53	*Lema nawu ghéa fi'i kanga*	That your tongue should be offered to the ritual centre,
54	*Lema sawé*	All spoke.
55	*Taa nebu 'ina*	But now,
56	*Dau ngao lo'o*	You must speak in a faint voice.
57	*Ho'o ngéré béré 'oro*	They said yes like chorusing streams,
58	*Pusu tuu ghéa tubu toko*	That your heart should be brought there to the altar stones.
59	*Mo'o pusu ma'é tuu ghéa tubu toko*	If you do not want your heart to be brought there to the altar stones,
60	*Kéa ria si*	Confess loudly,
61	*Lema ma'é nawu ghéa fi'i kanga*	If you do not want your tongue to be brought there to the ritual centre,
62	*Nosi mbeja si*	Tell everything.
63	*Poké kamba dui*	Spear a water-buffalo with long horns,
64	*Wéla wawi ngi'i*	Slaughter a pig with tusks,
65	*Mo'o doro digo*	In order to level the projecting part,
66	*Sako nggadho*	In order to shave the protuberant part,
67	*Baru garé wola*	Then talk again,
68	*Kéko walo*	Speak back.
69	*Mo'o pa'a ghéa tubu*	In order to make offerings there at the altar stones,
70	*Réwu ghéa kanga*	In order to scatter offerings there at the ritual courtyard,
71	*Mo'o loo ma'é roo*	In order that the trunk should not be painful,
72	*Weki ma'é baja*	The body should not be exhausted,
73	*Roo ma'é lita longgo*	Pain should not step on the back,
74	*Baja ma'é teni weki*	Exhaustion should not press the body,

75	*Rio wai dhika*	Let us bathe to be pure,
76	*Rasi wai masa*	Let us wash to be clean.

The ordeal

The traditional ordeal was held on the next day. Many villagers gathered, standing around the ritual courtyard, to witness the ordeal, a type of performance they had never seen. Before the ordeal, a divination called *kilé lai lako*, 'investigating the spleen of a dog', was carried out to judge whether the ordeal would be valid or not. The priests killed a dog in the ritual courtyard and cut out its spleen. It was red, which signalled that the ordeal would be valid. An old priest ate the spleen at the altar stone in the proper way. One of the accused men was absent. The accuser and the accused man drank the substance prepared by the priests for the ordeal, a mixture of palm wine, dirt, rust from a ritual knife, and fine powder from the altar stones. Before drinking, the accuser declared in ritual language that *dari nia pasé la'é 'o Léta Laka, demi 'aku nosi réwo, tana kaa watu pesa*, 'as a successor of Léta Laka, if I am lying the earth should eat me and the stones should consume me'. The accused man said in the style of daily speech, 'If I am lying I should die, or else the liar should die.' The old priest who had eaten the spleen of the dog chanted:

Text 4

1	*Nitu lédo*	May *nitu*-spirits make you lose your way,
2	*Pa'i pénggo*	May *pa'i*-spirits bend your way,
3	*Pa'i lai lowo*	*Pa'i*-spirits who walk along the rivers,
4	*Juu léta wolo*	*Juu*-spirits who walk on the mountains,
5	*Ho'o ngéré béré 'oro*	They said yes like chorusing streams.
6	*Pusu tuu ghaa tubu toko*	His heart should be brought here, to the altar stones,
7	*Mbotu Roka*	To Mount Roka.[12]
8	*Demi langga lola*	If one violated and offended,
9	*Roda boka*	Stab his lungs,
10	*Ma'é ngenda wola*	Do not forgive him,
11	*Lai langa dhanda tuu*	Take out his intestinal membrane and bring it to
12	*Watu Wanda*	Watu Wanda,
13	*Pena Kuwi Jawa*	Pena Kuwi Jawa,

14	*Pemo Dari Paga*	Pemo Dari Paga,
15	*Nua Nggojo*	Nua Nggojo,
16	*Doro Tana*	Doro Tana.[13]
17	*Kai ndoré*	He transgressed,
18	*Kai langga*	He violated,
19	*Wiki ngala 'iné naju 'amé naka*	He could steal *'iné naju 'amé naka*,
20	*Dau tana kaa*	The earth must eat him,
21	*Dau watu pesa*	The stones must exhaust him.
22	*Siko sia*	Strip him,
23	*Loru dari*	Undress him.
24	*Nggoro ghélé wolo*	Sliding down from the mountain,
25	*Sii nggoro fi'i joo*	Since the raft slid down,
26	*Kala ghélé kéli*	Crawling down the summit,
27	*Sii wa'u nopo néta*	Since the firewood came down.
28	*Kau lai langa léwa*	You took them away.
29	*Kami ta garé ndéna ngéré wai déka*	We, however, spoke as evenly as sliced dry areca nuts.
30	*Kau ngangé mésa*	You did not want to agree to any suggestion.
31	*'Ana lo'o ngéé leka tuka*	A little child, who was born from our abdomen,
32	*Koré ngangé mboré*	Does not want to dig into our ears,
33	*Teka ngangé bega*	Does not want to pierce into our ears,
34	*Ngao ngangé lo'o*	Does not want to speak to us in a faint voice,
35	*Ngguju ngangé dhengo*	Does not want to whisper to us in a low voice,
36	*Ghalé bu'u*	At the hearth,
37	*Ghalé waja*	At the fireplace.
38	*Bhisi roo leka koba wiwi*	He makes noise on the edge of the lips,
39	*Mo mbou laki*	To plunder the priests of their authority,
40	*Bhesa no ngalu lema*	He makes noise on the tip of the tongue,
41	*Mo ramba 'ongga*	To rob the elders of their prestige.
42	*Roda boka tuu ghélé Kéli Ndota*	Stab his lungs and bring them up to Mount Kéli Ndota.
43	*'Ana kota noa*	*Kota noa*-spirits,[14]

44	*Maé téi doga*	The soul cannot be seen.
45	*Noa 'uli pa'i*	*Noa*-spirits, who are friends of *pa'i*-spirits,
46	*'O nggela ngabi*	Who have a harelip,
47	*Tau sia ndai*	Will shred him,
48	*Noa méma ndai*	*Noa*-spirits will shred him.
49	*Kai naka nara ngai*	He stole because of uncontrolled desire,
50	*Jadi kai mo'o léwa laki*	By doing this, he wanted the priests to lose authority.
51	*Lai langa dhanda*	Take out his intestinal membrane.
52	*Tuu Watu Wanda*	Bring it to Watu Wanda,
53	*Pena Kuwi Jawa*	Pena Kuwi Jawa,
54	*Pemo Dari Paga*	Pemo Dari Paga,
55	*Nua Nggojo*	Nua Nggojo
56	*Doro Tana*	Doro Tana,
57	*Bagi sama sama*	Divide it into equal pieces.
58	*Dau tubu no kanga*	To the altar stones and the ritual centre,
59	*Wowo no naka*	To the *wowo* tree and *naka* tree.
60	*'Iné naka 'amé naju*	To the *'iné naka 'amé naju*,
61	*Du'a ria*	To the offering place,
62	*Lamba bapu*	To the ritual drum.
63	*Bhesa ngaju*	Eat and chew him,
64	*Tisi feri*	*Tisi feri*-spirits,
65	*Fénggé ré'é*	*Fénggé ré'é*-spirits,[15]
66	*Kami kuni*	We order you,
67	*Kami péé*	We command you,
68	*Pa'i lai lowo*	*Pa'i*-spirits who go along the rivers.
69	*Ngodo ma'é godo*	We should not sit long enough to feel tired.
70	*Téki bhamba*	Take the water container,
71	*Regu gogo*	Carry the water vessel,
72	*Bou ghélé tubu toko*	Gather at the altar stones,
73	*Mondo si loo*	Assemble the members,
74	*No'o kai 'o lima ngoo*	And he who stole,
75	*Loo 'ana lo'o*	Who is a little child,
76	*Lima lama*	Who has quick hands,
77	*Ndoré langga*	Who transgressed and violated,
78	*Ngebu no gaja*	*Ngebu*-snakes and elephants,[16]
79	*Segé no sawa*	*Segé*-snakes and *sawa*-snakes,

80	*Mori no gaja*	Crocodiles and elephants,
81	*'O raga ghalé tana*	Which crawl on the earth down there.
82	*Lai langga*	Take him away,
83	*Kobé rua ma'é nala*	Within two nights.
84	*Gaja no'o ngebu*	Elephants and *ngebu*-snakes,
85	*Weki kai rembu ngéré bhoti sepu*	His body will vanish like buried wood scraps,
86	*Nduu 'embu ki 'iwa welu*	Follow what the ancestors did not leave.
87	*Mbaa leka jala*	If he goes on a road,
88	*Kiku tetu*	*Kiku*-snakes will bite,[17]
89	*Watu laba*	Rocks will press him.
90	*Demi kai lima lama 'iné naju 'amé naka*	If he stole *'iné naju 'amé naka* with quick hands,
91	*Ngai kowa kowa kebhé*	May his boat capsize,
92	*Ngai rajo rajo melé*	May his ship sink,
93	*Tuku du'u*	May his flow be stopped,
94	*Tendu Tuka Tubu*	To be destined for Tuka Tubu, far off in the sea,
95	*Wesa ma'é kedha*	May he have his oars stuck in the sea,
96	*Tendu Béo Meta Pu'u*	To be destined for Beo Meta Pu'u,[18] far off in the sea.
97	*Kau kema téé*	You infringed
98	*'O nggoro la'é ghalé ghélé mi*	What had slid from the west up there,
99	*Kai téé kema*	He breached
100	*O Papo no Pera*	What Papo and Pera had left,
101	*O welu mbeja*	What they had already left,
102	*O tana welu*	What the earth had left,
103	*Dai liti*	Remaining in the right place,
104	*'Énga lata*	Staying in the proper place,
105	*'Iwa rewa sala*	Not wrong any longer.
106	*Demi kau ndoré*	If you transgressed,
107	*Kau langga*	If you violated,
108	*Kobé rua ma'é langga*	Within two nights,
109	*Mutu guu*	Mount Mutu will ululate,
110	*'Ia pai*	Mount 'Ia will call.
111	*Kobé ma'é roké*	You cannot sleep all night long,
112	*Leja ma'é mera*	You cannot sit all day long.
113	*Kolo tobhé tana*	Your head will plunge into the earth,

114	*Ha'i ngadho liru*	Your legs will look up to the sky.
115	*'Aku 'o bhéa*	I, who am doing *bhéa,*[19]
116	*'Éja kéra leka tegu béla*	Am a brother-in-law of the thunder and the lightning,
117	*Wuru wai 'uja 'angi*	Am allied to the rain and the wind,
118	*Wogha 'ongga*	Succeeded to the authority,
119	*Bagi laki*	Inherited the prestige:
120	*Wolo no'o Mité*	Wolo and Mité.[20]
121	*'Ola garé 'iwa nara ngai*	What I have declared does not depend on my personal desire,
122	*Nduu no wolo wai*	But follows the traditional mountain,
123	*Jala laki*	The authorised way.
124	*Waké si wani*	Beat the drum.

The drum was beaten in quick tempo and for a while the priest and the accuser danced around the altar stones to its beat.

After the ordeal

After the ordeal all the villagers, including the accuser and the accused, went back to their daily affairs. The problem of *'amé naka 'iné naju* was never discussed again in public. Though the old priest cursed the offender to die within two days, nothing happened to the accuser or to the accused. But the search for the statues was continued by some of the priests, including the 'origin priest'. It seemed that the search was based on information from diviners, but since neither the result nor the process was known publicly, their activities appeared obscure. Several times they secretly brought the news that the statues had been discovered to my main informant, one of the most influential priests but one not directly committed to the search. They said that they were busy arranging the ritual procedure to bring back *'amé naka 'iné naju* to the village. But this news proved to be false when, after a week or two of silence, they brought 'really true' news of discovery, which also turned out to be wrong. However, new stories of an alleged discovery continued.

Three months after the statues had disappeared, the 'great ritual' was held. The offerings which used to be made to the statues were made at the hut in which they had been kept. The priests seemed still to be continuing the search, but the villagers hardly expected that the search would be successful; they gossiped only occasionally about *'amé naka 'iné naju.* Then the district police suddenly conducted a search in the residence of a certain priest, a search demanded by the 'origin priest' and several other priests belonging to the faction opposed to that priest. The priest whose house was searched was one of the persons who had sued the 'origin priest' about ten years earlier, bringing about the present factional division among the villagers.

After this search, people became preoccupied with arguments about the factional conflict. People of either faction began accusing those of the other of offending traditional prohibitions. For example, some villagers accused a woman, who was said to be insane, of sowing before the 'great ritual'. They asserted that she deserved to be fined because several years ago an old woman related to them had had to pay a buffalo to the priests for having thrown out husks of paddy, which, by accident, sprouted.

The problem of the disappearance of *'amé naka 'iné naju* was thus replaced with the quotidian, persistent, latent, and evasive conflict between the two factions in the village. The *'amé naka 'iné naju*, which had once occupied a central place in the lives of the villagers, retired to the periphery of their concern.

The social roles of ritual language

In this section, through interpretation of the ritual speech cited above, I would like to explore Lionese views of their society and to make clear some of the social roles of Lionese ritual language.

The ritual utterances described the statues as important ancestral inheritances and the figures the statues represented as ancestral beings.

> Mother since the raft slid down,
> Father since the *néta*-wood crawled down,
> Since *poi*-grasshoppers showed it,
> *Nombi*-grasshoppers taught it.
>> (Text 1, lines 19–22; see also Text 4, lines 24–27, 98)
>
> What Papo and Pera left,
> What they had already left
>> (Text 4, lines 100, 101)

These metaphorical expressions refer to the primeval time. The primeval ancestors slid down, like rafts or *néta*-wood, from Mount Lépé Mbusu in central Lio, and they spread over the island and over the world. The first ancestors were ignorant about how to produce offspring until they saw grasshoppers copulating. Papo and Pera are the names of the villagers' ancestors.

In relation to the importance of *'amé naka 'iné naju*, the ritual utterances depicted their disappearance as a grave matter: not a private matter, but a matter with which the whole community, especially the priests, should be concerned.

> We came here not because of our personal desire,
> We arrived here not because of our personal judgement.
> But we came here because the great origin called,
> We arrived here because the high heaven summoned.
>> (Text 1, lines 1–4; see also lines 5, 6, 11, 12)

> Let us search for them to know,
> Let us look for them to discover,
>> (Text 1, lines 15, 16; see also lines 17, 18)

At the early stage of the sequence of events, the disappearance was expressed only as 'disappearance' or 'vanishing'.

> Because Mother disappeared,
> Father vanished.
>> (Text 1, lines 11, 12; see also lines 13, 14)

But, as the sequence unfolded, the disappearance was described as theft.

> The moving elbow,
> The quick hand,
> He stole.
>> (Text 2, lines 1, 2, 7; see also Text 3, lines 1, 17, 18, 27; Text 4, lines 19, 28, 49, 74, 76, 90)

This theft was described as abnormal at three levels: in emotion, in action and in social evaluation. The motive of the theft was described as uncontrolled personal desire.

> Because of the desiring liver,
> The gushing saliva,
> He stole.
> He stole because of uncontrolled desire,
>> (Text 2, lines 5–7; Text 4, line 49)

This motive contrasts with the socially oriented motives of the priests' conduct.

> We came here not because of our personal desire,
> We arrived here not because of our personal judgement,
> The priests carried it on their head without leaning,
> Carried it on their shoulder without averting.
>> (Text 1, lines 1, 2; Text 2, lines 26, 27; see also Text 1, lines 15–16; Text 4, lines 121–123)

The theft was represented as the particular motion of certain parts of the body.

The moving elbow,
The quick hand,
You bent at the elbow,
You turned at the wrist.
>(Text 2, lines 1, 2; Text 3, lines 17, 18; see also Text 3, lines 1, 27; Text 4, lines 74, 76)

The theft was defined as an offence against social order. This description was emphasised in the final stage of the sequence.

He transgressed,
He violated,
>(Text 4, lines 17, 18; see also lines 77, 97, 99, 106, 107)

Further, the thief's behaviour was presented as a challenge against the authority of the priests, since he did not heed the priests' effort and pain in searching for the statues.

After having sat long to feel tired,
Enduring hunger in the stomach,
Bearing thirst in the throat,
>(Text 3, lines 9, 10, 12; see also lines 29, 31, 32)

To plunder the priests of their authority,
To rob the elders of their prestige,
>(Text 4, lines 39, 41; see also line 50)

Though the person who had stolen the statues was thus accused, his wrong act was not attributed to his personality itself but to a part of his body, such as his elbow, hand, or wrist (see Text 2, lines 1, 2; Text 3, lines 1, 27; Text 4, lines 74, 76), or to his temporary condition.

Bursting sprout,
Spurting fecundity,
>(Text 2, lines 3, 4)

The boldness which had prompted him to commit the theft was compared to the ephemeral energy of sprouts and adolescents, whose sexual power is thought to increase explosively. This energy contrasts with the stable traditional authority of the priests, who are regarded as the elders of the village.

Succeeded to the authority,
Inherited the prestige.
What I have declared does not depend on my personal desire,
But follows the traditional mountain,
The authorised way.
>(Text 4, lines 118, 119, 121–123; see also lines 116, 117)

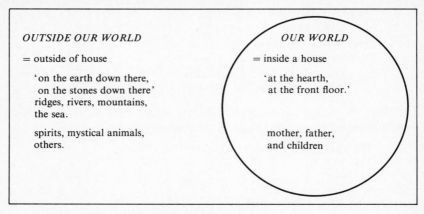

OUTSIDE OUR WORLD

= outside of house

'on the earth down there,
 on the stones down there'
ridges, rivers, mountains,
the sea.

spirits, mystical animals,
others.

OUR WORLD

= inside a house

'at the hearth,
 at the front floor.'

mother, father,
and children

Figure 7.1. Lionese views of their society

The ritual speeches reveal two ways that the priests dealt with this case. They asked the thief to come back, but they also cursed him. We can see clearly the Lionese concept of the world which brings about these contrastive ways. The Lionese people distinguish 'our world' from the area 'outside of our world' (Figure 7.1). In the ritual speeches, the former was represented as the inside of a house.

> Speak in a very faint voice at the hearth,
> Whisper in a very low voice at the front floor.
>> (Text 3, lines 38, 39; see also Text 4, lines 34–37)

The latter was compared to what is outside a house, such as the earthly world of rivers, ridges, mountains, the sea, and other alien places.

> Let us go out on the stones down there,
> Let us walk out on the earth down there.
>> (Text 2, lines 32, 33; see also Text 2, lines 19, 20; Text 3, lines 40–47; Text 4, line 81)

> *Pa'i*-spirits who walk along rivers,
> *Juu*-spirits who walk on ridges.
>> (Text 3, lines 48, 49; see also Text 4, lines 3, 4)

> Mount Mutu will ululate,
> Mount 'Ia will call.
>> (Text 4, lines 109, 110; see also lines 7, 42)

> To the people of the mast down there,
> To the people of the sail down there,
>> (Text 2, lines 35, 36; see also Text 4, lines 91–96)

Watu Wanda,
Pena Kuwi Jawa,
Pema Dari Paga,
Nua Nggojo,
Doro Tana.
(Text 4, lines 12–16; see also lines 52–56)

Mutu and 'Ia are the mountains located in central Flores which are said to be the destination of the dead. The locations of Watu Wanda, Pena Kuwi Jawa, Pema Dari Paga, Nua Nggojo, and Doro Tana are not known, or are secret and these places are thought to be where the ancestors originated.

The 'outside of our world' is occupied by alien beings such as various spirits, mystical animals, and the outsiders.

Kota noa-spirits,
Noa spirits, who are friends of *pa'i* spirits,
Tisi feri-spirits,
Fénggé ré'é-spirits,
(Text 4, lines 43, 45, 64, 65; see also Text 3, lines 44, 47–49; Text 4, lines 1–4, 46, 48, 68)

Ngebu-snakes and elephants,
Segé-snakes and *sawa*-snakes,
Crocodiles and elephants,
(Text 4, lines 78–80; see also line 84)

Thousands of others would know,
Hundreds of outsiders would know,
(Text 3, lines 43, 46; see also Text 2, lines 35–38)

The priests were described as mother and father, or only as mother: the offender was described as a little child.

If this child
Was born from the abdomen of Mother,
Was generated from the belly of Father,
(Text 2, lines 9–11; see also lines 12–16, 31, 34; Text 3, line 36; Text 4, lines 31, 75)

The priests are generously waiting for the offender to come back and whisper into their ears, as parents wait for their child to tell them something.

Mother here
Will never push him back with the wrist,
Will never shake him off with the back of the hand.

In order that the child comes back,
Returns again,
Whisper in a very faint voice,
Speak in a very low voice.
(Text 2, lines 12–18; see also Text 3, lines 2, 5, 8, 13, 28, 30,
34, 37–39, 56; Text 4, lines 29–35)

Just as the mischief of a child is forgiven in the house only if he shows respect to his parents, so the faults of a person in 'our world' are forgiven only if he defers to the authority of the priests. While relations in the house are familiar and merciful, like those between parents and their children, the order outside the house is forceful and alien. The implication is that, to solve the case, restoring normal relations between the priests and offender is preferable to casting the thief into the hands of alien beings. Because of this preference, after cursing the offender the priest still proposed to smooth away the fault by the sacrifice of a water-buffalo or a pig in order to restore normal relations.

Spear a water-buffalo with long horns,
Slaughter a pig with tusks,
In order to level the projecting part,
In order to shave the protuberant part,
Then talk again,
Speak back.
Let us bathe to be pure,
Let us wash to be clean.
(Text 3, lines 63–68, 75, 76; see also lines 57–62, 69–74)

But finally, the priests cursed the offender resolutely by invoking spirits and mystical animals, and entrusted the case into the hands of the authorities outside 'our world' (see Text 4, lines 1–23, 78–96, 108–114).

By interpreting these specific examples, we can comprehend an aspect of the social role of Lionese ritual language. Lionese ritual language not only presents a way of placing specific events, the theft of the statues, for example, in a socio-cosmological universe, but also reveals the contours of this universe as the Lionese people conceive of it.

Some sentences in Lionese ritual language can be understood as having a legal function, since they name sanctions against the offence.

You bent at the elbow,
You turned at the wrist,
You will have a swollen stomach,
You will have a sore throat.
He transgressed,
He violated.

He could steal *'iné naju 'amé naka*
The earth must eat him,
The stones must exhaust him.
>(Text 3, lines 17–20; Text 4, lines 17–21; see also Text 3, lines
>9–16; Text 4, lines 106–114)

Lionese ritual language shows that it is the beings 'outside our world' who should punish offenders, but if the matter is dealt with in 'our world', what the priests should do is restore the normal relations which were impaired by the offence. The words in Lionese ritual language are essentially different from words in our legal systems, in regard to sanctions. In legal systems words entitle an authority to punish the offender by using physical force as a sanction. In Lionese ritual language words do not function as the justification for physical force, but invoke the alien beings 'outside our world' to punish the offenders and inspire people with a common imagination which is culturally elaborated. In law, words define the conventional equivalence between two human acts, an offence and a sanction, while this equivalence cannot be logically proved. In Lionese ritual language, words, instead of making this logical leap, are given their power, as well as their effectiveness, by culture.

As poems strike our imagination, so ritual language moves the culturally elaborated imagination. It is no coincidence that ritual language reveals the same features found in poetry, such as parallelism, repetition, and metaphorical expression. The fact that living ritual language as a cultural phenomenon is now found only in a few scattered areas in the world may be consistent with the fact that most societies in the world now admit words as a cultural device to justify physical sanctions but do not regard words as affecting the supernatural source of power. From this point of view, the study of ritual language throws light on the relation between words and authority.

Lionese theory of the efficacy of words

In this last section, by exploring their explanations for the failure of the curses and by referring to another genre of magical speech, I would like to elucidate the Lionese theory of the efficacy of words.

Curses are very frightening to the Lionese people. When the priests invoked the spirits to punish the thieves, they saw the spirits flying around in the sky in the form of red rays, responding to the invocation. It seems that some people interpreted the accuser's fainting on the road as being related to the curses the priests had made.

Owing to the belief in the power of the curse to produce misfortune, a curse is also effective in social events. In the ritual utterances above, especially those in Text 3, the priests used cursing phrases to induce the thief to confess. The villagers were convinced that at least one of the villagers had committed the theft. In spite of their belief in the power of the curse, it was apparent that the thief did not die within two days of the ordeal, as the priest had intended. In spite of their confidence in the effectiveness of the curse, the thief did not reveal himself nor return the statues. Was it obvious to them that the curse was neither powerful nor effective?

In the Lionese speech genres there is another category of speech which is called *sua*. *Sua* is used defensively to counteract any assault, including the effect of ritual language, upon the person. Let us refer to an example of the use of *sua*.

About three generations ago there was a man called Sato Jopu. He was a very wily person because of his great knowledge of magical speech, especially *sua*. At one time a woman sued him for rape. He and the woman underwent a traditional ordeal called *kepo su'a*, 'holding the iron', in which a red-hot iron stick is put in the hands of the accused and the accuser. If anyone has lied, his hand will be burnt; if not, the iron stick will become cool. Though Sato Jopu had raped the woman, he walked around holding the red-hot iron stick in his hand, but the woman's hand was badly burnt as soon as the stick was put in it. To bring about this result Sato Jopu is said to have spoken a *sua* as follows:

Se toko léda sii nggoro fi'i joo	One stick fitted in since the time a raft slid down,
Mboko rua tura tuka sii nuwa 'ata du'a	Two balls riding on a belly since the age of ancestors.
Tuma péla kau 'iwa kéa	When a flea rapes you, you do not accuse loudly,
Koté pe'la kau 'iwa kéa	When your cloth rapes you, you do not accuse loudly,
Lima kau péla kau 'iwa kéa	When your hand rapes you, you do not accuse loudly,
Kau menga kéa téta kai 'aku mésa	You only accuse in order to shame me.
Méra no'o meta 'aku la'é dema	Red or green, I am not sure yet,
Demi 'éo réwo 'aku se mbé'o	It is possible that it was I who was wrong.
Keta gho su'a	You, the iron, cool down!

Sua is characterised by a more cryptic use of words, designed to confound the definition of facts and actions and turn back the power that would normally have struck the person without the help of *sua*.

Even though the ritual procedure was correctly performed, the ordeal concerning *'amé naka 'iné naju* failed the villagers. One informant explained the failure:

The ordeal was not valid, because the ordeal cannot be valid unless they say the words that the priests have prepared. The men who were subject to this ordeal know *sua* well; besides, one of them is a descendant of Sato Jopu. What does it mean when he said *dari nia pasé la'é 'o Léta Laka*? He made the ordeal invalid by referring to the name of an ancestor who is not common to all of us, because an ordeal should be based upon the names of ancestors who are common to all of us. We can find a similar thing in the chant which was made right after the ordeal. The priest evaded his responsibility by uttering the names Wolo and Mité.

As we see in his comment, the power of words is thought to be countered by other words. Ancestors are thought to be a source of the power and the authority. This kind of ordeal is regarded as an authoritative device supported by the common ancestors. In this context, uttering the name of the personal ancestor was suspected as the means of acquiring personal power that could neutralise or confuse the authoritative power of the ordeal. The priest was thought to have attempted to deflect the potentially dangerous power of the ordeal by declaring that it was not he but Wolo, the 'origin priest', and Mité, the 'great priest', who were responsible for the ordeal. It is said that people are always trying to shift threatening power in covert ways; although nothing appears to happen, the interaction of words occurs continually. This theory reconciles the failure of the curse with a belief in the power of words and a confidence in their effectiveness. Further, because this theory is unassailable, it maintains belief and confidence intact, regardless of whether or not a specific performance of ritual language is successful.

This Lionese village is in the process of changing. Wet rice cultivation is not only bringing about new residential patterns but it is also influencing the traditional ritual system based on swidden agriculture. The influence of Christianity is altering the traditional cosmology. Preference for the Indonesian language seems to be related to an increasing ignorance of traditional ritual language. Since these new influences are not uniform among villagers, cultural disparity within the society is increasing. In this regard, we can reason that because increasing cultural disparity has impaired the collective imagination on which the effectiveness of ritual language is based, the curses failed to induce the thief to submit to the authority of the priests. Thus we can predict that ritual language will lose its influence upon social events and will be replaced by other cultural devices and their influences. In these future situations, what might happen to the Lionese theory of the power of words? Will this seemingly invincible theory remain like 'a grin without the Cheshire cat'?

8

THE JOURNEY OF THE BRIDEGROOM: IDIOMS OF MARRIAGE AMONG THE ENDENESE

SATOSHI NAKAGAWA

Introduction

The purpose of this article is to analyse two ritual language texts gathered from the Endenese of central Flores and to consider the significance of some of the metaphors employed in them. These metaphors are not only common to other Endenese rituals, but also occur in the rituals of other societies in eastern Indonesia. Thus this paper may, I hope, contribute to a general comparative understanding of eastern Indonesian societies.

The two texts which I wish to examine are examples of what the Endenese call *mbuku*, a form of ritual speech employed at bridewealth negotiations. The principal metaphors in the two texts are spatial metaphors, involving the idea of a 'journey' as applied to marriage relations. Some basic background information on the Endenese and various forms of their marriage is necessary to make the texts and their recurrent metaphors comprehensible.

The Endenese are a people, numbering approximately 78,000, who live in central Flores. To the east of the Endenese are the people called the Lionese, who speak a dialect of Endenese. To the west of the Endenese live another group (sometimes called the Nga'o-nese[1]) whose language could also be classified as a dialect of Endenese. This situation of dialectal diversity provides each population with a wide range of vocabulary with which to create parallel couplets, since it allows the possibility of borrowing synonymous words from a neighbouring dialect. We thus find in the ritual language such dyadic sets as *nosi* (a Lionese word for 'to tell, to instruct')//*sodho* (an Endenese equivalent), *kerho* (an Endenese word for 'to forget')//*ghéwo* (a Nga'o-nese equivalent).

Marriage in Ende

Marriage is called, in Endenese, *wai rhaki*. The expression *wairhaki* has a wider range of meanings than that implied by the English word 'marriage'. The expression *wai rhaki* refers to the whole sequence of activities which is pertinent, in one way or another, to a marriage, ranging from the proposal of marriage to the wedding feast and subsequent rituals.

Marriage is important in Endenese society. Unlike the neighbouring Lionese people, the Endenese have no fixed social categories, such as named clans, which would classify people into pre-established categories. Rather, in Endenese society it is the articulation of relationships that regulates societal life. Marriage provides an opportune occasion to sort out relationships with other individuals and groups. There is also a corresponding difference between the Endenese and Lionese societies in their preference for types of marriage. Whereas the Lionese say a man *should* marry his mother's brother's daughter, the Endenese put a preference on the establishment of new relations (that is, with others not of the mother's natal group).

The Endenese recognise five types of marriage,[2] one of which is called *mburhu nduu//wesa senda*, 'following the path//connecting the way'. This is the marriage with a girl from one's mother's natal group, or, according to the Endenese, an alliance with one's old wife-giving group. The following expression, which alludes to marriage with the mother's brother's daughter, provides an illustration of the negative attitude towards this type of marriage:

Nirhu minu	Drink what has turned sour,
Ngesa pesa	Eat what has gone bad.

Thus, the ideal type of marriage for an Endenese is one that creates a new relationship, not one that merely continues a relationship already established.

A second form of marriage, called *'ana 'arhé* or 'asking' (or what is sometimes called *piso teké//rhambu remu*, 'holding a knife//carrying a jacket over the head'), designates the type of marriage contracted with a supposedly[3] unrelated group. A wife married in this fashion is usually regarded as more prestigious than any of her co-wives recruited in other ways. As opposed to *mburhu nduu//wesa senda*, in which practically no bridewealth is demanded, one must pay a considerable amount of bridewealth to conclude a marriage in this way. *'Ana 'arhé* also has a rigidly structured set of procedures consisting of various named stages.

In striking contrast to *'ana 'arhé* marriage is a third type of marriage, called *'ana paru dhéko*, 'run [and] follow'. This form of marriage is different from *'ana 'arhé* in that it is considered to be 'improper' (*petu*, 'hot'). In this case the girl plays the leading role, 'running' and 'following' the boy to his home. After the girl has run away, her parents' group must go to the boy's house and make aggressive demands (*jeké*) for bridewealth.

In this paper I will discuss these two contrasting types of marriage – *'ana 'arhé*, the marriage of asking, and *'ana paru dhéko*, the marriage of running and following – and consider the formal rhetoric which accompanies these forms of marriage.

'Jointed' narratives: mbuku

The texts examined here have a pragmatic purpose. They are not sung or chanted for communicating with deities or spirits; they are recited in demanding bridewealth (*ngawu*), specifically by the wife-giving group at a negotiation for bridewealth.

The texts are composed of couplets. One set of couplets is called a *mbuku*, 'a joint', and each distich in one *mbuku* is called *mata mbuku*.[4] These *mbuku* are the subject of this paper.

At a negotiation (*mbabho*) of bridewealth there can be many people present, both men and women; the *mbabho* is led by two, usually elderly, men who act as representatives of the two parties concerned. Speakers at a *mbabho* are considered to be skilled in this type of speech. There is no special term for the speakers, nor are their positions institutionalised.

A *mbabho* is occasioned by the wife-giving group's relating one couplet with a demand for some valuables, followed by the wife-taking group's bargaining. For example, in a *mbabho* for an *'ana 'arhé* marriage, a reciter might mention:

Kombé éé	[The bridegroom] is eager at night,
Rhera nara	Is longing in the daytime.

After reciting this couplet, the reciter demands from the bridegroom's group valuables such as an elephant tusk, a pair of gold items and a horse. Then the two groups negotiate until they reach an agreement. When the value of bridewealth for one couplet is settled, the two groups then proceed to the next couplet. This is referred to as 'climbing up the joint' (*nai mbuku*).

Asking for a bride: 'ana 'arhé

There are, roughly speaking, three stages of an *'ana 'arhé* marriage: *'ana 'arhé*, 'asking'; *tuu ngawu*, 'carrying bridewealth'; and *pe sia*, 'wedding'.

'Ana 'arhé is the first stage, in which a man from the bridegroom's side, sometimes accompanied by a second, goes to the girl's house and asks for the girl. The girl is sometimes referred to as a 'banana' (*muku*), or sometimes as a 'female sarong' (*rhawo*). The messengers are called *koré mboré//teka taso*, '[one who] digs out//tills through', or sometimes *rhérhu rharu*, 'the needle [for] cotton'. This second designation is in keeping with the metaphorical reference to the girl as a 'female sarong'.

If the marriage is approved by the bride's group, then, after a short while, the girl's group sends a messenger, called *padha rhéta*, 'one on the bridge', to the groom's group, announcing a date for the 'carrying of the bridewealth' (*tuu ngawu*).

The *tuu ngawu* comprises two stages: *téo tanda*, 'to hang the token', and *wenda tanda*, 'to detach the token'. The first is a provisional stage; the second is the main one. In the first stage the bridegroom's group brings a small portion of bridewealth to let others know that the girl is now engaged; and, in the second, the bridegroom's group, after accumulating a prescribed amount of bridewealth, brings all of it to prepare for the marriage feast.

Several days after *wenda tanda*, a feast (*pe sia*) is held in the bride's village. Pigs given by the wife-givers are slaughtered and served to the wife-takers, and the meat of water-buffaloes (or cows) given by the wife-takers is served to the wife-givers. Thus an alliance is concluded.

The 'joints' of a marriage of asking: mbuku 'ana 'arhé

Let us now consider the *mbuku* associated with an *'ana 'arhé* marriage. The text can be divided into two parts: couplets 2 to 28 describe the bridegroom's journey (*worho rarha*, 'the ridges and the roads'). This is followed by the other couplets (29 to 41), which mention the bride's specific kinsmen, to whom a portion of bridewealth should be paid. The latter part of the text is also common to the *mbuku* of *'ana paru dhéko*.

Text 1

1	*Woo wiwi bidi*	For fixing the trembling lips,
	Rhaka rhema rherhi	Lifting up the shivering tongue.
2	*Kombé éé*	[He] is eager at night,
	Rhera nara	Is longing in the daytime.
3	*Wa'u sa'o*	[He] goes out of the house,
	Tiro tenda	Jumps from the veranda.
4	*Wuru péré*	[He] appears out of the door,
	Deso ndeko	Is seen outside the village.
5	*Mbana rarha masa*	[He] goes along the neat road,
	Rhora wesa rhina	Walks along the clean path.
6	*Nggorhé worho*	[He] passes the ridges,
	Rhepo mbegho	Crosses the valley.

7	*Poro rhowo* *Dagé 'aé*	[He] enters the river, Comes out of the water.
8	*Nuka nua* *Tama manga*	[He] ascends into the hamlet, Enters the village.
9	*Rhéta wewa rhéwa*	[He] passes the long yard.
10	*Késo musu* *Rhangga nata*	[He] steps upon the altar, Walks across the forum.
11	*Rhako porhu* *Wawi besu*	Dogs are barking, Pigs are grunting.
12	*Piso teké* *Rhambu remu*	(He] is holding a knife, Carrying a jacket over his head.
13	*Ruri 'éri* *Parhé ngaté*	[He] goes through the ditch, Goes close to the edge [of the ditch].
14	*Padha tangi*	[He] climbs onto the ladder.
15	*Tika ténda* *Dhajo paso*	[He] climbs up the veranda, Sits on the balcony.
16	*Pai tarhu* *Niu oé*	[He] cries aloud [and we] answer, [He] calls [and we] reply.
17	*Mbé'o sa'o* *Nggesu ténda*	[He] knows the house, Is familiar with the veranda.
18	*Sa'o muri* *Ténda meta*	That new house, That fresh veranda.
19	*Kai péré* *Gheso 'usu*	[He] opens the door, Loosens the bolt.
20	*Rhérho rhoro* *Rhangga rhata*	[He] passes through the entrance, Walks across the threshold.
21	*Mbé'i mbu'u* *Dhaa ndawa*	[He] leans against the back wall, Stretches his legs on the floor.

22	*Nara mbé'o weta*	The brother knows his sister,
	Weta mbé'o nara	The sister knows her brother.
23	*Téo muku*	[He] hangs a token on the banana,
	Tanda tewu	Attaches a sign to the sugarcane.
24	*Mbupu jaga muku*	That the old one guards the banana,
	'Embu tipo tewu	That the elderly one protects the sugarcane.
25	*Peté negi*	[He] binds it tightly,
	Riké nggiki	Ties it securely.
26	*Ru'u tu'u*	[Until] the sign of prohibition is dried,
	Jaga rara	The amulet is broken.
27	*Wenda tanda*	[He] brings the token down,
	So'i ru'u	Detaches the sign of prohibition.
28	*Kuni ma'é taku*	Don't hesitate in ordering,
	Dudu ma'é kengu	Feel free in asking.
29	*Begu méngi*	[She who] carries *sirih*,
	'Uné wunu	The stuff of leaves.
30	*Weti moki*	*Sirih pinang* for the [mother's] mouth.
31	*Pesa réwo*	That we may eat freely.
32	*Mata mésa*	[She who] dies alone,
	Ré'é rhédhé	Feels sick by herself.
33	*Kombé pa'i*	[He who] sits up all night long,
	Rhera dari	Stands all day long.
34	*Piré rhaka 'iné*	For the taboo for helping the mother.
35	*Mbonggo mbeta*	[He who] is exhausted,
	Baja mbasa	Is drenched to the skin.

36	*Mbendi wéa méré*	[He who] wears the big golden weapon.
37	*Tubu musu* *Ora nata*	[He who owns] the stone altar, The village forum.
38	*Kepala Desa RK RT*	Village, hamlet heads.
39	*Pemuda*	Village youths.
40	*Weka té'é* *Soro rhani*	[He who] opens the mat, Arranges the pillow.
41	*Kema mbéki* *Rona soja*	[He who] sets up the sleeping room, Makes the bedroom.

Let me summarise the text and comment upon some of the lines. The initial couplet refers to the speaker of *mbuku*. After being given a gift prescribed in this *mata mbuku*, he prepares to recite the *mbuku*.

Couplets 2 to 28 describe the bridegroom's journey from his village to the bride's village (*worho rarha*, 'the ridges and the roads'). The bridegroom first thinks about his bride at home (couplet 2) and departs from his house (*sa'o//ténda*, 'the house//the veranda'). After leaving his house//village (*péré//ndeko*, 'the door//outside of the village'), he walks along the road (*rarha//wesa*, 'the road//the path') which lies between the two villages. After a few lines describing the topography (*worho//mbegho*, 'the ridge//the valley', *rhowo//'aé*, 'the river//the water', he enters the girl's village (*nua//manga*, 'the village//the hamlet') (couplet 8).

The text then proceeds to describe (couplets 9, 10, 11) the general structure of the village (*wewa*, 'village yard', *tubu musu//ora nata*, 'the stone altar//the village forum'), followed by a description of some domestic animals (*rhako//wawi*, 'the dogs//the pigs'). As a transition from the description of the village to that of the house, one couplet sketches the groom's appearance. This same couplet is also employed for the whole sequence of this type of marriage (*piso teké//rhambu remu*, 'holding a knife//carrying a jacket over the head') (couplet 12).

Couplets 14 to 21 form a group. They depict the groom's entering the bride's house: *ngaté//'éri*, 'the ditch around the house' [a kind of drain to prevent water running under the floor]; *tangi*, 'the ladder'; *ténda//paso*, 'the veranda// the balcony'; *sa'o//ténda*, 'the house//the veranda'; *péré// 'usu*, 'the door//the bolt'; *rhata//rhoro*, 'the threshold//the entrance', which marks a most important transition from the 'outer part of the house' to the 'innermost part of the house'; and *mbu'u//ndawa*, 'the back wall//the floor'.

Couplets 23 to 29 form another group within the set. This group relates the engagement and marriage process, comparing the girl to the banana// sugarcane (*muku//tewu*) and the boy to the owner of the plant. First of all, he attaches a token of prohibition to the banana//sugarcane (couplet 23), which corresponds to the second stage of the actual sequence of the marriage, the *téo tanda*. The token is fastened tightly to the plant (couplet 25) and the guardian (the girl's parent) looks after it (couplet 24) until it has dried (couplet 26). Then the groom comes to detach it (couplet 27), making the third stage in the actual sequence (*wenda tanda*).

Couplets 22 and 28 present an interesting contrast. In couplet 22, the only chiastic distich in the *mbuku*, the boy and the girl are called *nara* and *weta*, which refers to two structurally distinct relationships, that is, 'brother and sister' and 'mother's brother's son and father's sister's daughter'. These terms define a relationship in which marriage is prohibited. Thus, in couplet 22, before the procedure, the two are described as an 'unmarriageable' couple, even though they 'know each other well'. Yet, after going through the procedure, in couplet 28, the groom is asked not to hesitate in ordering. He has come to be regarded as a member of the family of the bride's group: the intended relationship is now established.

This is the end of the first part of the *mbuku*, the end of 'the ridges and the roads', *worho rarha*, through which the groom had to pass. The text goes on to refer to each specific person or kinsman of the bride's group who demands a gift.

The bride's mother is the most important figure in these *mata mbuku*. Couplets 29, 30, 32 allude to her: couplets 29 and 30, '[She who] carries *sirih*, The stuff of leaves' and '*Sirih pinang* for the mouth', can be considered together since the common metaphor concerns *sirih pinang*. But couplet 32 is the most significant of the three *mata mbuku* for the mother. This couplet is sometimes simply called '*iné*, '[one for] the mother'. For this, gold items of very good quality are demanded.

Couplet 32, which narrates the labour of the mother ('[She who] dies alone//Feels sick by herself'), contrasts with couplet 33, which describes the great effort the father has taken in bringing up the bride ('[He who] sits up all night long//Stands all day long'). This latter couplet is also, like couplet 32 for the mother, called '*ema*, '[one for] the father'. For this couplet, a longer elephant tusk is asked of the groom's group.

More important, according to the Endenese, than couplets 32 and 33, but less valuable (in the bridewealth ascribed to it), is couplet 35 ('[He who] is exhausted//Is drenched to the skin', which alludes to the pains to which the bride's father's father went in obtaining the bridewealth for the bride's mother. This couplet is called *waja*, '[one for] the old one'.

Couplet 34 ('For the taboo for helping the mother') alludes to the eldest sister of the bride, who works hard in the house, sometimes in place of the mother. And couplet 36 ('[He who] wears the big golden weapon') alludes to the protective role (metaphorically referred to as the 'big golden weapon') played by the bride's brother(s). Interestingly, each of these two units is composed of only one line and of three words (which is unusual, since most lines contain two words). Couplet 31 ('That we may eat freely') alludes to such non-agnatic relatives as the bride's mother's sisters; they are prohibited from eating the meat given by the groom's kin until they are given their portion of the bridewealth (hence the name 'that they may eat freely').

Couplets 38 and 39, ('Village, hamlet heads, Village youths') are both in Indonesian and must have been introduced quite recently; they are a straightforward listing of the persons who contribute in one way or another to the marriage ceremony. Couplet 37 ('[He who owns] the stone altar//The village forum') refers to the Lord of the Land of the village of the bride's family.

Couplets 40 and 41 allude to the most important figures among the bride's maternal relatives (that is, the bride's family's wife-givers): couplet 40 ('[He who] opens the mat//Arranges the pillow') is for the bride's mother's brother and couplet 41 ('[He who] sets up the sleeping room// Makes the bedroom') is for the bride's father's mother's brother. The mats (*té'é*) and the pillows (*rhani*) are items which constitute the gifts wife-givers give to their wife-takers.

Analysis of spatial symbolism

Among the several themes discernible in the text, I wish to focus on the use of spatial metaphors. In the text the social distance between the bride's and the groom's groups in the ritual sequence is translated into a spatial distance between two houses (or villages), and this is gradually reduced.

To understand fully this process in the text, we need consider the structure of the Endenese village and house. Rough sketches of the Endenese village and house are given in Figures 8.1 and 8.2. The village (*nua*) or the part inside the village (*'oné nua*) is juxtaposed with the outside part of the village (*rhonggo nua*). *Ndeko*, '[places] close to the village' forms a penumbra around the village, merging the village proper with the outside world. A village has its 'head' (*'úrhu*, the uppermost part of a village) and 'tail' (*'éko*); this pair sometimes has *ora'* 'centre', as an intermediary component. In the centre of the village, surrounded by a village yard (*wewa*), is a stone altar called *tubu musu//ora nata*, a symbol of the unity of the village as well as of the cosmos.

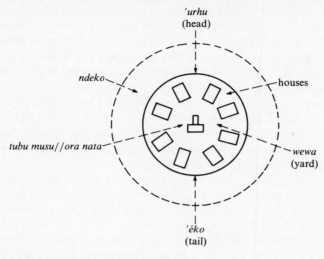

Figure 8.1. The village structure (*nua*)

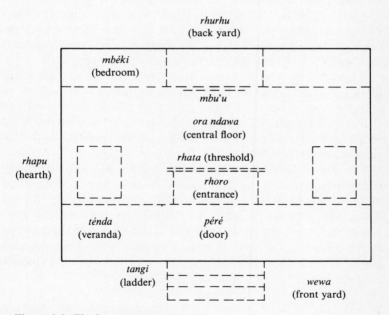

Figure 8.2. The house structure (*sa'o*)

The house, *sa'o*, or the space within, *réta 'oné* ('up inside'), is contrasted with the world outside, *rarhé tana* ('down on the ground'). In this opposition the ladder, *tangi*, functions as a connecting operator; in some other contexts, the yards, the one in front (*wewa*) or the one at the back (*rhurhu*), become an intermediary. Within the house structure, the house proper, *ora ndawa* ('the central floor'), is coupled with the veranda part, *ténda*; in this opposition the door (*péré*) forms the boundary between them. The veranda is a place where young men are supposed to sleep, whereas the bedrooms (*mbéki*) are for women; the central floor (*ora ndawa*) is for full-grown men. Within the *ora ndawa* the area farthest back is the most important: the place closest to the door is called *rhoro* (a place for slaves); then comes a sort of threshold, *rhata*, which marks the boundary between *rhoro* and *ora ndawa* proper; in the backmost part of *ora ndawa*, that is, against the wall of the *mbéki*, is a board called *mbu'u*, against which respected guests lean.

With this outline of the schemes of the Endenese spatial structure, let us now consider the text, especially those couplets which have spatial references, to see how canonical parallelism is imposed upon the scheme.

The spatial references begin with couplet 3, *sa'o*//*ténda*, 'the house//the veranda'. This pair is the only recurrent one in the whole text; it occurs in couplets 3, 17 and 18. This dyadic set occurs in other chants as well: chants for agricultural rituals (*soa sorha*) have this parallelism occasionally; for example, *sa'o méré*//*ténda rhéwa*, 'the big house//the long veranda', or *mera sa'o*//*ndi'i ténda*, '[we] live in the house//stay on the veranda'.

Then couplet 4 employs two items (the door//outside the village, *péré*//*ndeko*) which form a boundary in some schemes of house structure and village structure, thus making this couplet a transition from the preceding two introductory couplets that have a temporal dimension ('night//daytime'), and a spatial dimension ('the house//the veranda') to the following three topographical ones.

The next three couplets are closely related to each other. The three dyadic sets, 'the road//the path' (*rarha*//*wesa*), 'the ridge//the valley' (*worho*//*mbegho*) and 'the river//the water' (*rhowo*//*'aé*) occur in this sequence. Thus, one could say, at least, that the first item of each pair ('the road, *rarha*, 'the ridge', *worho*, and 'the river', *rhowo*) is syntagmatically related to the other. A brief look at other examples of the Endenese ritual language would show, moreover, that the three items are also paradigmatically related.

Worho rha'é wai	The ridges have not been crossed between the relatives,
Rarha rha'é rhaki	The roads have not been completed between the affines.

Nitu ndeka worho	The spirits [live] in the ridges,
Pa'i ndeka rhowo	The genii [live] in the rivers.

We see in the sequence of the three couplets (5, 6, 7) an axis of similarity projected onto the axis of continuity.

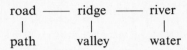

```
road —— ridge —— river
  |        |        |
path     valley    water
```

After this topographical sequence comes another three-couplet sequence (couplets 8, 9, 10), which describes the bride's village, followed by two non-spatial couplets (11 and 12). Supposing that non-spatial couplets serve to mark some semantically interconnected clusters, this sequence of the village description (couplets 8, 9, 10) is comparable to the next cluster (couplets 12, 13, 14) marked by the non-spatial couplet 16. This second cluster describes the outer house structure, as it were. In each sequence there occurs a one-line unit (couplets 9 and 14) which, in each case, refers to the intermediary item of some scheme (*wewa*, 'yard', and *tangi*, 'ladder').

Having finished the two clusters (couplets 8, 9, 10 and 13, 14, 15) with intermittent non-spatial couplets (11, 12, 16) as boundary markers, the text repeats the main theme twice in couplets 17 and 18, 'the house//the veranda'.

Then comes another cluster (couplets 19, 20, 21). This cluster is all about an inner house structure. The cluster begins with a description of the outermost structure of an inner house, 'the door//the bolt', followed by a description of the boundaries, 'the entrance//the threshold', and ends with a description of the most important area, that is, the area farthest from the door, 'the back wall//the floor'. The concentric scheme of the house is thus, tactfully, re-coded by canonical parallelism, while still retaining the frame work of the scheme intact.

The whole process of the bridegroom's journey as expressed in the text is recapitulated in Figure 8.3.

Marriage of running and following: *'ana paru dhéko*

As comparative material, let us examine another text which belongs to the same genre of ritual language. This text is about another form of marriage, *'ana paru dhéko*, the marriage of running and following.

Cases of *'ana paru dhéko* marriage vary considerably. Sometimes the girl enters the boy's house without letting him know beforehand. Sometimes the boy and girl come to an agreement and then ask some older woman to lead the girl to the boy's house at night.

When the girl is about to enter the boy's house, her legs should be

Theme
house//veranda
　　　Transition
　　door//outside village
　　　　　Topographical Cluster
　　　　　road//path
　　　　　ridge//valley
　　　　　river//water
　　　　　　　Village
　　　　　　village//hamlet
　　　　　　　yard
　　　　　　altar//forum
　　　　　　　　House
　　　　　　　ditch//edge of ditch
　　　　　　　　ladder
　　　　　　　veranda//balcony
　　　　　　　　　Theme
　　　　　　　　house//veranda
　　　　　　　　house//veranda
　　　　　　　　　　Inner House
　　　　　　　　　door//bolt
　　　　　　　　　entrance//threshold
　　　　　　　　　back wall//central floor

Figure 8.3. Outline representation of the bridegroom's journey

sprinkled with cold water to 'make her cool' (*pati keta*). If the bride's family does not yet know about the girl's running away, the boy's family has a choice. They can pay a prescribed amount of bridewealth as a kind of down payment, comparable to the *téo tanda* in a marriage of asking, which is intended to 'cool the heat down//put the warmth off' (*séwu petu//peré ara*). This payment is followed by an amicable negotiation of the rest of the bridewealth.

If the girl's group finds out about the girl's departure before the boy's group informs them, then they go to the boy's village and demand the bridewealth aggressively (*jeké*). They sit in front of the boy's house and swear at the boy's family, and do not let them out of the house. Sometimes they burn pepper and send its pungent smoke into the house. In response to these aggressive demands, the boy's group leaves the house and begins the negotiation of the bridewealth. In the Endenese rendering, once the *jeké* is finished, 'at night we are affines//in the daytime we are relatives', *kombé wai//rhera rhaki*.

The 'joints' of running and following: mbuku 'ana paru dhéko

In contrast to the *mbuku* in a marriage of asking, the *mbuku* of marriage of running and following is much more difficult to comprehend. The informant who provided this *mbuku* (Text 2) could not give a coherent account of what the narrative was about. Contrary to what could be expected from the description of this type of marriage, the informant asserted that the subject in couplets 1 to 7 in this text is the bridegroom, not the bride. Thus in the following *mbuku* there are two journeys for the bridegroom: one from the bride's village to his village with the bride on his back; and the other from his village to the bride's, presumably to conduct the marriage negotiation.

Text 2

1   *'Iné 'éru méré*   The mother is sound asleep,
    'Amé nandé ndaté   The father is sleeping well.

2   *Gedu mesu*   Sound of stamping, then they fall down,
    Nggigha nggorha   Noise of bumping, then they roll along.

3   *'Ura moo*   The muscles are tired,
    Siku nirhu   The elbows are sour.

4   *Dhoko to'o*   [He] brings [her],
    Wangga mbana   Carries [her] on his back.

5   *Saé sumbi*   [He] tears the fence,
    Teté kebé   Cuts down the railings.

6   *Nuka nua*   [He] ascends into the hamlet,
    Tama manga   Enters the village.

7   *Tunggu rhurhu*   [He] calls from the back garden,
    Pai wewa   Cries aloud from the yard.

8   *Woo wiwi bidi*   [He] fixes the trembling lips,
    Rhaké rhema rherhi   Lifts up the shivering tongue.

9   *Topo bongo*   The machete is dull,
    Taka baka   The axe is blunt.

10	*Nésa rarha*	[He] mows to make a road,
	Mbati wesa	Cuts the grass to make a path.
11	*Poké manda*	[He] stretches a board [on the thorny grass],
	Rero karo	Steps on the thorns.
12	*Ruri 'éri*	[He] goes close to the ditch,
	Parhé ngaté	Passes by the edge.
13	*Padha tangi*	[He] climbs up the ladder.
14	*Tika ténda*	[He] climbs up the veranda,
	Dhajo paso	Sits on the balcony.
15	*Pai tarhu*	[He] cries aloud [and we] answer,
	Niu oé	He calls [and we] reply.
16	*Mbé'o sa'o*	[He] knows the house,
	Nggesu ténda	Is familiar with the veranda.
17	*Sa'o muri*	That new house,
	Ténda meta	That fresh veranda.
18	*Kai péré*	[He] opens the door,
	Gheso 'usu	Loosens the bolt.
19	*Rhangga rhata*	[He] walks across the entrance,
	Rhérho rhoro	Passes the threshold.
20	*Mbé'i mbu'u*	[He] leans against the back wall,
	Dhaa ndawa	Throws his legs on the floor.
21	*Nara mbé'o weta*	The brother knows his sister,
	Weta mbé'o nara	The sister knows her brother.
22	*Kuni ma'é taku*	Don't hesitate in ordering,
	Dudu ma'é kengu	Feel free in asking.
23	*Begu méngi*	[She who] carries *sirih*,
	'Uné wunu	The stuff of leaves.
24	*Weti moki*	*Sirih pinang* for the [mother's] mouth.

25	*Pesa réwo*	That we may eat freely.
26	*Mata mésa*	[She who] dies alone,
	Ré'é rhédhé	Feels sick by herself.
27	*Kombé pa'i*	[He who] sits up all night long,
	Rhera dari	Stands all day long.
28	*Piré rhaka 'iné*	For the taboo for helping the mother.
29	*Mbonggo mbeta*	[He who] is exhausted,
	Baja mbasa	Is drenched to the skin.
30	*Mbendi wéa méré*	[He who wears] a big golden weapon.
31	*Tubu musu*	[He who owns] the stone altar,
	Ora nata	The village forum.
32	*Kepala Desa RK RT*	Village, hamlet heads.
33	*Pemuda*	Village youths.
34	*Weka té'é*	[He who] opens the mat,
	Soro rhani	Arranges the pillow.
35	*Kema mbéki*	[He who] sets up the sleeping room,
	Rona soja	Makes the bedroom.

Now let us consider the content of the *mbuku*, keeping in mind that it is about the journey of the groom and not the bride.

The narrative begins by describing the situation of the bride's house. The parents of the girl are awakened (couplet 2) from a peaceful sleep (couplet 1) because of the sound the man makes when he takes the girl away. The groom carries the bride on his back (couplet 4) until he feels exhausted (couplet 3). Before entering his own village (couplet 6) he has to tear down the fence around the village (couplet 5), *sumbi//kebé*, 'the fence//the railings'. He cries from outside his house (couplet 7) for someone to let them in. Couplet 8 is difficult to understand; it may refer to the account he gives to his parents about taking the bride.

With couplet 9 the second part of the story begins, that is, the groom's journey back to the bride's village. This second journey is made in the

same direction as that made by the groom in the *mbuku* of a marriage of
asking (see Text 1). As is the case of that *mbuku*, the groom in a marriage
of running and following also walks on the road (*rarha*//*wesa*, 'the
road//the path'); this time, however, he must make his road by himself
(couplet 10) (*nésa*//*mbati*), 'mow//cut the grass') and must pass through
the thorny grass (couplet 11) until his machete becomes blunt (couplet 9).

Couplets 12 to 20 are the same as in a marriage of asking; they describe
the groom's entering the bride's village and house. In the text of a marriage of asking, between the two couplets which described the transition
of groom's status was inserted a series of couplets which unfold the story
of the engagement in terms of planting metaphors (Text 1, couplets 22 to
26). Yet in the *mbuku* of a marriage of running and following (Text 2), this
part is truncated and the same two couplets (21 and 22, 'The brother
knows his sister//The sister knows her brother' and 'Don't hesitate in
ordering//Feel free in asking') are adjacent to each other without any
couplet standing between them. When the intended relationship is thus
established, the text shifts its focus to the *mata mbuku* about the kinsman,
which are also the same as in Text 1.

Comparison

As is discernible from the name of the first type of marriage, 'following
the road//connecting the path' (*mburhu nduu*//*wesa senda*), the relationship between two groups related by conjugal ties can be compared to a
road. When a man who has had a poor relationship with his wife-givers
(not only his wife's natal group but also his mother's natal group) dies,
then his agnates may be asked for extra death-payments, one of which is
called 'the path has become rotten//the road has become thickly covered'
(*wesa mbaru*//*rarha kapa*). Another relevant example is the expression
that refers to an established relationship (when all bridewealth has been
paid): 'the ridges have been crossed between affines//the roads have been
established between relatives' (*worho wai*//*rarha rhaki*).

The ridges and the roads (*worho rarha*) which the groom has to pass in
both texts are, thus, a metaphor of the relationship between his group and
the bride's group.

The two ritual sequences described in this paper deal with the very
different ways in which the establishment of new relationships is accomplished. The scenario of a marriage of asking abounds with botanic metaphors. It is expressed as one of agricultural activity. The relationship is
gradually formed. As opposed to the calmness of the scenario for a marriage of asking, that of a marriage of running and following presents a
war-like aspect. The idiom permeating the scenario is 'heat' (*petu*). The
bride, who comes into the bridegroom's house, is considered to be hot; so

she must be cooled down. In some regions the bride must be secluded in a hut for a few days before she enters the groom's house. For a year she is not allowed to talk with her parents, or to see them face to face. The bride's group is also hot; they have to be made cool. Without any ceremonial procedures, the two groups abruptly enter into the relationship of wife-giver and wife-taker. They stand, from the beginning, in a hostile relation (*papa ro'i*) and not in a harmonious relation (*papa pawé*). The scenario concerns itself with turning this 'heat' into 'coolness'. The wife-giver has given a woman, but not received anything from the wife-taker. Thus *jeké* is performed to gain balance. After *jeké* is concluded, everything becomes normal (*keta*, 'cool').

The contrast between the two scenarios finds expression, in the texts concerned, in the description of the bridegroom's journey. In the narrative of a marriage of asking, the bridegroom walks along *rarha masa//wesa rhina*, 'the neat road//the clean path'; whereas, in the narrative of a marriage of running and following, he becomes tired (couplet 3), slashes the grass to make his way (couplet 10) or tears the fence (couplet 5), before he gets to his destination. While the groom in a marriage of asking uses the normal junctures of inside and outside in the village (or the house), the groom in a marriage of running and following breaks the fixed boundary between outside and inside.

Furthermore, the bridegroom described in Text 2 never walks past the 'stone altar//the village forum' (*tubu musu//ora nata*), which symbolise the cosmic unity of the village. Thus, reference to 'the stone altar//the village forum' in the text of a marriage of asking (Text 1) expresses the cosmological acceptance of the bridegroom into the bride's group's world; the bridegroom in a marriage of running and following is never accepted in this way. In everyday life, Endenese often use the metaphor of a road in reference to a marriage relation: *ja'o mbana rarha kai*, 'I am going out for his road', meaning 'I am going out to his marriage negotiation (or arrangement)'. This is what could be called a conventional metaphor.

Yet the texts discussed here exhibit the productivity of that metaphor, which not only unfolds its rich spatial connotations in various parallel expressions but also contrasts, in narrative form, the types of relationships concluded by two different types of marriage.

Like other metaphors common to eastern Indonesian societies, the metaphor of the road or path presents a topic which needs minute, context-oriented analysis.

9

A QUEST FOR THE SOURCE:
THE ONTOGENESIS OF A CREATION MYTH
OF THE ATA TANA AI

E. D. LEWIS

> In ... the liberation of mythic thought and the separation of the
> person beginning to enter into his own history, there are no
> watertight partitions ... between the notions of person,
> intelligence, rationality, and myth.
>
> Maurice Leenhardt, *Do Kamo*

Introduction

The Ata Tana Ai (People of the Forest Land) inhabit the watershed and
tributary valleys of Napun Geté, the largest riparian system of the Regency of Sikka in eastern Flores. Tana Ai is a region of well-watered
forest land insulated from the neighbouring peoples of eastern Flores by
high mountain ridges to the east and west. Within their valley the Ata
Tana Ai have maintained a society and a ceremonial system that are quite
distinct from those of the peoples of central Sikka to the west and Larantuka (Regency of East Flores) to the east.

Despite increasing pressures from both the state and the Catholic
church, the Ata Tana Ai maintain their traditional religion and a ceremonial system that integrates clans and maternal houses into larger social
and political entities. Tana Ai is divided into several ceremonial domains,
called *tana* in the local language, each of which is led by a *tana puan*, who
is 'Source of the Domain' or 'Source of the Earth'. While they are generally comparable, the rituals and myths of the various *tana* of Tana Ai
comprise distinct traditions. The largest *tana* of Tana Ai, and the one
most important to the Ata Tana Ai themselves, is Tana Wai Brama. It is
this central domain whose myths and ritual language are the subjects of
this essay.

In the domain of Tana Wai Brama, the articulation of myth is a political activity. In the telling of a myth, the episodes included, the episodes
left out, and who tells a particular part of the sequence of a mythic
narration, are determined consciously by the men who organise, manage,

and enact the rituals that have as components the narration of history. The ritual specialists of Tana Ai all agree that the histories of the domains are immutably part of the Tana Ai world, but, given exigencies of performance, participants, and their purposes, there is an unlimited number of ways by which a history can be rendered as performed narration. Since performances are prior to texts, there are potentially as many texts of a myth as there are performed narrations of it. Texts of a single myth can exhibit differences of form, structure, and content of a degree equal to the radically different performances of a ritual of a single type. Any text of a myth thus reflects and is constituted by the state of relations among the ritual leaders of the community at the time of the myth's telling.

While the myth tellers of Tana Ai say that the histories they chant and the myths they relate are themselves timeless and without history, and are a given in the social world of the Ata Tana Ai, the access of the analyst to that world through texts is constrained by the circumstances in which a text is produced. The contingencies of circumstance must be charted if the text of a telling of a Tana Ai myth is to be understood. Indeed, an account of the circumstances of its telling is essential to any analysis of Tana Ai myth.

It follows that there are no *a priori* grounds for taking as definitive one particular text of a history as against another. All texts of the histories point the analyst in two directions simultaneously, both to the unchanging history of the domain as it is constituted in ideology and to the friable and permutable relations of individuals that, in the present, constitute the community.

This essay is about one man's rendering of a myth of the creation of the Ata Tana Ai and their world. It is about how that man came to articulate his version of the myth at a particular point in the history of his community and how a text of his myth came to be recorded. Rather than examining the text to puzzle out the myth, I wish to recount how the text of the narration of a history came into being, and to speculate about the reasons that its articulator spoke his myth in the form and with the content he did. I shall demonstrate that while the text of a linguistic event might seem to be coherent and discrete in itself, in the case of this creation myth it is in the narrator's act of creation itself that the myth's pragmatic and social meanings are to be found. The discovery of these meanings requires the analyst to explore the circumstances in which the myth was told and the desires and motives of its creator.

In the case to be reported here, the creation of one text of a history by one man led directly to the creation of other texts by other ritualists of the community. These additional texts were intended to fill in, clarify, and make more complete the original history. I shall examine here the way this composite text of Tana Ai ritual language was built up and amended by other chanters reacting to it, and shall draw some conclusions about what the process of creation implies for the study of Tana Ai myth and ritual generally. I shall argue that the way in which several chanters created over two years the texts presented here corresponds generally to the way in which Tana Ai ritualists co-operate in the tracing of the history of the domain in ritual. And I will show that the articulation of this particular myth in August 1979 to an ethnographer was intended to do more than just provide him with a text of a creation myth. It was a significant and successfully accomplished political act on the part of the myth teller.

The ceremonial system

The ceremonial system of the Ata Tana Ai consists of several different but related ritual cycles. Annual rites of agriculture are conducted by maternal descent groups, or *lepo* (houses), for all the gardens of their women. Members of a *lepo* organise the rites of burial for its members and once a year conduct the second-stage mortuary rites for members of the house who have died during the previous year.

Once every seven to fifteen years the membership of a clan, which consists of a number of affinally related houses, performs the third-stage mortuary rites for all the houses of the clan. By this ritual, the hair and fingernails of all the members of the clan who have died since its last performance are returned to the central, or 'source', reliquary basket of the clan, thereby elevating to the status of clan ancestors all those spirits of the dead.

Transfers of women from their mothers' clans to their fathers' in order to replace 'father's blood' occur regularly, but follow no fixed calendar. Male initiations are held when a cohort of potential initiates becomes large enough to justify the ritual. In addition, there are many smaller-scale rituals performed throughout the year for the opening of new gardens, the building of houses, hunting, curing, and to seek the sources of and reasons for illness and other misfortunes. All these rituals invoke and are addressed to the ancestors of the clans of the domain who act as intermediaries between the deity and the living members of the community.

Once every fifteen to twenty years the ritual life of the domain culminates, under the leadership of the *tana puan*, with the performance of *gren mahé*, the ceremony of ceremonies in Tana Wai Brama. In *gren mahé* the deity is addressed directly by the ritual leaders of Tana Wai Brama to correct all the accumulated imbalances in the domain and to ensure the fertility of the land and its people. *Gren mahé* requires contributions of personnel, animals, and rice from every clan and house of the domain, and the participation of virtually every member of the community. The ceremony requires a week to complete, but preparations and a variety of smaller-scale rituals leading to it begin many months before the forest site of the ritual is cleared and the special ceremonial houses are built.

The year of *gren mahé* is not determined by a fixed schedule, and the decision to hold a *gren* is the right and obligation of the *tana puan*. His decision takes into account many considerations, among them the pressures that build within the community for a *gren* to be held, the quality of harvests during the previous years, the availability of animals for sacrifice, and the length of time since the last *gren* was performed. Of great importance in deciding when to hold *gren mahé* is the estimation of the *tana puan* of the state of political relationships among the clans, houses, and territories of the domain.

While the *gren* is meant to draw together and to reassert the unity of the community as a whole, the performance of this culminal ritual provides the single most important arena for the potentially divisive political life of the domain. The *gren* occurs but once or twice during a person's adult life, but participation in it and satisfactory performance of its rituals provide men with the means of winning prestige as ritualists and of gaining political power within their clans. Of greater significance for the larger community, in *gren mahé* old allegiances are challenged and dissolved and new alliances are formed, and the leadership for a generation is produced. *Gren mahé* is thus a supremely political event as well as the single most important religious ceremony in Tana Ai. By it established leaders become ritual masters and elder statesmen of the community, and younger men begin to make their reputations for wisdom, ritual skill, and largesse, which put them on the path to a *gren* of their own.

When I began my fieldwork in Tana Ai in 1978 it had been seventeen or eighteen years since *gren mahé* had been held in Tana Wai Brama.[1] The 1970s had seen a succession of poor harvests. Half of the rice crop of 1978 was lost to late rains, and the rice and maize crops of 1979 were totally destroyed by simultaneous plagues of rice borers and mice. While the distribution of land holdings, the pattern of sharing of food within clans, and the availability of forest plants and animals prevent suffering due to the failure of crops in one year, two disastrously poor harvests in succession, following on several years of harvests that were below the expected norm, had left the community in a precarious position. In June and July of 1979 the *tana puan* of Tana Wai Brama received representations from several delegations of subaltern ritual leaders from different territories of the domain. All urged him to hold a *gren mahé* in October 1979, or in 1980 at the latest. The accepted view of the community was that *gren mahé* was the only means by which to restore the productivity of the gardens of Tana Wai Brama, the most likely cause of the suffering of the community being the long delay since the last *gren*.

This was the state of the community when, in July 1979, the *tana puan*, who had become during the previous two years my informant, friend, and sponsor in the community, approached me to suggest that we collaborate to record the myth of the creation of the world and the history of clan Ipir Wai Brama, the clan of the *tana puan*, whose ancestors were the founders of the domain of Tana Wai Brama.

The chanter and his office

During my first two years of fieldwork in Tana Ai, the *tana puan* of Tana Wai Brama was Mo'an Robertus Rapa Ipir Wai Brama. Mo'an Rapa never consented to give me an autobiography, and the events of his life and his role in them were not subjects that others in his community were willing to address. I know well his activities and role in Tana Wai Brama during the years 1978 and 1979, and from many conversations with him I can reconstruct some of the points of his life that distinguish him from other members of his house and clan.

Mo'an Rapa became *tana puan* of Tana Wai Brama around 1945. After World War II, and before the government of the Republic of Indonesia secured its authority in Flores in 1954, the island was ruled by a Council of Rajas and was, at least nominally, part of the Negara Indonesia Timur (State of East Indonesia). From 1950 to 1954 Rapa served as *kapitan* of Distrik Wérang under a Sikkanese noble who was *kapitan* of the division of Talibura. During his years as *kapitan*, Rapa established himself as a political force throughout Tana Ai and during his later years was often referred to as Pitang (from *kapitan*). In 1966 Rapa was again in Talibura to perform rituals of cooling following the '30 September Movement' of 1965. He was then one of several local leaders consulted on the question of the reorganisation of the Regency into *kecamatan* (district governments).

While Rapa saw material benefits for his community in the increasing influence of the Catholic church in Tana Ai during his lifetime, and his many children all attended the local Catholic primary school, he argued forcefully that Catholicism was merely a 'new addition' and that the real strength of Tana Wai Brama could be maintained only by adherence to the traditional religion and customs of Tana Ai. The last years of his life were marked by a feud with the local Catholic missionary over the question of his second wife, whom he married in the early 1960s. By 1976 the missionary realised that he could not hope to accomplish much in Tana Wai Brama without working amicably with its *tana puan*, and a tacit settlement of the dispute between *tana puan* and priest was reached. The missionary ignored Rapa's bigamy, and Rapa for his part ceased arguing against Catholicism, though he continued to promote the traditional religion and its rituals as better serving the spiritual needs of the domain.

The responsibility for the physical and spiritual well-being of a *tana* is vested in its *tana puan*, the 'centre, source, trunk, foundation' of the

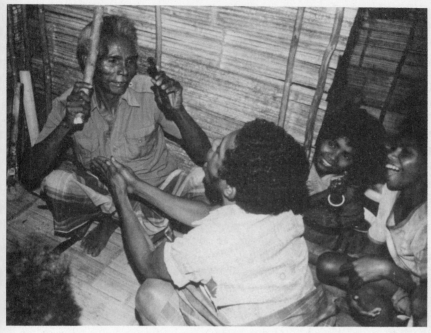

The *tana puan* of Tana Wai Brama 'chisels' a classificatory sister's son as part of the 'cooling' of his new house (1978). This rite, called *paltok*, 'opens' the mind to the *ngeng ngerang* of the domain. Note M'oan Rapa's daughters (right) looking on from the hearth of the house.

domain. It was in his capacity as *tana puan* that Rapa decided that *gren mahé* should be held in 1980. Preparations for the *mahé* celebration began in July 1979 when, a few weeks before his death, Mo'an Rapa 'spoke the words *gren mahé*' to the other ritual leaders of the domain, thereby setting into motion plans for its performance the following year.

The language of Tana Ai ritual

Published texts of ritual speech[2] from different communities in eastern Indonesia reveal many similarities with regard to the formal structures of composition and narrative by which this special genre of language can be distinguished from its ordinary counterparts. While there are few detailed linguistic studies of ritual languages or comparisons of the syntactic differences between ritual and ordinary languages,[3] the ethnographies of eastern Indonesia indicate that the circumstances in which ritual speech is employed and the uses to which ritual language is put vary from one society to another.

Rotinese ritual language, for example, is employed for a variety of purposes but 'it is not a vehicle for communication with the spirits ... nor is it a vehicle for the preservation of ancestral histories' (Fox 1971:221).[4] Rather, the ritual language of the Rotinese is primarily 'the language of formal social or ceremonial interaction' (*ibid.*). By contrast, among the Ata Tana Ai, chanting in ritual language is the only medium in which the myths of the creation of the world and its human inhabitants and the histories of the clans, which comprise the myths of the founding of the domains of Tana Ai, are recounted. As a part of offerings, ritual language is also the medium for invocations of ancestral spirits of clans and of communication with the deity. Ritual language is a necessary and ineluctable part of the performance of rituals; it is used for no other purpose, and is not employed outside of ritual.

The general term for 'language' in the dialect of the Ata Tana Ai is *sara*.[5] Thus Sara Tana Ai is the 'language' or 'speech of Tana Ai'.[6] The language of everyday discourse is distinguished from ritual language, the special idiom for communication with the ancestors and the recounting of the histories of the domain. To speak in ordinary language of quotidian matters is *marin plaun*, 'to speak simply, straightforwardly'.[7] The language of ritual, which comprises a separate linguistic field and is recognised by the Ata Tana Ai as a special genre of speech, is called *latu lawan* or *bleka hura*. *Bleka hura* is the most commonly used and perhaps the most general term for ritual chants. *Bleka* means 'rhythm' or 'cadence' and *hura* means 'pattern' or 'ordered (and orderly) sequence'; *bleka hura* thus means 'patterned speech', where the pattern is in the parallelism of words, phrases, and lines that comprise a couplet of ritual language. The word *bleka*, used singly in everyday language, means 'ritual chant'. The phrase *bleka hura*, itself exhibiting the semantic pairing of ritual language, is used synonymously with *latu lawan*, 'to speak boldly'.[8]

The Ata Tana Ai are a very soft-spoken people. Normal conversation has, to a Western ear, the quality of quiet murmuring, punctuated, to be sure, by laughter and rhetorical exclamations. The Ata Tana Ai themselves say that serious talk requires decorum and conformity to etiquette, which, they say, results in the subdued timbre and restrained registers that characterise their conversation. In contrast, ritual chanting involving more than one chanter is projected from the diaphragm and is intended to be heard by the crowds of people who attend large ceremonies. The term 'bold speech' thus characterises well the first distinction that the Ata Tana Ai make between their ordinary and ritual languages.

Not all ritual language is performed loudly. Invocations to the ancestors of individual houses, on occasions of small-scale rituals, are most commonly performed by a single chanter who addresses in ritual language not a crowd of people but a house post or small offering stone in a soft, murmurous, and syncopated monologue that is heard by no one other than the chanter himself and the ancestors. These muted performances are also referred to as *latu lawan*, which reveals the more fundamental distinction between ordinary and ritual speech. *Latu lawan* is bold, because addressing the ancestors and the deity is a dangerous business with the potential for inauspicious consequences. Errors of ordinary discourse can be corrected by additional talk but ritual language is not so correctable. Ritual language follows canons of sequence and formulae of its own and, if errors are made in performance, chanters cannot recall their words. The consequences of errors are the sanctions of the unseen and unknowable world of spirits which are visited upon the whole of the community. *Latu lawan* is bold speech because its performance requires bold and knowledgeable men.

The histories and their performance

The chants that employ bold speech are referred to by a number of terms and phrases. The phrase *kleteng latar*, which in ritual language is paired with the synonymous phrase *weten wenet*, is used in a general way to mean 'chant', but *kleteng latar*//*weten wenet* carries the connotation of 'history', and in its specific meaning refers to those chants that are histories of the journeys of the ancestors of the clans of Tana Ai to the valley where they founded their domains. These histories are more precisely called *ngeng ngerang*, a phrase which, in its strict sense, refers to a specific genre of chant but which is also used loosely as a synonym of *bleka*. Thus, the chanters of Tana Ai, when precise expression is required, speak of the *ngeng ngerang sukun*, 'the histories of the clans', while *kleteng latar* is a phrase used by people who are not themselves chanters and is heard more frequently in central Sikka (Tana Krowé) to mean clan history.

While all ritual speech employs the same ritual language, two broad categories of chants can be identified according to differences of themes and the different purposes they serve. In Tana Wai Brama all ceremonial events require the summoning and invocation of the ancestors of the group performing a ritual. Invocations make up the first category of chants, and are the most frequently performed chants. In so far as ritual always has an end or purpose, chanters invoke ancestral spirits to implore the spirits to attend the ritual, to take note of the rites being performed, and to secure a desired state of affairs, or end, for the living members of the group to which the spirits also belong. The chants employed in these invocations are called *neni plawi*, 'to request, to implore', or 'requests and entreaties'.[9] Each ritual specialist has his own style of chanting *neni plawi* and individual chants, and their contents, are composed and performed to reflect the exigencies of particular ritual occasions.[10]

The second category of chants is that to which the Ata Tana Ai refer generically as *sejara*.[11] *Sejara* are the 'histories and genealogies' by which the people of Tana Wai Brama recount and preserve origins and the sequences of events that have produced the physical and social worlds they inhabit. With the histories the Ata Tana Ai account for the contemporary conditions of those worlds. The chronicles of the *sejara* are broadly divided into three sequential parts which, it is said by the ritual specialists, comprise the *oda geté*, the 'great precedence', of the histories. The first part is the *Ngeng Ngerang Tota Nian Paga Tana*, which recounts the creation of the world. The second is the *Ngeng Ngerang Tota Iang Paga Bangu*, the history of the creation of humankind and the first human beings, Iang and Bangu. The third part consists of the *Ngeng Ngerang Tota Sukun Pulu Paga Wot Lima*, and comprises the histories of the 'fifteen clans' of Tana Ai.

Each of the major three parts of the histories is a *ngeng ngerang*, as is each of the individual histories of the various clans. An examination of this phrase and the class of narratives it denotes will demarcate a number of fundamental ideas that must be explained if the nature of the histories is to be understood. *Ngeng*, the noun formed by the affixation of the nominalising morpheme *-ng* to the root *ngé*,[12] means 'people' in the sense of 'race, tribe, nation, generation, family', that is, people who share a common origin and descent. *Ngerang* means 'to disperse, to spread, to scatter, to go out of'. *Ngeng ngerang* can thus be glossed as 'spread of the people', the journeys by which the world was created, peopled with human beings, and by which the ancestors of the clans of the Ata Tana Ai came to settle in their valley, to found there the ceremonial domains of Tana Ai, and then to create Tana Ai society.

The phrase *ngeng ngerang*, as used in ritual speech, also has connotations of genealogy, the history of the generations between the creation of the world and living Ata Tana Ai, traced in the sequence of the ancestors of the clans. The people who are spoken of as being one people, the Ata Tana Ai who are related by *ngeng ngerang*, are actually of many clans. Each clan is thought to have a different origin, and the *ngeng ngerang* recount how the ancestors, who were of different origins, came to share the same *tana*, 'earth' or 'domain'.

The names of the parts of the *ngeng ngerang* are extended by the phrase *tota ... paga*. *Tota* means 'to seek, to search, to look for something'.[13] These names for the histories that recount the creation of the world, the origin of human beings, the journeys of the ancestors of the clans to Tana Ai and their coming together in that empty valley to create the society of Tana Wai Brama, can thus be interpreted as:

ngeng	ngerang	tota	paga
people,	spread,	to seek,	to find,
generations	dispersal	to search	to attain

'the spread of the generations to seek and to attain'

Tota and *paga*, the seekings and attainings of the names of the parts of the *sejara*, refer to the finding of the world, the first human beings, and the clans, but have a dual meaning. First, the narratives recount epic searches: of the creator for dry land, as well as for plants, animals, and people to inhabit it; and the journeys of the ancestral Ata Tana Wai Brama for a 'broad earth and a wide, empty land' in which to settle. Second, the ritual specialists conceive the recounting of the histories on ceremonial occasions to be quests, through ritual language, for the sources and origins of things by which the order of the world is re-established. While the events recounted in the histories follow one another in mythologically established sequences, the chanters view their quests as moving backward from contemporary states of affairs to their sources and origins. *Sejara* recount origins, and in each recounting chanters, speaking in ritual language, engage in a quest for the source.

In ritual speech, chanters seek not only the cosmic origins of the world but also, in the invocatory chants of the *neni plawi*, they seek *waké puan réan wangun*, 'to construct the source, to recreate the growth (or development)' of a particular event or state of affairs that has had an unfortunate effect on the life of the community, a house, or one of its members. Every event, whether it is a storm or plague that affects the whole of the valley or an accident or illness that befalls a person, has a source or cause. Causes are discoverable by tracing the history, that is, by seeking the source, of the event in past actions of the community or in a person's life and activities. In *neni plawi* chanters seek these sources, which are discovered by communion with the ancestors who reveal causes, and to whom offerings are made to correct errors and to re-establish balance and order in the life of an individual or of the community. Thus, both invocations and histories are quests for sources, but they are quests of different kinds and are distinguishable in terms of the structures, themes, and characters of their performance. Some of the differences between *neni plawi* and *ngeng ngerang* can be tabulated as below.

Neni Plawi (Invocations)	*Ngeng Ngerang* (Histories)
Quest for the source of an event, illness, or state of affairs.	Quest for the source (that is, the origins of the world, human beings, clans) as the beginning and history of the domain.
Waké puan réan wangun.	*Tota Oda*

Performed by solitary chanter.	Usually performed by groups of chanters.
Language is chanted in monotone or relatively uninflected tone of voice.	Language is chanted or sung more slowly and rhythmically; voice more dynamic and loud; may be accompanied by dancing or swaying in place.
Texts of performances by a single chanter show uniformity of style and content from one performance to another.	Segments of histories are passed from one chanter to another in turn; one mentions a theme which is then developed by the next chanter. Structure of chant more amorphous, though general line of thematic development can be perceived.

The *ngeng ngerang* of the Ata Tana Wai Brama, were they ever to be recorded fully, would form a vast corpus of texts of ritual speech. That corpus is potentially endless for two reasons. First, ritual speech requires the use of a special language and, as with any language, the variety of utterances in it is unlimited. Second, the corpus of the histories is potentially unlimited because the history it recounts is not yet fully played out. The view of the Ata Tana Wai Brama with regard to their *sejara* is that many, perhaps most, of the events that will come to pass in the domain have been ordained by the ancestors but have not yet occurred. As things happen, and the histories unfold as events, they are recounted by ritual specialists through the composition of new verse. The chanters of Tana Ai do not, however, view the composition of 'new' *sejara* as a creative activity of individual men; rather, such additions are occasions of the chanters 'remembering' some part of the history that had not been chanted previously, or at least had not been heard previously, by the living chanters of the community. In the same way, no part or episode of the *sejara* is ever truly lost by being forgotten. Episodes never before heard by living ritual specialists can be recovered by the 'remembering' of chants, as when a gifted younger chanter 'inherits' the knowledge of a classificatory mother's brother who has been dead for many generations.

While there are many talented chanters in Tana Wai Brama, their abilities are not thought to reflect individual intelligence, talent, or creative ability, but are thought to be gifts of the ancestors. In the view of the ritual specialists of Tana Wai Brama, the knowledge of all great chanters is passed to one among their classificatory sisters' sons. Young chanters acquire their knowledge of ritual language not by study or by memorising chants but by receiving their knowledge of the language of the histories and the histories themselves in a single flash of insight and understanding when, it is said, they *himo wa déa li'ar*, 'receive the tongue and take the voice' of their ancestors' knowledge. Thereafter, having received knowledge of the language of ritual, they can add to that knowledge the skills of performance that come from practice and hearing the performances of other experienced chanters. Only a few men are chosen and there is no predicting who, among the living members of the community, the ancestors will choose to receive the voice.

Knowledge of the histories, as it exists in the community in a given generation, is distributed among men who form the corps of the chanters of the domain. Each man is said to hold a part of the whole. The *sejara* begin with the creation of the world and proceed in a strict sequence through the creation of humankind to the detailed histories of the clans of the domain. Similarly, an order of ritual precedence, determined by the hierarchical ranking of clans within the domain, governs how various parts of the sequence of the histories are distributed among the chanters of the domain. Proximity of status to the *tana puan* determines which part of the sequence is held by a chanter, with 'source' ritualists holding the episodes of the creation while 'peripheral' ritualists hold the *ngeng ngerang* of their clans and territories. At the centre and head of the system of ritual precedence is the *tana puan*, who holds the *Ngeng Ngerang Tota Nian Paga Tana*, the history of the search for land and finding of earth, in which the creation of the world is recounted. The *tana puan* is said to be the only person who knows also the overall sequence of all the chants of the domain, and therefore it is he alone who is qualified to organise *gren mahé*.

The Source of the Domain is always of clan Ipir Wai Brama, which, as the senior and founding clan of the domain, is 'source' (*puan*) among the five principal clans of the domain. Chanters of clan Ipir Wai Brama also hold the *Ngeng Ngerang Sukun Ipir Wai Brama*, the history of that clan. Chanters of clan Tapo, the second clan in the ranking of ritual precedence, hold the *Ngeng Ngerang Tota Iang Paga Bangu*, the history of the origins of human beings. The three remaining clans hold various auxiliary histories (including the histories of hunting, the acquisition of dogs, the making of fire, and the building of houses) that are considered of lesser significance in the *oda geté*, the 'great precedence', of the *sejara*.[14] In addition, men of each clan are responsible for holding the knowledge of the histories of their clans, and for the proper performance of those histories in *gren mahé*, the culminal rituals of the ceremonial system of the domain.

In the course of a career as a ritual specialist, a chanter acquires considerable knowledge of the histories of clans other than his own, and the *ngeng ngerang* of the creation. Holding rights to particular segments of the whole, vested in chanters by virtue of their clan affiliation and ritual status, does not imply a complete exclusivity of knowledge. Rights to parts of the *sejara* entail an obligation and responsibility of individual chanters to see that, in a performance of that part of the whole they hold, their segments are chanted in the proper place within the sequence of the whole, and that the elements of their segments are chanted in the proper order. In chanting the *oda geté* of the domain, or any individual *ngeng ngerang*, the sequence of the chant is crucial in so far as the events and genealogies recounted in the histories must follow one another in proper succession.

Chants of *neni plawi* accompany all rituals of the annual agricultural cycle and events marked ritually in the life-cycle of individuals. *Neni plawi* are also required for many kinds of rituals for the correction of *halan hulir*, 'errors and forgettings', that result in illness, the death of animals, disputes, and other misfortunes. These chants are performed almost daily in the domain. In contrast, the *sejara* of the domain, which encode its history and the great precedence, are performed very infrequently and only on the occasion of *gren mahé*. *Gren mahé* are the only celebrations of the domain that require the participation of every clan and house of Tana Wai Brama and of every member of the community.

Gren mahé entwines two principal strands of ritual. One is a sequence of animal sacrifices sponsored by the houses of the domain. The blood of sacrificial animals is the agent of 'cooling' the earth and its people, who, during the intervals between *gren mahé*, accumulate dangerous ritual 'heat'. This heat threatens the fertility of humans and their gardens and puts at risk beneficial relations between the worlds of living people and the spirits and deity. The other thread of ritual in the *gren* is the chanting of the *sejara*, by which balance is restored to the world and its human community by restructuring the sources and origins from which the community arose. The quest for the source consists of chanting the *oda geté*, the complete sequence of the *ngeng ngerang*, beginning with the creation of the world and ending with the histories of the clans.

The ritual specialists of Tana Wai Brama say that the histories of the domain are narrated completely only on the infrequent occasions of *gren mahé*. But even then, if the *gren* of 1980 is taken as a guide, the unfolding of the *sejara* is less than complete. While in principle the narration of the complete *sejara*, with all its episodes chanted in proper sequence, is required for the performance of *gren mahé*, this seems not to happen in the actual event. In the performance of the histories in 1980 reference was made to all the essential episodes of the *sejara*, but in chanting some of those episodes were elaborated more fully than others, to which only elliptical references were made. The chanters themselves point out that there is no ideal text which they, in performance, seek to reduplicate or by which they judge a performance. In the narration of a particular history there are bound to be parts that are 'not remembered' by contemporary chanters. The notion of 'remembering the history' implies that the complete history, while it may never be chanted in one performance, is never lost, and that parts unknown to contemporary chanters are quite likely to be 'remembered' by future chanters. Remembering parts of any *ngeng ngerang* that have not been heard by living chanters is possible because the 'voice' of the chanter is supposed to be inherited directly by a living chanter along with the spirit and knowledge of *hadat* ('custom', 'tradition') he acquires from deceased ritual experts.

While much of the incompleteness of chanting can be attributed to differences in the skills of the chanters, or more generally to the impossibility of performing flawlessly a ritual as complex as *gren mahé*, there is perhaps a more fundamental principle at work, a principle of efficacious incompleteness. The performance of the histories requires the participation of many chanters who co-operate in the total performance.[15] Each chanter represents a division of society that has rights to the ceremony and specified obligations to contribute to its performance. The presence of a chanter as a representative of his group (either house or clan), and his contribution to the performance, is sufficient of itself to fulfil the requirements of the *oda* and guarantee the efficacy of the ritual as a whole. Beyond that, there is no requirement that his contribution to the performance of the histories be complete or flawless. The purpose of the *gren* is to re-establish a specific order in society; less attention is devoted to the content of the framework established by that order. No chanter aims at a complete rendering of the history he holds, and indeed, a degree of ellipsis in performance is not only tolerated but is thought to be desirable.[16]

Ritualists are holders of a special and recondite knowledge. It is expected that they know the histories, but it is never expected that they will fully divulge that knowledge. To chant a history fully would undermine the pregnancy of ritual speech as the most powerful of ritual operators. Thus, while words are required for ritual, the Word itself is never fully articulated, for to do so would be to arrogate power that properly belongs to the ancestors and the deity.[17]

The text and its origins

The *gren mahé* of 1980 followed by a year the death of Mo'an Robertus Rapa Ipir Wai Brama, the Source of the Domain of Tana Wai Brama. Because a new *tana puan* had not been recognised in November 1980, the *Ngeng Ngerang Tota Nian Paga Tana*, which was within the purview of the *tana puan* and would normally have been chanted by him during the *gren*, was not chanted as part of the publicly performed rites of the *gren*.

Instead, other chanters performed this crucial first component of the *sejara* in one of the many closed rites, attended only by the ritual specialists, during several weeks of preparations for the *gren mahé*. Thus no record exists of the creation myth as it is actually performed by the Source of the Domain in the *gren*. I was fortunate, however, to obtain a text of the myth in another way.

Six weeks before his death in August 1979, and during the middle of the ceremonial season of that year, Mo'an Rapa proposed to me that the history of his clan, Sukun Ipir Wai Brama, should be set down in writing. Mo'an Rapa was pre-eminently qualified to undertake the recording of the history of his clan. In a happy coincidence of clan affiliation, ritual position, and individual talent, not only was he the ritual head of his people and the domain that bears the name of his clan, but he was also regarded by the people of the domain as the most accomplished of the chanters of Tana Ai. Any rendition of a myth by Mo'an Rapa would be regarded as authoritative by the other chanters of the community.

Mo'an Rapa would not agree to making a sound recording of his chanting, saying that his voice was not a good one and that chanters, in actual performances of the histories, include too many repetitions in their narratives and are liable to put parts of a history out of their proper sequence. These aspects of ritual speech in performance Mo'an Rapa found objectionable. In fact, Mo'an Rapa had a very fine chanting voice, and the few recordings of his chanting that I made on other occasions reveal an unusual elegance of composition and lack the faults he claimed his chanting would display. He also pointed out that it is proper to perform the history only on occasions of *gren mahé*. It is therefore likely that he felt it to be inappropriate to perform the chant vocally on other than a truly ceremonial occasion, and that it was for this reason that he preferred writing the history.[18]

I provided Mo'an Rapa with pencil and paper, and on three consecutive evenings he dictated the history to his daughter, who was at that time seventeen years of age and attending the middle school (SMP) in Talibura on the north coast of Flores. Mo'an Rapa considered his project to be of sufficient importance to recall his daughter from the coast in order to assist him in writing down the history.[19]

Once it was completed, I typed the manuscript and then elicited Mo'an Rapa's comments on the chant. I first recited the text back to him, making corrections, emendations, and minor rearrangements of the sequence of some couplets as he suggested changes. I then solicited, line by line and word by word, his exegesis of the text with regard to the meanings of its lexicon and to elucidate metaphor and points of structure.[20]

Throughout our collaboration Mo'an Rapa was intent on providing the clearest and most orderly text of the history. One of the reasons for undertaking the project was, as he told me, that none of the younger men of the community knew well the whole chant and none knew the proper sequence in which its episodes and couplets should be revealed; writing the chant would provide a means of preserving for the chanters of his clan this important aspect of the history of the domain.

The project required five weeks and was completed to Mo'an Rapa's satisfaction on 10 August 1979. Then, at noon on 14 August, Mo'an Rapa died.[21] Following his death, I typed the text of the history, bound a copy of the typescript, and presented it to Mo'an Rapa's daughter as a memento of my collaboration with her father. The bound copy of the text soon became an object of scrutiny and debate among the ritual leaders of the domain, who visited Rapa's house from all parts of the valley to examine the typescript, to hear its contents read, and to argue its merits and correctness. Never before had a written text of a history been made available to chanters of the domain.

For two weeks following his death no mention of the *gren mahé* was made within my hearing. In September, as my wife and I were preparing to leave Flores, one of the men who would be instrumental in bringing the *gren* to a successful conclusion told me, in response to my query, that the *gren* was certain to be held in 1980. The 'words *gren mahé* [had] been spoken', and the community and its ritual leaders were thus enjoined to perform the ceremonies. Terrible calamities would befall the domain if the words were not followed by action.

The celebration of the domain is initiated when the *tana puan*, taking a decision of his own initiative, 'speaks the words *gren mahé*'. In speaking the words, he informs the ritual specialists of the domain that a *gren* is to be organised and performed following the next harvest. Mo'an Rapa 'spoke the words' in July 1979 and thereby initiated the *gren* that was held in November 1980.[22] When he proposed to set down the history of his clan, Mo'an Rapa had already decided that a *gren* would be performed, and he knew I would be leaving Flores in September 1979. The *gren* and the *sejara* were undoubtedly already in his mind.

The history of the people of clan Ipir Wai Brama and their founding of the ceremonial domain of Tana Wai Brama are the *Ngeng Ngerang Sukun Ipir Wai Brama*. The history provided by Mo'an Rapa is prefaced by a briefer account of the creation of the world, to which Mo'an Rapa gave the title *Sejara Tota Nian Paga Tana*, 'The History of the Search for Land and Finding of Earth'.

Ngeng Ngerang Tota Nian Paga Tana
(The History of the Search for Land and Finding of Earth)

Mo'an Robertus Rapa Ipir Wai Brama

1	*Sugung wura wae lau*	Dive downward through the oily sea,
2	*Bawang olé wae wawa*	Swim below the ocean waves,
3	*Da'a lau tahi taru*	Reach downward into the viscous waxy sea,
4	*Toma wawa naro naké*	Reach below into the substance of the black void,
5	*Hulut hulut wae wawa*	See, see below,
6	*Halet halet wae wawa*	Look, look below,
7	*Muok du'e tahi unen*	Fashion with the hands the substance that lies within the sea,
8	*Botin du'e wair ' loran*	Knead with the hands what lies in the midst of the waters.
9	*Ia gu*	Then,
10	*Sugung sugung wae wawa*	Dive, dive below,
11	*Wawa wau wuor neti*	Below, go downward and carry the lumps,
12	*Bawan bawan wae wawa*	Swim, swim below,
13	*Wawa wau popor lawat*	Beneath, go downward and collect the piles.
14	*Ia gu*	Then,
15	*Sugung wura wae réta*	Dive upward through the oily sea,
16	*Bawan olé wae réta*	Swim upward through the ocean waves,
17	*Réta a wuor tegu*	Go upward and throw out the lumps of mud,
18	*Réta a popor leong*	Go upward and throw into a pile,
19	*Bitak hak nian anak*	Broken but the land was small,
20	*Gegar hak tana kesik*	Shattered but the earth was small.
21	*Ia gu*	Then,

22	Sugung mole wa'i ha	Dive again once more,
23	Bawan mole ha homa	Swim once again,
24	Wawa wau wuor eti	Descend below and take a lump,
25	Wawa wau popor lawat	Go downward below and collect the piles.
26	Ia gu	Then,
27	Sugung wura wae réta	Dive upward through the oily sea,
28	Bawan olé wae réta	Swim upward through the ocean waves,
29	Topo bliro lari aman	Call the father of the Brahminy kite,
30	Hawong gak nobon bura	Summon the white hawk,
31	Bliro na bur wor	The Brahminy kite to go strewing [mud] to add to [the land],
32	Gak na teto kesa	The hawk to go distributing [mud] to increase [the earth],
33	Nian newan we'en geté	The land was enabled to grow larger,
34	Tana newan wekang klewang	The earth was enabled to increase its breadth.
35	Ko	But,
36	Bemo ganu kebo wuan	Soft like the fruit of the bemo tree,
37	Klémur ganu padu daha	Mushy like the ripe papaya.
38	Ia gu	Then,
39	Wori lé'u guman rua	Dried for two nights,
40	Pak lé ' u leron telu	Baked in the sun for three days,
41	'Odo woko sikit di'in	Order the woko bird to run lightly and make footprints in the earth,
42	Gareng kang sega tadan	Command the crow to hop up and down and make marks on the earth,
43	'Odo woko dodo inan	Order the mother of the woko dodo bird,

44	*Kang raga jawa aman*	And the father of the crow of Larantuka,
45	*Sikit hat wu'un boga*	To run lightly over the ground but its bones were broken,
46	*Sega hak larun bewar*	To hop up and down but its bones split,
47	*Terang ganu watu napan*	[The ground was] hard like a stone protruding from the earth,
48	*Mangan ganu tana inan*	Strong like the mother of the earth,
49	*Gi' it biri baru sinan*	Sturdy as the *biri baru* tree of China,
50	*Mangan bao ara jawan*	Strong as the banyan tree of Larantuka.
51	*Ko*	But,
52	*Detun poin désak poin*	Only level and flat,
53	*Koben poi naman poi*	Only smooth and unobstructed,
54	*Topo rutun bukun ploi*	Call the porcupine to burrow and clear the [path of] grass,
55	*Hawong béhar lera sesa*	Summon the giant forest rat to scoop and scratch [a path].
56	*Ia gu*	Then,
57	*Wair newan ba bajang*	The water was enabled to flow far,
58	*Watu newan gogo pout*	And the rocks were enabled to roll down to the land's end [the sea shore],
59	*Dopo ... ... [?]*	Call ... ... [?]
60	*Hawong wodon géri wolon*	Summon the *wodon* bird to scrape up the hills,
61	*Ilin di newan tawa*	The mountains were also enabled to rise up,
62	*Wokan di newan léma*	The peaks were also enabled to climb upward.
63	*Ko*	But,
64	*Nian la'en wulu tawa*	On the land vegetation had not yet grown,

65	*Tana la'en héron léma*	From the earth green plants had not yet risen,
66	*Pati du'a Nipa inan*	These were dibbled by the mother of the woman Nipa,
67	*Mula tena nian wulu*	[Who] planted to make the vegetation of the land,
68	*Oba mo'an Néhok aman*	Dibbled by the father of the man Néhok,
69	*Pa'at tena tana héron*	[Who] planted to make the green plants of the earth,
70	*Nian di wulu tawa*	The land then grew with vegetation,
71	*Tana di héron léma*	On the earth green plants came up.
72	*Huk mole wa'i ha*	Think again one time,
73	*Nera mole ha homa*	Meditate again once more,
74	*Lau wau tedu watu*	Descend downward breaking the rock,
75	*Wawa wau mela ai*	Descend downward cutting the trees,
76	*Watu riat newan bitak*	The coral stone could be broken,
77	*Ai lajat newan boga*	The trees could be parted,
78	*Da'a wawa rumang dadin*	Descend down to where dark[ness] is,
79	*Toma wawa iteng totan*	Get to the place below where blackness is found,
80	*'Litin wawa napan wutun*	Sit below on the protruding stone and the final reach,
81	*'Lér wawa repit puan*	Lean against the cliff at the centre of the earth,
82	*Nian wawa dudak rumang*	Below the land was obstructed and dark,
83	*Tana wawa eho teker*	The earth below was tight and constricted,
84	*'Odo ui getin etin*	Order the crab to open a path with its dorsal spines,
85	*Laba watu wae réta*	To chisel upward through the stone,
86	*Gareng umen donen oan*	Command the snail to show the path,
87	*Korek tana wae réta*	To bore upward through the earth,

88	*Topo guna puku nulu*	Call the *guna*-spirit to lead the way,
89	*Hawong déwa gawi wa'a*	Summon the *déwa*-spirit to step at the front,
90	*Guna kobu 'i'ur patar*	*Guna*-spirit as a crocodile with a broken tail,
91	*Déwa éto brae brana*	*Déwa*-spirit as an *éto*-fish savage and vicious,
92	*Laba watu wae réta*	Chisel upward through the stone,
93	*Korek tana wae réta*	Bore upward through the earth,
94	*Da'a réta liwun napan*	Reach upward to the pool and protruding stone,
95	*Toma réta rani hading*	Arrive upward at the ladder lying across the stream.
96	*Huk mole wa'i ha*	Think again one time,
97	*Nera mole ha homa*	Meditate again once more,
98	*Laba watut wae réta*	Chisel upward through the stone,
99	*Korek tana wae réta*	Bore upward through the earth,
100	*Da'a réta nobe no*	Reach upward climbing hand over hand,
101	*Toma réta kedo kolot*	Arrive atop the stairs and look over the top,
102	*Tuna inan manu goko*	The mother of the eel and the chicken that pecks open,
103	*Legi 'lora wair matan*	Reach the centre of the spring,
104	*Tuna 'inan deten térang*	The mother of the eel leads the water along the bamboo aqueduct,
105	*Posi loli go'i wair*	Digs an opening for the water,
106	*Wair di ba bajang*	The water then flowed freely,
107	*Watut di gogo pout*	The stones then rolled down to the edge of the land,
108	*Laba laba wae réta*	Chisel, chisel upward,
109	*Korek korek wae réta*	Bore, bore upward,
110	*Toma ba'a kung bio*	Until the cord of heaven and earth is reached,
111	*Sapé ba'a tali plou*	Until the hanging cord is reached,
112	*Léma depo kung bio*	Ascend following the cord of heaven and earth,
113	*Kung bio honeng gorek*	Cord of heaven and earth like a ladder,

114	*Pikit tetu tali plou*	Climb up following the hanging vines,
115	*Tali plou wulu lodan*	Hanging vines like a golden bamboo necklace,
116	*Da'a réta timu tawa*	Reach upward the place of the sun's rising,
117	*Réta timu tawa dogon*	Upward the sun rises on its sloping path,
118	*Sapé réta lero léma*	Until is reached the rising sun,
119	*Réta lero léma lekir*	Upward the sun climbs its inclined road,
120	*Léma depo wae réta*	Climb following upwards,
121	*Pikit detu wae réta*	Mount leading upwards,
122	*Da'a bliro lari aman*	Reach the father of the Brahminy kite,
123	*Bliro réta soka ukung*	The Brahminy kite that dances backwards,
124	*Sapé gak nobon bura*	Up to the white hawk's realm,
125	*Gak réta nani baler*	The hawk that floats backwards,
126	*Léma tepo wae réta*	Climb following upwards,
127	*Pikit tetu wae réta*	Mount leading upwards,
128	*Da'a kiku lilu doen*	Reach the suspended butterfly,
129	*Sapé blilo blalo horo*	Get to where the black wasp flies,
130	*Réta mitan maro tear*	Upward to the black void of the sky,
131	*Réta bura baga liga*	Upward to where the white clouds roll open and closed.
132	*Huk mole wa'i ha*	Think again one time,
133	*Nera mole ha homa*	Meditate again once more,
134	*Huk mole wua wutun*	Think again atop the areca palm,
135	*Poton mole glok lolon*	Raise up the new sheath of the areca palm,
136	*Hoe hok ora lohor*	Descend the picked-clean areca palm,
137	*Ora lero wulan lohor*	As the sun and moon descend,
138	*Oi wekok ora léma*	Dig up and pick up as it rises,
139	*Ora nian tana léma*	As the land and earth rises.
140	*Huk mole wa'i ha*	Think again one time,
141	*Nera mole ha homa*	Meditate again once more,

142	*Teri laba ora lepo*	Settle down and chisel the joists of the clan house,
143	*Era pa'at ora woga*	Stand up and construct the guests' pavilion,
144	*Lepo geté ulu sinan*	The great clan house with its sitting room of China,
145	*Woga blon balé jawan*	The long guests' pavilion and platform of Larantuka,
146	*Dan kadak soro ehur*	Steps of the house ladder, ritually cooled at the corners,
147	*Gebi blasi soro sinan*	The walls of the clan house cooled with the coconut of China.
148	*Huk mole wa'i ha*	Think again one time,
149	*Nera mole ha homa*	Meditate again once more,
150	*Puka ora klugeng guer*	Cut the trees around the small garden,
151	*Ha'e ora rewuk mapan*	Lay the cut tree trunks athwart the slope,
152	*Pati hak ai géri*	Cut, but the trees cry out,
153	*Heti hak tali klangit*	Chop, but the vines weep,
154	*Ai blapi nala géri*	The sacred trees cry out in pain,
155	*Tali lekeng nala klangit*	The forest place sheltered by vines weeps,
156	*Teri ala kedo ukung*	Sit and step back [into the house],
157	*Era ala pano waler*	Stand up and return [home],
158	*Wali a urat luhen*	Go and tear the cloth in offering,
159	*Wali a rahe paré*	Go and scatter rice [in ritual].
160	*Ia gu*	Then,
161	*Pati ewan ai bile*	Cut and the trees are silent,
162	*Heti ewan tali meket*	Chop and the vines are silent,
163	*Topo Siang Lima api*	Call Siang Lima who knows the making of fire,
164	*Hawong Gega lama holo*	Summon Gega who knows the ritual chants,
165	*Wali na kiho boro*	Bring hither the fire-drill,
166	*Wali na sarit rati*	Come hither and shred the coconut husk,

167	*Boro boro wae wali*	Rub, rub across the bamboo fire-drill,
168	*Kapa lait wali mai*	Hither come the first wisps of smoke,
169	*Ojor ojor wae wali*	Up and down across the fire-drill,
170	*Pua pebo wali bawo*	Smoke rises up out of the fire-drill,
171	*Tut ba'a 'érin lau*	The lower half of the garden is burned,
172	*Sewing ba'a rain réta*	Fire is set to the upper half of the garden,
173	*Gula newan puka puan*	Fire was able to fell the tree trunks,
174	*Go'o newan lagé katek*	Burning was able to cut the brush,
175	*Ulan bura wekak hepang*	White ash flew like cockatoos,
176	*Tubon mitan kang tobon*	Crows perched on the blackened tree trunks,
177	*Wuri ora puhun bura*	Scatter the white grain seed,
178	*Teto ora keron mérak*	Broadcast the red fruit seeds,
179	*Puhun bura 'érin lau*	White seeds in the garden's lower half,
180	*Keron mérak rain réta*	Red seeds in the garden's upper half,
181	*'Érin lau uma koja*	In the garden's lower half grows the almond,
182	*Rain réta tua niur*	In the garden's upper half grows the lontar palm and coconut,
183	*Uma anak rudi ihin*	Though the garden was small it yielded,
184	*Tua kesik rudi dolo*	Though the lontars were small their juice flowed copiously,
185	*Da'a ihin witin geté*	Until the harvest filled large baskets,
186	*Toma dolo waran berat*	Until the flow of lontar juice filled heavy bamboo tubes,
187	*Oa rehin tau to'o*	The surplus food traded for heirlooms,
188	*Inu rehin hobu balik*	The excess drink traded for wealth.
189	*Huk mole wa'i ha*	Think again one time,

190	*Nera mole ha homa*	Meditate again once more,
191	*Blau wa'i lima lelin*	Fearful of the legs and hands trembling,
192	*Blemuk tur loi lesok*	Senseless from pain of the knees collapsing,
193	*Gahu gahu teri réhi*	From the heat and fever cannot dwell,
194	*Rou rou era loar*	From the heat and hotness cannot stand up,
195	*Nian du'e buluk buluk*	The land lies close by [the sky and sun],
196	*Tana gera blepeng blepeng*	The earth stands enclosed [by the sun],
197	*Topo du'a boro puhen*	Call the woman to cut the umbilical cord,
198	*Boro nian tana puhen*	Cut the umbilical cord of the land and earth,
199	*Hawong mo'an bohak oha*	Summon the man to untie the knots,
200	*Bohak lero wulan oha*	Untie the knots of the sun and moon,
201	*Nian du'e dagi laing*	The sky lies tied to a hook,
202	*Tana gera tali taon*	The earth stands knotted with cord,
203	*Nian la'en boro puhen*	The umbilical cord of the sky is not yet cut,
204	*Tana la'en bohak oha*	The knot of the earth is not yet untied,
205	*Topo Dong du'a Létu*	Call the woman Dong Létu,
206	*Hawong Laga Baleng aman*	Summon the father of Laga Baleng,
207	*Réta na boro puhen*	To go up and cut the cord,
208	*Réta na bohak oha*	To go up and untie the knots,
209	*Boro nian tana puhen*	Cut the umbilical cord of land and earth,
210	*Bohak lero wulan oha*	Untie the knots of sun and moon,
211	*Nian bejo wae réta*	The sky floats upward,
212	*Tana nené wae wawa*	The earth sinks downward,
213	*Blatan wair sina mitan*	Cool as the water of the black Chinese,

214	*Ro kabor bali bura*	Cool as the water of the white coconut of Bali.
215	*A'u Ipir leten geté*	I am clan Ipir, the great ebony tree,
216	*A'u sodor wodon ilin*	I am exalted like the large birds of the mountains,
217	*Wai Brama Wolobola*	The domain of Wai Brama and Wolobola
218	*Ratu wutun Balénatar*	Raja as far as Balénatar,
219	*Ora nian tana kiring*	Speaking to the sky and earth,
220	*Ora lero wulan harang*	Addressing the sun and moon,
221	*Nian tana pi pitu*	Sky and earth of seven levels,
222	*Lero wulan tedang walu*	Sun and moon of eight layers,
223	*Wawa soru wawa bere*	The pillars below, the supporting base below,
224	*Wawa loet wawa 'lo'at*	Foundation below, the supporting trunk below,
225	*Soru bere loet 'lo'at*	Pillar, base, foundation and trunk,
226	*Pun pati repa gala*	[I who] spread my hands over the great rice basket and place,
227	*Wawa tepu wawa rebu*	Below the forging, below the iron,
228	*Wawa hena wawa brané*	Below the sturdiness, below the strength,
229	*Tepu rebu tuba nian*	Forge the iron for the sky to lean on,
230	*Hena brané ha'an tana*	Place the strength of the compacted earth,
231	*Nian di newan gi'it*	The sky is also enabled to be strong,
232	*Tana di newan mangan*	And the earth is also made sturdy,
233	*Gi'it biri baru sinan*	Strong as the areca palm and *baru* tree of China,
234	*Mangan bao ara jawan*	Sturdy as the banyan and fig of Larantuka.

The episodes of the text

The text of the *Ngeng Ngerang Tota Nian Paga Tana* can, for analytic purposes, be divided into five major sections. The first, which consists of the first 107 lines, recounts a sequence of four creations of the land and some of its physical features:

(1) the creation of dry land from the sea (lines 1–50);
(2) the creation of the physical features of the Tana Ai landscape (lines 51–62);
(3) the creation of vegetation (lines 64–71);
(4) the creation of springs (lines 74–107).

The second section (lines 108–119) describes the connection of the firmament and the earth by an umbilical cord and golden chain (lines 112–115). The third section recounts the creation of the first clan house (lines 142–147) and the first garden (lines 150–188). The fourth section (lines 191–214) then tells of the separation of the sky and the earth following the failure of the first garden to yield a harvest.[23] The fifth and final section (lines 215–234) comprises a 'clan boast' (kahé) of clan Ipir Wai Brama, the clan of the chanter.

Chants in ritual language are punctuated with a variety of words and phrases employed as rhetorical pauses. The most common words used for this purpose are *ia gu*, 'thus, then', and *ko*, 'or, but'. In particularly elegant recitations, a chanter can use formulaic couplets rather than single words or short phrases as rhetorical pauses in his chant. Couplets used as rhetorical pauses are considered to be more elegant because they better preserve the flow and parallelism of the narrative. The most common couplet employed for this purpose is:

Huk mole wa'i ha	Think again one time,
Nera mole ha homa	Meditate again once more.

Ritual specialists say that in the performance of a chant the rhetorical pauses give the chanter a chance to catch his breath[24] and provide a moment to organise his thoughts before launching the following section of his chant. Given that rhetorical pauses characterise the performance of chants, it was puzzling to me that Mo'an Rapa carefully dictated a number of them to be included in the text of his history.[25] But the rhetorical pauses in ritual speech serve a function other than that identified by the ritual specialists.

Mo'an Rapa's rhetorical pauses serve to demarcate the beginnings and ends of episodes of the narrative that make up the whole of the history. In the first episode of the first section of the text, the creator:

(i) dives through the ocean to find the mud from which to fashion lumps of earth (lines 1–8);
then (*ia gu*, line 9);
(ii) the creator collects the lumps of earth into piles (lines 10–13);
then (*ia gu*, line 14);

(iii) the creator dives upward through the water and throws the lumps of earth out of the ocean. But these piles produce only small and broken bits of land (lines 15–20);
then (*ia gu*, line 21);

(iv) the creator returns under the sea and repeats the collection of lumps of earth (lines 22–25);
then (*ia gu*, line 26);

(v) the creator summons the Brahminy kite and white hawk to assist in distributing the lumps to make the land (lines 27–34);
but (*ko*, line 35);

(vi) the land was soft and mushy (lines 36–37);
thus (*ia gu*, line 38);

(vii) the land was allowed to dry and bake in the sun (lines 39–50);

and so on. Thus rhetorical pauses are not merely rests for the chanter, but delineate the episodic structure of the chant and bound its constituent parts.

During fieldwork in 1980 and 1982 another significance of the rhetorical pauses that punctuate both Mo'an Rapa's history and chants recorded under natural conditions in Tana Ai became clear, and one of the reasons for Mo'an Rapa's desire to record his *ngeng ngerang* emerged. In those years, on several different occasions, I recited Mo'an Rapa's text to a number of different ritual specialists. In every case these men expressed admiration for the chant while emphasising that it was incomplete and that its episodes were radically abridged. One ritualist commented that the reasons for summoning the *bliro* (Brahminy kite) and *gak* (falcon) (lines 29–32) should be explained. He proceeded to chant a brief segment of the history that told how, when the dry land was to be enlarged (lines 33–34), the kite and the falcon divided the work between them, the *bliro* enlarging the land of Tana Ai while the *gak* (which is not a bird seen often in the valley) enlarged the earth *lau wawa*, that is, outside of Tana Ai and including the land of the white people.

Later in the narrative it is said that when the first garden was being cut from the forest, the trees cried out and the vines wept (lines 152–155). Mo'an Rapa's narrative continues with the cultivators returning home to make an offering of torn cloth and sprinkled rice before attempting once again to cut the trees and vines of the forest (lines 156–162). Another chanter explained that there was a reason for the pain of the trees and vines to which only an indirect allusion is made in Mo'an Rapa's text, and offered the following couplets as an addition to the text to be inserted at this point (between lines 155 and 156) in the history:[26]

235	*Lupa lé'u guna piren*	The forbidden *guna*-spirits had been forgotten,
236	*Hulir lé'u déwa glaran*	The sacred *déwa*-spirits had been neglected,
237	*Guna 'a'un lau wolo*	My *guna*-spirit down the mountain,
238	*Déwa 'a'un lau ledin*	My *déwa*-spirit down in the valleys,
239	*Naha nodi oti wua*	First areca nut must be offered,
240	*Naha wajak[27] oti bako*	First tobacco must be provided,
241	*Na'i nora to'o halan*	Placed with wealth [given over] for the errors,
242	*Na'i nora balik hulir*	Placed with heirlooms in atonement for the forgettings,
243	*Guna nala ga wua*	The *guna*-spirit takes and eats the areca nut,
244	*Méra sero wiwir wutun*	The end of its lips drool red areca juice,
245	*Déwa 'a'un ninu bako*	My *déwa*-spirit drinks the tobacco,
246	*Gahu lagé ahan pu'a*	The heat of the burning tobacco produces smoke,
247	*Huja lopo uma 'lora*	Evil spirits do not occupy the garden's centre,
248	*Bujo lopo tua wutun*	Mischievous ghosts do not remain in the lontar palms of the garden's periphery,
249	*Ina 'a'un*	My mother,
250	*Urat ora luhen tipa*	Tears the *patola* cloth as an offering,
251	*Rahe ora paré bura*	Sprinkles white rice in offering,
252	*Luhen tipa eman mérak*	The *patola* cloth with its red patterns.
253	*Paré bura koko rojo*	The white rice will then yieldfruit
254	*Héni wali blapi puan*	Light the fire at the forest's central sacred place,
255	*Hokot wali lekeng wutun*	Clear the trees to the edge of the sheltering forest,
256	*Pati é'o nimu klangit*	I can cut the trees and they will not cry out,
257	*Oba é'o nimu géri*	I can chop the vines and they will not weep.

A third chanter noted that part of the narrative of the separation of the earth and the firmament is left out of Rapa's text. The first garden (lines 150–188) failed to yield a crop because the land and the earth were too close to one another. Thus the ancestors sought to separate the sun and moon from the land and earth. The cutting of the umbilical cord that connected the earth and the sky, and the cooling of the earth, are described in lines 195–214. But before the woman Dong Du'a Letu and the man Laga Baleng Aman were called to cut the cord and to untie the knots (lines 205–210), the ancestors decided to make war on the sun and moon as a means of reducing the heat of the land. Thus, following line 190, the chanter amended Rapa's text with this insertion:

258	*Au timu tawa mai*	You who come rising from the east,
259	*Au lero léma ba'u*	You the sun that rises and sets,
260	*Au Du'a Sepu olor*	You have ignited Du'a Sepu,
261	*Au Mo'an Salak larak*	You have roasted Mo'an Salak,
262	*Naha nuhu nian tana*	[We] must make war on the land and earth,
263	*Naha kata lero wulan*	[We] must fight the sun and moon.

The ancestors, Igor and Engar, refused to fight, and advised the other ancestors:

| 264 | *Lopo nuhu nian tana* | Don't make war on the land and earth, |
| 265 | *Loa kata lero wulan* | Don't fight the sun and moon. |

Instead, the ancestors summoned Dong Du'a Letu and Laga Baleng Aman to cut the cord and to untie the knots that bound the sky and earth together (lines 197–214).

After that had been done, the chanter continued, the earth and the sky parted (lines 211–212), but the earth was still too hot for human life. In the end, the ancestors contrived to cause a war between the land and earth and the sun and moon,[28] and as a narrative of that battle the chanter inserted, following line 214:

266	*Nian du'e gahu la'en*	The land still lay hot,
267	*Tana gera rou la'en*	The earth still stood in heat,
268	*Gahu gahu teri réhi*	From the heat and fever [humans] could not live,
269	*Rou rou gera loar*	From the heat and hotness they could not stand,
270	*Wulan wali buluk nan*	The moon goes close to the earth,

271	*Lero réta gahar bawo*	The sun moves upward [in its daily journey],
272	*Nian deri buluk buluk*	The land lies close by,
273	*Tana gera blepeng blepeng*	The earth stands enclosed [by the sun],
274	*Réta bawo buluk la'en*	[The sun] climbs upward but is still near,
275	*Wali ba'u blepeng la'en*	Descending near and still enclosing,
276	*Lero wulan ro'o la'en*	The sun and moon are still close by,
277	*Ro'o nian tana la'en*	Still near the land and earth,
278	*Ora nian tana nuhu*	The land and earth made war,
279	*Ora lero wulan kata*	The sun and moon fought,
280	*Pati ora wulan bao*	Beat the moon's banyan tree,[29]
281	*Oba ora lero matan*	Strike the sun's eyes,
282	*Bao ha papa rapé*	Half the branches of the moon's banyan tree fell off dead,
283	*Matan ha papa léwek*	One of the sun's eyes fell and rolled away,
284	*'Alu alo sudar wulan*	Rice pestles then supported the softened moon,
285	*Léan[30] towa jok lero*	The sun hung tethered to a bamboo drying pole,
286	*Nian bejo wae réta*	The sky floats upward,[31]
287	*Tana nené wae wawa*	The earth sinks downward,
288	*Blatan wair sina mitan*	Cool as the water of the black Chinese,[32]
289	*Ro kabor bali bura*	Cool as the dew that falls from the white coconut of Bali,
290	*Huk mole wa'i ha*	Think again one time,
291	*Nera mole ha homa*	Meditate again once more ...

Thus, finally, the ancestors brought about the cooling of the earth for human habitation.

More additions to Rapa's text have been volunteered by and elicited from the chanters of Tana Wai Brama since his narrative was first written. Other addenda to Rapa's history relate the origin of animals and their domestication, the first distillation of gin from the juice of the lontar palm, the origin of weaving, the first hunt, the origin of rice, the origins of earthquakes, and the source of Europeans. These and other similar episodes are considered to belong to the *Sejara Tota Nian Paga Tana* and to the history of Iang Bangu, the first human beings. Indeed, the largest part of the histories that were not given by Rapa is the *Sejara Iang Bangu*, the history of the creation of the first human beings, which would properly begin before the clan boast (lines 215–234) of Rapa's narrative. Thus it is possible that these divers histories can be synthesised into a single text of multiple authorship in accord with the notions of sequence and precedence established by Rapa's text.[33]

Rhetorical pauses are points of transition between discrete episodes in a history. They are thus points at which a history is, or can be, abridged, and they are also points at which a given chant can be expanded. In chants performed as part of large-scale ceremonies in which many chanters co-operate in the performance of a history by taking turns, rhetorical pauses are junctions at which the chant can pass from one chanter to another, or mark points in the chant of one ritualist that might be elaborated by a following chanter. While I have not heard a ritualist in Tana Ai refer to them in such a way, the rhetorical pauses of a chant have the character of the *matan* of the joint between sections of bamboo, the node from which new branches emerge and grow.[34] Rhetorical pauses in Tana Ai ritual speech are truly pregnant pauses from which can emerge elaborations and refinements of a given theme in a chant. They also mark the points at which a chanter has chosen, for reasons of economy or according to the exigencies of time, place, or the importance of a given ceremonial occasion, to collapse a potentially longer chant into a briefer form. This implicitness of Tana Ai ritual speech allows ritualists to maintain that the 'whole' of a history has been spoken when what is actually chanted is only a few disjointed couplets.

The temporality of ritual events in Tana Ai

The life of a community can be charted in the flow of occurrences that take place in it. Ethnographers record occurrences, things that happen, in a community and from them, and the order of social relations among members of the community they manifest, extract principles of organisation that account for observed occurrences. But occurrences can be happenings that lack plan, intent, or volition on the part of the people who are part of them. Many occurrences taken by an ethnographer as paradigmatic of community affairs are merely incidental; they are to members of the community themselves trivial and deemed unworthy of attention. Events are occurrences, but they are, for the people studied, worthy of remark and are unusual or significant occurrences in the community. Events differ from mere incidents and happenings because they are thought to be important; events are important or significant, and thereby differ from happenings, because they are the issue, outcome, result, or consequence of other events and because they are themselves viewed as causes, necessary or potential, of events yet to transpire. A happening may be a significant event, but determination that it is so must be made by reference to the significance attributed to it by the people of the community.

Events are never discrete, unique occurrences, but are part of and constitute the continuity of time. Unlike mere incidents and happenings, informed events follow one another as they do because they are connected temporally in necessary sequences; events form progressions in causally ordered sequences. While happenings manifest chance and randomness, from which they arise, events manifest the order of the world and the end and fate of its inhabitants. Events are occurrences inscribed with significance. Events transcend occurrences because in the succession and sequence of events can be read meaning, purpose, and order of importance to the community.

It is not always easy for an ethnographer to distinguish events from mere happenings. Once the distinction is made, the two kinds of occurrences must be treated in different ways. Charting occurrences leads to an objective description and appraisal of the life of a community while the ethnographer is present, but can fail to reveal the essences of community life. Appreciating events, however, is not possible without becoming a member of the community; otherwise events can be mistaken for merely incidental happenings, no more or less significant than hundreds of other occurrences, when in reality they are, to the community, of considerable significance. Happenings just happen; events are created. To an Ata Tana Ai, an occurrence such as falling from a cliff, which might be recorded by an ethnographer as a chance happening, is never an accident but is caused by transgressions against forest spirits, ancestors, or *hadat*. To recognise an occurrence as an event it is necessary to know the person to whom it is expected and attributed; to comprehend an event fully it is necessary to 'know the mind' of its creator, his purposes, will, and intentions. The extended temporality of events means it is unlikely that an ethnographer, who spends but a few months continuously in a community, will know well the antecedents of an occurrence, or will be present to appreciate its consequences.[35] It is by virtue of having antecedents and causes, consequences, and results that occurrence is constituted as event.

Several times, beginning in 1978, I asked Mo'an Rapa to chant the history of the domain. After two or three refusals, Rapa suddenly volunteered to provide a creation myth. It did not occur to me at the time that his change of mind was significant or that it would result in more than just a recitation for my benefit. Rapa's text, for me, was a good, though incomplete and somewhat jumbled, example of ritual language; its telling an incident in the course of my gathering information on ritual language. But for Rapa the text was a tool for the expression of his will and intentions regarding the *gren mahé*, a major event in the life of his community, of which I was wholly ignorant at the time. For the other ritual specialists of the domain, Rapa's telling of the myth marked the start of an important event in the life of the community, whose results would not be manifest for more than fifteen months until the *gren mahé*. The text was a significant distillation of the event that was to be, and the only window that the ritual specialists had, after his death, to Rapa's intentions for the *gren*.

The text of Mo'an Rapa's rendering of the *Ngeng Ngerang Tota Nian Paga Tana* generated considerable interest among other ritual specialists of the domain. After Rapa's death in 1979, and again before the *gren mahé* in 1980, I was asked several times to read the text to men who were close to Rapa and who were to be the principal organisers of the cere-monies. These readings generated much discussion both of the episodes that Rapa had chosen to include in his text and of details of the language in which the text was phrased.[36] One result of the reading of the text to other ritual specialists was that Rapa's part of the *oda geté* was available to the other chanters of the domain even though Rapa died before the *gren mahé*. A second result was an indication of how the histories are built up by co-operation among chanters from basic lines of chanting laid down by one chanter, a practice that was manifested in the chanting of the *oda geté* in the *gren*.

One of the imponderable questions raised by the events of 1979 and 1980 is whether Mo'an Rapa knew, when he dictated his history, that within a few weeks he would suddenly fall ill and die. That question is beyond knowing with certainty, but subsequent events suggest that he perhaps did know, and that recording his history at the time and in the form he did was a means of exercising power over the performance of the *gren* and ensuring that ritual authority in the domain remained with people close to his house within clan Ipir rather than shifting to ritualists from another part of the domain. During the early stages of the preparations for the *gren*, a man named Déwa from a branch of clan Liwu in another area of Tana Wai Brama made a claim to the position of *tana puan*.[37] This claim gained some support in the domain. Meanwhile, two men genealogically and politically very close to Rapa had begun the organisation of the rituals. Realising that to attempt to choose a new *tana puan* at that time would have diverted the community from the task of carrying out the *gren*, they proceeded by invoking Rapa's name and arguing that, since he had initiated it, the *gren* was properly his, and thus leadership must remain with his house. A compelling element in their argu-ment was that the knowledge of the *gren* was held by Rapa's close associates, knowledge to which the new claimant to the position of *tana puan* did not have access. A part of that knowledge was the text of Rapa's history, to which (at that point in the affair) only Rapa's allies had had access. In the end, the claims to leadership by Déwa were rejected, and in the *gren* two of Rapa's associates shared the position of *tana puan* in his name.[38]

Mo'an Rapa insisted that his text was a history of the creation of the world. But more than one third of the text consists of episodes that recount the construction of the first clan house (lines 142–147), the opening of the first garden (lines 150–188), the separation of the sky and earth (lines 191–214), and a *kahé* (clan boast) of Sukun Ipir Wai Brama (lines 215–234). There is some evidence that the first three of these parts of Rapa's history belong to the *Sejara Iang Bangu*, the history of the first human beings, and not properly to the *Sejara Tota Nian Paga Tana*. Certainly the *kahé* with which Rapa ended his narrative belongs to the history of clan Ipir Wai Brama. This being so, it appears that, rather than providing just the history of the creation of the world, what Rapa actually did was to provide a radically abridged précis of the whole of the histories as he wished them to be chanted in the *gren*.

When Mo'an Rapa suggested recording his history of the creation of the world and of clan Ipir Wai Brama he commented that other chanters of the domain knew only fragments of the *sejara*, and that none knew the whole. Whether in fact this was true, it can be presumed that he wished to ensure the proper sequence of the episodes of the myth was preserved. Since power lies in the knowledge of the sequences and order of things, the dictation of Rapa's history helped to ensure that the political alignments within the ceremonial system of Tana Wai Brama would remain unchanged, at least until the *gren mahé* following the one he planned for 1980. Recording the *sejara* through the medium of the ethnographer provided a means of preserving the sequence without delegating that knowledge directly to a political and ritual heir while Rapa was still in effective control of the domain. Judging from the response of other chanters to his history, and the success of the ceremonies in 1980, in this he was successful.

In Tana Ai the significance of most events is inversely proportional to the predictability or expectability of their occurrence. As a rule, the less expected an occurrence the greater is the interest in and concern about it. Conversely, the more an occurrence is expected the less the interest shown in it and the less the significance attached to it. Performances of rituals are perhaps the most predictable occurrences in the life of Tana Ai communities, and the more important the ritual the more certain it is to take place. If, on the surface, ritual in Tana Ai is expected, its performance probable, and its conclusion and outcome predictable, how can ritual be a major event in the life of the community? I refer here not to the myriad and ephemeral rituals of healing and guarding, or the rituals of etiquette, all of which inform the continuous episodes of daily life, but to the rarer and major events of the ceremonial cycle of Tana Ai that bring together the whole of the valley, and all its clans, houses, and individuals, at great expense in time, energy, and material goods. In Tana Ai it is predictable that *gren mahé*, the culminal ritual of the domain, will occur. What is less certain is when it will occur; even less predictable is who will manage it; and least predictable of all is the new configuration of political power that will emerge in the community after its conclusion. *Gren mahé* is far from being a means for ensuring the preservation of a *status quo;* it does not reaffirm the community as it was and is. It is instead a means of enabling radical changes to take place in the social order, and legitimates such changes.

For the ritual specialists of Tana Wai Brama, the central rites of the *gren mahé*, some of which occur outside the public domain,[39] are the chanting of the histories of Tana Wai Brama. Ritual language is for the ritual specialists of the domain if not for the community as a whole, the thread that holds the fabric of the ceremonies together. While there are many other parts of the ceremonies, such as the sacrifice of dozens of animals, the chanting of the histories over the period of a week, from the beginning of the world to the present day, is what, for the ritual men of the domain, the *gren mahé* is about. The chanting of the histories normally begins with the secret *nara wowa* rite a few days before the public ceremonies begin, but fourteen months before the *gren* of 1980 took place, Rapa produced his text which outlined the structure and sequence of the histories as he would have had them performed in the *gren*. Rapa's dictation of his chant in August 1979 and the performance of the histories of the domain in November 1980 were not simply related occurrences, they comprised a single event. In a larger sense, for the ritualists of Tana Wai Brama the 1979–80 performance of the histories was not a discrete event, but an episode in a larger continuity of events stretching back to the founding of the domain of Tana Wai Brama.

The function of ritual language, the code of the histories, and the histories themselves, is not to separate or make discrete that which, in the view of the Ata Tana Ai, is continuous, but to make continuous, or lend continuity to, that which might otherwise be mistaken as discrete, the events that comprise the history of the domain. All events in Tana Ai involve agencies, whether of the deity, the ancestors, the ubiquitous and sometimes capricious spirits of earth, water, and forest, or human beings. The ritualists of Tana Wai Brama say that *gren mahé* is required by *hadat*; they also say that the *gren* occurs only when it is willed by men. Between the requirements of *hadat*, history and custom, and human agency there is considerable latitude for the play of secular will, intention, and individual creativity. *Gren mahé*, ritual language, and individual persons all quest for the source, of things that are and configurations that will be. In seeking the source, responses to the exigencies of existence and changes in the community are brought into history, to be reconciled with the past, to be legitimately of force in the present, and to bind the future to the will of the community and its members.

10

THE TREE OF DESIRE: A TORAJA RITUAL POEM

CHARLES ZERNER and TOBY ALICE VOLKMAN

Introduction

Sulawesi, Indonesia's third largest island, lies between Borneo and the Moluccas, with its peninsular arms extending in every direction. The fertile plains of the island's southwestern arm rise into rugged mountains formed of limestone and volcanic tuffs in the north. These mountains, through which the Sa'dan River and its tributaries flow, are the homeland of 320,000 Sa'dan Toraja people. At altitudes between 3000 and 4000 feet, the Toraja cultivate rice in irrigated fields carved into the mountainside, supplemented by cassava, corn, and Arabica coffee as a cash crop. Water buffalo, pigs, and chickens are raised for both food and ritual purposes. Recently, international tourism and labour outmigration have begun to play a role in the economy. Religious change, begun in the Dutch colonial period with Protestant missionising, has accelerated since Indonesian independence as the Toraja increasingly convert to Christianity.[1] Language is changing as well. Although all Toraja speak a Malayo-Polynesian language known to the Dutch as *Tae'* (after the local word for 'no'), and known to the Toraja simply as *basa Toraya* ('Toraja language'),[2] most younger educated Toraja also speak Indonesian, a trend likely to continue as education and outmigration increase.

The Toraja are famous in Western travel brochures and throughout Indonesia for their exuberant ritual life. In particular, spectacular funerals with hundreds or thousands of guests, scores of sacrificed buffalo and pigs, and dizzying cliff burials have attracted the attention of adventurers, film-makers, and scholars. Less attention, however, has been paid to the speech that plays a vital role in this ritual tradition. In spite of changes occurring throughout Toraja culture, speech continues to be a source of power and pleasure, in both ritual and everyday life.

Speech as pleasure is manifest in the delight Toraja take in ordinary conversation, labelled affectionately as *basa bo'bo'*, 'rice language'. As a playful pastime, speech takes the form of stories told to children while the rice is still growing in the fields (*ulelean pare*, 'rice stories'), or riddles (*karume*), or songs for children or adults. Speech as power is most clearly actualised in the complementary roles of the two most respected village leaders: the *ambe' tondok*, or village head, and the *tominaa*, a ritual priest. Although an *ambe' tondok* must claim noble lineage and wealth, without eloquence and the skilful use of language these other attributes are diminished. This is even more clearly the case for the *tominaa*, who need not be a man of great ancestry or riches. The paramount criterion for a *tominaa* is his mastery of language, in particular of 'high speech'.[3]

'High speech' is one of the distinctive features of Toraja language and

Men gather around the base of the *bate*, firmly planting it in the ground. The spine and side poles of the *bate* are tightly wrapped in old Toraja batik cloths lashed with rattan.

custom of which both Christian and 'animist' Toraja are proud. It is called 'the speech of *tominaa*' (*basa tominaa*), or 'the words of *tominaa*' (*kada tominaa*). *Tominaa*, more precisely, are 'those whose knowledge and thoughts are wide'. A man becomes a *tominaa* by listening since childhood to 'ancestral words' that enter his 'breath' or 'spirit' (*penaa*), and are stored in his 'stomach' (*tambuk*). As an adult he must flawlessly reproduce those potent words, speaking, singing, or chanting them in ritual performances, whether rituals of life or of death. It is the *tominaa* who calls in high speech to the spirits to bless the house or rice fields, and it is he who knows the special language to chase away plagues or cure the sick.[4]

One scholar who did attend to speech in Toraja culture was the great Dutch linguist, Dr. H. van der Veen. Van der Veen, as the Netherlands Bible Society resident linguist in Toraja for over forty years, became fascinated with Toraja language both in its ordinary and in its more elevated form. His dictionary (1972) is an extraordinary work in which Toraja poetry and metaphor are interwoven with plain speech. Although much of the material he collected was lost during the Japanese occupation, an enormous amount survived, including two monumental transcriptions of chants, one (1965) recited at the *merok* feast, and one (1966) sung for the dead. Van der Veen's translations are prefaced by detailed descriptions of the rituals, providing a mine of information, and the texts themselves reveal a wealth of erudition and imagery. Although inspired by van der Veen, the scope of the present paper is far more limited. By focusing on one small but lively fragment of a contemporary ritual speech performance, we hope to unfold the symbolic riches that are embedded within the verses, articulating key cultural themes and meanings condensed and reiterated throughout the poem.[5]

The fragment, called *ma'pakumpang*, forms part of a week-long recitation at the *maro* ritual. In 1977 we taped two versions at separate *maro* performances in the same region of Mount Sesean. Although recited by different *tominaa*, the texts are strikingly similar, and we have chosen to deal exclusively with the longer version (see Reference Text at end of this paper). Translation, as of any ritual speech, was no simple process. From tapes to transcripts typed in lines we already lose the oral/aural quality of the recitation, in which only breaths punctuate the phrases. From transcribed '*tominaa* language' to ordinary speech, 'rice language' (*basa bo'bo'*), is an uncertain leap. For although ritual speech consists of variations (metaphorical and sometimes obscure) on everyday speech, most Toraja claim not to understand it. We were fortunate to find two highly skilled and sensitive interpreters of these verses, although, not surprisingly, they sometimes disagreed.[6] With these translators we also worked to bridge the gap from everyday Toraja to Bahasa Indonesia. We then translated the Indonesian version into English, which is itself by no means transparent. Although it is perhaps obvious, we should say that our 'text' makes no claim to be a definitive version. Other researchers might have discovered, after all these layers of translation, a rather different *ma'pakumpang*.

The context: the maro ritual

In October, when the rice seedlings planted on the slopes of Mount Sesean are about four inches tall, it is time for the *maro*: a ritual associated with the fertility of the fields; with a movement from death toward the affirmation of life; and with the fulfilment of desires for wealth, for children, and for the greatness of ancestral houses and their descendants.[7]

The *maro*, like all Toraja rituals, is embedded in a cycle based on opposing hierarchies of rituals, one associated with death ('smoke-descending'), the other with fertility and growth ('smoke-rising'). On Mount Sesean, in the northern region of Tana Toraja, the rice harvest occurs in June, and during the next few months the rituals of death are carried out. By September the funeral season is over and, as seed is sown in the terraced fields, the series of life-affirming rituals begins. If the seed grows well, and if a family has sufficient wealth (and, in former days, sufficient status), it may be decided to hold a *maro* before transplanting.

One other consideration influences the decision to hold a *maro*. If, during previous years, a relative from an ancestral house had been honoured with an elaborate seven-night funeral, then the ghost of this deceased relative may be transformed into a spirit or *deata* through the performance of the '*maro* of reversal', *maro pa'balikan*.

This transformation is visually represented by the reversal of a cloth and bamboo tower. At a funeral, the tower or *bandera* is erected with the bamboo's growing tip thrust down into the earth. At the '*maro* of reversal', an almost identical construction called the *bate* (lacking only the shirt, betel pouch, and umbrella of the *bandera*) is erected, with the bamboo pointing toward the sky, the direction in which it once grew. The *bate* as an inverted *bandera* refers to the deceased, but it is the growth-oriented, positive direction that is stressed in the *maro*.

As a spirit, an ancestor is thought to bestow blessings upon the descendants of the house, or *tongkonan*. The entire family of deceased ancestors may partake in this process, following the pattern of life on earth, where relatives and followers are imbued with at least some of their leader's status, wealth, and good fortune. The transformation of ancestral ghosts promises parallel gains for the living. It is the hope of fulfilment of the wishes of the living that underlies the *ma'pakumpang* poem. In this cluster of *maro* ritual verses, the cloth and bamboo *bate* becomes an image of a 'tree of desire'.

At dawn on the seventh day of the *maro* the *bate* is assembled, erected, and given offerings. Several *bate* may be prepared by different households, depending on the clustering of families within the larger *tongkonan* and the particular ancestors being honoured. Each *bate* is carried in boisterous procession to a ritual field known as the 'market'. There, under the hot noon sun, to the sounds of chanting *tominaa*, all kinds of spirits are said to descend, draw near, and enter the bodies of those dancing and entranced on the field. Possession by the spirits may last several hours, revealed by 'tricks' such as self-laceration with iron swords. The chanting, the whirling, and the frenzy that signify the coming of the spirits take place within the space ringed by the *bate*, if there are several, or marked by it if there is only one.

In the late afternoon the spirits depart and the exhausted trancers go home or are helped home. Then the *tominaa* bless the *bate*, symbolically 'cool' it, and take it apart. Cloths and swords are returned to their owners, and the bamboo frame is carried to the rafters of the ancestral house that was responsible for its creation.

Although this day is the highlight of the ritual, its most public and dramatic expression, it is made possible only by many hours of ritual speech that prepare the way for the spirits' communications with the living. For six days before trancing occurs, a group of *tominaa* assemble in the house of the sponsoring family, where they chant and sing throughout the night. The content of the songs and chants ranges widely over Toraja mythology and genealogy. The form is encompassed by the word *gelong*.

Gelong refers to ritual speech used at the *maro*, in contrast, for example, to that used at mortuary rituals (speech forms include *ma'badong, ma'londe, ma'retteng*) or at other life affirming ceremonies such as *ma'bua'*. Like some other forms of Toraja ritual speech, *gelong* are characterised by octosyllabic phrasings, as van der Veen originally noted (1965:17). To achieve eight syllables the *tominaa* may at times create additional syllables by drawing out a single sound; conversely, they may drop a syllable or two when necessary. The octosyllabic form is not always strictly followed: late at night, tired *tominaa* may compress their lines, abbreviating or deleting stock phrases (see, for example, lines 173–183).

Different kinds of *gelong* are associated with particular aspects of the *maro* ritual: 'verses of the possessed people', *gelong to ma'deata*; 'verses to feed the *tominaa*', *gelong ma'pakande tominaa*; or, in the present instance, 'verses of those who make requests', *gelong to malaku*. All *gelong* 'open, reveal, scoop up, or ladle out our lives', as one Toraja man expressed it.

Metaphor and multiplicity

In the *gelong* known as *ma'pakumpang*, requests are made. The language of *ma'pakumpang*, like that of other Toraja ritual speech forms, is based on both metaphor and multiplicity.

Metaphor takes various forms. *Ma'pakumpang* opens, for example, with these lines (1–2):

> I will search for gold,
> The wishes of gold dust.

More than gold itself is sought; gold essentialises the highest value in all that could be desired. The verses continue (lines 3–8):

> Different are the requests of [Tumbang]
>   she who is called 'to jump',
> Distinct are the desires of [Banaa]
>   she who is called 'rice vessel',
> The wishes of [Pangria Banang]
>   she who holds the winnowing tray.
> Different are the requests of the cock,
> Distinct are the desires of the man,
> The wishes of the decorated man.

Tumbang, Banaa, and Pangria Barang are the titles held by the three most ritually elevated women in *ma'bua'*, the pinnacle ceremony in the life affirming ritual cycle. Their mention here clearly evokes 'woman', particularly 'woman' as she is associated with fertility and increase. 'Man' appears both literally as 'man' and also as 'cock' and 'decorated man', the latter two suggesting his qualities as a warrior.

In a more general way, the whole structure of *ma'pakumpang* is an extended metaphor. The word *ma'pakumpang* is formed by the addition of a verb indicator *ma'* and the causative prefix *pa* to the root *kumpang*. *Kumpang* is usually translated into Indonesian as either *mengarah*, 'to point, aim, or direct', or *mencondong*, 'to lean, incline toward, or be sympathetic'. *Ma'pakumpang* suggests both longing and leaning, desire and movement. The performance of *ma'pakumpang* signifies the act of seeking and bringing back the objects of desire, whether near or from afar. Images of extension in space are also images of intention, of inclination in both senses.

The central portion of *ma'pakumpang* consists of a series of requests, stated indirectly, through insertion into an artfully constructed verse form. This verse provides a kind of armature for a 'shopping list' of what is desired from the spirits. Take, for example, the verse in which porcelain bowls are requested (lines 65–70):

> It bends like a tree-top toward Bone,
> It sways for a while,
> It becomes branches of white porcelain bowls,
> Becomes leaves of all kinds,
> Everything that is used,
> All that is eaten.

By changing the place (Bone) and the object (white porcelain bowls), the *tominaa* can extend the list of requests endlessly. But because the spirits, not ordinary mortals, are addressed, the request is embedded in elaborate imagery. One cannot simply say to a spirit, 'Hey, give me sugar'. Instead, the subject of these lines, the 'it', is a metaphorical tree representing the pooled desires of the family, a tree that 'bends' and 'sways' in the direction of those desires. With each new six-line verse of this section, new places and desired objects are inserted, while the spirits, presumably, continue to be enticed by the artfulness of the requests. Perhaps they are honoured as well; indirection in either physical or linguistic usage is a sign of respectful distance between actors of unequal status.

The other underlying principle in the language of *ma'pakumpang* is multiplicity or repetition. In the central section of the poem the key six-line verse is repeated thirty-three times, with varying place names and objects. In the portions that precede and follow the central section, phrases are typically repeated, with parallel meanings or closely related variations, two or three times (lines 12–14).[8]

> Different are the requests of the children,
> Distinct are the desire of the little ones,
> The wishes of those who know nothing at all.

For the Toraja, to have much of one thing is not merely to possess a collection of neutral multiples, but to generate power. To have one child is a promising beginning, but not enough. To have many children and descendants (*lolokna*, literally 'buds') is to be rich and full, as clusters of rice grains weigh down the stems of plants at harvest time. To be a 'big man' (*to kapua'*) is to be at the apex of a pyramid of kinsmen and followers who are both supportive and supported. And a ritual without many participants is not only incomplete, it is less than effective. A ritual must be *marua'*: crowded, noisy, alive with a bustling multitude of people. In a similar way, the speech of *tominaa* must be full, made powerful through the repetition of words and images.

The setting

It is evening, 11 p.m., in October 1977. The village is Limbong, a three-hour walk northwest of Rantepao. Five small houses are clustered under tall bamboo on a promontory, surrounded by *sawah* separated by slippery, muddy paths. The house at the end of the row feels old. It is not elegantly incised with carvings. It is small, and its roof is made of traditional shingles, rarely used these days. Although the house does not emanate an aura of prosperity, rows of buffalo horns hung in front remind us of funerals past, of meat divided among the living.

Inside the house a small central room is lit only by a hissing pressure lamp that reveals ten men sitting on mats on the wooden floor, facing each other in a ring. Small boys sprawl over the old men's legs, others lie in dark corners of the room, asleep. In the centre of the room are one-foot high bamboo spittoons, suspended on ropes from the rafters and passed among the men. Women busy themselves over a hearth along the east wall, preparing rice and boiling water for coffee.

The men, all *tominaa*, are old and wrinkled, except for one whose face glows. He sports a bright red shirt and red bandanna, his lips stained even redder with betel juice. This is Ne' Lumbaa, the skilled young *tominaa* who leads the older men with his mellifluous voice, exacting memory, and unquestionable air of authority. As the initial disruption of our unexpected entry subsides, the men begin to ignore us and to resume their chanting. Lumbaa leads; he is the 'mother of the *gelong*', *indo'na gelong*, and the others follow his cues. After a while they break for coffee or betelnut. Laughter, joking, and argument about the proper sequence of the verses punctuate the recitation, to which some of the family and neighbours crowded into the room seem to listen enthralled while others sleep or gossip in back corners. After several hours, in the early morning, the *gelong ma'pakumpang* begins. Lumbaa leads in a softly musical, compelling recitation of the first verses, a prelude to the requests. All the old *tominaa* are silent. Then, at the completion of Lumbaa's solo, they join together (some jostled out of their sleep), robustly chanting

Diong tallang!   Under the bamboo!

and simultaneously they bow their heads. Almost everyone in the house wakes up and participates in this portion of *ma'pakumpang* by shouting suggestions to the *tominaa*.

Prelude

Ma'pakumpang begins with the wish and search for gold, the epitome of all that is valued (lines 1–2).

> I will search for gold,
> The wishes of gold dust.

'I' in the first line becomes, in the lines that follow, a complex subject: 'the family bamboo clump', *ma'rapu tallang*.[9] And the family bamboo clump becomes differentiated, in this prelude, into women, men, children, buffalo boys, herders, little ones, and those 'who know nothing at all'. Even the spring, the waterfall, and cool water itself (all associated with the spirits) are said to have desires (lines 15–17):

> Different are the requests of the spring,
> Distinct are the desires of the waterfall,
> The wishes of cool pure water.

The family bamboo clump and its parallel, 'the whole cluster of coconuts', refuse to accept substitutes for their desires (lines 21–23):

> It refuses to be healed with the citrus fruit,
> Or with the *ta'bi* flower,
> Massaged by the sour citrus fruit.

If things are well ordered, the satisfaction of the family's desires is possible (lines 25–27):

> Arranged are the thoughts,
> Put in motion are the wants,
> Truly flowing in the chest.[10]

The well-ordered sounds which state the wishes of the family are not only the voices of chanting *tominaa*, but also the sounds of the heirloom drum and gong (lines 28–30):

> The path of the drum's thoughts,
> The wants of the gong,
> The heart's desires.

The drum, which is beaten throughout the *maro*, is sometimes said to represent the family leader who speaks in public meetings, orchestrating the diverse desires and conflicting claims within the group. Both drum and gong are sacred, sound-making heirlooms, presences with their own thoughts and wants.[11]

Other heirlooms are cited (lines 31–38):

> Do not moan, drum,
> Do not whine, bamboo violin,
> Do not moan, cordyline,[12]
> Do not whine, *seke* plant,
> Do not moan, bamboo,
> Do not whine, bamboo shoots,
> Do not moan, *maa'* cloth,[13]
> Do not whine, multicoloured.

These are among the most obscure lines in *ma'pakumpang*. If we may venture an interpretation, the lines seem to enjoin the heirlooms, which concentrate the spirits' powers, to be in a state of quiet calm.

A full and fully aware family awaits the recitation of further verses (lines 48–52):

> Here is the family bamboo clump,
> The whole cluster of coconuts,
> Without end it is recited,
> Without debts it is said,
> Without changes it is spoken.

What is the link between debt and desire? Toraja social life is constituted by exchanges and a net of debts. In *ma'pakumpang* everything is requested and nothing is offered in exchange, or so it seems. However, even this apparently one-sided transaction implies a debt. What is given in exchange for the fulfilment of the family's desires is *ma'pakumpang*, an oratorical performance accompanied by profuse offerings to the spirits. The recitation of *ma'pakumpang* is itself an offering, of beautiful, well-ordered speech and sound, of couplets and triplets, of synonyms and substitutions, of metaphors and multiples.[14]

The *tominaa*, who mediates between the family and the spirits, inquires (lines 53–54):

> Whatever more do you desire,
> Demanded by your heart?[15]

Many things are desired, as we shall see in a moment. Then, following the prelude, the *tominaa* pause for coffee, and talk among themselves.

> Now we will bow, to gather in many things, so that clothing of all kinds will be piled high. The wealth is drawn toward us. The *bate* is bounced up and down. Let's take it! Let's *ma'bate*.

The Tree of Desire

An offering of betel-nut is made and *tominaa* Lumbaa, the 'mother' of the *gelong*, cues his fellow speakers, saying 'bamboo first'.

Diong tallang!	Under the bamboo!
Diong tallang!	Under the bamboo!
Diong tallang!	Under the bamboo!
Diong lamba'!	Under the *lamba'* tree!
Diong lamba'!	Under the *lamba'* tree!
Diong lamba'!	Under the *lamba'* tree!

As they speak these lines (55–60), the *tominaa* bow emphatically at the end of each phrase, miming the movements of bamboo in the wind, or the *bate* itself, and the metaphorical *bate* of the poem which inclines and sways repeatedly toward that which is desired.

An image of the *bate* inclining toward a particular locality begins each six-line verse in which a request is embedded (for example, lines 89–90):

| *Ia kumpang lako Makki* | It bends like a tree-top toward Makki, |
| *Ia kakumbaya baya* | It sways for a while, |

'It', the *bate*, is a family tree composed of heirloom cloths and swords contributed by branches of the extended family. It contains both male (iron) and female (cloth) elements, signifying the ancestors and spirits from whom the heirlooms were obtained. The fullness of the *bate*, the density of folded, fringed cloths of many colours from many houses, represents the desired fullness of the family, its extensivity in space and time. The *bates*'s bamboo frame, 'dressed in cloths', is said to suggest a tall *lamba'* tree and a protective umbrella; it is said to be handsome, beautiful, and sacred. Within the *maro* ritual the *bate* becomes a powerful centre, creating a field in which spirits make their appearance. In the *gelong*, the *bate* is addressed as it leans in the direction of the family's desires (lines 91–94):

Ia mentangkean lola'	It becomes branches of gold bracelets,
Mendaunan sanda sanda	Becomes leaves of all kinds,
Annga dipokalalanna	Everything that is used,
Mintu' dikande kandena	All that is eaten.

As a man-made tree, the *bate* not only leans toward the source but actually generates or 'plucks' that which is desired. It becomes a fabulously generative cornucopia, producing porcelain bowls and gold, salt and palm wine, even customs and cars.

The cornucopia

Ma'pakumpang is based on the principle that good things come from other places, and that every place exudes a speciality, as fruit grows on a tree. An old man well-versed in custom noted: 'Even if it's from the edge of heaven, it is requested.' In *ma'pakumpang*, said another man, 'we ask for the wealth of others, from everywhere'. In the words of a young English teacher: 'Wherever the *bate* points, there is profit and hope. We might *kumpang* to Hong Kong, the Ming Dynasty, or Egypt or Rome. All over the world there is produce and fruit that can be picked.'

Ma'pakumpang is directed toward the gathering in of the necessities of life and the objects of the 'breath's wishes' from villages in the Toraja heart-land, and from more distant sources of Sulawesi's coasts and across the seas in Java. If the prelude is a meditation upon the needs and composition of the 'family bamboo clump', the verses that follow sound like a shopping list.

From the outer limits of the known world, which exude more exotic and perhaps more magically powerful stuff (porcelain bowls, *maa'* cloths, money, automobiles), the list moves around the peripheries of Toraja territory and calls for salt, daggers, and gold bracelets. From the peripheries, the *bate* moves to within the Toraja heartland, where it seeks everything from cooking pots to custom (*aluk*). Also chickens, water buffalo, horses, cats, dogs, fish, rice, citrus fruit, scallions, bananas, honey, sago, coffee, palm wine, cool water, bamboo, rattan, wooden plates for feeding pigs, small knives, and woven sun hats. Also shell bracelets, gold bracelets, gold neck pieces, and gold itself. Also people, descendants, drums, and mythical spinning wheels.

The verses provide a kind of economic map of what different regions have to offer. Tondon, for example (line 176), is known for its fertile rice fields, Madandan (line 161) for its plaited baskets, Balusu (line 178) for its white shell bracelets, called *balusu*. Interspersed with these contemporary places and economic realities are movements back and forth in time, revealing what different areas have had to offer in the past. Money (*ringgit*, line 109) is plucked from Enrekang, south of Tana Toraja and an area through which coins entered the Toraja hinterland in the pre-colonial period. Other goods, such as salt, have probably been obtained from the coastal lowlands of Palopo (line 125) for as long as the Toraja have lived in the mountains. Slightly less essential and less timeless is the request for automobiles from Mangkasa' (line 113), the old Toraja name for the modern city of Ujung Pandang.

Other requests are less material. *Kada siturut*, for example, are sought in both Makale and Pangala (lines 169, 205); literally 'words of agreement', the expression refers to government. Makale became the seat of Toraja government in the Dutch administration, and Pangala, today the capital of one of the regency's nine districts, was an important centre in pre-colonial times. The village of Limbong, in which these verses were recited, is situated in the Pangala district. *Tuntungan bia'*, 'the glowing torch of Suloara', a semimythical *tominaa* who brought knowledge of custom to the people of the northern regions, is sought on the uppermost crest of Mount Sesean (line 226). Custom (*aluk*) itself is requested from Tikala (line 221), a fertile region at the base of Mount Sesean to which many people of the mountain trace their ancestry.

Other requests are more specific: the drum, for example, from Randanan (line 239), is said to refer to Ne' Sulo, a living priest famous for making drums 'speak' with his feet. A mythical element, the spinning wheel of the ancestress Lambe Susu, is sought from the village of her legendary origin (line 233).

In a version of *ma'pakumpang* that we collected in the village of Tanite, the *bate* travels up to heaven in order to obtain the sacred *maa'* cloths. In the Limbong version, Java is the source of these cloths. A Toraja who read these verses commented that 'these days *tominaa* may ask for rank from Java instead of *maa*'. In each case, that which is valued and powerful is found at the far reaches of the known world.

Transportation: centre and periphery

As water from the slopes of Mount Sesean is gathered in bamboo conduits which lead to villages and fields, so do the golden waterworks of these verses guide the flow of blessings and desired objects home. In this economy based on wet-rice agriculture (lines 244–246),

> We make a water channel for you to come,
> We build a stone bridge for you,
> We make a golden waterworks.

Reaching the village, diverse stuffs flow uninterruptedly around the 'earth', that is, the village (lines 247–249):

> It will arrive here,
> The sea will encircle the world,
> There will be no brokenness.

A circle of goods surrounds the family, the village, the earth, as water surrounds rice plants in a field.

Historically, the Toraja have conceived of power and precious things as originating in centres beyond the boundaries of the Toraja heartland. Such a distant centre was the kingdom of Luwu on the Gulf of Bone, ruled by a *datu* who was regarded by the Toraja as semidivine. The *datu* of Luwu sat immobile in the court at Palopo, while a stream of humbler visitors and emissaries arrived from southern and central Sulawesi, bringing tribute in the form of gold, rice, rattan, fish, or whatever else the hinterland had to offer. The Toraja travelled periodically to Palopo to perform a ceremony called *me'datu*, in which offerings were given to the *datu* in exchange for blessings conferred upon Toraja rice seed. *Me'datu* was a movement from the highland village to the powerful coastal centre, and a return to the centre at home. The movements of the metaphorical *bate* in *ma'pakumpang*, reaching toward the external centres and sources of wealth, parallel the movements of *me'datu*, from which Toraja returned with precious salt (in exchange for rice) and the assurance of fertility and abundance.[16]

The family bamboo clump

The family, in gathering from dispersed settlements throughout Tana Toraja, the island of Sulawesi, and as far away as Kalimantan, Java, and

Irian Jaya, creates a nucleus or powerful centre, like the *datu* itself, toward which everything moves. The branches of the family become 'the family bamboo clump', *ma'rapu tallang*, or 'the whole cluster of coconuts', *mintu' ma'limbo kaluku*. In this ceremonial setting the family is referred to as 'those of one thousand slender bamboo trees', or 'those of one ritual unit'. This powerful image is generated not only by the physical presence of so many people, but also by the collective symbol of itself that the family creates, in both the material and the metaphorical *bate*: one of cloth and bamboo, the other of speech. Erect, handsome, admired, in the centre of the ceremonial field, the *bate* which sweeps across the landscape, across the mountains and coasts of Sulawesi and beyond, is an image of the arc of desire. The *bate* concentrates the pooled wishes of the family, which range from the 'edge of heaven' to the village across the ridge, into a single, ephemeral, multicoloured centre.

Conclusion: the dream

Ma'pakumpang concludes with verses, again spoken solely by the *tominaa* Lumbaa, which emphasise the central intention. Bounty will flow into the village, now a centre, through a golden waterworks, and, as a circle completes and unifies, this bounty will encircle the earth, softly and without brokenness.

While *ma'pakumpang* verses obtain diverse things through verbal performance, the family, on the receiving end, is exhorted to secure their treasure by any means possible (lines 252–255):

> Be clever at catching it!
> Be smart at snatching it!
> You will catch the wealth
> In a wide embrace.

Catch it like a football, grab it, and run quickly; be wily if necessary, squeeze it like a lemon to the last drop; take care of it! And in lines 258–259:

> Lock it up! Make it safe!
> Do not let it become less than full.

In the final *gelong*, the *tominaa* speaks again to the family (line 262):

> You become a *datu*.

Fulfilment of desire means great wealth and position. It is hoped that the family in the village will become, like a *datu*, a powerful centre of abundance.

The dreams of the night, and those of the late afternoon sleep, are thought by the Toraja to portend the future, to be the dreams 'through which everything can be obtained'. Like the elusive wish that sets a dream in motion, or the absent object that prompts a child to draw a hobby horse, it is the wishes of 'the family bamboo clump' that move the *bate* from place to place. These collective wishes appear not as the images of dreams or paintings, but as the spoken, chanted *gelong* of *ma'pakumpang*. And the speaking of these words in the context of the *maro*, in the presence of the invited *deata* spirits, makes the imagined, wished-for outcome a possibility. It is the Toraja who tell us that that is so: that *ma'pakumpang*, like the dreams of the night and the late afternoon, brings toward them the fulfilment of their desires (lines 263–268):

> Complete are the dreams of the night,
> With the sleep of the late afternoon,
> So that the banyan tree is tall,
> So that the *lamba'* tree gives shade.
> Here is the family bamboo clump,
> The whole cluster of coconuts.

In a reflexive movement, the text of *ma'pakumpang* refers to itself. The verses begin at the centre, the village and the ancestral house, and move outward. At the conclusion of the poem, both the orators and the listeners, like the stuffs procured 'outside', have returned home. It is this extended family, transformed into the image of a swaying, leaning, sacred tree of cloth, which is the agent of its own fulfilment.

Reference text

Ma'pakumpang

1	*La unnanga'na' bulaan*	I will search for gold,
2	*Panguntean rau rau*	The wishes of gold dust.
3	*Senga' palakunna Tumbang*	Different are the requests of she who is called 'to jump',
4	*Laen anga'na Banaa*	Distinct are the desires of she who is called 'rice vessel',
5	*Panguntean Pangria Barang*	The wishes of she who holds the winnowing tray.
6	*Senga' palakunna londong*	Different are the requests of the cock,
7	*Laen anga'na muane*	Distinct are the desires of the man,
8	*Panguntean telo telo*	The wishes of the decorated man.
9	*Senga' palakunna pasang*	Different are the requests of the grassy buffalo place,

10	*Laen anga'na pangkambi*	Distinct are the desires of the herders,
11	*Panguntean ponglaa tedong*	The wishes of the buffalo boys.
12	*Senga' palakunna pia'*	Different are the requests of the children,
13	*Laen anga'na baitti'*	Distinct are the desires of the little ones,
14	*Panguntean tang unnissan*	The wishes of those who know nothing at all.
15	*Senga' palakunna bubun*	Different are the requests of the spring,
16	*Laen anga'na turunan*	Distinct are the desires of the waterfall,
17	*Panguntean sakke malino*	The wishes of cool pure water.
18	*Inde to ma'rapu tallang*	Here is the family bamboo clump,
19	*Mintu' ma'limbo kaluku*	The whole cluster of coconuts.
20	*Inde gandangna ma'rapu*	Here is the drum of the family,
21	*Nanoka didampi lemo*	It refuses to be healed with the citrus fruit,
22	*Sia ta'bi kayu bale*	Or with the *ta'bi* flower,
23	*Dipamurru' lemo laa'*	Massaged by the sour citrus fruit.
24	*Inde to ma'rapu tallang*	Here is the family bamboo clump.
25	*Dirundunan inayanna*	Arranged are the thoughts,
26	*Diolan pa'poraianna*	Put in motion are the wants,
27	*Tungka lolong di ara'na*	Truly flowing in the chest.
28	*Lalan inayanna gandang*	The path of the drum's thoughts,
29	*Pa'poraianna bombongan*	The wants of the gong,
30	*Passitanan inayanna*	The heart's desires.
31	*Manggi' sumarroi gandang*	Do not moan, drum,
32	*Mengkaoa'ri tandilo*	Do not whine, bamboo violin,
33	*Manggi' sumarroi tabang*	Do not moan, cordyline,
34	*Mengkaoa'ri lan seke*	Do not whine, *seke* plant,
35	*Manggi' sumarroi tallang*	Do not moan, bamboo,
36	*Mengkaoa'ri to tiang*	Do not whine, bamboo shoots,
37	*Manggi' sumarroi maa'*	Do not moan, *maa'* cloth,
38	*Mengkaoa'ri masura'*	Do not whine, multicoloured.
39	*Ke la tarun raka para'?*	Is it not clear blue?
40	*Ke la sido raka para'?*	Will it not be sea blue?
41	*Ke la riri raka para'?*	Will it not be yellow?
42	*Ke sarita raka para'?*	Is it not a blue and white cloth?
43	*Ke la bassi raka para'?*	Will it not be iron?

44	*Dirundunan inayanna*	Arranged are the thoughts,
45	*Diolan pa'poraianna*	Put in motion are the wants;
46	*Tungka lolong di ara'na*	Truly flowing in the chest.
47	*Ke la bate raka para'?*	Will it not be a tree of cloth?
48	*Inde to ma'rapu tallang*	Here is the family bamboo clump,
49	*Mintu' ma'limbo kaluku*	The whole cluster of coconuts.
50	*Tang pura pura disa'bu*	Without end it is recited,
51	*Tang ma'indan dipokada*	Without debts it is said,
52	*Tang leluk di pau pau*	Without changes it is spoken.
53	*Apa sia pa mu anga'*	Whatever more do you desire,
54	*Natuntun lan inayanmu?*	Demanded by your heart?
55	*Diong tallang!*	Under the bamboo!
56	*Diong tallang!*	Under the bamboo!
57	*Diong tallang!*	Under the bamboo!
58	*Diong lamba'!*	Under the *lamba'* tree!
59	*Diong lamba'!*	Under the *lamba'* tree!
60	*Diong lamba'!*	Under the *lamba'* tree!
61	*Diong lamba' tunduk tunduk*	Under the *lamba'* tree leaning,
62	*Kateang kumbaya baya*	The bamboo branch sways,
63	*Kateang kumbaya baya*	The bamboo branch sways,
64	*Kateang kumbaya baya*	The bamboo branch sways.
65	*Ia kumpang langan Bone*	It bends like a tree-top toward Bone,
66	*Ia kakumbaya baya*	It sways for a while,
67	*Ia mentangkean pindan*	It becomes branches of white porcelain bowls,
68	*Mendaunan sanda sanda*	Becomes leaves of all kinds,
69	*Angga dipokalalanna*	Everything that is used,
70	*Mintu' dikande kandena*	All that is eaten.
71	*Kita lo kasari sari*	We take palm wine from someone else's tree,
72	*Kitete to ala' kari'*	We use the forest people's bridge,
73	*Kisaruran bulayanni*	We make a golden waterworks.
74	*La rampo inde mo tende*	It will arrive here,
75	*La tasik lengkoi lino*	The sea will encircle the world,
76	*Tang la kalimban limbanan*	There will be no brokenness.
77	*Ia kumpang lako Jawa*	It bends like a tree-top toward Java,
78	*Ia kakumbaya baya*	It sways for a while,

79	*Ia mentangkean maya*	It becomes branches of *maa'* cloths,
80	*Mendaunan sanda sanda*	Becomes leaves of all kinds,
81	*Angga dipokalalanna*	Everything that is used,
82	*Mintu' dikande kandena*	All that is eaten.
83	*Ia kumpang langan Seko*	It bends like a tree-top up to Seko,
84	*Ia kakumbaya baya*	It sways for a while,
85	*Ia mentangkean bassi*	Becomes branches of iron,
86	*Mendaunan sanda sanda*	Becomes leaves of all kinds,
87	*Mintu' dipokalalanna*	Everything that is used,
88	*Mintu' dikande kandena*	All that is eaten.
89	*Ia kumpang lako Makki*	It bends like a tree-top toward Makki,
90	*Ia kakumbaya baya*	It sways for a while,
91	*Ia mentangkean lola'*	It becomes branches of gold bracelets,
92	*Mendaunan sanda sanda*	Becomes leaves of all kinds,'
93	*Angga dipokalalanna*	Everything that is used,
94	*Mintu' dikande kandena*	All that is eaten.
95	*Ia kumpang ri Mamasa*	It bends like a tree-top toward Mamasa,
96	*Ia kakumbaya baya*	It sways for a while,
97	*Ia mentangkean bulayan*	It becomes branches of gold,
98	*Mendaunan sanda sanda*	Becomes leaves of all kinds,
99	*Angga dipokalalanna*	Everything that is used,
100	*Mintu' dikande kandena*	All that is eaten.
101	*Ia kumpang sau' Duri*	It bends like a tree-top south to Duri,
102	*Ia kakumbaya baya*	It sways for a while,
103	*Ia mentangkean tedong*	It becomes branches of water buffalo,
104	*Mendaunan sanda sanda*	Becomes leaves of all kinds,
105	*Angga dipokalalanna*	Everything that is used,
106	*Mintu' dikande kandena*	All that is eaten.
107	*Ia kumpang ri Enrekang*	It bends like a tree-top toward Enrekang,
108	*Ia kakumbaya baya*	It sways for a while,
109	*Ia mentangkean ringgi'*	It becomes branches of coins,

110	*Mendaunan sanda sanda*	Becomes leaves of all kinds,
111	*Angga dipokalalanna*	Everything that is used,
112	*Mintu' dikande kandena*	All that is eaten.
113	*Ia kumpang ri Mangkasa'*	It bends like a tree-top toward Mangkasa',
114	*Ia kakumbaya baya*	It sways for a while,
115	*Ia mentangkean oto*	It becomes branches of automobiles,
116	*Mendaunan sanda sanda*	Becomes leaves of all kinds,
117	*Angga dipokalalanna*	Everything that is used,
118	*Mintu' dikande kandena*	All that is eaten.
119	*Kikaloran komi sae*	We make a water channel for you to come,
120	*Kitetean batuan komi*	We build a stone bridge for you,
121	*Kisaruran bulayanni*	We make a golden waterworks.
122	*La rampo inde mo tende*	It will arrive here,
123	*La tasik lengkoi lino*	The sea will encircle the earth,
124	*Tang la kalimban limbanan*	There will be no brokenness.
125	*Ia kumpang ri Palopo*	It bends like a tree-top toward Palopo,
126	*Ia mentangkean gayang*	It becomes branches of gold daggers,
127	*Ia mentangkean sia*	It becomes branches of salt,
128	*Mendaunan sanda sanda*	Becomes leaves of all kinds,
129	*Angga dipokalalanna*	Everything that is used,
130	*Mintu' dikande kandena*	All that is eaten.
131	*Ia kumpang rokko Ala'*	It bends like a tree-top down to Ala' [Palopo or Masamba],
132	*Ia kakumbaya baya*	It sways for a while,
133	*Ia mentangkean manuk*	It becomes branches of chickens,
134	*Mendaunan sanda sanda*	Becomes leaves of all kinds,
135	*Angga dipokalalanna*	Everything that is used,
136	*Mintu' dikande kandena*	All that is eaten.
137	*Ia kumpang ri Baruppu'*	It bends like a tree-top toward Baruppu',
138	*Ia kakumbaya baya*	It sways for a while,
139	*Ia mentangkean lola'*	It becomes branches of gold bracelets,
140	*Mendaunan sanda sanda*	Becomes leaves of all kinds,

141	*Angga dipokalalanna*	Everything that is used,
142	*Mintu' dikande kandena*	All that is eaten.
143	*Ia kumpang rokko Awan*	It bends like a tree-top down to Awan,
144	*Ia kakumbaya baya*	It sways for a while,
145	*Ia mentangkean busso*	It becomes branches of stone cisterns,
146	*Mendaunan sanda sanda*	Becomes leaves of all kinds,
147	*Angga dipokalalanna*	Everything that is used,
148	*Mintu' dikande kandena*	All that is eaten.
149	*Ia kumpang ri Bittuang*	It bends like a tree-top toward Bittuang,
150	*Ia kakumbaya baya*	It sways for a while,
151	*Ia mentangkean bonga*	It becomes branches of piebald buffalo,
152	*Mendaunan sanda sanda*	Becomes leaves of all kinds,
153	*Angga dipokalalanna*	Everything that is used,
154	*Mintu' dikande kandena*	All that is eaten.
155	*Ia kumpang sau' Piongan*	It bends like a tree-top south to Piongan,
156	*Ia kakumbaya baya*	It sways for a while,
157	*Ia mentangkean serre'*	It becomes branches of cats,
158	*Mendaunan sanda sanda*	Becomes leaves of all kinds,
159	*Angga dipokalalanna*	Everything that is used,
160	*Mintu' dikande kandena*	All that is eaten.
161	*Ia kumpang ri Mandanan*	It bends like a tree-top toward Madandan,
162	*Ia kakumbaya baya*	It sways for a while,
163	*Ia mentangkean baka siroe'*	It becomes branches of baskets strung together,
164	*Mendaunan sanda sanda*	Becomes leaves of all kinds,
165	*Angga dipokalalanna*	Everything that is used,
166	*Mintu' dikande kandena*	All that is eaten.
167	*Ia kumpang ri Lamun*	It bends like a tree-top toward Lamun,
168	*Mentangkean kurin*	It becomes branches of clay cooking pots,
169	*Kumpang sau' Makale*	It bends like a tree-top south to Makale,

170	*Mentangkean kada situru'*	It becomes branches of the words of agreement,
171	*Mendaunan sanda sanda*	Becomes leaves of all kinds,
172	*Angga dipokalalanna*	Everything that is used,
173	*Mintu' dikande kandena*	All that is eaten.

174	*Ia kumpang langan Buntao'*	It bends like a tree-top up to Buntao',
175	*Mentangkean ao'*	It becomes branches of slender bamboo,
176	*Kumpang tama Tondon*	Bends like a tree-top entering Tondon,
177	*Mentangkean pare*	Becomes branches of rice sheaves,
178	*Kumpang rekke Balusu*	Bends like a tree-top north to Balusu,
179	*Mentangkean balusu*	Becomes branches of white shell bracelets,
180	*Kumpang rekke Pia'*	Bends like a tree-top north to Pia',
181	*Mentangkean tau*	Becomes branches of people,
182	*Mendaunan sanda sanda*	Becomes leaves of all kinds,
183	*Angga dipokalalanna*	Everything that is used,
184	*Mintu' dikande kandena*	All that is eaten.

185	*Kumpang Sangbua'*	Bends like a tree-top to Sangbua',
186	*Mentangkean tuak*	Becomes branches of palm wine,
187	*Kumpang Batu*	Bends like a tree-top to Batu,
188	*Mentangkean sarong*	Becomes branches of woven sun-hats,
189	*Mendaunan sanda sanda*	Becomes leaves of all kinds,
190	*Angga dipokalalanna*	Everything that is used,
191	*Mintu' dikande kandena*	All that is eaten.

192	*Kikaloran kami sae*	We make a water channel for you to come,
193	*Kitetean batuan komi*	We build a stone bridge for you,
194	*Kisaruran bulayanni*	We make a golden waterworks.
195	*La rampo inde mo tende*	It will arrive here,
196	*La tasik lengkoi lino*	The sea will encircle the earth,
197	*Tang la kalimban limbanan*	There will be no brokenness.

198	*Kumpang ri To' Tille*	Bends like a tree-top toward To'Tille,
199	*Mentangkean sarambu*	Becomes branches of a waterfall,
200	*Kumpang Lo'ko Lemo*	Bends like a tree-top to Lo'ko Lemo,
201	*Meptangkean lemo sambai' mai*	Becomes branches of citrus fruits from there,
202	*Mendaunan sanda sanda*	Becomes leaves of all kinds,
203	*Angga dipokalalanna*	Everything that is used,
204	*Mintu' dikande kandena*	All that is eaten.
205	*Ia kumpang ri Pangala'*	It bends like a tree-top toward Pangala',
206	*Ia kakumbaya baya*	It sways for a while,
207	*Mentangkean kada situru' lo' mai*	Becomes branches of the words of agreement,
208	*Mendaunan sanda sanda*	Becomes leaves of all kinds,
209	*Angga dipokalalanna*	Everything that is used,
210	*Mintu' dikande kandena*	All that is eaten.
211	*Kumpang Ke'pe*	Bends to Ke'pe,
212	*Mentangkean kabubu'*	Becomes branches of creeping tuberous vegetables,
213	*Mendaunan sanda sanda*	Becomes leaves of all kinds,
214	*Angga dipokalalanna*	Everything that is used,
215	*Mintu' dikande kandena*	All that is eaten.
216	*Kumpang Lolai*	Bends like a tree-top to Lolai,
217	*Mentangkean bale*	Becomes branches of fish,
218	*Mendaunan sanda sanda*	Becomes leaves of all kinds,
219	*Angga dipokalalanna*	Everything that is used,
220	*Mintu' dikande kandena*	All that is eaten.
221	*Kumpang Tikala*	Bends like a tree-top toward Tikala,
222	*Mentangkean aluk*	Becomes branches of custom,
223	*Mendaunan sanda sanda*	Becomes leaves of all kinds,
224	*Angga dipokalalanna*	Everything that is used,
225	*Mintu' dikande kandena*	All that is eaten.
226	*Kumpang langan Sesean*	Bends like a tree-top to Sesean,
227	*Mentangkean Tutungan Bia' domai*	Becomes branches of the torch of glowing embers,

228	*Mendaunan sanda sanda*	Becomes leaves of all kinds,
229	*Angga dipokalalanna*	Everything that is used,
230	*Mintu' dikande kandena*	All that is eaten.

231	*Kumpang Pangden*	Bends like a tree-top to Pangden,
232	*Mentangkean lolo tau domai*	Becomes branches of umbilical cords from there,
233	*Kumpang Batu*	Bends like a tree-top to Batu,
234	*Mentangkean unuran*	Becomes branches of spinning wheels,
235	*Kumpang Sapan*	Bends like a tree-top to Sapan,
236	*Mentangkean tuak*	Becomes branches of palm wine,
237	*Kumpang rekke Pengkaroan Manuk*	Bends like a tree-top north to Pengkaroan Manuk,
238	*Mentangkean manuk*	Becomes branches of chickens,
239	*Kumpang rekke Randanan*	Bends like a tree-top north to Randanan,
240	*Mentangkean gandang*	Becomes branches of drums,
241	*Mendaunan sanda sanda*	Becomes leaves of all kinds,
242	*Angga dipokalalanna*	Everything that is used,
243	*Mintu' dikande kandena*	All that is eaten.

244	*Kikaloran kami sae*	We make a water channel for you to come
245	*Kitete batuan kami*	We build a stone bridge for you,
246	*Kisaruran bulayanni*	We make a golden waterworks.
247	*La rampo inde mo tende*	It will arrive here,
248	*La tasik lengkoi lino*	The sea will encircle the world,
249	*Tang la kalimban limbanan*	There will be no brokenness.

250	*Inde lako to ma'rapu*	Here is the family,
251	*To mai sang pemalaran*	Those of one ritual community.
252	*Manarangko untimangngi!*	Be clever at catching it!
253	*Pandeko unsarande ki!*	Be smart at snatching it!
254	*La untimang timang sugi'*	You will catch the wealth
255	*La unsarande kalua'*	In a wide embrace.
256	*Mutangga' tau senga'!*	Trick other people!
257	*Tang la mupatumbangmo!*	Do not let it go!
258	*Sulu'i! pemanda'i!*	Lock it up! Make it safe!
259	*Temboi lodang lodanganni!*	Do not let it become less than full!
260	*Mukaridisanni lemo!*	Squeeze the citrus fruit to the last drop!

261	*Mutammanni sarre ala'mu!*	Chew the fragrant lemon grass!
262	*Mupopadatu datumo*	You become a *datu*.
263	*Sundun tindo bonginna*	Complete are the dreams of the night,
264	*Sola mamma' karoenna*	With the sleep of the late afternoon,
265	*Anna barana' kalando*	So that the banyan tree is tall,
266	*Anna lamba' paonganan*	So that the *lambar* tree gives shade.
267	*Inde to ma'rapu tallang*	Here is the family bamboo clump,
268	*Mintu' ma'limbo kaluku.*	The whole cluster of coconuts.

NOTES

Introduction

1 The literature on biblical parallelism continues to grow. Four recent publications on the subject are of particular note: W.R. Watter's *Formula criticism and the poetry of the Old Testament* (1976), S.A. Geller's *Parallelism in early biblical poetry* (1979), and M. O'Connor's *Hebrew verse structure* (1980) apply new linguistic approaches to the study of Hebrew and Ugaritic poetry; while J.L. Krugel's *The idea of biblical poetry: parallelism and its history* (1981) gives an account of the development of the study of parallelism.

2 For some idea of this substantial literature on parallelism in Chinese, see Hervey-Saint-Denys 1862; Schlegel 1896; Tchang Tcheng-Ming 1937; Boodberg 1954–55a,b,c; Hightower 1959; V.Y.C. Shih 1959; T'sou 1968; Jakobson 1970.

3 Among the more important collections of texts in which parallelism figures prominently are those published by Paulhan (1913) for the Merina, by Lagemann (1893, 1906), Sundermann (1905), and Steinhart (1934, 1937, 1938, 1950, 1954) for Nias, by Schärer (1966) for the Ngaju Dayak, by Dunselmann (1949, 1950a, 1950b, 1954, 1955, 1959a, 1959b, 1961) for the Mualang and Kendayan Dayak groups, by Sabatier (1933) for Rhade, by van der Veen (1929, 1950, 1965, 1966, 1972) for the Sa'dan Toraja, by Dunnebier (1938, 1953) for Bolaang Mongondow, and by Middelkoop (1949) for the Atoni Pah Meto of west Timor. For the peoples of eastern Indonesia, this present volume, whose coverage is only partial, should give some indication of the extent of the use of parallelism within the region.

4 For a discussion of some of these notions, see Kemmer 1903; Malkiel 1959; Meyer 1889; Salomon 1919; Lloyd 1966.

5 'Weyéwa' and 'Wewewa' refer to the same domain in west Sumba where Kuipers and Renard-Clamagirand have done separate fieldwork. In their writings, these two researchers have adopted different transcription systems for rendering the Weyéwa/Wewewa language.

6 This is a further excerpt from the funeral chant, *Ndi Lonama ma Laki Elokama*, quoted in my paper in this volume. For the full text, see Fox 1972a: 34–43.

7 Notably, as Forth points out, the people of Rindi distinguish between ritual language use in invocations addressed to the ancestors, which they designate as *hamayangu*, and the language used in negotiations, which they refer to as *luluku*.

8 See Kuipers 1982:89, for example; he distinguishes eleven genres requiring ritual speech.

1. Etiquette in Kodi spirit communication

The research on which this paper is based was supported by grants from the US Social Science Research Council, the Fulbright Commission and the US National Science Foundation, and was conducted in west Sumba, Indonesia under the auspices of Lembaga Ilmu Pengetahuan Indonesia. I would like to thank Markos Rangga Ende, Martinus Maru Mahemba, Hermanus Rangga Horo and Lota Rehi, my Kodinese informants whose words and wisdom are reported here.

1 Rarely have I encountered a description of an indigenous cosmology which is so explicitly presented as a communication system. Although the universe itself is said to be made up of six levels of land and seven levels of sky (*nomo ndani cana*//*pitu ndani awango*), my informants were both unable and unwilling to express the order that they perceived in the spirit world in terms of the visual or spatial metaphors familiar to our Western pantheons. They refused to speak of certain spirits as living at certain levels, or of a more abstract integration of the levels in a wedding-cake-like structure. Despite their emphatic insistence that some spirits were 'higher' or 'more important' than others, they could only articulate this in terms of the rules governing how the spirit concerned could be addressed, not where he or she was located in an ethereal kingdom of uncertain physical dimensions. I was finally forced to conclude that the contours of the spirit hierarchy can be most clearly discerned through an examination of the speech etiquette followed in ritual.

2 My use of the male pronoun here is in fact inappropriate, since the Creator is presented as a double-gendered deity who combines male and female aspects in the unitary source of all being. Usually referred to as the Binder and the Smelter (*Amawolo Amarawi*), the longer version of this name is the Mother Binder of the Forelock//Father Creator of the Crown (*Inya wolo hungga*//*Bapa rawi lindu*). The female activity of binding the hairs at the brow (just as women bind the threads of *ikat* cloth) is paired with the male activity of smelting the hard skull at the crown of the head. Forth (1981) notes that the east Sumbanese have a similar name for the Creator, *na wulu*//*na majii*, the maker and plaiter of mankind.

3 The same division between the forces of the inside and the outside is found in the eastern domain of Rindi, as documented by Forth (1981). He notes, however, that in Rindi the term *marapu* is more directly connected to human forebears and would not apply to altars, medicines, totem animals, heirloom objects or to the wild spirits of uninhabited land. Certain other authors who have written on east Sumba, notably Lambooy (1930, 1937), discuss more varied senses for the term. This is also true of early writers on west Sumba (van Dijk 1939; Onvlee 1973), so that regional shifts in the way that the spirit world is conceived would seem to present an intriguing comparative problem.

4 Pyoke and Mbyora were the names of the first ancestors to die; they are always invoked to remind men of their own mortality and the inevitability of their passing. Kodi acceptance of universal mortality does not, however, alter their conviction that the precise time of death is always related to the anger of a spiritual agent. Some transgression or failure to propitiate the proper deities must have caused them to revoke their protection, exposing their human charges to the forces of illness and disaster.

5 The original divination spear is said to have been brought from Savu many generations ago, and by now it has largely displaced the earlier method of rope divination. The Kodi name for the divination rite itself is still *parupu kaloro* (lit. 'blowing on the ropes'), even though, in fact, the spear is used almost exclusively. Thus, the earlier couplet, the 'mat which is rolled out//the ropes which are blown upon', refers to the work of the diviner.

6 Cucumber milk is a whitish, watery liquid whose cooling, nourishing force is probably intended to suggest the generous fertility of the Great Mother, just as his wide thighs suggest the welcoming acceptance of the Great Father.

7 These phrases refer to the use of stealth in taking someone else's belongings within the village. Raiding conducted on other clans is not punished by the ancestral deities.

8 The noisy birds who strut about arrogantly refer to disputes within the family. Ironically, the movements described are the same as those of dancers in the prestige feasts who display their grace and bravery by dancing with ankle bells (the women) and beating their chests with spears (the men).

9 The dirty-minded creatures of the sea represent those guilty of incest or adultery.

10 This phrase is a way of asking whether the proper offerings were not made when people left for a stone-dragging ceremony to build a grave in the ancestral village. The hamlet deity should be honoured first with a meal of chicken and rice dedicated to him to secure his permission for departure.

11 When the spear strikes the pillar in response to this question, it indicates that the tree where the hamlet deity resides has not been properly consecrated. In the section that follows, the diviner has begun to speak directly, as if he were the deity.

12 Byokokoro is the hare-lipped gatekeeper of the flood waters of the heavens. He is represented as the mythological figure who traded the waters of the sky for fire from the earth back in the time of the first ancestors. Ever since then he has been the deity prayed to for rainfall and for fertility of the crops. Manjalur is described as his servant and guardian.

13 The image of plentiful meat and abundant water is complemented by the human skulls whose presence shows that the lords of the upper world are also brave headhunters whose splendour and daring knows no bounds. The Kodinese themselves are former headhunters who greatly esteem the heroic bravery of their ancestors.

14 Sibling rivalry is especially strong at prestige feasts, because whenever one brother decides to sponsor a feast in his own name, all of his brothers and affines are required by custom to contribute to the slaughter. In effect, every man who seeks to 'make his own name' in the ceremonial field is also deeply dependent upon aid from his kin. In this particular instance the rite had been sponsored to renew an earlier contract with the spirit of metal-working, and the elder brother, himself a metal-worker, was the only one who stood to benefit from it. Other residents of the garden hamlet of Kere Homba, which held the rite in 1977, were unwilling to commit themselves to such heavy expenditures because they did not see them as serving the common interest. As the time for the sacrifice approached, they protested that the younger buffalo

were needed to reproduce the herd, and several of them withdrew entirely. Embarrassed, the host still felt obligated to feed his guests, and therefore killed his own buffalo in a special area outside of the central ceremonial field. This ceremony, held in 1981 in the same garden hamlet, was basically an attempt to rectify those problems and re-establish a harmonious relationship with the spirits to whom the sacrifices had originally been dedicated.

15 These images of dense and fertile growth are meant to show the assumption of the higher deities that unless this feast is being held for a good reason, then it is simply a celebration of the abundance of the harvest. The instructions given by the ritual orator constitute a specific denial of the cheery picture of a bountiful life which he presents.

16 The souls of earlier offerings – the roasted pig meat and boiled buffalo, the scattered tobacco and areca nut – are all said to hover impatiently around the house, where their presence is detected by divination. Until they are officially sent off to the upper world with the proper invocations, they will continue to be stuck outside, causing trouble because of their impatience.

17 The red heat of the metal symbolises the anger of the spirits, which is always associated with excessive heat. The holes in the cloth represent the human suffering of illness and hunger which have afflicted the members of this garden hamlet since the time of that fateful feast.

18 These are more specific references to fevers and malarial delirium which have attacked members of the household sponsoring the rite.

19 Here, the orator asserts that it was only the illness and suffering of the people inside the house which pushed them to make the preparations for this feast. The post for the upright drum and the stand to hang the gongs are explicit references to *woleko* feasting, because they are not used in any of the simpler rites. Here he implies that they realised that it was only by sponsoring a full-scale *woleko* that the souls of the original offerings could be ushered up to their final resting place in the sky.

20 The Mother of the Earth, Father of the Rivers is, of course, the hamlet deity, who is asked to represent the human community to the higher deities of the ancestral village.

21 At times, this contrast between the modern world and the supposedly unchanging words of the ancestors produces an almost comic sort of irony. At a rite which I attended in 1980 the host entered on a motor cycle which was described as a 'thundering jet-black horse', and proceeded to leave – with his extensive shares of sacrificial meat – in a minibus rented for the occasion, described as a 'herd of long-horned buffalo'. Since there are, of course, no traditional couplets which explicitly describe such modern objects, the Kodinese seem content to settle for metaphorical extensions.

22 The liver is the seat of wisdom, while the throat is the organ of verbal articulation and skill with words. Thus, the spider is seen as a being with no knowledge, and the snail as an animal with no words.

23 White teeth represent youth and inexperience because they are not yet betel-stained from extensive chewing of the reddish quid, usually mixed with tobacco. The 'blue' hair is actually blue-black.

24 The concept of a wild-spirit familiar is also present in east Sumba, where it has been described by Forth, who calls it an *ariyaa* or 'guest, associate' (1981:107),

and by Adams, who analyses the encounter as a psychological experience (1979:96). Significantly, Adams states that the snake may try to tempt its interlocutor into marriage, a dangerous union certain to result in early death. Forth notes, in another context, that the Kodi term for wild spirit, *yora*, is used in the eastern district of Rindi as a metaphor for an illicit lover (1981:429). The secretive and dangerous character of such liaisons, whether with spirits or human beings, emphasises their 'outside' character. Another implication which can be drawn from this association of terms and of concepts is one which Kodinese informants made clear to me: people are inclined to contract such pacts with wild spirits of the opposite sex.

25 *Tangero ba na muyo, emenikya a bei kabani, ha ghughuna a maloyo mono a laki.*
  'Nggaranghu nana?' wena a bei kabani.
  'Oo, yayo do kiyo, ambu,' wena.
  'A pena ba yinghu?'
  'Oo, halako ndikya njaka kingguni, ambu, oro mate inya mate bapa nggu.'
  'Yayo marongo ghughu dougha,' wena a bei kabani. 'Pa marongo ghughu waingo, ba ngehe kandakuroka ha ghughu nggu, mate eloloka!'
  'Oo, milya kalu kinjaka, ambu. Milya mate inya kiyo, dara mate bapa kiyo.'
  'Wonggu ana langhuta mu hawu,' wena a marango ghughu.
  Na wonanikya a laghuta hawuyo. Na pokoroyaka a laghuta, na dekeya a ihina a kicolo, na bandaloka la. Na pa rongo naka liyo a marongo ghughu: 'Mu baka hitu, kerenda mono watu lahunda!'
  'Pena ba hei kingo yoyo, ba pa rongo liyo, ambu?'
  'Di douka ha marapu ngg yayo,' wena a marango ghughu.
  Mengeka, a mohengoka.

2. Method in the metaphor

My research in Wanukaka, west Sumba, was conducted under the auspices of Lembaga Ilmu Pengetahuan Indonesia and with the assistance of a travel grant from the Centre of Southeast Asian Studies, Monash University. Many Wanukakans gave generously of their time and knowledge in teaching me to understand something of their language. Drs Kering Hama, Ngailu Dappa, Lydia Kalumbang Weru and Weingu Bora were particularly helpful, but no one was more industrious in transcribing and translating texts, or more patient in explaining the subtleties of the language, than Jusuf Poho Potty. For him it was a labour of love.

1 The clan history of the Matolangu clan of Lewa Paku, east Sumba, is recounted in considerable detail by Oemboe Hina Kapita in his book *Sumba di dalam Jangkauan Jaman* (1976a:218–242). Although for the most part the story is told in paraphrase, several short passages are given in ritual language and literally translated into Indonesian. The clan histories which in Wanukaka are known as *kanuga* are known as *lii ndai* in most east Sumba dialects.

3. Li'i marapu

This paper, but without Wewewa linguistic formulae, was first published in French in a special issue on oral literature of ASEMI (1979, 10:49–58).

1 Although it does not appear in the transcription, one must keep in mind that there exists in Wewewa an opposition between short and long vowels. For example, *koba* with a long ō means the half-shell of a coconut, and *koba* with a short ŏ means 'bland, without taste, without poison or harmless, permitted' when opposed to *eri*, which means 'sacred, forbidden'. But I have insufficient information to be able to take into account this opposition in the present transcription.

2 My identification of animals and plants has been made through Indonesian translations of Wewewa terms.

3 There are different *marapu*, each having his own character and occupying a specific point in space; but such a subject requires a whole study in itself, and in this paper I use the general term *marapu* even where a particular *marapu* is mentioned.

4 The fact that the collective clan rituals are not performed any more may amplify this tendency to competition, since there is no longer the confrontation and the discussion that always preceded the rituals in which each and every one was reminded of the role and the position given to him by custom.

4. The pattern of prayer in Weyéwa

The ethnographic research on which this study is based was carried out from 1978 to 1980 with the sponsorship of the Biro Penelitian of Universitas Nusa Cendana in Kupang, and the Indonesian Institute of Sciences (LIPI). This support is gratefully acknowledged. Versions of this paper were delivered at the Departments of Anthropology at the Universities of Chicago, Rochester and Michigan in the spring of 1983. I am grateful to the members of those Departments, some of whose suggestions have been incorporated in this paper.

5. Fashioned speech, full communication

Fieldwork in Rindi was carried out between February 1975 and December 1976 under the auspices of the Lembaga Ilmu Pengetahuan Indonesia, and was funded from a Social Science Research Council Project Grant awarded to Professor Rodney Needham of the University of Oxford, under the terms of which I was engaged as a research assistant.

1 In a limited number of cases everyday words may undergo minor phonetic change when used in ritual language. Examples of this include the use of *a* or *à* for *e* (for example, *eti*, 'liver'→*ati*) and the placing of a consonant before an initial vowel (for example, *unungu*, 'to drink' → *ngunungu*). Such transformations, however, appear to characterise the oratorical rather than the invocatory use of ritual language; hence they were explained as facilitating the comparatively rapid speech of the former style and as a way of ensuring clarity in this regard.

2 It is relevant here that the Rindi claimed that ritual language cannot be translated, either into ordinary speech or into Bahasa Indonesia (cf. Fox 1971:224).

3 Since eastern Sumbanese ritual speech generally displays a pronounced metre,

with paired lines usually comprising an equal or nearly equal number of syllables, in some cases such divergences from ordinary language might be attributable to the metrical requirements of this speech style. Yet it is not difficult to find instances where this consideration appears not to apply; and, in any case, as metrics is a topic I have yet to consider in any detail, I would leave this question open. What does seem clear, though, is that metre has little direct effect on the semantics of ritual language pairings (cf. Fox 1971:230 n.5).

4 By itself, *ama bokulu* ('great father') can also mean 'elder' and 'clan, lineage headman'. Thus the adjectives *mahamayangu* and *mauratungu*, both of which can be generally glossed as 'who performs invocations', specify a person within the category of *ama bokulu* who regularly carries out priestly duties. The two words can also be used on their own, as substantives, with the sense of 'priest'.

5 The earliest clear reference to the eastern Sumbanese tradition of ritual speaking is found in Roos (1872:73–75), who provides a fairly detailed and accurate description of the use of 'interpreters', 'spokesmen', or 'speakers' in 'important transactions' between two parties. As he notes that the speech employed on such occasions is called *loloek*, he is clearly referring to the oratorical use of ritual language. Roos, however, makes no mention of the formal features of this verbal style, although he does note, correctly, that the speech of orators is conveyed in a loud voice and is uttered rapidly (see note 8). The first published examples of eastern Sumbanese parallelistic language are the texts of a number of songs recorded by Wielenga (1909:115–128; see also Wielenga 1917: 76–96). Other early sources which deal with this tradition, particularly as it relates to problems of biblical translation, include Onvlee 1934, 1953 (reprinted in Onvlee 1973:232–239) and Lambooy 1932.

6 That connectedness is a major attribute of ritual language is further suggested by the native equation of the word *ndekilu*, which refers to a term with which another is paired, with *ndetu*, 'connection' (see Kapita 1974:182).

7 Although priests and orators are not formally paid for their services, the former receive a share of the meat of sacrificial animals, while the latter may participate in the exchanges of prestations that accompany oratorical performances.

8 This contrast is in accord with another difference between oratorical and invocatory performances. Thus, while orations are generally carried out in a louder than normal voice, the speech of invocations is very often softer than normal, and indeed sometimes barely audible. In this latter regard, I was told that priests often lower their voice in order to gloss over passages which they do not properly know, or to obscure ones which, because they touch upon weighty matters, they wish to conceal from other, especially younger, persons who may be present. The speech of both priests and orators also displays something of a staccato quality, although this is more pronounced in the case of oratorical speech, which is also characteristically rapid. Invocatory speech, too, is usually more rapid than ordinary speech, but rather less so than oratorical speech.

9 This was said for the benefit of a young Rotinese official from Kupang who, at the time, was temporarily assigned as an adviser to one of the several *desa*

(Bahasa Indonesia 'village', the smallest administrative unit of the Indonesian government) into which Rindi is currently divided. His constant complaint while in Rindi was that he could never get anyone to talk with him.

10 *Pamangihingu* is occasionally rendered as *pamangihilungu*, which apparently derives from *ngihilungu*, 'to move, be in motion' and 'to turn, rotate'. Possibly, then, this term expresses the idea of ritual language as speech which is 'moving', or which produces a definite effect.

11 In this respect Traube contrasts Mambai ritual language with that of the Rotinese, whom she characterises as creating 'elaborate webs of verbal deception purely out of appreciation and respect for verbal skill' (1980:291 n.1).

12 *Kajangu*, in fact, appears as a reference to divine protection afforded by beneficent spirit in the lexicon of ritual language itself, where it is paired with *maü*, 'shadow, shade, shelter' (see Reference Text 2, lines 21–22).

13 The fact that the stationary orators are the superior of the two types of speakers agrees with a more general theme in eastern Sumbanese thought which is revealed especially in ideas concerning inactive and active, and immobile and mobile, manifestations of divinity (see Forth 1981:97).

14 In one major oratorical performance I witnessed in Rindi, one party, the ruling noble clan, was in fact represented by another speaker, an experienced orator, who spoke on their behalf to the stationary orator, and moreover did so in ritual language. This man, however, was not joined by a deputy, and in other ways as well did not fully take the part of an orator (among other things, he did not repeat the speech given to him by the stationary orator) but merely acted as a spokesman for the noble clan. Thus it would be incorrect to say that in this situation three pairs of speakers, or three orators, were employed.

15 Although an orator actually addresses his opposite number's deputy, here and in what follows I shall for convenience speak as though it were the orators who directly address one another.

16 Further communications can be required if, for example, a prestation is considered inadequate by the party to whom it is presented.

17 It is worth mentioning in this connection that informants explained the phrase *Puruwa Umbu*, 'Descend, Lord', which is a usual way of beginning an invocatory speech, as meaning that the ancestor 'descends' (that is, makes known his will) in the entrails of the fowl. Furthermore, this idea was propounded by some informants in opposition to the more literal interpretation that the ancestor himself (or his spirit) actually descends on such occasions. As regards the representation of fowls' entrails as a means of communication between spirit and man, it seems relevant to note also that the Rindi frequently compare these, as well as the livers of larger sacrificial animals, to 'books', and hence the act of divination to 'reading'. For a discussion of the relation between sacrifice, divination, and ritual language use in western Sumba (Weyéwa), see Clamagirand 1979.

18 This applies particularly to metal items. On the one hand, pendants of gold and silver (or alloys thereof), and copper chains, together with horses, compose prestations given to wife-givers, while, on the other, pieces of gold and silver are offered to spirits in a variety of rites designated as *pakalokangu kawàdaku* (see Reference Text 1). The term *kawàdaku* also refers to pieces of metal

consecrated to the clan ancestor (*marapu*), which are stored in the peak of an 'ancestral', or senior, house of a clan and form part of a class of goods named 'ancestral possessions' (*tanggu marapu*; see Forth 1981:94–96). Interestingly, also included among these possessions is a stallion called the 'ancestral horse' (*njara marapu*).

19 In designating this instrument as a 'comb' I am following the usage of Kapita (1974:284) and Indonesian-speaking Rindi informants who referred to it with the Bahasa Indonesia word *sisir* ('comb'). Adams (1973:271), in contrast, translates *wunangu* as 'heddle', which is quite possibly a more accurate gloss, particularly as this author's knowledge of eastern Sumbanese weaving technology is much greater than my own.

20 Another instance of weaving imagery, though one that does not relate specifically to oration or ritual language, is the dyadic expression *hupu lii lakunda// hupu lii lawàdi*, 'first winding on of the thread//first tying of the warp' (see Reference Text 1, lines 22–23), which refers to the beginning of things, and more particularly to the inauguration of ritual life and social order by the earliest ancestors.

21 Although 'line' is, of course, mostly an artificial construct when applied to an unwritten language such as eastern Sumbanese, it is a notion that is clearly indispensable to the analysis of parallelism. What constitutes a line in any given instance, however, is partly dependent on the particular form of the parallel language in question, and especially the extent to which dyadic elements appear as components of easily distinguishable paired phrases. Where they do not, it seems that the decision as to how a passage is to be treated in this regard must always be somewhat arbitrary.

22 By contrast, in Rotinese ritual language the maximum number of dyadic elements per line is four, though lines containing two or three elements are apparently more common (Fox 1971:238). This difference from eastern Sumbanese is consistent, then, with the fact that a greater variety of types of elements form dyadic sets in Rotinese, and that eastern Sumbanese, accordingly, appears to make greater use of repetition in paired lines.

23 As is consistent with the fact that *papa* refers to a wide variety of binary relations (see Forth 1981:59, 416), according to what I was told the term is applicable not only to elements of dyadic sets and to entire parallel lines but also to dyadic combinations occurring within single lines (regardless of whether these are elements which otherwise occur in parallel lines or not), and even to terms, such as nouns and modifiers, which do not form dyadic sets but which nevertheless regularly appear together in ritual language phraseology. In addition, *papa* can refer to a reply or response to an earlier communication in oratorical performances, and to a counter-prestation.

24 Referring to Rotinese ritual language, Fox remarks that dyadic elements form 'neutral, unordered pairs' since 'it is largely irrelevant which element of a set occurs first or second in a single line or in parallel lines' (1971:239). To some degree, this characterisation also applies to eastern Sumbanese ritual language. However, in this tradition probably the majority of paired terms occur in a particular order with such regularity that there is apparently some principle of subordination at work here. That this should be so is moreover in

accordance with the native idea that (in principle at any rate) elements of dyadic sets are distinguishable as 'male' and 'female' (Forth 1981:19, 416), although it should also be mentioned that, even among instances where this distinction can be clearly specified, in not every case is the 'male' element, for example, placed first.

25 It may also be relevant that two of these three lines (namely, lines 25 and 28 of Reference Text 2) could themselves be interpreted as forming a pair of sorts, since in this context they both express the same idea: namely, that of the two parties to this transaction being equal in the sense that, formally speaking, both share in bereavement.

26 In ordinary speech *ngilu* simply means 'wind', but here it has the sense of the derivative word *hangilu* ('to blow'). This, then, provides an example of how, in eastern Sumbanese ritual language, as in related traditions, the meanings of words can deviate from those encountered in everyday discourse, and, furthermore, of how such meanings can be clarified by reference to paired elements (see Fox 1971:231, 232).

27 According to the Rindi, when thus combined these six words collectively designate what in ordinary speech is called the *hamangu* ('soul'); and, as I have shown elsewhere (1981:73–82), their individual meanings overlap considerably. Thus, even supposing it were possible to do so, to assign to each a single discrete English gloss would be highly artificial and misleading. This circumstance, which is by no means unique to this case, of course highlights a more general problem in the translation of dyadic elements in ritual language, and particularly ones that appear to be more or less synonymous: that is, how to reproduce in one language the precise degree of identity and differentiation that obtains between two terms in another.

28 The first set of four terms, for example, expresses the idea of 'cleansing, purification', while those in the third are applied to things considered 'hot' (*mbana*) in the sense of 'threatening', 'excessive', 'prohibited', etc. Interestingly, it seems that in each instance of this pattern one or two elements refer more directly, or literally, than do the others to the idea they are intended to convey (see also note 25), and these usually appear in the first pair of the series. In fact, this observation appears to be more generally applicable to forms of pairing in ritual language. Thus, in a number of cases, Rindi informants specified one element of a pair as being primary while describing the other as merely a paired term.

29 A similar regularity is also found in the ritual language of the Tzotzil Maya (see Fox 1977:75).

30 In this regard it would be more useful to compare a number of eastern Indonesian ritual languages, particularly as comparison within such a restricted ethnographic and linguistic field would be more likely to provide insight into possible factors influencing the occurrence of parallelism and repetition in different traditions. One factor which might be worth exploring in this connection is the different uses to which ritual speech is put in different societies.

31 This would, of course, also apply to the repetition of lines and phrases in various places within a single speech. In contrast, the repetition of a message

as it is passed between a number of speakers obviously *decreases* the chances of it being communicated correctly to the ultimate addressee. Hence, in this respect, other forms of repetition may be seen as a counterbalance to this latter feature.

32 Cf. Tambiah 1979:134 *et seq.*, who treats parallelism as an instance of a broader category of repetition (or redundancy) which is characteristic of ritual performances in general.

33 Of course, since some terms can form pairs with more than one other, the wider linguistic and ritual context in which a given term occurs must also be assumed to play a part here.

34 The reference here is actually to the entrails of the sacrificial fowl, and more particularly to the desired condition of these.

6. Manu Kama's road, Tepa Nilu's path

The research on which this paper is based spans a considerable period. It has involved extended fieldwork on Roti in 1965–66 and again in 1972–73, as well as brief visits in 1977 and 1978. This research has been supported by grants from the United States National Institute of Mental Health (MH–10,161; MH–20,659), the United States National Science Foundation (2NS–7808149 A01), and The Australian National University. In Indonesia, all research was conducted under the auspices of the Lembaga Ilmu Pengetahuan Indonesia and in co-operation with the University of Nusa Cendana in Kupang.

1 Jonker published the original text in double columns with unnumbered lines. I have numbered the lines for identification and made a number of minor corrections: line 43, *lelena* for *lelea*; line 103, *Lide* for *Lede*; line 131, *Doli* for *Dali*. In lines 163 and 164 *do* should probably be read as *o*, which would be grammatically correct. In lines 218 and 220 the same *do* appears again but is less easily interpretable. Only one line in the entire text made little or no sense. This was line 232, which originally appeared as '*lope lea de neu*' and was corrected, on Rotinese advice, to '*lelo afe de lope*', which is the correct formulaic parallel to line 231, '*fo'a fanu de la'o*' (see lines 155–156). In addition, in lines 123, 126, 166, and 200 I have shifted the word *nae*, 'to say, to speak', from the following line. Nothing is changed except line length, which is variable; the shift facilitates, however, overall phrasing. I have also simplified Jonker's transcription of Rotinese words.

2 Jonker does not identify the chanter from whom he obtained the *Manu Kama ma Tepa Nilu* text. In his preface to *Rottineesche Teksten* he thanks D.A. Johannes, a native religious instructor in Keka, for his assistance in the gathering of written texts and J. Fanggidaej, the Head of the native school at Babau, for checking and correcting the manuscripts.

3 With the exception of one short excerpt from the chant *Sua Lai ma Batu Hu*, all of the contemporary material I quote in this paper is taken from *Rotinese Ritual Language: Texts and Translations* (Fox 1972a).

4 In ritual language, *Sela(n) do Dai(n)* or *Sela Sule do Dai Laka* refers to a distant, unspecified land. Some Rotinese, however, claim that this place name refers to the island of origin of the Rotinese people, though this in itself is

somewhat dubious since Rotinese disagree about their origins. The argument is based on sound similarity: *Sela(n)* is sometimes identified with the island of Ceram in the Moluccas and sometimes with the island of Ceylon. In the text no such association is hinted at and no such exegesis was suggested by Meno.

5 Formally, it is possible to define repetition as the linkage of an element with itself. By this convention all elements would have a potential range of one. Repetition, though it occurs, is not an admired feature of ritual language and, since it would be difficult to differentiate between the potential for repetition and the actual repetition of certain words, I have chosen not to adopt this convention.

6 The linguistic situation on Roti is one of diversity. Each of the eighteen former domains on the island claims to have its own 'language'. In turn, these domain 'languages' may be sorted into roughly six dialect areas. Although ritual language varies less than ordinary language across these dialect areas and, in fact, uses words from different dialects to form synonymous pairs, there are none the less noticeable differences in ritual language. Within each dialect area there are standard forms that even affect the way specific formulae are phrased.

7 In lines 57 and 59 I have translated the double dyadic set *timu dulu*//*sepe langa* as 'dawning east'//'reddening head'. I have done so because these terms are followed by a pluralising marker *-la* which reflects back to the subject, the blackbirds//green parrots: *ala mai* – 'they come'. In other poems this set might better be interpreted as a place name designating some region in the east. And, as a place name, this set can also be taken up as a personal name. This occurs, for example, in the poem *Kea Lenga ma Lona Bala* by Seu Bai. An auspicious pair of bats are referred to as *Soi Ana Sepe Langa*//*Bau Ana Timu Dulu*, 'Tiny Bat of Dawning East'//'Flying Fox of Reddening Head', and they form part of a family with *Timu Tongo Batu*//*Sepe Ama Li*, 'Dawn Tongo Batu'//'Reddening Ama Li', and his daughter, *Buna Sepe*//*Boa Timu*, 'Flower Reddening'//'Fruit Dawning'.

8 Hints of an earlier view of life as a process ending in ultimate return can still be detected in Rotinese ritual, but these are now muted or reinterpreted to conform to contemporary views. In the late 1950s and early 1960s a congregational rupture occurred in the Timorese Protestant Church (GMIT: Gereja Masehi Injilih Timor). The split was largely Rotinese-inspired and Rotinese-based and the new group that was formed at the time called itself the *Gereja Musafir*, 'The Pilgrim Church'. The label 'Pilgrim' typifies what has now become the traditional view that the Rotinese have of themselves.

7. The case of the purloined statues

The research on which this paper is based was conducted in Indonesia in 1982–83, under the auspices of Lembaga Ilmu Pengetahuan Indonesia and the University of Nusa Cendana in Kupang, and was supported by the INPEX Foundation.

1 In this paper, 'ritual language' refers to a category of language, performance of which accompanies a ceremonial setting or brings about a context which is distinct from an everyday context. See Fox 1971:221, 222.

2 In this paper I do not use actual personal names.

3 I also did research among the Nga'o-nese, the west Endenese and the east Endenese, who are different from one another in culture and language.

4 This figure is based on *Nusa Tenggara Timur dalam Angka gka tahun 1979* (Kantor Sensus dan Statistik Propinsi Nusa Tenggara Timur 1980).

5 The correspondence between the basic vocabularies of the Endenese language and the Lionese language is 86 per cent.

6 Wolo Waru was the site of the administrative office of Kerajaan Lio and is a subdistrict capital.

7 *Nua puu* literally means 'a village since the primeval time'. There is a village named Nua Puu.

8 This figure is based on Sensus Kecamatan Detusoko 1983 (unpublished).

9 In Lionese cosmology, an incestuous relationship between a brother and sister is thought to be one of the sources of magical power.

10 *Néta* is a kind of forest vine.

11 *Nitu*-spirits, *pa'i*-spirits, *juu*-spirits are different kinds of spirits.

12 Mount Roka is on Palue Island about 30 kilometres off the north coast.

13 Watu Wanda, Pena Kuwi Jawa, Pemo Dari Paga, Nua Nggojo, Doro Tana are places which are thought to be sources of power, the locations of which are secret. *Watu*, 'stone, rock'; *wanda*, 'a kind of traditional dance'; *pena*, 'salty soil, to drop'; *kuwi*, 'handful, to pinch'; *jawa*, 'corn, Jawa, Jawanese, foreign places, foreign'; *pemo*, 'place for water-buffalo to bathe'; *dari*, 'to stand'; *paga*, 'span, a kind of divination by spanning'; *nua*, 'village'; *nggojo*, 'beings similar to crabs (*kojo*)'; *doro*, 'to flatten'; *tana*, 'earth, land, soil'.

14 *Kota noa*-spirits and *noa*-spirits are explained by informants as kinds of *nitu pa'i*-spirits.

15 *Tisi feri*-spirits and *fénggé ré'é*-spirits are spirits in forests likely to do harm to persons who encounter them.

16 *Ngebu, segé*, and *sawa* are snakes; *mori* is a crocodile; *gaja* is an elephant. These animals have extraordinary magical power and are rarely seen.

17 *Kiku* is a kind of poisonous green snake which is thought to have magical power.

18 Tuka Tubu and Beo Meta Pu'u are places far away in the deep sea. *Tuka*, 'belly'; *tubu*, 'the altar stones, stump'; *béo*, 'whirl, whirl of the hair, top [a kind of toy]'; *meta*, 'green, unripe, unfinished'; *pu'u*, 'trunk, origin'.

19 *Bhéa* is a category of Lionese ritual language which is performed before starting a dance called *wogé*.

20 Wolo and Mité are fictitious names which I have substituted for the real names of the present 'origin priest' and 'great priest'.

8. The journey of the bridegroom

The research on which this paper is based was supported by the Ministry of Education, Japan, and by The Australian National University. It was carried out under the auspices of Lembaga Ilmu Pengetahuan Indonesia, during two periods of fieldwork, the first from 1979 to 1981 and the second in 1982. I am specially thankful to James J. Fox for his guidance and helpful comments.

1 By 'Nga'o-nese' I refer to the people who dwell in an administrative region

which was once called Tanah Rea, now stretching from Kabupaten Ende to Kabupaten Ngada.

2 The five types are: (1) *'ana 'arhé*, marriage of asking; (2) *'ana paru dhéko*, marriage of running and following (elopement); (3) *'ana mburhu nduu//wesa senda*, marriage of following the road and connecting the path (marriage with one's mother's brother's daughter); (4) *'ana dhéi dhato*, marriage of loving by themselves (marriage of free will); (5) *'ana poi*, marriage of taking away (marriage of plunder).

3 Even when two groups are in the wife-giver and wife-taker relation, in concluding a marriage the wife-givers sometimes may claim that the marriage be in the form of *'ana 'arhé*, basing their claim upon a fact that their relation has not been well maintained (because of the wife-taker's neglect of duty).

4 *Mata*, a pan-Austronesian word, in this usage is close to a modern Indonesian usage such as in *mata pelajaran*, in which the word means 'a unit in a set'.

9. A quest for the source

1 People in Tana Wai Brama speak of an aborted *gren mahé* organised some time in the late 1960s or early 1970s. The *tana puan* and others of the domain are reticent about that ceremony and I have been unable to discover why it is considered to have been a failure and whether it actually took place. There are indications that the ritual specialists of the domain were unable to bring that *gren* to a successful conclusion because of interference by the local government, abetted by the church.

2 It is useful to distinguish ritual language and ritual speech. By ritual speech I mean the performance of chants in ritual language, while ritual language is a genre of Sara Tana Ai distinct from ordinary language in terms of register, structure, syntax, and lexicon.

3 See Kuipers 1982 for one such study.

4 Myths of origins, the histories of the Rotinese domains, and genealogical histories must be distinguished. Origin myths are composed in ritual language, while genealogies and the histories of the domains of Roti are not. Furthermore, Rotinese myths of origins are not tied to myths of creation as they are in Tana Ai histories (James J. Fox, personal communication).

5 *Sara* is a cognate of the Malay word *cara*, 'fashion, method, manner, way, idiom'.

6 The language of the Ata Tana Ai is a dialect of the Sikkanese language which, along with Lamaholot (the dialects of Larantuka and East Flores), belongs to the Timor Area Group (Flores–Lembata [Lomblen] subgroup) of the Austronesian languages (Wurm and Hattori 1983). The Tana Ai dialect of Sikkanese is spoken by approximately 12,000 people.

7 *Plaun* means 'one half of something (that is usually paired with something else)', that is, one of a pair of matching things, such as a knife without its sheath: *Tudi aun lapi ne na to'é? O, tudi plaun*, 'Is the sheath of your knife behind there? Oh, there is just the knife itself.' Thus, *marin plaun* is ordinary speech and connotes half speech, simple speech, or speech on one side, that is, speech without the parallelism of ritual language.

8 *Latu* is 'to speak forcefully or truly' and connotes a quality of loudness. *Lawan*, which is cognate with the Malay word, means 'opposite, antithesis, counterpart, match, to oppose, to sit opposite'. This term for ritual speech thus implies the parallelism of ritual language. Both phrases are used as nominal terms for ritual speech as a genre of language and as verbal phrases for speaking in ritual language.

9 For examples and texts of *neni plawi* see Lewis 1982a.

10 Though not without a large portion of a given chant consisting of more or less formulaic couplets.

11 The word *sejara* is a cognate of the Malay word *sejarah* which means 'history'.

12 *Ngé* means 'to grow, to become larger, to advance, to make headway'. The phrase *ngé noran* in ordinary speech means 'to happen, to occur, to come about, to come to pass'.

13 The word *tota* is paired in ritual language either with the word *toma* ('to get, to find, to obtain, to attain a place or state of being') or *paga*. *Paga* means also 'to find' or 'to attain', but a dual meaning informs the phrase *tota ... paga*. *Paga* is the span between the extended thumb and index finger, a sign that is used to indicate distance. *Paga* means also 'to stretch' (as in stretching the hand to measure a length with the span of the thumb and index finger), 'to spread' (as spilt water spreads over a flat surface), and, by extension, means distance, space, emptiness. Thus in ordinary speech, *paga ha* means 'a distance, at a distance, distant', that is, any distance both in space and time.

14 Some chants, such as one held exclusively by the *tana puan* for the increase of pig herds, are hereditarily restricted to men of certain clans and houses.

15 In the *gren mahé* of 1980, as many as two dozen men were involved in chanting the *oda geté* of the domain during the week of the rituals themselves and for the smaller rites of preparation that took place during the months preceding the *gren*.

16 During the *gren mahé* of 1980 the central ritualists of the domain complained frequently of a lack of chanters qualified to perform the *oda geté* properly. The principal chanters were occasionally called upon to assist or replace chanters of lower ritual status in the performance of the clan histories to ensure that the histories were chanted correctly. The elision of parts of some of the lesser chants can thus be attributed to the physical exhaustion of the central chanters. Once the *gren* was completed, these same chanters were satisfied that the *oda geté* had been properly performed.

17 Thus an ethnography of the ceremonial organisation of Tana Wai Brama cannot establish as definitive a particular text of a myth. The procedure for recording ethnographically the histories of the domain must conform to the practice of chanters themselves in their performances, whereby one ritualist establishes a theme or structure which is then filled in and elaborated by the contributions of other chanters.

18 It was only after Rapa produced his text that I learned that he was contemplating calling for a *gren* the following year (he may already have made the announcement to other ritual specialists of the community when the history was written). Thus to have chanted the history at that time would have been even more inappropriate. I have found it impossible to elicit from chanters

complete and coherent texts of ritual language in interviews, except for the occasional couplets cited by informants in reply to my queries about matters of *hadat*. In Tana Ai the myths are only performed on ritual occasions, and the only way to record a myth is to be present at such a performance. The dictation of the history by Rapa remains the one exception to this conclusion during my fieldwork. While other reasons for this restriction have become apparent since 1979, chanters simply cite *hadat* as the reason for restricting the chanting of the histories.

19 The work that Rapa and his daughter produced consisted of the history of clan Ipir Wai Brama (*Ngeng Ngerang Sukun Ipir Wai Brama*), which ran to 440 lines. Prepended to it were 234 lines of the history of the origin of the world, the *Ngeng Ngerang Tota Nian Paga Tana*, which I discuss here. I plan to write about the histories of the clans elsewhere.

20 The notes from this work are incorporated into my translation of the history.

21 His death did affect the performance of the *gren* and left the ritual specialists of the domain disorganised and in disarray, but it did not, in the end, result in the cancellation of the *gren*. Once the words are spoken, responsibility for organising and conducting the rituals is delegated to other senior ritual specialists of the community and, in any case, speaking the words lays on the community a ritual imperative to conclude the *gren* that can in no way be abrogated.

22 In 1980, knowing that the *gren mahé* was planned, I returned to Tana Ai and, in collaboration with Timothy and Patricia Asch, filmed the rituals and the events that took place during several weeks before the *gren* (Lewis, Asch and Asch, in production).

23 This myth of the separation, which is of key significance in the mythology of the Ata Tana Ai, has been treated elsewhere (Lewis 1982b).

24 Indeed, in chanting, performers often articulate the rhetorical expressions *ia gu* and *ko* when drawing a breath. These pauses thus serve the function of rests in vocal music.

25 Thus the pauses *ia gu* or *ko* constitute lines 9, 14, 21, 26, 35, 51, 56, 63, and 160 of the text, while the couplet, *huk mole wa'i ha//nera mole ha homa* forms lines 72–73, 96–97, 132–133, 140–141, 148–149, and 189–190.

26 It is significant that most of the addenda offered by other chanters in the months following the writing of Rapa's text pertain not to the history of the creation of the world, which is thought to be held exclusively by the *tana puan*, but to those parts of Rapa's history that belong to the history of the first human beings.

27 *Wajak* is a dish or porcelain plate used for offering a guest areca-nut and tobacco; as a verb, the word means to offer hospitality to a guest.

28 This is an interesting and significant point in the mythology of the Ata Tana Ai, since *Nian Tana Lero Wulan*, the Land and Earth, the Sun and Moon are four attributes by which the deity is known to mankind.

29 The face of the moon is believed by the Ata Tana Ai to present the image of a banyan tree.

30 *Léan* is a bamboo frame from which clothes are hung to dry.

31 On the ambiguity of the word *nian* as both 'land' and 'sky' see Lewis 1982b.

32 The precise meaning of this couplet, one of the most common in the chants of

cooling rituals, is obscure. *Blatan* means 'cool' or 'cold'. *Ro* is the dew that forms on coconuts and drips to the ground on cool nights. *Wair sina mitan*, 'water China (Chinese) black', given the syntax of Sara Tana Ai, can mean variously, 'black water of China' or 'water of the Black Chinese'. In the first sense it may refer to the blood of sacrificial animals, which is an agent of ritual 'cooling' in Tana Ai. In parts of eastern Indonesia the Topasses, or 'Black Portuguese', were sometimes called Black Chinese. A connection is thus suggested between the holy water of Catholic priests and coconut water: both are sprinkled in their respective rituals in similar fashion. In any case, this couplet expresses the 'cooling' function of ritual.

33 Work on that synthesis is proceeding, but more field research will be required to collect texts of all the episodes of the *Sejara* and, with the assistance of the chanters of Tana Wai Brama, to establish their proper sequence. I plan in the future to publish a synthesis of these histories, along with the histories of the clans of the domain.

34 For a description of the significance and pervasiveness of the morphology of the bamboo as a complex of metaphors in Tana Ai thought and speech, see Lewis 1982a (esp.96–105) and Lewis 1983.

35 A fundamental problem for the ethnography of ritual is the synchronicity of events. If an event is by its nature diachronous, then how can any event be described satisfactorily when the history of the event is unavailable to the ethnographer? This is a particularly vexing obstacle for the analysis of rare events, such as *gren mahé*. The *gren* is unquestionably of considerable importance in an account of the social organisation of the people of Tana Wai Brama, but the ethnographer can rely on only one performance for his description. A record of more than one occurrence of *gren mahé* would be required before general conclusions about its nature could be drawn, yet the temporal scale of fieldwork is insufficient to encompass multiple performances. One not entirely satisfactory solution is to record the roughly contemporary performances of *gren mahé* in different ceremonial domains of Tana Ai. This approach would shed light on the range of variation in the performance of the rites of the *gren*, assuming relevant differences in the societies of the domains can be controlled, but still would not contribute to a fuller understanding of the *gren* in a single community.

36 Some of the points of the text discussed by other chanters were quite detailed. For example, in 1982, after reading the text once again, an argument arose between one of Rapa's sons and two men of other clans about the word *tepu* in lines 227 and 229. Rapa's son argued that Rapa should have used the verb *tetu* 'to pound, to beat (as in working iron into a desired shape)'. *Tepu* means 'to be strong, capable of hard work (as in being strong enough to bend iron with the hands)'. The two theories were later put to the senior chanter of the domain, who upheld Rapa's use of the word *tepu* in these lines. Rapa himself defined *tepu* in the chant as meaning 'to make the earth strong, as in forging iron'.

37 Déwa's claim was supportable. While the *tana puan* must be of clan Ipir Wai Brama, the founding mother of Déwa's house was originally from clan Ipir. Furthermore, Déwa was widely acknowledged to be *ata jentiu*, a pagan, whereas most of Rapa's people are, at least nominally, members of the Catholic church.

38 *Gren mahé* become associated with particular men, usually their organisers, and are thereafter referred to by the names of those men. Before the *gren mahé* of 1980 was undertaken, it was referred to by the ritual specialists of the domain as 'Mo'an Rapa's *gren*'. After its performance it came to be referred to as 'the *gren* of Mo'an Sina and Mo'an Koa', the two ritual leaders of the domain who organised and managed the rituals and whose responsibility they became.

39 For example, *nara wowa*, 'the collection of the ancestral stones', in which the men who will conduct the *gren mahé* gather at the house of a particular clan of the domain and away from public scrutiny in order to reveal their ancestral stones, from which comes the power to chant the histories of the domain.

10. The tree of desire

The research on which this paper is based was carried out in 1977 and 1978. We gratefully acknowledge the support of a Fulbright Hays Doctoral Dissertation Research Abroad Grant (Volkman), the support of the Cornell Southeast Asia Program (Zerner and Volkman), and that of the US National Science Foundation (Volkman). We are also grateful to the Lembaga Ilmu Pengetahuan Indonesia (LIPI); to the Toraja who patiently translated and explicated this text with us; and to Mama' Agus Lies Kombonglangi' who made the work possible.

1 For discussions of tourism, migration, and change, see Adams 1984, Crystal 1977 Volkman 1982a, 1982b, 1984, 1985, and Zerner 1982. The effects of recent changes on Toraja language may be far-reaching, as educated youth are more interested in learning English than in mastering the linguistic forms of high speech discussed in this paper. For most people, it is no longer worth the effort of memorising copious verses when such things are easily stored in books.

2 Roger Mills has traced Tae' to a 'Proto South Sulawesi' language family that includes Makassarese, Bugis, and Mandarese (Mills 1975).

3 Women cannot become *tominaa*, although women who talk excessively in public contexts are jokingly referred to as *tominaa baine*, 'female *tominaa*'. Neither can there be female *ambe' tondok*, literally 'fathers of the village'.

4 Although in this paper we concentrate on speaking, it should be pointed out that *tominaa* must know how to reproduce ritual actions as well as words. They must prepare perfect offerings of betel nut and rice, and arrange in order a host of ritual elements. In Toraja ritual, which is neither predominantly oratorical nor ostensive (see Fox 1979), both speech and acts are crucial. The *maro* would be fruitless without betel, plates of steaming rice, red sugar, the brilliantly coloured *bate*, and the distribution of hundreds of scrawny chickens to the *tominaa*, the 'wages of speaking'.

5 A related poem, the '*bate*-song', was translated by van der Veen before his death in 1977, but unfortunately it has not yet been published (Nooy-Palm 1979: 222).

6 We are indebted to Pak J.T.P. Pirri, a Christian schoolteacher in Rantepao who grew up on Mount Sesean, where he listened avidly to the speech of *tominaa*; to Pak Banti Pempe, also a Christian schoolteacher in Rantepao, from the

Sa'dan region; and to Pak Kila', descended from a family of *tominaa* in the Sesean area and now a representative in the Makale DPRD (Peoples' Consultative Assembly). Kila' is an active figure in the movement to revitalise traditional Toraja religion (Alukta) and its language, including the ritual language of *tominaa*. We are thankful also to other Toraja friends who, although initially hesitant to translate ritual speech, found themselves engrossed in the project once it had begun. Consequently, obscure or difficult phrases sometimes yielded rather different, although coherent, results. For example, *mintu'-ma'limbo kaluku*, 'the whole cluster of coconuts', became, for some, *mintu'ma-'lindo kalua'*, 'all with the expansive face'. Other lines seemed more doubtful: for instance, *mutammanni serre ala'mu*, 'chew for the forest cat', seemed more convincing as *mutammanni sarre ala'mu*, 'chew the fragrant lemon grass'.

7　For a fuller discussion of the *maro* ritual, see Volkman 1985, and Zerner 1981.

8　In spite of the parallelism, this phenomenon is not nearly so thorough or precise as in the Rotinese speech analysed by Fox (1974).

9　The 'family bamboo clump', like the 'whole cluster of coconuts', reflects the botanical imagery and idiom which pervade Toraja kinship expressions. 'To marry', for example, is 'to plant a kitchen', *mentanan dapo'*. The ancestral house is sometimes thought of as a plant, with nurturing heirlooms (cloths, drums, swords, gongs) stored in the southern 'root' and conducting blessings northward. The rice plant's structure is sometimes used as an idiom through which family groupings are described. In high speech the representation of the family as a bamboo clump or a coconut cluster emphasises both the concentration of family power at rituals and the organic connections between the family's separate shoots and fruits.

10　This line may also be translated as 'the debt-claim flows in the chest'. Debts and desires are reconciled in that, for the Toraja, the debt-claim flowing is tantamount to being alive, fully human, and conscious of social interconnections.

11　The sounds of drums and gongs signal phases within the life-affirming and life-waning rituals.

12　*Cordyline terminalis*, known as *tabang*, is associated with the spirits, and planted at sacred spots or in front of the houses of nobility. Its long red leaves are believed to prevent the flow of blood from wounds, including those inflicted during *maro* trances.

13　*Maa'* include a wide variety of textiles regarded as having sacred origins and special powers. Many *maa'* were Indian trade cloths or Dutch imitations used as currency in the spice trade (see Gittinger 1982:149, 153–155).

14　We would suggest that the spirits are thought to perceive and be pleased by the presence of offerings that can be heard, seen, smelled, or consumed. A *tominaa* once said, 'Spirits are drawn by our words, which rise into the sky like the fragrant smoke of roasting coffee.' Words in the patterned sequences of high speech may be as compelling as the aromas of incense or coffee, or the appearance of a finely carved bamboo altar. See Arendt 1978 for a pertinent discussion of aesthetic delight.

15　'You' may refer to either the spirits or the 'family bamboo clump', both of which are interrogated during this performance.

16　See Kruyt 1922 for a discussion of *me'datu*.

REFERENCES

Adams, K. 1984. Come to Tana Toraja, 'Land of the Heavenly Kings': travel agents as brokers in ethnicity. *Annals of Tourism Research* 11(3):469–485.

Adams, M.J. 1971. Designs in Sumba textiles, local meanings and foreign influences. *Textile Museum Journal* 3(2):28–37.

1973. Structural aspects of a village art, East Sumba, Indonesia. *American Anthropologist* 75:265–279. Reprinted as 'Structural aspects of East Sumbanese art' in J.J. Fox (ed.), *The flow of life: essays on Eastern Indonesia*, pp.208–220. Cambridge, Mass: Harvard University Press, 1980.

1979. The crocodile couple and the snake encounter in the *tellantry* of East Sumba, Indonesia. In A.L. Becker and A.A. Yengoyan (eds.), *The imagination of reality: essays in Southeast Asian coherence systems*, pp.87–104. Norwood, New Jersey: Ablex.

Ahlqvist, A. 1863. *Suomalainen runousoppi kielellisteltä kannalta* (Finnish poetry from a linguistic standpoint). Helsinki.

Allen, N.J. 1978. Sewala puja bintila puja: notes on Thulung ritual language. *Kailash* 6(4):237–256.

Arendt, H. 1978. *The life of the mind.* New York: Harcourt Brace & Jovanovich.

Austerlitz, R. 1958. *Ob-Ugric metrics* (Folklore Fellows Communications no. 174). Helsinki: Suomalainen Tiedeakatemia, Academia Scientarum Fennica.

Beckwith, M.W. 1951. *The Kumulipo.* Chicago: University of Chicago Press.

Berthe, L. 1972. *Bei Gua: itinéraire des ancêtres.* Paris: Editions du Centre National de la Recherche Scientifique.

Bloomfield, M. 1916. *Rig-Veda repetitions* (2 vols). Cambridge, Mass: Harvard University Press.

Boodberg, P.A. 1954–55a. Syntactical metaplasia in stereoscopic parallelism. *Cedules from a Berkeley Workshop in Asiatic Philology*, 017–541210. Berkeley, California.

1954–55b. On crypto-parallelism in Chinese poetry. *Cedules from a Berkeley Workshop in Asiatic Philology*, 001–540701. Berkeley, California.

1954–55c. 'T'/'M' parallelism once more. *Cedules from a Berkeley Workshop in Asiatic Philology*, 030–550420. Berkeley, California.

Boster, J. 1973. K'ekchi' Maya curing practices in British Honduras. A.B. thesis, Harvard University.

Bricker, V.R. 1974. The ethnographic context of some traditional Maya speech genres. In R. Bauman and J. Sherzer (eds.), *Explorations in the ethnography of speaking*, pp.368–388. Cambridge: Cambridge University Press.

Cajanus, E. 1697. *Linguarum ebraeae et finnicae convenientia.* Abo.

Clamagirand, B.R. 1979. Li'i marapu: parole et rituel chez le Wewewa de Sumba Ouest. *ASEMI* 10:49–58.

Clementi, C. 1904. *Cantonese love-songs*. Oxford: Clarendon.

Conklin, H.C. 1958. *Betel chewing among the Hanuno'o*. Quezon City: National Research Council of the Philippines.

Crystal, E. 1977. Tourism in Toraja (Sulawesi, Indonesia). In V.L. Smith (ed.), *Hosts and guests: the anthropology of tourism*, pp.109–125. Philadelphia: University of Pennsylvania Press.

Dahood, M. and Penar, T. 1970. The grammar of the psalter. In M. Dahood, *Psalms III:101–150* (The Anchor Bible, 17A), pp.361–456. New York: Doubleday.

Davis, J.F. 1830. On the poetry of the Chinese. *Transactions of the Royal Asiatic Society of Great Britain and Ireland* 2:393–461.

De Bono, E. 1970. *Lateral thinking: a textbook of creativity*. London: Ward Lock.

Dijk, W. van 1939. Het begrip Marapoe in West Soemba. *Bijdragen tot de Taal-, Land- en Volkenkunde* 98:497–516.

Dunnebier, W. 1938. De plechtigheid 'waterscheppen' in Bolaang Mongondow, *Tijdschrift voor Indische Taal-, Land- en Volkenkunde* 78:1–56.

1953. *Bolaang Mongondowse teksten* (Koninklijk Instituut voor Taal-, Land- en Volkenkunde). 's-Gravenhage: Martinus Nijhoff.

Dunselman, D. 1949. Bijdrage tot de kennis van de taal en adat der Kendajan Dajaks van West-Borneo. *Bijdragen tot de Taal-, Land- en Volkenkunde* 105:59–105, 147–218.

1950a. Over de huwelijksadat der Moealang-Dajaks van West Borneo. *Bijdragen tot de Taal-, Land- en Volkenkunde* 106:1–45.

1950b. Bijdrage tot de kennis van de taal en adat der Kendajan-Dajaks van West-Borneo II. *Bijdragen tot de Taal-, Land- en Volkenkunde* 106:321–373.

1954. Kana Sera of Zang der Zwangerschap. *Bijdragen tot de Taal- en Volkenkunde* 110:52–63.

1955. *Kana Sera* (Verhandelingen van het Koninklijk Instituut voor Taal-, Land- en Volkenkunde, 17). 's-Gravenhage: Martinus Nijhoff.

1959a. Gezangen behorend tot het huwelijksceremonieel der Mualang-Dajaks. *Anthropos* 54:460–474.

1959b. *Uit de literatuur der Mualang-Dajaks* (Koninklijk Instituut voor Taal-, Land- en Volkenkunde). 's-Gravenhage: Martinus Nijhoff.

1961. Ngebau tadjau, een kosmogonie der Mualang-Dajaks. *Anthropos* 56:409–437.

Edmonson, M.S. 1970. Notes on a new translation of the *Popol vuh*. *Alcheringa* 1(1):14–23.

1971. *The Book of Counsel: The Popol vuh of the Quiche Maya of Guatemala* (Middle American Research Institute publication no. 35). New Orleans: Tulane University.

Emeneau, M.B. 1937. The songs of the Todas. *Proceedings of the American Philosophical Society* 77:543–560.

Field, D.Z. 1975. With a flower, with a candle, with a prayer. A.B. thesis, Harvard University.

Fokos, D. 1963. *Osztják (Chanti) Hösénekek: Reguly A. és Papay J. Laqyatéka*. (Reguly-Könyvtár,3). Budapest: Akadémia Kiadó.

Fortes, M. 1975. Tallensi prayer. In J.H.M. Beattie and R.G. Lienhardt (eds.),

Studies in social anthropology: essays in memory of E.E. Evans-Pritchard, pp.132–148. Oxford: Clarendon.

Forth, G.L. 1981. *Rindi: an ethnographic study of a traditional domain in Eastern Sumba* (Verhandelingen van het Koninklijk Instituut voor Taal-, Land- en Volkenkunde, 93). The Hague: Martinus Nijhoff.

——— 1983. Time and temporal classification in Rindi, Eastern Sumba. *Bijdragen tot de Taal-, Land- en Volkenkunde* 139:46–80.

Fox, J.J. 1971. Semantic parallelism in Rotinese ritual language. *Bijdragen tot de Taal-, Land- en Volkenkunde* 127:215–255.

——— 1972a. Rotinese ritual language: texts and translations. Unpublished multilith.

——— 1972b. Dictionary of Rotinese formal dyadic language. Unpublished multilith.

——— 1973. On bad death and the left hand: a study of Rotinese symbolic inversions. In R. Needham (ed.), *Right and left: essays on dual symbolic classification*, pp.342–368. Chicago: University of Chicago Press.

——— 1974. Our ancestors spoke in pairs: Rotinese views of language, dialect, and code. In R. Bauman and J. Sherzer (eds.), *Explorations in the ethnography of speaking*, pp.65–85. Cambridge: Cambridge University Press.

——— 1975. On binary categories and primary symbols: some Rotinese perspectives. In R. Willis (ed.), *The interpretation of symbolism* (ASA Studies no. 3), pp.99–132. London: Malaby Press.

——— 1977. Roman Jakobson and the comparative study of parallelism. In C.H. van Schooneveld and D. Armstrong (eds.), *Roman Jakobson: echoes of his scholarship*, pp.59–90. Lisse: Peter de Ridder Press.

——— 1979. The ceremonial system of Savu. In A.L. Becker and A.A. Yengoyan (eds.), *The imagination of reality: essays in Southeast Asian coherence systems*, pp.145–173. Norwood, New Jersey: Ablex.

——— 1980a. Introduction. In Fox, 1980c, pp.1–18.

——— 1980b. Obligation and alliance: state structure and moiety organization in Thie, Roti. In Fox, 1980c, pp.98–133.

——— 1980c. (ed.), *The flow of life: essays on Eastern Indonesia*. Cambridge, Mass: Harvard University Press.

——— 1982. The Rotinese chotbah as a linguistic performance. In A. Halim, L. Carrington and S.A. Wurm (eds.), *Papers from the Third International Conference on Austronesian Linguistics*, vol. 3: *Accent on variety*, pp.311–318 (Pacific Linguistics C–76). Canberra: Department of Linguistics, Research School of Pacific Studies, The Australian National University.

——— 1983a. Review of *Sijobang, sung narrative poetry of West Sumatra* by Nigel Phillips. *Asian Folklore Studies* 42(2):310–312.

——— 1983b. Adam and Eve on the island of Roti. *Indonesia* 36:15–23.

Freedman, D.N. 1972. Prolegomenon to G.B. Gray, *The forms of Hebrew poetry* (orig. 1915), pp.vii–liii. New York: KTAV.

Gabelentz, H.C. von der 1837. Einiges über mongolische Poesie. *Zeitschrift für die Kunde des Morgenlandes* 1:20–37.

Garibay, A.M. 1953. *Historia de la literatura Nahuatl* (2 vols). Mexico: Biblioteca Porrua.

Geller, S.A. 1979. *Parallelism in early biblical poetry* (Harvard Semitic Monographs). Missoula, Montana: Scholars Press.

Gervitz, S. 1963. *Patterns in the early poetry of Israel* (Studies in Ancient Oriental Civilization no. 32). Chicago: Chicago University Press.

Gittinger, M. 1982. *Master dyers to the world: technique and trade in early Indian dyed cotton textiles*. Washington DC: The Textile Museum.

Goffman, E. 1981. *Forms of talk*. Philadelphia: University of Pennsylvania Press (Publications in Conduct and Communication).

Gonda, J. 1959. *Stylistic repetition in the Veda* (Verhandelingen der Koninklijke Nederlandse Akademie van Wetenschappen, Afd. Letterkunde n.s.65(3)). Amsterdam: N.V. Noord-Hollandsche Uitg.

Gossen, G.H. 1974a. To speak with a heated heart: Chamula canons of style and good performance. In R. Bauman and J. Sherzer (eds.), *Explorations in the ethnography of speaking*, pp.389–413. Cambridge: Cambridge University Press.

1974b. *Chamulas in the world of the sun*. Cambridge, Mass: Harvard University Press.

Granet, M. 1919. *Fêtes et chansons anciennes de la Chine*. Paris: Editions Ernest Leroux. (English translation, *Festivals and songs of ancient China*, 1932.)

Gray, G.B. 1972. *The forms of Hebrew poetry*. New York: KTAV. (Orig. 1915, London.)

Greuter, H. 1946. Beknopte Lionese grammaire. Unpublished.

Guildford, J.P. 1967. *The nature of human intelligence*. New York: McGraw-Hill.

Gumperz, J. 1982. *Discourse strategies*. New York: Cambridge University Press.

Hanson, O. 1906. *A dictionary of the Kachin language*. Rangoon: Baptist Board of Publications.

Hardeland, A. 1858. *Versuch einer Grammatik der Dajackschen Sprache*. Amsterdam: F. Muller.

Herder, J.G. 1782. *Vom Geist der ebräischen Poesie*. Dessaux. (English translation, *The spirit of Hebrew poetry*, 1833.)

Hervy-Saint-Denys, M.J.L. 1862. *Poésies de l'époque des Thang*. Paris.

Hightower, J.R. 1959. Some characteristics of parallel prose. In S. Egerod and E. Glahn (eds.), *Studia Serica Bernhard Karlgren Dedicata*, pp.60–91. Copenhagen: Ejnar Munksgaard.

1966. *Topics in Chinese literature* (Harvard–Yenching Institute Studies no.3). Cambridge, Mass: Harvard University Press.

Jablonski, W. 1935. *Les 'Siao-ha (i-eu) l-yu' de Pekin: un essai sur la poésie populaire en Chine*. (Prace Komisji ojentalistycznej no. 19). Cracow: Nakladem Polskiej Akademii Uniejetnosci.

Jakobson, R. 1960. Closing statement: linguistics and poetics. In T.A. Sebeok (ed.), *Style in language*, pp.350–377. Cambridge, Mass: MIT Press.

1966. Grammatical parallelism and its Russian facet. *Language* 42(2): 399–429.

1970. The modular design of Chinese regulated verse. In J. Pouillon and P. Maranda (eds.), *Echanges et communications: mélanges offerts à Claude Lévi-Strauss à l'occasion de son 60ème anniversaire*, I: 597–605. The Hague: Mouton.

1973. *Questions de poétique*. Paris: Editions du Seuil.

Jakobson, R. and Halle, M. 1956. *Fundamentals of language*. 's-Gravenhage: Mouton.

Jonker, J.C.G. 1911. *Rottineesche teksten met vertaling.* Leiden: E.J. Brill.
   1913. Bijdrage tot de kennis der Rottineesche tongvallen. *Bijdragen tot de Taal-, Land- en Volkenkunde* 68:521–622.
   1915. *Rottineesche spraakkunst.* Leiden: E.J. Brill.
Juslenius, D. 1728. *Oratio de convenientia lingua Fennicae cum Hebraea et Graeca* (Schwedische Bibliotek I). Stockholm.
Kantor Sensus Dan Statistik Propinsi Nusa Tenggara Timur 1980. *Nusa Tenggara Timur dalam Angka tahun 1979.* Kupang.
Kapita, Oe. H. 1974. Kamus Sumba Timur–Indonesia. Unpublished MS.
   1976a. *Sumba di dalam jangkauan jaman.* Waingapu: Panitia Penerbit Naskah-Naskah Kebudayaan Daerah Sumba Dewan Penata Layanan Gereja Kristen Sumba.
   1976b. *Masyarakat Sumba dan adat istiadatnya.* Waingapu: Panitia Penerbit Naskah-Naskah Kebudayaan Daerah Sumba Dewan Penata Layanan Gereja Kristen Sumba.
Kemmer, E. 1903. *Die polare Ausdrucksweise in der griechischen Literatur* (Beiträge zur historischen Syntax der griechischen Sprache, 15). Würzburg.
Kern, W. 1956. *Commentaar op de salasilah van Koetai* (Verhandelingen van het Koninklijk Instituut voor Taal-, Land- en Volkenkunde, 19). 's-Gravenhage: Martinus Nijhoff.
Koestler, A. 1964. *The act of creation.* New York: Macmillan.
Kowalski, T. 1921. Ze studjów nad forma poezji ludów tureckich. *Mémoires de la Commission orientale de l'Académie polonaise des sciences et des lettres*, no. 5. Cracow.
Kramer, F.W. 1970. *Literature among the Cuna Indians* (Ethnologiska Studier, no. 30). Göteborg: Elanders Boktryckeri Aktiebolag.
Krugel, J.L. 1981. *The idea of biblical poetry: parallelism and its history.* New Haven, Conn.: Yale University Press.
Kruyt, A.C. and Kruyt, J. 1922. Een reis onder de Toradjas van Sa'dan en Mamasa (Celebes). *Tijdschrift Aardrijkskundig Genootschap* 49:678–717.
Kuipers, J. 1982. Weyéwa ritual speech: a study of language and ceremonial interaction in Eastern Indonesia. PhD dissertation, Yale University.
Lagemann, H. 1893. Das niassische Mädchen von seiner Geburt bis zu seiner Verheiratung. *Tijdschrift Bataviaasch Genootschap* 36:296.
   1906. Ein Heldensang der Niasser. *Tijdschrift Bataviaasch Genootschap* 48:341.
Lambooy, P.J. 1930. De Godsnaam op Soemba. *De Macedoniër* 34:275–284.
   1932. Evangelie-prediking in Oosterschen vorm. *De Macedoniër* 36:134–144.
   1937. Het begrip 'Marapoe' in den godsdienst van Oost Soemba. *Bijdragen tot de Taal-, Land- en Volkenkunde* 95:425–439.
Lang, E. Forthcoming. Proceedings of the colloquium in memory of Wolfgang Steinitz, 26–27 February 1985. Linguistische Studien. Zentralinstitut für Sprachwissenschaft, DDR. Berlin.
Leenhardt, M. 1979. *Do Kamo: person and myth in the Melanesian world* (transl. B.M. Gulati). Chicago: University of Chicago Press, (Orig. 1947.)
Lewis, E.D. 1982a. Tana Wai Brama: a study of the social organization of an Eastern Florenese domain. PhD thesis, The Australian National University, Canberra.

1982b. The metaphorical expression of gender and dual classification in Tana Ai ritual language. *Canberra Anthropology* 5(1):47–59.

1983. Opposition, classification and social reproduction. Working paper presented at research seminar on 'Gender, ideology and social reproduction', Department of Anthropology, Research School of Pacific Studies, The Australian National University, Canberra. MS.

Lewis, E.D., Asch, P. and Asch, T. In production. *Gren mahé* (16mm. film made in Tana-Ai, July–November 1980). Watertown, Mass.: Documentary Educational Resources Inc.

Lloyd, G.E.R. 1966. *Polarity and analogy.* Cambridge: Cambridge University Press.

Lotz, J. 1954. Kamassian verse. *Journal of American Folklore* 67:369–377.

Lowth, R. 1834. *Isaiah.* Boston. (English translation of *Isaiah X–XI*, 1778.)

1971. *Lectures on the sacred poetry of the Hebrews* (2 vols). New York: Garland. (Reprint of English translation (Boston, 1829) of *De sacra poesia Hebraeorum praelectiones academicae,* Boston, 1753.)

Malkiel, Y. 1959. Studies in irreversible binomials. *Lingua* 8:113–160.

Marmier, X. 1842. De la poésie finlandaise. *Revue des Deux Mondes* 32:68–96.

Meyer, R.M. 1889. *Die altgermanische Poesie nach ihren formelhaften Elementen beschrieben.* Berlin.

Middelkoop, P. 1949. *Een studie over het Timoreesche doodenritueel* (Verhandelingen van het Koninklijk Bataviaasch Genootschap van Kunsten en Wetenschappen, 76). Bandoeng: A.C. Nix.

Mills, R.F. 1975. The reconstruction of Proto South Sulawesi. *Archipel* 10:205–224.

Mitchell, I.G. 1981. Hierarchy and balance: a study of Wanukaka social organisation. PhD thesis, Monash University, Victoria.

Needham, R. 1980. Principles and variations in the structure of Sumbanese society. In Fox 1980c, pp.21–47.

Newman, L.I. and Popper, W. 1918–23. Studies in biblical parallelism. *University of California Publications in Semitic Philology* 1(2–5).

Nguyen Dinh Hoà. 1955. Double puns in Vietnamese: a case of 'linguistic play'. *Word* 11: 237–244.

1965. Parallel construction in Vietnamese. *Lingua* 15:125–139.

Nooy-Palm, H.1979. *The Sa'dan-Toraja: a study of their social life and religion.* Vol. 1, *Organization, symbols and beliefs* (Verhandelingen van het Koninklijk Instituut voor Taal-, Land- en Volkenkunde, 87). The Hague: Martinus Nijhoff.

O'Connor, M.O. 1980. *Hebrew verse structure.* Winona Lake, Indiana: Eisenbrauns.

Onvlee, L. 1934. Voorbereidend werk. *De Macedoniër* 38:321–334.

1953. Van zang en psalm. *De Heerbaan* 6:16–23.

1973. *Cultuur als antwoord* (Verhandelingen van het Koninklijk Instituut voor Taal-, Land- en Volkenkunde, 66). 's-Gravenhage: Martinus Nijhoff.

1977. The construction of the Mangili Dam: notes on the social organization of Eastern Sumba. In P.E. de Josselin de Jong (ed.), *Structural anthropology in the Netherlands,* pp.151–163. The Hague: Martinus Nijhoff.

1984. *Kamberaas (Oost-Soembaas): Nederlands Woordenboek.* Dordrecht: Foris.

Paulhan, J. 1913. *Les Hain-Teny Merinas*. Paris: Librairie Paul Teuthner.

Poppe, N. 1958. Der Parallelismus in der epischen Dichtung der Mongolen. *Ural-Altaische Jahrbücher* 30(3–4):195–228.

Porthan, H.G. 1766–68. *De poesi fennica*. Helsinki.

Reichard, G. 1944. *Prayer: the compulsive word* (Monographs of the American Ethnological Society no. 7). Seattle: University of Washington Press.

Ridder, R. de 1979. Van modder en mais. Doctoraalscriptie, Universiteit Leiden.

Roos, S. 1872. Bijdrage tot de kennis van taal, land en volk op het eiland Soemba. *Verhandelingen van het Bataviaasch Genootschap van Kunsten en Wetenschappen* 36:1–126.

Rosner, V. 1961. The Bhak Katek ritual in use among the Sadars of Jashpur, Madhya Pradesh (India). *Anthropos* 56:77–113.

Rothenberg, A. 1971. The process of Janusian thinking in creativity. *Archives of General Psychiatry* 24:195–205.

Sabatier, L. 1933. La chanson de Damsan. *Bulletin de l'Ecole Française d'Extrême-Orient* 33:143–302.

Salomon, G. 1919. *Die Entstehung und Entwicklung der deutschen Zwillingsformeln*. Göttingen.

Sankoff, G. 1977. Le parallélisme dans la poésie Buang. *Anthropologica* (n.s.) 19(1): 27–48.

Scarborough, W. 1875. *A collection of Chinese proverbs*. Shanghai: American Presbyterian Mission Press.

Schärer, H. 1966. *Der Totenkult der Ngadju Dajak in Süd-Borneo*. (Verhandelingen van het Koninklijk Instituut voor Taal-, Land- en Volkenkunde, 51, parts I and II). 's-Gravenhage: Martinus Nijhoff.

Schirmunski, V. 1965. Syntaktischer Parallelismus und rhythmische Bindung im alttürkischen epischen Vers. In *Beiträge zur Sprachwissenschaft, Volkskunde und Literaturforschung*. Berlin: Akademie-Verlag.

Schlegel, G. 1896. *La loi du parallélisme en style chinois: démonstrée par la préface du 'Si-yü-ki'*. Leiden: E.J. Brill.

Schulze, B. 1982. Der Wortparallelismus als Stilmittel der ostjakischen Volksdichtung. Dissertation, Akademie der Wissenschaften der DDR, Berlin.

Sherzer, D. and Sherzer, J. 1972. Literature in San Blas: discovering the Cuna Ikala. *Semiotica* 4(2): 182–199.

Sherzer, J. 1974. Namakke, Sunmakke, Kormakke: three types of Cuna speech event. In R. Bauman and J. Sherzer (eds.), *Explorations in the ethnography of speaking*, pp.263–282. Cambridge: Cambridge University Press.

Shih, V.Y.C. 1959. *The literary mind and the carving of dragons* (translation of Liu Hsieh's *Wen-hsing Tiao-lung*). New York: Columbia University Press.

Sibree, J. 1880. *Madagascar: the great African island*. London.

Siskel, S. 1974. With the spirit of a jaguar: a study of shamanism in Zinconton, Chamula. A.B. thesis, Harvard University.

Smith, A.H. 1902. *Proverbs and common sayings from the Chinese*. Shanghai: American Presbyterian Mission Press.

Stein, R.A. 1972. *Tibetan civilization*. London: Faber & Faber.

Steinhart, W.L. 1934. Niassche teksten met Nederlandse vertaling en aanteekeningen. *Tijdschrift voor Taal-, Land- en Volkenkunde* 74:326–375, 391–440.

1937. *Niassche teksten* (Verhandelingen van het Koninklijk Bataviaasch Genootschap van Kunsten en Wetenschappen, 73). Bandoeng: A.C. Nix.

1938. *Niassche priesterlitanieën* (Verhandelingen van het Koninklijk Bataviaasch Genootschap, 74). Bandoeng: A.C. Nix.

1950. Niasse teksten met Nederlandse vertaling en aantekeningen. *Tijdschrift voor Taal-, Land- en Volkenkunde* 84:33–109.

1954. *Niasse teksten*. Koninklijk Instituut voor Taal-, Land- en Volkenkunde. 's Gravenhange: Martinus Nijhoff.

Steinitz, W. 1934. *Der Parallelismus in der finnisch-karelischen Volksdichtung* (Folklore Fellows Communications no. 115). Helsinki: Suomalainen Tiedeakatemia, Academia Scientarum Fennica.

1939–41. *Ostjakische Volksdichtung und Erzahlungen aus zwei Dialekten*, Teil 1 und 2. Tartu and Stockholm.

Strehlow, T.G.H. 1971. *Songs of Central Australia*. Sydney: Angus & Robertson.

Suchtelen, B.C.C.M.M. van 1921. *Endeh (Flores)* (Mededeelingen van het Bureau voor de Bestuurszaken der Buitengewesten, bewerkt door het Encyclopaedisch Bureau no. 26). Weltevreden: Papyrus.

Sundermann, H. 1905. *Niassisch–Deutsches Wörterbuch*. Moers: J.W. Spaarmann.

Tambiah, S.J. 1979. A performative approach to ritual (Radcliffe-Brown lecture). *Proceedings of the British Academy* 65:113–169.

Tchang Tcheng-Ming, B. 1937. *Le parallélisme dans les vers du Cheu King* (Variétés Sinologiques no. 65). Paris: P. Geuthner.

Thompson, J.E.S. 1950. *Maya hieroglyphic writings: an introduction*. Washington DC: Carnegie Institution of Washington (Publication 589).

Traube, E. 1980. Mambai rituals of black and white. In Fox 1980c, pp.290–314.

T'sou, B.K. 1968. Some aspects of linguistic parallelism and Chinese versification. In C.E. Gribble (ed.), *Studies presented to Roman Jakobson by his students*, pp.318–328. Cambridge, Mass: Slavica.

Veen, H. van der 1929. Een wichel-litanie der Sa'dan Toradjas. In *Feestbundel uitgegeven door het Koninklijk Bataviaasch Genootschap van Kunsten en Wetenschappen bij gelegenheid van zijn 150–jarig bestaan 1778–1928*, Vol. II. Weltevreden: G. Kolff & Co.

1950. De samenspraak der beide priesters, de woordvoerders van bruid en bruidegom bij de huwelijksplechtigheid der Sa'dan Toradjas. In *Bingkisan Budi* (Een bundel opstellen aan Dr Philippus Samuel van Ronkel), pp.291–306. Leiden: Sijthoff.

1952. Gebruik van literaire of dichter-taal bij de vertaling van poëtischen gedeelten van de Bijbel in de Indonesische taal. *De Heerbaan* 5(5): 211–240.

1965. *The Merok feast of the Sa'dan Toradja* (Verhandelingen van het Koninklijk Instituut voor Taal-, Land- en Volkenkunde, 45). 's-Gravenhage: Martinus Nijhoff.

1966. *The Sa'dan Toradja chant for the deceased*. (Verhandelingen van het Koninklijk Instituut voor Taal-, Land- en Volkenkunde, 49). 's-Gravenhage: Martinus Nijhoff.

Veen, H. van der (with J. Tammu). 1972. *Kamus Toradja-Indonesia*. Rantepao: Jajasan Perguruan Kristen Toradja.

Vergouwen, J.C. 1964. *The social organisation and customary law of the Toba-Batak of North Sumatra*. The Hague: Martinus Nijhoff.

Volkman, T.A. 1982a. Tana Toraja: a decade of tourism. *Cultural Survival Quarterly* 6:3.

— 1982b. Mortuary tourism in Tana Toraja. Paper presented at American Anthropological Association meetings, Washington DC.

— 1984. Great performances: Toraja cultural identity in the 1970s. *American Ethnologist* 11:152–169.

— 1985. *Feasts of honor: ritual and change in the Toraja Highlands* (Illinois Studies in Anthropology no. 16). Urbana and Chicago: University of Illinois Press.

Watson, B. 1971. *Chinese rhyme-prose*. New York: Columbia University Press.

Watters, W.R. 1976. *Formula criticism and the poetry of the Old Testament*. Berlin: Walter de Gruyter.

Wielenga, D.K. 1909. *Schets van een Soembaneesche spraakkunst (naar't dialect van Kambera)*. Batavia: Bataviaasch Genootschap van Kunsten en Wetenschappen.

— 1917. Vergelijkende woordenlijst der verschillende dialecten op het eiland Soemba en eenige Soembaneesche spreekwijzen. *Verhandelingen van het Bataviaasch Genootschap van Kunsten en Wetenschappen* 61(6):1–96.

Winokan, M.G. 1960. Sedjara singkat dari bekas daerah Flores dan kepulauannja. Unpublished.

Wrigglesworth, H.L. 1980. Rhetorical devices distinguishing the genre of folktale (fiction) from that of oral history (fact) in Ilianen Manobo narrative discourse. *Philippine Journal of Linguistics* 11(1):45–80.

Wurm, S.A. and Hattori, S. 1983. *Language atlas of the Pacific area*. Part II: *Japan area, Taiwan (Formosa), Philippines, mainland and insular South-East Asia* (Pacific Linguistics C–67). Canberra: Australian Academy of the Humanities, in collaboration with the Japan Academy.

Yeats, W.B. 1903. *Ideas of good and evil*. London: Bullen.

Zerner, C. 1981. Signs of the spirits, signature of the smith: iron forging in Tana Toraja, *Indonesia* 31:89–112.

— 1982. Tourism and the arts in Southern Sulawesi. *Cultural Survival Quarterly* 6:4.

Zsirai, M. 1951. *Osztják (Chanti) Hősénekek: Reguly A. és Papay J. Lagyatéka* (Reguly-Könyvtár, 2). Budapest: Akadémiai Kiadó.

INDEX

Adams, M.J. 65, 74, 75, 82, 310 n.24, 314 n.17

adat/*hadat* 62, 259, 287, 281

affines 49, 88, 89, 107, 131, 132, 138, 240, 244, 308 n.14

alliance 231

altar 18, 22, 31, 32, 38, 42, 55, 204, 208, 214, 218, 236, 245

ancestors (*see also* spirits) 13–14, 30–31, 39, 49, 57, 59, 87, 97, 207, 208, 219, 223, 227, 248, 254, 256, 281, 285–286, 292, 306 n.7, 313 n.17, 314 n.18

antonymy 154

Ata Tana Ai, Tana Ai 13–14, 16, 19, 20, 21, 246ff., 319 n.4, 321 n.18

augury (*see also* diviner, divination) 40–42, 143

Boodberg, P. 28

border, boundary (*see also* inside/outside) 33, 59, 238–239, 245

botanic idiom (*see* metaphor, botanical)

canonical parallelism (*see* parallelism)

Catholic Church (*see* Christianity)

centre/periphery (*see* inside/outside)

chant, chanter (*see also* orator, priest) 13, 14, 17, 67–68, 75, 88, 92–95, 96–97, 100, 101–103, 164, 178, 188–190, 208, 247, 248, 250–251, 252–259, 273–276, 279, 281, 289, 291, 320 n.16, 322 n.36

Christianity 19, 24, 30, 52, 166, 169, 189, 205, 226, 246, 250, 282, 317 n.8

Clamagirand, B.R. 313 n.17

clan (*see also* descent group, lineage) 14, 31, 67–68, 71, 105, 107, 132, 167, 229, 248, 257–258, 280, 310 n.1, 314 n.18

colloquial speech (*see* ordinary language, ordinary speech)

Conklin, H. 110

connective devices (*see also* text structure) 108, 109, 147, 272, 273, 277, 321 n.24–n.25

cooling (*see* metaphor, of heat/cooling)

couplets (*see also* dyadic sets) 7, 10, 12, 20, 23, 28, 30–31, 53, 56, 64, 65, 68, 69, 70–72, 75–76, 107, 108–109, 111, 129, 176, 179, 182, 228, 230, 237–238, 252, 272, 291

curse 102, 202, 218, 222, 224, 225, 227

power of 225–226

Dahood, M. 6

Davis, J.F. 7

dead, souls of (*see also* spirits) 39, 48, 49, 91

De Bono, E. 80

deity (*see also* divinity) 30, 32, 34, 37, 39–40, 42, 49–52, 62, 109, 248, 252, 281, 308 n.12, 321 n.28

delegation 321 n.21

descent group (*see also* clan, lineage) 48, 49, 248, 256

diviner, divination (*see also* augury) 15, 34–44, 55, 89, 97, 104, 209, 215, 218, 308 n.5, 308 n.11, 313 n.17

divinity (*see also* deity) 131, 136

domain 246–248, 254, 257, 261, 317 n.6

double names 36, 37, 44, 168, 181, 307 n.2

drum, gong 17, 18, 21, 27–28, 44–48, 52, 88, 90, 92, 95–96, 98, 100, 101, 173, 218, 290, 324 n.11

dualism 26, 27, 69

dual symbolic classification 130, 141

Dutch 76, 159, 165, 203, 282

Dutch East India Company (VOC) 165

dyadic elements 130, 147, 314 n.21–n.24, 315 n.27

dyadic language (*see also* parallelism) 1, 2, 26–27

dyadic sets (*see also* couplets) 129–130, 145–152, 176–179, 181, 183–184, 186, 204, 228, 238, 314 n.22–n.23, 315 n.24, 317 n.7

Edmonson, M.S. 7

Endenese, Ende 23, 203, 228–229, 236–238, 318 n.3–n.5

episode (*see also* narrative structure) 169–176, 180–190, 246, 256–257, 271–277, 279

error 19, 21, 49, 166, 258

exchange   69, 107, 110, 131, 138, 140,
      142, 143–144, 159

feasting   32, 43–44, 48ff., 92, 93, 94–95,
      97, 231, 308 n.14, 309 n.15
Flores   12, 14, 20, 223, 228, 246, 250
formulae, formulaic   10–12, 24, 87, 101,
      129, 130, 161, 162, 165, 166, 178–180,
      182, 184–189, 272, 317 n.6, 320 n.10
Fortes, M.   117
Forth, G.   105, 307 n.3
Fox, J.J.   24, 64, 66, 69, 129, 144, 147,
      150, 152, 153, 204, 314 n.24, 317 n.1
Freedman, D.N.   6

genealogy (*see also* histories)   13, 20, 44,
      102, 180–181, 319 n.4
genre   24, 145, 204, 226, 239, 306 n.8
Gervitz, S.   6
Goffman, E.   116
grave, tomb (*see also* mortuary rites)   49,
      61, 188, 308 n.10
Gray, G.B.   5, 6
Greuter, H.   203
Guildford, J.P.   80
Gumperz, J.   108

Hanson, O.   8
Hardeland, A.   9
heat (*see* metaphor, of heat/cooling)
hierarchy   14, 18, 29, 31, 54, 63, 88, 101,
      103, 144, 205, 257, 285, 307 n.1
   of houses   88–89
histories (*see also* genealogy, origins)   13,
      20, 52, 67–68, 247–248, 252, 253–259,
      260, 261ff., 281, 310 n.1, 319 n.4
Hopkins, G.M.   3, 4

incest   104, 105, 107, 111, 308 n.9, 318 n.9
inside/outside   25, 31–34, 52ff., 105, 113,
      222–225, 234–235, 236–238, 239, 245,
      294, 295–296, 307 n.3, 309 n.24
invocation   20, 44, 88–89, 90–101,
      130–131, 141–145, 155, 208, 224, 225,
      248, 252–253, 255, 312 n.8
   participation in   92–95
   prologue   93–96

Jakobson   3, 4, 6, 11, 24, 178, 179
Jonker, J.C.G.   161, 162, 316 n.1
journey (*see* metaphor, of journey)

Kapita, Oe. H.   131, 134, 145, 312 n.7,
      314 n.19
Kodinese, Kodi   11, 13, 15, 21, 28, 29ff.,
      307 n.4, 308 n.5, 310 n.24
Koestler, A.   80

knowledge   2, 13, 18, 24, 94, 101–102,
      133, 136, 143, 204, 226, 256–259,
      279–280

ladder   18, 22, 37, 45, 49, 88, 101, 238
Lambooy, P.J.   312 n.5
lineage (*see also* clan, descent group)   14,
      32, 48, 49, 61, 167, 285, 286
Lionese, Lio   14, 18, 22, 202–205, 219,
      226–227, 228–229, 318 n.5
literacy   2, 19, 261, 279
Lowth, R.   2–3, 4–5, 6, 68

Mambai   135–136, 313 n.11
marriage   69, 71, 83, 228–230, 319 n.4
   types of   229, 239, 319 n.2
   stages of   230–231
matriclan   32
mediation, mediator (*see also* spokesman,
      speaker)   17, 18, 30–31, 33, 34, 43,
      52, 54, 62, 63, 69–70, 72, 88, 89,
      92–93, 96–97, 101–103, 136, 141,
      142–143, 190
message, messenger   139–141, 230
metaphor   2, 3, 4, 7, 12, 24, 25, 28, 54,
      57, 59, 61, 64, 65, 70–72, 74–75,
      77–84, 87, 104–105, 110–113, 130,
      145, 165, 166, 167, 170, 204, 219–225,
      228, 230, 245, 249, 286, 287, 288, 291,
      308 n.8, 309 n.17, 309 n.21
   alimentary   105, 110, 111–112
   botanical   17, 18, 50, 51, 54, 167, 169,
      183, 189, 235, 244, 289, 290, 291, 294,
      295, 322 n.34, 324 n.9
   of heat/cooling   27, 28, 31, 37, 49, 59,
      240, 244–245, 258, 275–276, 285, 286,
      309 n.17, 322 n.32
   of journey   21, 22, 23, 44, 46, 47,
      112–113, 168, 169, 174, 175, 176,
      182, 234, 245, 253, 254, 317 n.8
   spatial   222, 228, 234–235, 236,
      238–239, 244
   temporal   219
metonym   4, 178
metre, metrics   11, 28, 311 n.3
Mitchell, I.G.   67, 69, 83
mortuary rites (*see also* grave, tomb)   16,
      58, 164, 165–166, 176, 182, 187, 190,
      248, 282, 285, 306 n.6

names, naming   31, 34, 44, 49, 52, 317
      n.7, 323 n.38
narrative, narrative structure (*see also* text
      structure)   20–23, 67, 169, 179, 182,
      185, 188, 189, 234–236, 243–244, 245,
      246–247, 251, 256–258, 272–273
Needham, R.   82

negotiation   20, 23, 24, 42, 56–57, 67,
    69–73, 138, 228, 230, 235, 240, 306
    n.7
Nga'o-nese   228, 318 n.3

offerings, gifts   14, 34, 36, 51, 60, 64, 67,
    69, 70, 89–92, 96, 100, 107, 108–109,
    110, 111, 112, 131, 138, 139–140, 142,
    143, 144, 155, 206, 231, 234, 235, 255,
    273, 286, 291, 308 n.10, 309 n.16, 313
    n.16–n.18, 324 n.14
omen (*see also* sign)   88, 90–91, 101
Onvlee, L.   65, 75, 82, 312 n.5
orator, oration (*see also* chant, chanter,
    priests)   14, 17, 44, 92–95, 96–97,
    131–133, 138–141, 142–145, 158–159,
    312 n.7–n.8, 313 n.13–n.14, 314 n.23,
ordeal   209, 214–218, 226–227
ordinary language, ordinary speech   13,
    26, 56–57, 61, 64, 66, 67, 70, 72, 75,
    81, 129–130, 131, 134, 251–253, 282,
    284, 315 n.27
origins (*see also* histories)   19, 20, 31, 48,
    189, 247, 250, 252, 254–255, 260,
    261ff., 272, 276, 278, 280, 316 n.4, 319
    n.4, 321 n.26

pairs, pairing (*see also* couplet, dyadic
    set)   1, 3, 6, 11–12, 18, 23–27, 30,
    53–54, 57, 61, 87, 101, 108, 129–130,
    146–152, 153–154, 169, 176–179, 187,
    252, 290, 312 n.3, 312 n.6, 314
    n.22–n.24, 315 n.25–n.28, 316 n.33,
    317 n.6, 319 n.4, 320 n.13
parallelism   1–12, 26–27, 28, 68–69, 72,
    73, 74–75, 76–77, 104, 108, 129, 130,
    131, 141, 142, 146–147, 149, 150–151,
    153–154, 168, 179, 183, 186, 228, 252,
    288, 306 n.3, 314 n.21–n.23, 316 n.32,
    324 n.8
    canonical   4, 6–11, 23–26, 27, 162,
        176–179, 189, 238–239, 306 n.1, 306
        n.4
    traditions of:
        Australian   10
        Austronesian   8, 9
        Chinese   7–8, 306 n.2
        Indo-European   10–11
        Mainland Southeast Asia   8, 9
        Middle America   7
        Near Eastern   5–6
        Papuan   10
        Semitic   2, 3, 4–6, 24–25, 68, 306 n.1
        Ural-Altaic   6, 7
patrilineage   32, 107
performance   13–14, 17–20, 27–28,
    67–68, 75, 106–107, 130, 132,

139–141, 142–143, 164, 214, 218, 247,
    249, 252, 253–259, 280, 287, 322 n.35
power   27, 48–49, 204, 207, 225, 227,
    280–281, 288, 294, 295, 318 n.9, 318
    n.13, 318 n.16–n.17
    of curse   225
prayer   7, 33, 53, 59, 104, 105, 106–108,
    109–113, 115, 116–117
prestations (*see* offerings, gifts)
priest (*see also* chant, chanter, orator)   14,
    18, 131–133, 136, 137, 142, 143, 204,
    205, 207, 208–209, 214, 218–219, 220,
    221–227, 283–284, 286, 289, 312 n.4,
    312 n.7–n.8, 323 n.3–n.4

recitation   19, 20–21, 23, 24, 272, 284,
    289
Reichard, G.   114
repetition   10–11, 12, 24, 27–28, 114–115,
    116, 140–141, 142, 150–154, 179, 225,
    288, 315 n.31, 316 n.32, 317 n.5
requests, entreaties   18, 43, 49, 52, 54,
    167, 171, 172, 253, 285–288, 292–294,
    295–296
Rindi   14, 17, 25, 26, 129, 132, 133,
    134–135, 139, 145, 159, 306 n.7, 307
    n.3, 310 n.24, 311 n.2, 313 n.14, 313
    n.17
ritual language, ritual speech   1–4, 11–14,
    17–20, 23–26, 28, 29, 30–32, 53, 57,
    61, 64–65, 66–68, 70, 71–74, 84–86,
    87, 88, 94, 101–103, 104, 107, 108,
    129–132, 133, 134–138, 145–155, 161,
    164, 176–179, 189, 202, 203–204,
    219–225, 251–253, 256, 281, 282–285,
    286, 291, 296, 313 n.11–n.12, 317 n.1,
    319 n.2, 320 n.8
ritual objects   18, 35, 38, 44, 48, 204,
    206–207, 218, 219, 285–286, 291–292,
    323 n.39, 324 n.13
    theft of   207–211, 220–221
rock and tree   15, 32, 38, 42, 55, 58
Roos, S.   312 n.5
Rothenberg, A.   80
Rotinese, Roti   14, 16, 19–20, 21, 23–24,
    25, 27, 28, 32, 147, 153, 161ff., 180,
    187, 189, 204, 252, 316 n.4, 317 n.8

sacrifice   42, 48, 52, 57, 59, 61, 87, 88,
    89–92, 99, 100, 102, 104, 142, 159,
    208, 224, 281, 308 n.14, 313 n.17
Sa'dan Toraja (*see* Toraja)
Savu   308 n.5
secrecy   31, 35, 58, 62, 204, 207, 218, 318
    n.13
semantic associations   4, 24–27, 76–84,
    177, 239, 315 n.26–n.27

Sibree, J.   9
sign (*see also* omen)   88, 90–91, 97, 101, 214
Sikkanese, Sikka   203, 246
singer, singing   43, 44–48
spirits (*see also* ancestors)   30, 32–33, 56–63, 66–67, 87ff., 104, 106, 108, 109, 110–111, 112, 113, 131, 137, 142–144, 155, 208, 223, 224, 225, 281, 285–286, 309 n.24
spokesman, speaker (*see also* mediation, mediator)   17, 30, 31, 34, 38, 48, 54, 104, 106, 107, 108, 110–112, 114, 230, 234
Steinitz, W.   6
Strehlow, T.G.H.   10
Suchtelen, B.C.C.M.M. van   203
Sulawesi   12, 282
Sumbanese, Sumba   17, 18, 64ff., 87ff., 104, 105
   east   11, 14, 20, 24, 25, 65, 129ff., 309 n.24
   west   12, 14, 20, 66, 307 n.3
synonymy   87, 130, 154, 228, 315 n.27

Tambiah, S.J.   113, 114, 316 n.32
text structure (*see also* narrative, narrative structure)   19, 107–108, 169ff., 230, 238–239, 247, 259ff., 271–277, 279–281, 320 n.17

scenes   107–108, 109–112, 113, 114–115
stanza   107, 108, 109, 113–115
theft   18, 207–211, 218, 220–221, 308 n.7
Toraja   12, 14, 18, 24, 27, 282, 284, 323 n.1–n.2
Traube, E.   135, 136, 313 n.11

Van Gennep, A.   113
Veen, H. van der   284, 286, 323 n.5
Vergouwen, J.C.   72, 80
voice, taking of voice   13–16, 17–20, 26, 28, 40–44, 257, 312 n.8

Wanukaka   12, 20, 66, 67, 69, 70, 73, 76, 79, 80, 310 n.1
weaving   17, 145, 314 n.19, 314 n.20, 324 n.13
Wewewa/Weyéwa   12, 14–15, 17–18, 20, 21–22, 24, 87, 102, 104ff., 306 n.5, 311 n.1
Wielenga, D.K.   312 n.5
wife-giver   131, 138, 144, 159, 230–231, 235–236, 240, 244–245, 313 n.18, 319 n.3
wife-taker   131, 138, 144, 230–231, 240, 245, 319 n.3
Winokan, M.G.   203

Yeats, W.B.   85